From L S $5

W9-AEJ-988

From L S $5

W9-AEJ-988

An Illustrated History
of the
United States
Navy

Chester G. Hearn

Foreword by Norman Friedman

PUBLISHED BY
SALAMANDER BOOKS LIMITED
LONDON

A Salamander Book

Published by
Salamander Books Ltd.
8 Blenheim Court
Brewery Road
London N7 9NY
United Kingdom

© Salamander Books Ltd., 2002

A member of the Chrysalis Group plc

ISBN 1 84065 343 4

All rights reserved. Except for use in a review, no part of this book may be reproduced, stored in a retrieval system or transmitted in any form or by any means, electronic, mechanical, photocopying or otherwise, without prior permission of Salamander Books Ltd.

All correspondence concerning the content of this volume should be addressed to Salamander Books Ltd.

Credits

Project Manager:
Ray Bonds

Art Director:
John Heritage

Designer:
Peter Laws

Production:
Phillip Chamberlain

Picture Research:
Anne Lang

Commissioned photography:
Don Eiler

Colour reproduction:
Media Print (UK) Ltd

Produced by MetroPrint Ltd

Printed in China

The Author

Chester ("Chet") G. Hearn is a former member of the United States armed forces. He has written more than a dozen books on U.S. military history, including *Naval Battles of the Civil War* (published by Salamander), and *George Washington's Schooners: The First American Navy*, *Admiral David Glasgow Farragut*, and *Admiral David Dixon Porter* (published by the U.S. Naval Institute Press). Three of his titles have been "alternate selections" for the History Book Club of America. He graduated from Allegheny College with a B.A. in Economics and a minor in History, and spent much of a civilian career as an executive in industry. He now spends all his time writing and researching – when he is not afloat on Lake Erie, Pennsylvania, or at a local pool keeping in shape for competitive swimming.

Norman Friedman

Norman Friedman is a highly respected defence analyst specialising in strategic and technical issues, consultant to U.S. government agencies, and former deputy director of national security studies at the Hudson Institute. He holds a Ph. D. in Physics from Columbia University and has written many successful books on navy ships and weapons, combining technical analyses with discussions of the historical, political, and economic influences on design and development. He also writes regularly for international defence journals and contributes a monthly column on world naval developments to the US Naval Institute's *Proceedings* magazine.

Acknowledgements

The publishers wish to thank the U.S. Department of Defense, the U.S. National Archives, and the Library of Congress for contributing many rare photographs and copies of valuable paintings for this book. In particular, gratitude is due to Dr. J. Scott Harmon at the U.S. Naval Academy Museum and Dr. Edward Furgol at the U.S. Navy Museum for making available many artefacts for photography.

Contents

FOREWORD

We have come to take for granted that the United States is the world's premier sea power. What many forget is how recent a growth that supremacy is. This book helps remind us that U.S. naval power was hardly pre-ordained. It also reminds Americans of just what the investment in a powerful fleet has bought. U.S. seapower made it possible for the United States to project decisive forces into Europe in two World Wars, and to maintain powerful forces there during the Cold War. U.S. seapower made victory in the Pacific in World War II possible. In the aftermath of the Cold War, the U.S. Navy makes it possible for the United States to secure its interests abroad, rather than waiting for some threat at home.

When the United States was formed, it was a largely maritime country; indeed, the colonies supplied many of the sailors (and much of the materiel) of Britain's Royal Navy. However, the new country developed inland, not towards the sea. The classic precondition of naval power, a massive merchant marine (requiring protection), largely disappeared. The great burst of naval growth in the middle of the nineteenth century was intended to win the Civil War, and the Civil War navy was largely discarded in the decade that followed. By the 1880s, several South American navies were much more powerful than the U.S. Navy. As importantly, when Americans thought of the Navy at all, they thought in terms of coast defense – of fending off possible attacks from abroad while perhaps discouraging an enemy through commerce raiding.

The modern U.S. Navy, which did so much to win first World War II and then the Cold War, was the creation of a few nineteenth-century visionaries, such as Captain (later Rear Admiral) Alfred Thayer Mahan, the father of modern concepts of naval strategy. Where many Americans saw the oceans washing their coasts as barriers to any enemy, those visionaries saw the seas as highways. They argued that the United States could never disengage from the world. Its wealth would make it either a target or a dominant world power. It would be far better to engage potential foreign threats abroad than to wait for their approach.

This idea, that the United States can best defend itself by engaging abroad, is the basis of modern U.S. military strategy. It justified the creation of an oceanic navy capable of challenging the most powerful foreign fleets. The visionaries might well have failed; other great countries have turned away from the sea, and from engagement in the larger world. The United States faltered, but ultimately it did not turn away. The perception that the sea is a highway rather than a barrier explains why, in two World Wars, the U.S. government recognized that the fate of Europe, across the Atlantic, was linked to its own. Similarly, the perception of the sea as a highway explains why the United States helped form a North Atlantic Treaty Organization to stave off the Soviet attempt to conquer Europe, and why the United States is currently engaged in East Asia. Oceans bring both Asia and Europe close to the United States in a way that no map expresses. The existence of a powerful U.S. Navy helps insure that the United States will be able to exert pressure on potential enemies where they live, rather than where Americans live at home.

This book, then, is the story not only of a remarkable growth but also of remarkably good luck, not only for Americans but also for many others who have benefitted so much from shared American power.

DR. NORMAN FRIEDMAN, PH.D.

INTRODUCTION

In 1775, delegates from tiny Rhode Island, the smallest colony in the America, took the first step in creating what two centuries later would become the largest and greatest navy in the world. They proposed an American fleet – a united navy for the colonies' joint protection. Samuel Chase of Maryland made his most remembered rebuttal, calling the suggestion "the maddest idea in the world." George Washington agreed with the Rhode Islanders, and while the Continental Congress debated, he commissioned the first colonial navy under the auspices of his own army. The general's first vessel was a small 74-ton fishing schooner named *Hannah*, armed with four 4-pounder pop-guns and a few swivels and blunderbusses mounted in pivot. Washington would go on to become the first president and "father of the country," but fiery John Adams of Massachusetts, the second president, most deserved the sobriquet "father of the American Navy." Adams understood that the natural defense of any nation depended upon naval power, yet there was probably never a nation so reluctant to create one than the confederation of American colonies.

Since those early days of debate in the Continental Congress, no armed service in the United States has ever gone through more convolutions than the U.S. Navy. In 1775 America went to sea to protect its liberty. In the early 1800s, America went back to sea to protect its commerce. In the 1860s, America again went to war to reunify the country. In the 20th century it went to war to stop aggression. In between wars, America forgot about its navy. For a parsimonious Congress, a powerful navy was just too expensive to maintain during peacetime. But every time a navy was needed, the patriots who served her distinguished themselves with valor, boldness, fearlessness, and competence.

Every war has made the Navy a stronger and more cohesive force, building a legacy of pride within the service. Recognition, growth, and success did not come easily. Today the U.S. Navy stands proudly as the only armed service having its own fleet, its own air force, and its own ground force, the latter being the Marine Corps. It is the most complex of all the armed services, in weaponry, technology, and readiness.

This book conveys the history of that force, from the fishing schooners of George Washington's navy to the supercarriers, nuclear submarines, aircraft, and weapons of the 21st century. It relates how the Navy grew during the wars it fought and why it had to grow to meet the challenges of nations who would weaken and suppress the natural development of the United States. It speaks of the officers and men who fought the battles and created the strategies that now take the nation into the first decade of a new century. And it traces the progress and expansion of technology and tactics from the early colonial days of privateering to shielding the United States from ballistic missiles armed with chemical, biological, or nuclear warheads.

Most people accept the U.S. Navy as a fact without really understanding what it is or how it came to be. Few people, even many of the sailors themselves, fully understand the fascinating story behind the origins and development of the service, or the future role the Navy must play in all of our lives. So much history has been lost between the days of the lookout perched in a crow's nest on a sailing ship to the technicians of today who gather intelligence from satellites and aircraft that have become the eyes of navy command centers.

The book is also about the evolution of sea power for the generation of today, a sharing of knowledge plainly written that belongs to the legacy of every American. One needs not "to go down to the sea in ships" to become a part of the Navy. The story is here, between the pages.

CHESTER G. HEARN
Erie, Pennsylvania

CHAPTER ONE

THE REVOLUTIONARY WAR

Above right: In 1775, while every state was developing its own special flag, the Continental Navy, on December 3, adopted the first Navy Jack.

Right: On December 16, 1773, a number of Bostonians dressed up like Indians to protest an attempt by Parliament to confer upon their own East India Company a monopoly on the importation of tea into the colonies. The so-called Indians ripped open 342 chests of tea valued at $90,000 and dumped them into the harbor. The famous Boston Tea Party led to harsher British laws, the convening of the First Continental Congress, and the Revolutionary War.

The seeds for the conflict occupying George Washington's attention in 1781 were sown in 1763 after the British emerged victorious from the Seven Years' War. Without a rival, the Union Jack flew from the polar regions of Canada to the sun-drenched keys of Florida.

Because the war had taken a heavy toll on Britain's Royal treasury, King George III looked to the colonies for fresh capital. Collecting it required new taxes and a stricter enforcement of the Acts of Trade and Navigation. The Acts, which colonial merchants had previously ignored or evaded, subordinated the economic interests of the colonists to those of the British crown. Because the colonies had fought beside Britain in the suppression of France in North America, they expected more appreciation and less interference from the king's ministers. Instead, they received the opposite. The Royal Navy became the ministerial tool to collect duties and, because their ships were shorthanded, they impressed American sailors. Oppression bred resentment, and by early 1775 the fury in New England against the king's ministers reached breaking point.

Great Britain could barely afford another war, especially against its thirteen colonies. Defeating France had greatly diminished the Royal Navy, leaving it with 264 armed vessels to protect the king's growing empire. Few of the vessels were in top shape and all needed repairs. To compound the problem, many of Britain's finest officers had no appetite for fighting fellow Englishmen and refused service on the American coast. The ministers feared a land war with the colonies and believed the only way to subdue a potential rebellion was to blockade America's ports, thereby escaping a heavy cost in blood and treasure. They miscalculated the resolve of the colonists as well as their own ability to patrol 1,800 miles of coastline with twenty-nine ships of war. They also overlooked another fact. The colonists had become adept at building fast ships capable of carrying up to forty-four guns.

In 1774, the first Continental Congress met at Philadelphia to discuss the problems raised by Britain's Intolerable Acts, or Restraining and Coercive Acts, those being a series of five parliamentary acts passed for the purpose of punishing the colonists for the Boston Tea Party of December 16, 1773. The first meeting accomplished little, but on April 18-19, 1775, bitterness towards the king's ministers erupted in flashes of musket fire, first on the village green of Lexington, Massachusetts, and then at nearby Concord. A thousand British soldiers, sent by General Thomas Gage to seize the arsenal at Concord and Acton, limped back to Boston with heavy casualties.

Soon thereafter, the Continental Congress met

again, this time constituting itself a provisional government with the objective of organizing an army to make war on Great Britain. In June they formed a Continental Army and on the 17th named George Washington its commander. Before adjourning in July, they authorized the issue of two million paper dollars to finance a navy. Prior to that date, five colonial legislatures had already made provisions for arming vessels to protect their harbors.

Forty-three-year-old George Washington collected his small force around the outskirts of Boston and commenced a siege. Knowing that Gage's garrison would be supplied from the sea, he did not wait for Congress to create its new Continental Navy. He took the initiative and recruited sailors from among the infantry. While Congress debated the wisdom of establishing a navy, where opponents such as Samuel Chase of Maryland called it "the maddest Idea in the World," Washington began fitting out and arming eight fishing schooners to interdict British transports sailing to Boston with supplies and reinforcements. He sorely needed gunpowder, muskets, lead, and cannon, and hoped to pluck from the sea a British vessel heavily laden with arms and munitions. Washington made his schooners an arm of the Continental Army but gave his commanders typical navy commissions.

LARGE, FAST PRIVATEERS

On September 5, 1775, when the general's first armed schooner *Hannah* went to sea, the ports along coastal New England were already refitting their fastest sailing vessels with cannon and converting them into privateers. To differentiate their creations from pirate vessels, privateers received a letter of marque and reprisal issued by the government, which protected captured crews from being hanged. Privateers were expected to bring their prizes into port for adjudication, after which the owners and crews would pocket shares from the sale of the ship, its contents, and cargo. Washington's schooners operated under the same restrictions as privateers, except that they were legitimate warships of the army. Unlike Washington's schooners, many of the privateers were large, fast vessels fully capable of doing battle with British armed sloops and schooners, but a privateer's objective was profit, not battle, and they preyed upon lightly armed British merchant vessels.

The outbreak of war in New England disconnected thousands of seafaring men from their professions of fishing, whaling, slaving, and trading. Farming the poor, rocky soil along the coast had never been a profitable option for those born near the sea, so the men became sailors and shipbuilders. John Luttrell, speaking before Britain's House of Lords in March, 1775, predicted that

"the King's ships cannot keep the seas in safety, in the northern parts of the coasts of America, for more than half the year." In the same debate he brought to the House's attention America's great nursery, "where seamen are raised, trained and maintained in times of peace to serve [their] country in times of war...." So it should have been no shock to the British when Washington's eight schooners, joined later by hundreds of privateers, sailed in search of British merchantmen. Washington's eight little schooners took fifty-five prizes, one being the 250-ton brig *Nancy* captured by Capt. John Manley and loaded from stem to stern with enough arms, munitions, and equipage to field an army of two thousand men.

In November, 1775, Congress adopted a naval policy, but mainly to give codification to the operating policies already governing Washington's navy. They had already created the

Above: *A page from the* Journal *of the Continental Congress contains part of the resolution that led to the formation of the Continental Navy. (October 13, 1775; Papers of the Continental Congress, National Archives, RG 360.)*

NOVEMBER 25:
Congress authorizes privateering against British vessels.

NOVEMBER 28:
Congress promulgates the first naval regulations.

DECEMBER 22:
Congress approves the building of thirteen frigates, appoints the first eighteen officers of the Continental Navy, and names Commodore Esek Hopkins commander in chief.

Above right: *General George Washington beat the Continental Navy to sea. In September 1775, he commissioned the 78-ton schooner* Hannah *to prey upon British shipping. Fitted out with an additional topsail and armed with 4-pounders and swivels, she sailed from Beverly, Massachusetts, in search of her first prize.*

Continental Navy without actually calling it such, partly because they had not yet formally declared their independence. In December they formed two standing committees on naval matters, the seven-member Naval Committee to lay the foundation for the Continental Navy, and the Marine Committee, the latter assuming responsibility for Washington's fleet and the acquisition of more ships.

The Naval Committee met at a waterside tavern after each day's congressional meetings ended and prepared in a remarkably short span of time a plan of action. They purchased merchant vessels, converted them into men-of-war, armed them with cannon, and manned them with officers, sailors, and marines. John Adams presented a draft for "Rules for the Regulation of the Navy of the United States," and on November 28 Congress passed it into law. Adams's "Rules,"

which remained in effect throughout the war, mirrored those of the Royal Navy but called for more humane treatment of sailors, limiting corporal punishment to a dozen lashes. The committee also named Esek Hopkins fleet commander, established operational policies, and authorized a limited naval war against British commerce and the Royal Navy. The limited war continued to expand, so in March 1776, Congress extended its policy to include a naval war against all British shipping.

Privateering became so popular that colonies forming state navies could not find enough men to fill their crews, and when the states began to turn their vessels over to the Continental Navy, neither could the Marine Committee. Privateers paid Jack Tar higher wages and a greater share of prize money, so why should a sailor operating out of his local port want to dedicate his career afloat to the uncertainties of an experimental navy operating out of cities like Philadelphia? Historians give little credit to the privateers for winning the war, but those vessels exacted a huge toll on the enemy, capturing, according to British records, 2,208 of His Majesty's ships worth in aggregate more than $66 million. The Continental Navy, an improvisation of a wary Congress, never came close to matching the great fleet of privateers.

In addition to privateers operating from American soil, Continental agents in Europe and the Caribbean also issued letters of marque, bringing the total of commissioned privateers to more than 2,000. For England, trade with the West Indies was particularly hard hit. The Royal Navy began running convoys back and forth across the

Comparative list of American-armed vessels (1776-1782)

Class	1776	1777	1778	1779	1780	1781	1782
Continental	31	34	21	20	13	9	7
Privateers	136	73	115	167	228	449	323

Comparative number of guns carried on the above vessels

Class	1776	1777	1778	1779	1780	1781	1782
Continental	586	412	680	462	266	164	198
Privateers	1,360	730	1,150	2,505	3,420	6,735	4,845

Atlantic, but vessels never sailed at the same speed. Privateers followed the convoys, and the poor sailor who fell behind became among the first captured. One convoy leaving England with sixty vessels arrived at its destination with thirty-five fewer, leaving one British subject to reflect, "God knows, if this American war continues much longer we shall all die from hunger."

BIRTH OF THE NAVY

In September, 1775, it had been John Adams of Massachusetts who suggested fitting out a congressional navy. Pennsylvania already had a squadron of row galleys operating on the Delaware River. Massachusetts, Connecticut, and Rhode Island had armed a number of ex-merchant vessels that stood about half-ready for action. On October 13, Congress provided funds for "fitting out of two armed vessels to be employed against British military transports," the *Andrew Doria* and *Cabot*. According to the United States Navy, the date also marked the birth of the Continental Navy, though it was far from being effectively organized. In late October, Congress appropriated $100,000 to fit out two larger vessels, *Alfred* and *Columbus*, specifically designating them to be employed "for the protection and defense of the united Colonies."

Debate over further action continued until December 13, after which Congress authorized the construction of thirteen frigates, a bold step

having gathered momentum from the capture of the munitions brig *Nancy* by Washington's navy. At a rough average cost of $66,667 each, five frigates would carry 32 guns, five would carry 28, and the remaining three 24. These collective actions, whether fully intended or not, created the Continental Navy.

In order to entice crews from privateers, Congress raised the wages of able-bodied seamen from $6.67 a month to $8.00 and fixed the monthly pay of Esek Hopkins, the commander in chief, at $125.00. Because Congress had formed two committees — the Naval Committee and the Marine Committee — they tended to overlap and

Above: *On November 2, 1775, Congress authorized the Naval Committee $100,000 to purchase and obtain eight ships of war. Alfred, 24 guns, became the first warship to be fitted out and armed for service on the high seas and the first flagship of the Continental Navy. On December 3, 1776, Lieutenant John Paul Jones raised the new Grand Union Flag on the vessel at Philadelphia.*

Left: *The 8-gun sloop of war Wasp, among the original eight warships of the Continental Navy, joined the squadron of Captain Esek Hopkins in the first armed attack against a British colony when the fleet attacked New Providence in the Bahamas.*

▶ 1776

MARCH 3: The Continental fleet under Esek Hopkins captures New Providence Island in the Bahamas.

APRIL 4: Capt. Abraham Whipple, commanding *Columbus*, captures the British schooner *Hawk* in the first engagement with an enemy vessel.

JULY 4: Congress issues the Declaration of Independence.

AUGUST 8: John Paul Jones is promoted to the rank of captain and, commanding the sloop *Providence*, captures sixteen prizes.

Right: *On March 3, 1776, the guns of* Wasp *cover the landing of 300 men under Captain Samuel Nicholas of the Continental Marines as they prepare to storm Forts Nassau and Montagu on New Providence Island in the Bahamas.*

Below: *On November 16, 1776, Captain Isaiah Robinson, commanding the 14-gun brig* Andrew Doria, *sailed into the Dutch port of St. Eustatius and took the opporunity to exchange the salute to the American flag.*

keep each other in a state of partial paralysis. Esek Hopkins of Rhode Island would soon elevate the problem to a higher level by demonstrating how not to command a squadron of men-of-war.

Fifty-seven-year-old Esek Hopkins, a merchant seaman and former privateer, seemed to have the right credentials for commanding the new Revolutionary fleet, most of which had not yet been built. With a squadron of eight converted merchant ships bought and refitted by the Naval Committee, Hopkins received orders to take his squadron into Chesapeake Bay and attack and destroy a bothersome flotilla under Lord Dunmore, the deposed royal governor of Virginia who had been terrorizing Yankee shipping. If weather conditions proved adverse, Hopkins had a green light to operate as he wished. Without informing Congress that he intended to ignore his orders, Hopkins headed for New Providence (Nassau) in the Bahamas, where, he learned, the British had stockpiled large quantities of arms and powder.

FIRST AMPHIBIOUS ATTACK

Hopkins set sail with two converted merchant-men – *Alfred* and *Columbus* – rated as frigates and mounting 24 guns; a pair of 14-gun brigs, *Andrew Doria* and *Cabot*; two 10-gun sloops, *Providence* and *Hornet*; and the 8-gun schooners *Fly* and *Wasp*. While plunging through a gale on a dark, wind-swept sea, *Hornet* and *Fly* collided and drifted off into the night. With the remaining six ships Hopkins plowed ahead and waited in vain at Great Abaco for the two missing vessels.

Meanwhile, Hopkins captured two island sloops, which he filled to capacity with sailors and marines. He planned to send them into the harbor at New Providence for a surprise attack on two forts. His plan miscarried because he failed to keep his ships below the horizon. A puff of smoke spewed from the fort, followed by the rumble of cannon and a splash of a round shot near one of the captured sloops. Having been discovered, Hopkins veered away and sailed to the opposite end of the island. On March 3, 1776, with *Wasp* and *Providence* covering the landing, 250 marines and sailors splashed ashore in America's first amphibious attack. Marching overland,

Hopkins's landing party assaulted the fort from the undefended rear and forced the garrison's surrender. Though the gunpowder mysteriously disappeared, Hopkins loaded 88 cannon, 15 mortars, and tons of other equipment on his vessels. Two weeks later he headed home, having pulled off the first successful naval operation of the war.

Though beset by storms and an outbreak of smallpox during the homeward passage, Hopkins had yet another opportunity to garner a little glory. Though *Wasp* had wandered away during another storm, the remaining five vessels stumbled upon the 20-gun British frigate *Glasgow*. The frigate should have made an easy prize, but her captain fought furiously, and after a four-hour engagement Hopkins gave up the fight and recalled his ships. Nicholas Biddle, commanding the *Andrew Doria*, confided to his brother James that Hopkins lacked leadership. As historian Nathan Miller observed, "Although the depletion of Hopkins's crews by sickness and their inexperience were extenuating factors, this inept action made it all too clear that patriotism

was not enough to create a navy."

At first, Esek Hopkins looked like the right man for the job. His amphibious assault on the British arsenal at New Providence had netted a handsome supply of artillery, but his failure to capture the British frigate *Glasgow* raised a few eyebrows, especially among officers of his own squadron. Members of Congress cried foul when they learned that Hopkins had ignored his orders to rid the lower Chesapeake of Lord Dunmore. Then, after Hopkins returned home, he did nothing further to promote the war, allowing his ships to wallow in idleness at Narragansett Bay.

Disgusted by their indolent commander, men like Nicholas Biddle of the *Andrew Doria*, Abraham Whipple of the *Columbus*, and John Paul Jones of the *Alfred*, all of whom had been promoted to captain, ran their ships through the British blockade and set off on cruises of destruction. While Hopkins rocked at anchor, Jones cruised off Nova Scotia and on November 12, 1776, captured the armed transport *Mellish*, laden with 10,000 winter uniforms. After women

Left: *Captain Esek Hopkins parades the deck of his flagship while he considers engaging the British frigate* Glasgow.

BUSHNELL'S *AMERICAN TURTLE*

David Bushnell grew up on a farm at the mouth of the Connecticut River, entered Yale in 1771 at the age of thirty-one, and while there experimented with underwater explosives. By 1775 he had developed a clockwork mechanism that would allow a man to plant the device and clear from the area before it exploded. Having solved one problem, Bushnell began building the *American Turtle*, a tiny twin-shelled submarine capable of delivering a mine filled with 150 pounds of powder.

In 1775 Ben Franklin witnessed a successful trial and came away convinced that with a few refinements *Turtle* could become a formidable weapon against the British fleet anchored off New York. The interior of the 6 by 7$\frac{1}{2}$-foot shell was rammed with levers and handles. The vessel contained a conning tower, a rudder, two propellers – one for moving vertically, the other for going horizontally – ventilation tubes, a ballast tank, and a screw for boring into a wooden ship's hull for attaching the mine. The vessel could remain underwater for about thirty minutes, but it took a man much stronger than Bushnell to operate it.

Three attempts were made to destroy a British vessel, but they all failed. The first was much like the others when Ezra Lee, a hurriedly trained operator, set out on September 6, 1776, to destroy *Eagle*, Admiral

"Black Dick" Howe's flagship. Lee had the misfortune of trying to drill into the metal strap holding *Eagle*'s rudder. Instead of moving *Turtle* over wood, Lee gave up and headed for shore. Discovered by a British boat, he released the mine. When it exploded, throwing up a huge gusher of water, the British fled in one direction and Lee the other. The Bushnell device did no damage, but it threw a scare into Black Dick, who moved his squadron away from its anchorage.

Above left: *The* American Turtle *creeps into the harbor off Staten Island to attack HMS* Eagle, *64-gun flagship of the British fleet.*

Above: *David Busnell's* Turtle *was a product of Yankee ingenuity composed of so many levers and gadgets that only one man ever agreed to test her against the enemy.*

SEPTEMBER 7: David Bushnell invents the *American Turtle*, America's first submarine.

OCTOBER 11-13: During the battle on Lake Champlain, General Benedict Arnold's fleet delays the British invasion of northern New York.

NOVEMBER 29: Capt. Lambert Wickes sails the first Continental ship *Reprisal* into European waters, conveying commissioners Benjamin Franklin, Silas Deane, and Arthur Lee to France.

1777

JANUARY 23: Congress authorizes the construction of two more frigates.

Below: *On May 10, 1776, John Paul Jones received his first independent command, the 12-gun USS* Providence.

re-dyed the uniforms blue, the army carted them over the roads to Washington's suffering troops at Valley Forge.

What to do with Esek Hopkins became a sensitive issue for Congress. Stephen Hopkins, a member of the Naval Committee, was Esek's brother. Four of Esek's captains, Abraham Whipple, Nicholas Biddle, John Paul Jones, and Dudley Saltonstall, were all connected in some way to the Hopkins family, either by marriage or through other members of the Naval Committee. To sort out the confusion created by an excess of nepotism in the Naval Committee, Congress suspended Esek Hopkins and transferred the responsibilities of the Naval Committee to the Marine Committee, whose organization consisted of one member from each of the thirteen colonies. Finding no justification for keeping Esek Hopkins on suspension, the committee dismissed him from the service.

The Marine Committee met during the evening and appointed a chairman, vice chairman, and secretary. Five members represented a quorum. For every busy coastal district they appointed a naval agent and a prize agent, often being a single person wearing both hats. The naval agent handled arrangements for buying, refitting, and manning ships of war; the prize agent dealt with the disposition of captured prizes. In cities such as Boston and Philadelphia, the work became so immense that naval boards were formed.

During the war, the fortunes of the Continental Navy ebbed and flowed, causing a continuum of organizational changes. In 1779, Congress dis-

NAVY PAY

The commander of the sloop *Providence*, Captain John P. Rathbun, earned $48 a month; Marine Captain Trevett, $30; and Lieutenants Vesey and Bears and Sailing Master Sinkins, $24. Surgeon Ebenezer Richmond received $21.67; the three master's mates, $15; and two midshipmen, $12. Gunners, boatswains, and carpenters each received $13 a month and their mates $9. Wages for the rest of the crew ranged from $10 for the steward and sailmaker to $9 for the coxswain, cooper, gunner's yeomen, and master at arms, $8.50 for the cook and quartermaster, $8 for seamen, and $6.67 for marines. Without a cash advance, most men would not enlist, and those whose wage averaged less than $8 a month received an average advance of $75. If blessed with good fortune, all men shared prize money.

The men were supplied clothing from the ship's slop chest, which was charged to their account and averaged about $30 per person – about four months' work. The slop chest contents were valued more for their warmth than their style.

There was no official uniform for sailors of the Revolution. Most wore loose pants and shirts of brown homespun. Headgear consisted of a knitted cap or a scarf tied around the head to protect the ears when a cannon discharged. Footwear ranged from heavy shoes to bare feet. Some men drew pay, dipped into the slop chest, and deserted.

(From *Valor Fore and Aft*, Hope S. Rider.)

solved the Marine Committee and replaced it with a five-member board consisting of two congressmen and three knowledgeable members from the public. Two years later, when the navy reached its lowest ebb, Congress decided to put the fortunes of its creation under a single executive and on February 18, 1781, created the Secretary of Marine. No one wanted the post, but Congress goaded Robert Morris, a signatory of the Declaration of Independence and the secretary of finance, into accepting the office because of his prior experience in maritime matters.

Eight months passed before Morris agreed to take the office, preferring the less auspicious title of Agent of Marine. Morris endured more than three years of frustration as he watched the navy decline to virtual oblivion, caused by shortages of men and money. By 1784 the Continental Navy all but ceased to exist, and after three years of pledging his own credit to keep vessels afloat, Morris departed from office a disheartened man.

But at sea, not all was lost. Eleven states raised their own navies, eclipsing the number of ships put in service by the Continental Navy. Most of the vessels were lightly armed shallow-draft barges and galleys suited best for inland defense. Only Massachusetts, and to a lesser extent South

Carolina, set about commissioning seagoing vessels, but mainly for commerce raiding. The weaknesses of the state navies became apparent in November 1777, when the Royal Navy entered the Delaware River, captured Philadelphia, and vanquished the Pennsylvania Navy.

Of the thirteen frigates authorized by Congress on December 13, 1775, only seven ever got to sea. The other six were destroyed on the stocks to prevent their capture. The Naval Committee awarded frigate contracts to shipyards from Portsmouth, New Hampshire, to Baltimore, Maryland, but not enough skilled labor could be found to build them quickly. Privateering enterprises dominated the market. Investors granted more lucrative contracts to shipyards and paid in coin, not Continental scrip. They outbid the Continental Navy for arms and munitions, paid higher wages to the crew, granted more prize money, and gave lucrative bonuses to successful skippers.

For the American cause, privateering became both an asset and a liability. On the one hand it provided the colonies with arms, munitions, supplies, and vessels while crippling British commerce and disrupting the king's efforts to land reinforcements. On the other hand it siphoned off men, ships, and weapons desperately needed by the Continental Navy. During the span of the war, the privateers represented a destructive force that the weak Continental Navy could not have achieved.

RECRUITMENT PROBLEMS

Captains of Continental warships had to recruit their own crews. In the early days of the conflict, men needing employment joined during spirited rallies in the local alehouse. If more men were needed, sailors and marines marched through town waving banners, beating drums, and raising a patriotic and drunken ruckus. Men who signed-up returned from sea broadcasting their miserable experiences, and interest in joining the navy disintegrated. As one disillusioned sailor wrote, "Our officers…carry [a] stick with bullets and Ropes ends to beat us with and are kept from morning till night upon deck and have scarce time to eat…. We are used like dogs on Board the *Providence*. We hope that you will find a new Captain or a new Vessel."

After Jack Tar reached shore and received his pay in worthless Continental currency, he looked for employment elsewhere. When bonuses were offered, some men signed for a second tour, pocketed the cash and disappeared. If later discovered serving on a privateer, they were removed and treated as deserters.

Harsh treatment on board was sometimes justified. The army got rid of their malcontents, and prisons emptied their cells of felons, provided that the men agreed to serve in the navy. On occasion, and much to the chagrin of the public, naval officers impressed men loitering about the waterfront. Some British sailors falling into the hands of American commerce raiders agreed to join the navy rather than rot in jail. One group of impressed English sailors conspired to seize the frigate *Alliance*, murder her officers, and sail her to the nearest British port. The plot, discovered at the last moment, almost succeeded.

The Continental frigates able to get to sea led careers every bit as unremarkable as the quality of the crews they recruited. Any one of the vessels typified the misfortunes of the others.

In January 1777, the Marine Committee ordered *Randolph*, commanded by Captain Nicholas Biddle, and *Hornet* out of Philadelphia when the British began a westward thrust across New Jersey. Biddle needed a crew. He offered a $20 advance to waterfront idlers, but they turned it down. Every other able-bodied sailor had been marched off to war to serve in the artillery. Congress gave Biddle approval to fill out his crew using prisoners incarcerated in Philadelphia jails. Before he could gather a crew, ice blocked the river.

On the night of February 6, 1777, the 32-gun *Randolph* finally slipped down the Delaware River and passed the capes. She would be the first Continental warship to get to sea, but Biddle still had no crew, only a company of marines. He then reached the conclusion that he must be master of an unlucky ship. On a cruise northward to locate the pestiferous HMS *Milford*, which had been harassing New England shipping, *Randolph* sprang her foremast and then lost her mainmast. Biddle beat down to Charleston, South Carolina, for repairs. With a new pair of masts, the frigate prepared to clear Charleston's bar when struck twice by lightning. With both masts shattered, she limped back to Charleston.

After *Randolph*'s short, unsuccessful cruise during the summer of 1777, Biddle teamed up in February with ships of the South Carolina Navy to first clear the coast of British men-of-war and then destroy enemy merchantmen hailing for the

Left: *Benedict Arnold, who became one of Washington's best generals before he became one of the nation's greatest traitors, built the squadron on Lake Champlain that detained the invasion of the British by losing, during October 1776, the Battle of Valcour Bay. (This fanciful work is provided by the Anne S. K. Brown Military Collection, Providence, R.I.)*

MAY 28: Capt. Lambert Wickes commands the first squadron in European waters – *Reprisal*, *Lexington*, and *Dolphin* – capturing eighteen prizes off Britain.

JUNE 14: Congress adopts a national flag.

OCTOBER 1-NOVEMBER 22: To avoid capture, the Pennsylvania and Continental Navies destroy their ships on the Delaware.

1778

FEBRUARY 6: France signs a treaty of commerce and alliance with the United States.

FEBRUARY 14: France salutes the American flag as Capt. John Paul Jones enters Quiberon Bay.

APRIL 22-23: John Paul Jones, commanding the sloop *Ranger*, invades Whitehaven on England's west coast, marking the first time since 1667 that an enemy landing party set foot on British soil.

JUNE 17: France officially enters the war.

Above right: *During the summer of 1776, Brigadier General Benedict Arnold began a furious shipbuilding program to dispute command of Lake Champlain. The British, under the command of Major General Sir Guy Carleton, brought some of his vessels down from Montreal and built the others on the shores of the lake. In a running battle on October 11-13, 1776, off Valcour Island, Arnold lost the fight to a superior force, but delayed Major General John Burgoyne's advance into New York until the spring of 1777.*

YANKEE

The name Yankee became familiar around the world, but its origination is still cloaked in a little mystery. Early American sea captains were known to drive hard bargains. Their main competition came from the Dutch, who were also determined negotiators. Whenever the two crossed paths, the Dutch referred to Americans as "Yankers," meaning wranglers, and the moniker still persists.

West Indies. Under Biddle, the little fleet cooperated well but failed to accomplish its objective. On the evening of March 17, 1778, Biddle ran afoul of the 64-gun *Yarmouth*. After an engagement lasting fifteen minutes, *Randolph* exploded with the loss of all but four of her 305 men.

As a fighting force, General Benedict Arnold's freshwater navy on Lake Champlain had no better success against the British than the Continental Navy's salt water flotilla, but Arnold, though he did not know it at the time, held the key to one of the turning points of the Revolution – the Battle of Saratoga.

Long, slender Lake Champlain touched the border of Canada to the north and emptied into the Hudson River. Late in 1775 an American army invaded Quebec, hopeful of making it a fourteenth colony. In the spring of the following year the British navy arrived with reinforcements and sent the Yankees back across the border. With no American force between the St. Lawrence and the northern route into Lake Champlain, Washington's army at New York lay vulnerable to a British incursion down the Hudson River.

Arnold's three small schooners were the only armed vessels on the lake when the British decided to build a small fleet on the St. Lawrence and portage it across the route to Lake Champlain. General Sir Guy Carleton, the British commander, had the resources to construct vessels far more powerful than anything Arnold could build. When Arnold discovered Carleton's intentions, he accepted the challenge and engaged in a furious boat-building race.

ARNOLD DELAYS THE BRITISH

Thirty-five-year-old Benedict Arnold was one of Washington's best generals and became one of America's most despised traitors. Four years would separate the two events. Born in Connecticut, Arnold began his career as a druggist and bookseller in New Haven. Finding life dull, he became a merchant and sailed his own ships to Europe and the Caribbean. During those years, his quick mind grasped the fundamentals of ships and shipbuilding. In 1775 he and Ethan Allen captured Fort Ticonderoga, a remote outpost on Lake Champlain. Then, in perhaps the most exhausting expedition of the war, he brought his army through the forests, rivers, and mountains of Maine in an unsuccessful effort to capture Quebec City, during which he suffered a wound. Promoted brigadier general in 1776, Arnold now found himself back at Fort Ticonderoga where he set to work designing and building his fleet. A handful of skilled workers cut lumber, shaped planks, fitted together four two-masted row galleys with lanteen sails and mounted the boats with guns, the largest being 24-pounders. They also built nine gondolas, each with one short mast that carried two square sails. Four small schooner- and sloop-rigged craft made up the remainder of the flotilla. Each vessel carried two or three small guns with an 18-pounder mounted in the bow. Arnold divided his "motley crew" of 750 soldiers into sailors, marines, and gunners but made oarsmen out of most of them.

Meanwhile, Carleton built a fleet designed to overwhelm anything the Yankees could cobble together at Fort Ticonderoga. The 18-gun sloop-of-war *Inflexible*, built at Quebec, had to be knocked down into sections and hauled overland to Lake Champlain. While the army reassembled *Inflexible*, Carleton's shipwrights built a two-masted scow and mounted enough firepower on her to send Arnold's entire squadron into oblivion. To further augment his fleet, Carleton added twenty gunboats and a few small sailing vessels, each mounting a single cannon in the bow. Satisfied with his creations, and knowing that General Horatio Gates wanted Fort Ticonderoga as a base for future operations, Carleton pushed off on October 11, 1776, and in a favorable breeze headed down the lake with his army.

Arnold expected the visit and anchored his vessels in the narrow bay between Valcour Island and the New York shore. As anticipated, the British fleet sailed by. After Carleton discovered his error, he tacked and beat slowly back against the wind. While the British squadron struggled to get into position, Arnold opened with all his guns. For several minutes, Yankee gunners had

their way, pouring a devastating fire into the disorganized British flotilla. Once Carleton moved into range, trained British gunners went to work, tearing to pieces the flimsy American fleet, dismounting guns, and soaking Arnold's craft with soldiers' blood. Fog settled in at nightfall, and Arnold escaped through the British cordon with the remnants of his battered boats. He and his survivors took to the woods. He had lost the fight but postponed the British attack until the following summer. British General John Burgoyne would not find the going so easy when he marched his redcoats onto the meadows of Saratoga.

As for Arnold, having quarreled with civil authorities, in 1780 he began communicating with British General Sir Henry Clinton. Arnold conspired to surrender West Point, but the plot was discovered, forcing him to flee to the British camp. He commanded British forces during raids in Virginia and Connecticut, burned the town of New London, and spent the rest of his life in poverty and disgrace in England and Canada.

BEN FRANKLIN'S PRIVATEERS

When seventy-year-old Benjamin Franklin went to France, his primary mission was to draw Louis XVI into a conflict with Great Britain. At first, France refused to do anything that might lead to war, but agreed to lend money and ships, and allow American privateers to use her ports. Beyond this she would not go, and all the clever diplomacy of Franklin was for a time in vain. Still determined to bring France into the war, Franklin used every trick to disrupt relations between

Left: *In 1776 two new Continental warships took to the high seas, the 16-gun brig* Lexington, *Captain John Barry, and the 18-gun brig* Reprisal, *Captain Lambert Wickes. Barry captured the British sloop* Edward *off the Virginia Capes, and Wickes sailed to the Caribbean where he engaged the British sloop-of-war* Shark.

▶ **1779**

FEBRUARY 7: The French government purchases for John Paul Jones a vessel he renames *Bonhomme Richard.*

JUNE 21: Spain declares war on Great Britain without recognizing the independence of the United States.

Right: *Gustavus Conyngham, a Philadelphia shipmaster who became stranded in Europe at the outbreak of war, went to Paris looking for a commission. He received a captaincy from Ben Franklin, who told him to go shopping for a ship.*

Below: *On February 6, 1778, Captain John Paul Jones, commanding the 18-gun* Ranger, *sailed into Quiberon Bay and exchanged salutes, the first to the American flag by a Frenchman, the admiral's flagship* Robuste.

Britain and France by using the latter's own policies on privateering to infuriate the British. So when John Paul Jones went to L'Orient to transform an old East Indiaman into the 50-gun *Bonhomme Richard,* Franklin knew he could commission more vessels to cruise out of French ports and held blank commissions signed by John Hancock, President of the Continental Congress, to do so.

Franklin came to France having no interest in naval affairs, a matter he admitted knowing nothing about. Operating without any specific instructions from Congress, and finding himself drawn into contentious issues over naval escapades caused by Americans sailing French-owned privateers, Franklin envisioned an opportunity to

'*Until I arrived in France and became acquainted with that great tactician Count D'Orvilliers, and his judicious assistant the Chevalier du Pavillon, who each of them honored me with instructions respecting the science of growing operations, etc., I must confess I was not sensible how ignorant I had been, before that time, of naval tactics.*'

—JOHN PAUL JONES
TO NAVY DEPARTMENT IN
SELECT NAVAL DOCUMENTS.

implicate France in the war after meeting Stephen Marchant. A shipmaster from Boston, Marchant had escaped from a British prison, landing in Dunkirk, France, with a number of sailors. M. Sutton de Clonard, a nobleman with maritime experience, suggested to Franklin that Marchant be given command of a 16-gun cutter lying idle at Dunkirk. Franklin knew that commissioning a privateer would involve him in more trouble, but for several months he had been unsuccessful in exchanging British sailors for captured Americans, mainly because he had no British seamen to trade. Privateering gave him a source. It also gave him an opportunity to enroll France in more trouble with the British. Franklin dispatched the commission to Marchant with orders to bring all prisoners to France "because they serve to relieve so many of our Country-men from the Captivity in England."

account of themselves.

Franklin found the Comte de Vergennes, foreign minister to King Louis XVI, not anxious to provoke another war with Britain until convinced that the colonists possessed the resolve to sustain the fight for independence. France also wanted time to rebuild her navy. In the meantime, Franklin worked out a scheme with Vergennes for shipping arms and supplies to America through a dummy gunrunning company having no traceable antecedents.

Wickes, however, brought his prizes into France. When Britain protested and insisted that *Reprisal* be ejected from port, Vergennes parried the demand, giving Wickes time to repair his sloop. Meanwhile, the 14-gun Continental brigantine *Lexington* and the lightly armed cutter *Dolphin* arrived from the colonies and on May 28, 1777, sailed with *Reprisal* into the Irish Sea. During a one-month cruise the squadron captured eighteen prizes, causing a panic among British merchants who in turn placed demands upon the Royal Navy for protection. Chased by the 74-gun HMS *Burford*, Wickes beat a hasty retreat for the safety of a French port, jettisoning his guns to make the escape. The British were furious, leveling an ultimatum on France that she expel *Reprisal* or suffer the consequences. For

Once Franklin made a decision, nothing stood in his way of executing it. Marchant renamed his cutter *Black Prince* and went to sea. Joined later by the *Black Princess* and *Fearnot*, the three privateers during 1779-1780 captured 114 prizes, scuttling 11 and ransoming 76, out of which they paroled 161 prisoners to France for exchange. In 1780 Louis XVI decided that having American privateers operate out of France was not such a good idea, but by then the British and the French were at war.

One of the most useful missions of the Continental Navy was transporting Benjamin Franklin to France. Had the navy accomplished nothing else, placing Franklin in Paris may have been enough. France had supported America's war for independence since its inception and was anxious to use the conflict to retaliate against the British for taking Canada. Captain Lambert Wickes drew the assignment. He loaded the elderly American statesman on the 18-gun sloop-of-war *Reprisal*, and in December, 1776, deposited him on French soil.

Wickes then sailed "directly on the coast of England," which made him the first Continental sailor to make war in Britain's home waters. In early January he captured three brigs, a ship, and a snow (similar to a small brig-rigged ship with a slightly different sail pattern). During the fight with the snow, *Reprisal*'s first lieutenant lost his arm. Wickes's marines — two officers and thirty men — were some of the same whom at Lake Champlain Arnold had called "the refuse of every regiment," but in the North Sea they gave a good

Left: *Captain Conyngham bought a cutter at Dunkirk, fitted her with 14 guns, named her* Revenge, *and sailed her into British coastal waters. There he took more than twenty prizes, often finding his ship engaged by two enemy vessels at the same time.*

Below: *On October 5, 1775, John Barry, commanding the merchant ship* Black Prince, *told Congress of two British vessels laden with munitions en route to Quebec. Congress, wishing to intercept these vessels, promptly bought* Black Prince *and converted her into the 24-gun brig* Alfred. *Though* Alfred *never made it to sea to interdict the British munitions ships, she was among the first to engage an enemy frigate, the sloop-of-war* Glasgow, *off Block Island, Rhode Island.*

JULY 19–AUGUST 17: The largest American joint army-navy amphibious operation of the war ends in disaster at Castine, on the Penobscot River.

SEPTEMBER 23: John Paul Jones, commanding *Bonhomme Richard*, captures the HMS *Serapis* off Flamborough Head.

1780

MAY 12: Capt. Abraham Whipple surrenders four vessels when the British capture Charleston.

Above right: *John Paul Jones (1747-1792) rose quickly in the ranks, from lieutenant in 1775 to captain in 1776. Born in Scotland, he entered the war as a rather obscure person and won battles that matched the romantic victories of Sir Francis Drake and Sir John Hawkins. He ended his career as an admiral in the Russian navy, still looking for a fight.*

Right: *What memorabilia exists from the life of John Paul Jones's career in the Continental Navy is his cuirass and what is believed to be his sextant.*

JOHN PAUL JONES

John Paul Jones, born John Paul, Jr., grew up on an estate on the shores of Solway Firth, where his father worked as a gardener. In 1761, at age thirteen, he went to sea, taking voyages that eventually landed him in Virginia, where in Fredericksburg his older brother William worked as a tailor. But John Paul chose the sea as his profession, and at the youthful age of twenty-one became a captain.

In 1773 his life became mysteriously muddled at Tobago. According to his own account, he killed a mutinous sailor in self-defense. Urged by his friends to flee, he disappeared. Twenty months later he reappeared in Fredericksburg under the name of John Paul Jones. As Jones, he applied for a commission in the Continental Navy and became first lieutenant on the frigate *Alfred* during the New Providence expedition. There he met men such as Nicholas Biddle and Abraham Whipple. As a reward for distinguished service on *Alfred* and *Providence*, the Marine Committee gave him command of the 18-gun sloop-of-war *Ranger*. Late in 1777 he sailed *Ranger* across the Atlantic and into British waters, initiating a new era for American naval vessels operating abroad, taking the war to the enemy.

> *'I wish to have no Connection with any Ship that does not sail fast, for I intend to go in harm's way.'*
>
> JOHN PAUL JONES
> TO JACQUES DONTIEN LE RAY DE CHAUMONT ON SECURING A FRENCH MAN-OF-WAR.

Vergennes, the time had not yet come for a new war with Britain, so *Reprisal* and *Lexington* sailed for home. The British captured *Lexington* off the coast of France, and *Reprisal* foundered off Newfoundland, drowning Wickes and all but one of his crew.

Raids in British waters did not end with the eviction of Wickes. Gustavus Conyngham, a Philadelphia shipmaster, became stranded in Europe at the outbreak of the war. Awarded a captain's commission in the Continental Navy, he obtained a lugger, named it *Surprise*, and captured a British mail packet carrying sensitive doc-

uments that he dispatched to Franklin. The British howled in protest, so Vergennes appeased them by arresting Conyngham and seizing the lugger. Vergennes held Conyngham only long enough for the Continental Navy to supply him with another vessel. By the end of the year Conyngham was back in business with the 14-gun cutter *Revenge*. For eighteen months he prowled in and out of the North Sea, captured sixty prizes, and did such damage to British commerce as to bring France and Britain to the brink of war.

Toward the end of 1777 John Paul Jones, commanding the 18-gun sloop *Ranger*, sailed across the Atlantic to bring the war to the doorstep of the enemy. By the time he reached France, the Continental Army had fought the Battle of Saratoga and put the redcoats to shame. France signed a treaty of alliance with the United States and opened her ports, which had been closed to American commerce. Unlike Wickes and Conyingham, Jones found France fully receptive to his presence.

Determined to make a statement, Jones sailed *Ranger* into Quiberon Bay, the anchorage of the French fleet, and unfurled the Union banner. He sailed past the French flagship, gave her a thirteen-gun salute, and received nine in return – the first salute to the Stars and Stripes by a foreign man-of-war.

JONES INVADES BRITAIN

Satisfied by his reception, Jones set sail on April 10 for the Irish Sea, having in mind an attack on Whitehaven, a town on the northwest coast of England near his place of birth. He knew the harbor and expected it to be filled with shipping. And so it was, but as his two boatloads of volunteer firebrands circulated through the docks they were too hasty setting the ships ablaze. The townsfolk, aided by a rainstorm, rushed to the waterfront and soon extinguished the fires. Chagrined by his lack of success at Whitehaven, Jones crossed Solway Firth in the morning and landed on St. Mary's Isle, the home of the Earl of Selkirk. He intended to kidnap the earl and

exchange him for American seamen in British prisons, but Selkirk was away. While Jones contemplated his next move, *Ranger's* landing party collected Selkirk's family silver. Jones did not stop them, but he later bought it from the crew and returned it to the earl.

News of the American invasion spread quickly, but instead of seeking safety in a French port, Jones remained in the Irish Sea and intercepted the 20-gun sloop-of-war *Drake*. Though the vessels were evenly matched in firepower, Jones had the better crew. The Americans forced *Drake* to strike, which was exactly what Jones wanted. Now he had a trophy, a British man-of-war, something to carry back to France as justification for a more powerful ship.

Eight months passed before the resourceful Ben Franklin scraped up an old 900-ton East Indiaman, the 42-gun *Duc de Duras*. Having seen better days, the vessel did not overly impress Jones, but she was twice the size of *Ranger* and carried good French guns. In deference to Franklin, he re-christened her *Bonhomme Richard*, using as his reference the French translation of the doctor's popular *Poor Richard's Almanac*.

Above: *No more famous words came out of the Revolutionary War than John Paul Jones's response, on September 23, 1779, to Captain Richard Pearson's demand that Jones surrender the* Bonhomme Richard *to the HMS* Serapis. *With his ship in flames and slowly sinking, Jones shouted back, "I have not yet begun to fight," and then proved it by forcing Pearson to surrender. Two days later the battered* Bonhomme Richard *sank. Jones removed his prisoners and crew to* Serapis *and on October 3 sailed into Trexel.*

Below: *A model of Bonhomme Richard, which was nothing akin to the sleek frigates built by the Continental Navy, but rather an old East Indiaman Le Duc de Duras, of 850 to 900 tons burthen. It took Jones six months to arm and outfit his new command, and he never improved her much beyond the slow, leaky, and wallowing craft she had become in the French merchant service.*

Jones pulled together a mixed crew of 380 officers and men. Seventeen of the 20 officers were personally handpicked Americans. Of 43 petty officers, half were Americans, the other half being British deserters or prisoners of war. The sailors and marines were mostly French or British with a smattering of other nationalities. Only 46 were Americans – recent escapees from British prisons – and they believed that with Jones there would be an opportunity to square accounts.

On August 14, 1779, Jones put to sea. With him went the 32-gun American frigate *Alliance*, commanded by an eccentric Frenchman, Pierre Landais, three ships of the French navy, and two French privateers which soon deserted. Jones could not control Landais, who made it clear to the commodore that he intended to follow his

own breezes. Jones captured several rich prizes in the Irish Sea, crammed his hold with 200 prisoners and, after creating a new wave of terror for British shipping, sailed his squadron around the Orkney Islands and into the North Sea.

On the evening of September 23 off Flamborough Head, Jones fell in with a large southbound convoy shepherded by the powerful 44-gun HMS *Serapis*, commanded by Capt. Richard Pearson, and the 20-gun sloop-of-war *Countess of Scarborough*. Jones wanted to break up and capture the convoy with its valuable naval supplies, but Pearson interposed his frigate between Jones's squadron and the merchantmen. Although night was falling, Jones ordered an immediate attack, but Landais wandered off, taking with him the other French vessels.

Left to fight *Serapis* alone, Jones opened with a broadside that was answered by one from Pearson. As both vessels maneuvered to rake the other, Jones heard a detonation on the lower gun deck that shook *Richard* from stem to stern. Two of the ship's 18-pounders had exploded, wiping out the gun crews and sending the stench of burning flesh mixed with screams of the wounded through a hole blown in the upper deck.

Having lost two of his best guns, Jones now realized that *Richard* was a poor match for *Serapis*. He tried to board her, but Pearson used his ship's superior speed to out-maneuver *Richard*. In a panicky effort to come alongside, *Richard* accidentally steered into the stern of *Serapis*, leaving Jones unable to fire while Pearson pounded away with his after guns. Thinking he had won the day, Pearson called out,

Right: *On September 23, 1779, the eve of the Battle off Flamborough Head, John Paul Jones was mainly interested in attacking a British convoy of 41 sail homeward-bound from the Baltic, but* Serapis, *50 guns, and* Countess of Scarborough, *20, moved between Jones and the merchantmen.* Pallas, *32, under the command of Captain Denis-Nicholas Cottineau, engaged* Countess *so Jones could concentrate on* Serapis. *After a grueling combat of more than three hours, both British vessels struck their colors.*

▶ **1781**

FEBRUARY 7:
Congress creates the office of Secretary of Marine to manage all naval affairs.

MARCH 1: Congress adopts the Articles of Confederation.

MAY 21: Vice Admiral François Comte de Grasse, commanding the French fleet, prepares to sail for the American coast.

AUGUST 4: The British army under Lord Cornwallis camps at Yorktown, Virginia, to await supplies.

AUGUST 30: de Grasse's French fleet arrives off the Chesapeake.

SEPTEMBER 5: The French fleet meets the British fleet under Admiral Thomas Lord Graves in a drawn battle..

SEPTEMBER 14-28: General Washington, aided by French troops, puts Cornwallis's army under siege.

OCTOBER 19: Lord Cornwallis surrenders.

"Has your ship struck?" Jones trumpeted back, "I have not yet begun to fight!"

Of such a nervy reply, Pearson had his doubts, but *Bonhomme Richard* sheered off and caught wind from *Serapis*. Sliding by, Jones conned his ship across *Serapis*'s bow. Pearson countered to avoid a raking broadside, but in the confusion *Serapis*'s bowsprit struck *Bonhomme Richard*'s poop deck, snarled in the mizzen rigging, and locked the two vessels together.

"Well done!" shouted Jones. "We've got her now!"

MORTAL COMBAT

The two men-of-war, touching barrel to barrel in mortal combat, blazed away until fires broke out on both vessels. With all guns knocked out except for two 9-pounders on the quarterdeck, Jones brought a third over from the idle port side, intending to use it to bring the down the enemy's mainmast.

Before Jones could get the gun in position, the *Alliance* emerged suddenly from the darkness, and Landais fired a broadside into the stern of *Richard*. The survivors aft shouted to Landais that he had fired on the wrong ship, only to be met with a second broadside. In the smoke and turmoil, Landais might not have recognized *Richard*, and he stopped firing once Jones raised the proper recognition signal. But Jones, whose

> *'The victory was wholly and solely due to the immovable courage of Paul Jones. The* Richard *was beaten more than once; but the spirit of Jones could not be overcome.'*
>
> CAPT. ALEXANDER SLIDELL MACKENZIE, *THE LIFE OF PAUL JONES.*

relations with Landais had been turbulent, believed the broadsides had been deliberate. Later, he brought charges against Landais, causing him to be dismissed from the Navy.

A British prisoner escaping from *Richard* informed Pearson that Jones's ship was sinking. This gave Pearson little encouragement because his own decks were being swept by musket fire from *Richard*, causing his gunners to leave their guns. Powder monkeys continued to bring up cartridges faster than they could be consumed, and small piles began to gather along the gundeck. One of Jones's sailors, carrying a basket of hand grenades, crawled out to the end of a yard overhanging *Serapis*'s deck and scattered the grenades on the enemy vessel. One rolled onto the gundeck, exploded among the cartridges, and started a chain reaction. An enormous explosion rocked the gundeck, instantly killing twenty British sailors and scorching dozens of others. Rattled by the explosion and seeing his mainmast tottering, Pearson feared that he would now be attacked by

Above left: *On September 25, 1779, John Paul Jones waved a last farewell to* Bonhomme Richard *as she sank beneath the sea. Captain Pearson (left) of* Serapis *watched with guarded satisfaction as he observed the ship that beat him make her final departure.*

1782

November 30: The United States and Britain sign a preliminary peace treaty.

1783

SEPTEMBER 3: In Paris, American and British commissioners conclude a peace settlement.

1785

Congress terminates the Continental Navy and orders the sale of the nation's last armed vessel.

Above right: *In 1779, after more than three years of fighting, the Continental Navy finally created its official seal.*

Below: *On June 28, 1776, a British fleet of 10 ships and 30 transports carrying 2,500 troops under Sir Henry Clinton were repulsed at Charleston, South Carolina. In 1780, the British tried again, and this time they succeeded.*

Alliance and surrendered. After three-and-one-half hours of battle, blood covered the deck so deep in places that it ran, as one of Jones's lieutenants recalled, "over one's shoes."

Two days later, from the deck of *Serapis,* Jones watched as the gallant old *Bonhomme Richard* plunged to the bottom of the North Sea. He sailed *Serapis* back to France, along with the *Countess of Scarborough*, which had been captured by the French frigate *Pallas.* For Jones, it was a glorious moment. He went on to become captain of *Alliance, Ariel,* and the 74-gun *America*, and when life became dull after the war, he joined the Russian navy as an admiral. He gave the Continental Navy a legacy it direly needed – a tradition for valor without regard for the costs.

The Continental Navy continued its struggle in home waters, with little success. On the night of March 31, 1778, Capt. James Nicholson, the Continental Navy's senior officer, tried to run the 28-gun frigate USS *Virginia* through the British blockade. The pilot put her aground under British guns off the Virginia capes. On April 1 – "All Fool's Day" – Nicholson abandoned his ship and crew, leaving both to be captured by the enemy.

Two other expeditions by the Continental Navy also ended in disaster. In July, 1779, Capt. Dudley Saltonstall, commanding the 32-gun frigate *Warren* and a force of some nineteen vessels, attempted to capture a British base on Maine's Penobscot River. A thousand men from Massachusetts joined the expedition, but a dispute over tactics between the two forces led to a lengthy siege instead of a lightning attack. When a British relief force hove in sight in August, the infantry fled to the woods, leaving the navy without support. Saltonstall lost all control of his

men. They ran their ships ashore, set them on fire, and followed the army into the thicket.

Nine months later, the ineptness of Continental forces again manifested itself during the defense of Charleston. Early in 1780 three frigates, *Boston*, *Providence*, and *Queen of France*, and Jones's old sloop of war *Ranger*, hurried down to Charleston to prevent General Sir Henry Clinton from capturing the city. The British blockaded the harbor, and Clinton sent his regiments ashore. Instead of defending the city, the Continental Navy found itself trapped inside the harbor, and when the city surrendered on May 12, the navy did the same. In this manner ended the short and not so glorious career of the Continental Navy.

Fearing an attack on New York by the combined forces of Washington and the Comte de Rochambeau, Clinton hurried north, leaving the ambitious Lord Cornwallis in charge of southern operations. Thinking he could recruit enough Tories to destroy American resistance in the south, Cornwallis launched a bloody campaign that on August 1, 1781, brought his straggling army of 7,000 men to Yorktown, Virginia, where he looked to the Royal Navy for aid. What Cornwallis did not know was that two fleets were converging on the same point at the same time, one of them French.

In mid-July 1781, while Clinton remained in New York, General Washington and Rochambeau marched quickly south while the French fleet under the Comte de Grasse moved from the Caribbean toward the Chesapeake. As de Grasse sailed north, Admiral Sir Samuel Hood divided his West Indies squadron and, to escape the hurricane season, sent half of it home, leaving him with fourteen ships scarred by long service in the

tropics. Those he sent to the American coast in pursuit of de Grasse, who had retained all twenty-eight of his warships. During their respective voyages north, the two fleets saw nothing of each other. Hood reached the Chesapeake first and, seeing no evidence of a French fleet, went on to New York.

In Long Island Sound Admiral Hood rendezvoused with Admiral Thomas Graves, who had been blockading a small French squadron at Newport, Rhode Island. Though Graves was senior officer, Hood persuaded him to join forces, sail to the Chesapeake, and rescue the besieged Cornwallis. The two admirals combined forces and with nineteen ships found de Grasse's squadron stretched across the mouth of the Chesapeake and backed by both the wind and the tide. Admiral Graves delayed the attack, and this enabled de Grasse to work to sea and reorganize his command.

Each fleet formed in a single line, faced off against a ship of equal strength, and for two hours blasted away at each other. Poor preparation and mistaken signals prevented some of the British vessels from getting into the action. When night fell, neither side had lost a ship, but the British vessels had suffered heavily. For several days, both fleets maneuvered off the Chesapeake without ever engaging. On October 19, 1781,

> '...whatever efforts are made by the Land Armies, the Navy must have the casting vote in the present contest.'
>
> GEORGE WASHINGTON
> TO COMTE DE GRASSE,
> OCTOBER 28, 1781.

Cornwallis gave up all hope of rescue and surrendered to his besiegers, giving Washington and his French allies the decisive victory of the war.

On September 3, 1783, Great Britain signed the Treaty of Paris, relinquishing her claim to the United States. The few ships still in possession of the Continental Navy went swiftly to the auction block, all except John Barry's *Alliance*. Some members of Congress wanted to keep her as a symbol of the Revolutionary navy, others for protection against a growing infestation of pirates, but the country could not afford the gallant old vessel. Like the Continental Navy itself, *Alliance* vanished into obscurity. But there were men who had earned their stripes in the nation's first navy and at another time, some of them would be called into service again.

Below: *Captain Joshua Barney (1759-1818) served through the American Revolution on* Wasp, Sachem, Virginia, *and* Saratoga. *Though he fought valiantly, he had the dubious distinction of being captured three times by the British.*

JOSHUA BARNEY AND JOHN BARRY

After the victory at Yorktown, where no ship of the Continental Navy participated, two young captains kept alive the war at sea. Eighteen months would pass before the conflict ended, and though the Continental Navy had all but disintegrated, Joshua Barney and John Barry gave it new spirit.

Barney had the distinction of being a captain of a merchant vessel at the age of sixteen, a privateersman, a three-time prisoner of the British, and in between, an officer in the Continental Navy. On April 8, 1782, twenty-three-year-old Barney sailed out of Delaware Bay in charge of *Hyder Ally*, an old Philadelphia merchantmen put into service to protect a fleet of trading vessels. On his way to sea he ran afoul of two British blockaders, the 20-gun HMS *General Monk*, which he attacked, and the frigate *Quebec*, which, backed by the wind, could not get into the action. To mislead the captain of *Monk*, Barney shouted false orders to his helmsman. The British skipper went one way and Barney the other, enabling *Hyder Ally* to fasten onto *Monk*'s bow and rake the vessel into submission, thereby enabling the merchantmen to escape.

Captain John Barry, commanding the frigate *Alliance*, had been operating on his own during most of the war. He had pitted his ship against sloops-of-war and won. But in March 1783, he had a new challenge – to bring the *Duc de*

Lauzun, loaded with 100,000 Spanish dollars, safely back to an American port.

On March 10, 1783, the situation looked desperate when he observed three British men-of-war, the 32-gun *Alarm*, the 28-gun *Sybil*, and the 18-gun *Tobago*, all converging on him. When the British attempted to separate *Alliance* from *Lauzun*, Barry fought them off and, though his ship was riddled with shot, held his fire until coming abreast of the fast *Sybil*. At close range, he opened with a broadside that shattered *Sybil* and sent her scampering for safety. Three days later the war ended.

Left: *Captain John Barry (1745-1803) commanded the brig* Lexington *(and many others) and captured the first British ship of the war. On February 22, 1797, President Washington presented Barry with a captain's commission in the new United States Navy.*

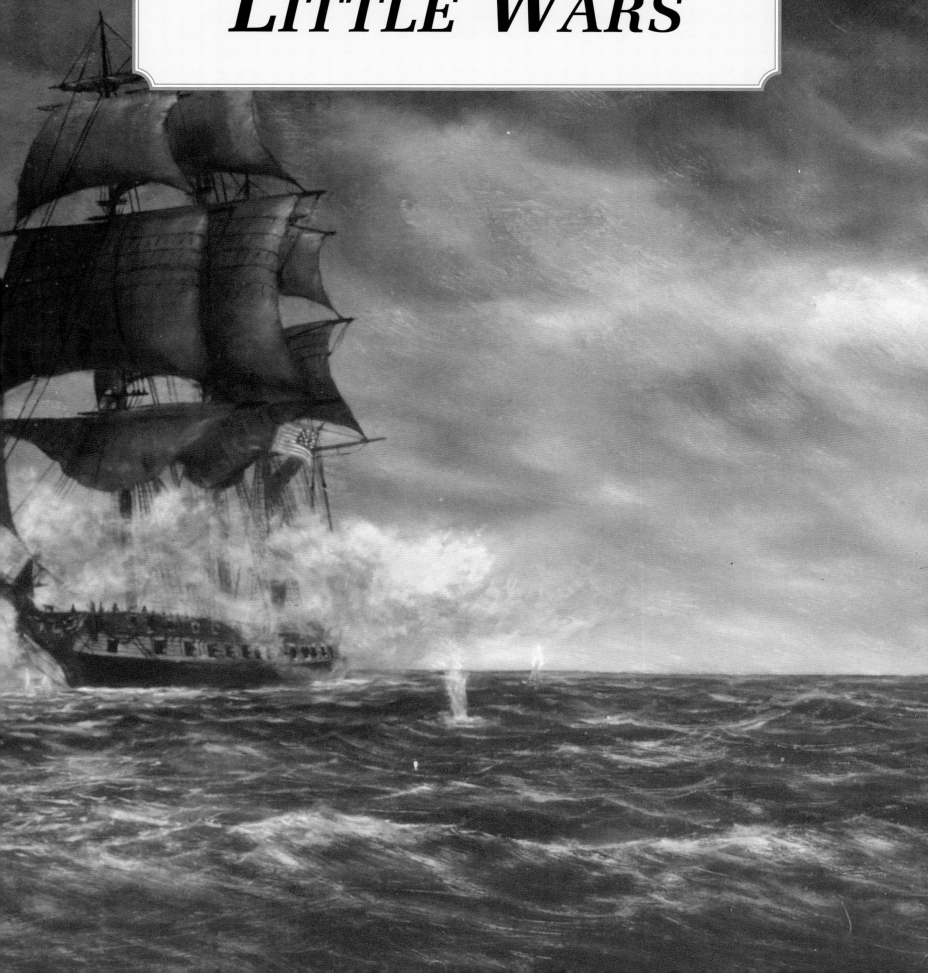

CHAPTER TWO

THE LITTLE WARS

TIMELINE

1791

JANUARY 6: Barbary States demand tribute from the United States.

1794

MARCH 27: Congress approves six frigates, all to be canceled if an agreement is struck with Algiers.

1796

SEPTEMBER 5: A treaty with Algiers is negotiated.

1796

MARCH 2: Construction of six frigates is stopped upon ratification of the Algerian treaty.

APRIL 20: Congress releases *Constellation*, *Constitution*, and *United States* for completion.

1797

MAY 16: President John Adams asks Congress to strengthen the Navy because of French attacks on commerce.

Right: *The USS* Constitution, *44 guns, launched from Boston on October 21, 1797, was among the first of the American frigates to carry its guns on a double tier. Her sister ships,* President *and* United States, *did the same. The Navy designed* Constitution *to outfight and outrun enemy ships of the line, yet planked her heavily with timber.*

When the Continental Navy auctioned off its last warship on August 1, 1785, and sailed into oblivion, the Yankee merchant fleet had spread its sheets to the wind, calling upon ports of the world. Without a navy to protect them, traders carrying the Stars and Stripes into the Mediterranean fell prey to the roving corsairs of the Barbary States — Algiers, Tunis, Morocco, and Tripoli. This centuries-old business operated like a floating tollgate, levying tribute upon the commerce of all nations. Unless skippers paid bribes, brigands seized the ships and held the occupants for ransom. Yankee traders had forgotten this threat, having for so many years been safeguarded by the Royal Navy.

Now they were vulnerable, having neither a navy for protection nor a readiness to pay tribute to a pack of waterborne thieves.

The same year that Congress dissolved the Continental Navy, Algerian corsairs captured two Yankee merchantmen and held their crews for ransom. Algeria demanded $59,496; Congress offered only $4,200. Having been charged with negotiating a solution, John Adams and Thomas Jefferson, ministers to England and France, said it would be cheaper to build a navy to protect American shipping than to pay tribute. Since Congress had no money to pay tribute, they also had no money for a navy, so for four years nothing was done to discourage the Barbary bunch from continuing their raids on Yankee vessels.

Were it not for the Barbary problem, the Constitution of 1789 may never have authorized Congress "to provide and maintain a navy." When Jefferson returned to America in 1791 to become Secretary of State, he again recommended that a navy be fitted out to suppress the Mediterranean pirates. Secretary of War General Henry Knox had been handling naval affairs and obtained quotes for building a few frigates. Finding such costs beyond the means of the country, Congress tabled the matter.

BRITAIN AND FRANCE AT WAR

In 1793 Britain and France were at war again, a conflict that was to span two decades. The conflict had an immediate effect on American shipping. The Portuguese, who had effectively kept corsairs confined to the Mediterranean, removed their Strait of Gibraltar blockade to appease the British. Barbary vessels poured into the Atlantic and in two months captured twelve Yankee ships and imprisoned their crews. Some in Congress believed that the British had coaxed the Portuguese into lifting their blockade for the sole purpose of discouraging Americans from trading in southern Europe.

The attacks stimulated debates in Congress, which on January 20, 1794, resulted in a proposal to build six vessels, four of 44 guns and two of 20 guns (later 36 guns). The cost, $600,000, created a heated sectional debate. Northern Federalists favored it; the southern landed gentry opposed it. On March 27 Congress passed the bill, but with a condition: if peace terms could be negotiated with Algeria, work on building a navy would stop. Congress then voted to spend $800,000 – more than the cost of a new navy – to obtain a treaty with Algeria that would free about a hundred American captives.

While some in Congress lobbied for arming merchantmen, President George Washington told General Knox to build new ships, not the kind cobbled together during the Revolution. Knox agreed. He informed the men called together to work on the project that the president wanted vessels of "strength, durability, swiftness of sailing, and force, as to render them superior to any frigate belonging to the European powers." The design committee, influenced by shipbuilder Joshua Humphreys of Philadelphia, developed a frigate that was longer, wider, and more streamlined than any vessel previously built in America. The frigates could outrun any British man-of-war and outmaneuver any vessel of the same size. Instead of 44 guns, some frigates carried 56 and, in place of the usual 18-pounders, they mounted 24s and a battery of heavy short-range, stubby-barreled 32-pounder carronades.

To save money the government by accident

'*Prepare, and always be prepared, for War by sea.*'

JOHN PAUL JONES TO JOHN JAY.

'*A Naval power, next to the militia, is the natural defense of the United States*'

JOHN ADAMS TO CONGRESS, MARCH 4, 1797.

As was customary with government appropriations, six states participated in the building program:

Chesapeake, 44 guns	Baltimore, Maryland
Congress, 36 guns	Portsmouth, New Hampshire
Constellation, 36 guns	Norfolk, Virginia
Constitution, 44 guns	Boston, Massachusetts
President, 44 guns	New York City
United States, 44 guns	Philadelphia, Pennsylvania

made a good decision. Instead of awarding contracts to individual shipbuilders, they rented yards, hired constructors and agents, specified materials, appointed captains, and by default sowed the seeds for operating permanent naval shipyards. The building program was well underway when in September 1795 the Dey of Algeria agreed to a treaty: the cost, $525,000 in bribes and ransom money and a 36-gun frigate. In compliance with the terms of the Navy Act of 1795, all work stopped on the frigates. Washington scolded Congress for allowing such waste, forcing another furious debate. The Legislature reached a compromise, enabling *Constellation*, *Constitution*, and *United States* to be completed.

Meanwhile, the Treaty of Alliance of 1778 with France began creating problems for the United States. The government had an obligation to open its ports to French privateers, but most Americans wanted to stay out of the war. Even Washington, who favored the British, and Jefferson, who liked the revolutionary spirit of the French, both agreed that the nation should remain neutral. John Jay's treaty with Britain in 1794 resolved many residual issues from the Revolution but angered France. During the summer and early fall of 1796, Frenchmen seized more than 300 American vessels. When John Adams became president on March 4, 1797, he demanded that the other three frigates on which construction had been suspended be completed. Congress ruminated until July 1, 1797. Federalists pressed through a new Navy Act giving Adams his ships. Three captains were named – John Barry, *United States*; Thomas

▶ 1798

APRIL 27: Congress approves President Adams's request for twelve ships.

APRIL 30: Congress forms the United States Navy, providing for a Secretary of the Navy.

MAY 18: Benjamin Stoddert becomes the first Secretary of the Navy

MAY 28: The Quasi-War with France begins.

JULY 11: President Adams approves an act creating the U.S. Marine Corps.

JULY 16: Congress releases *Chesapeake*, *Congress*, and *President* for completion

Above right: Benjamin Stoddert earned his laurels after becoming the first Secretary of the Navy and among the best for many decades to come. He made the cabinet post what it later became – an essential factor in the growth and security of the United States. For Stoddert, there were no standards, no precedents, and no job description to follow, so he carved out his niche and gave the new navy a life that continued to grow and expand for two centuries.

BENJAMIN STODDERT

Forty-seven-year-old Benjamin Stoddert did not pursue the new office of Secretary of the Navy; rather, he fell into it as John Adams's second choice because the president's first choice refused the post. Considering the secretary's background, Adams made a good decision. Stoddert operated a prosperous mercantile firm, had fought in the Continental Army, served as Secretary of the Board of War, and his years of experience with men, material, and finance prepared him for the work ahead. When the Senate confirmed his appointment on May 18, 1798, Stoddert laconically remarked, "It was unfortunate that in conferring the appointment…upon me, the President could not also confer the knowledge necessary."

While Stoddert took a month's leave to settle personal affairs, Congress responded to the war crisis by passing some twenty acts. One led to creating a Marine Corps; another appropriated funds for fitting-out twenty-four more ships.

Stoddert set about searching for officers of merit, declaring, "We had better have no Navy than have it commanded by indifferent men; and it shall be my study to rid the service of such men, as fast as possible." Stoddert kept his word. When he left office on March 31, 1801,

he also left a legacy. Charles Goldsborough, who had served as clerk in the office until 1843 and observed thirteen different secretaries of the navy, gave Stoddert highest praise: "To the most ardent patriotism he united an inflexible integrity, a discriminating mind, a great capacity for business and the most persevering industry."

Stoddert expedited every task falling under his jurisdiction. During the Quasi-War with France he reacted with urgency to protect American shipping. He placed naval agents in key ports and held them responsible for obtaining ships, ordnance, supplies, and crews. During his thirty-three months in office, the Navy grew to fifty-four vessels. He raised a force of 750 officers and more than 5,000 men for the Navy and 1,100 officers and men for the Marine Corps. He raised the pay of able-bodied seamen from $8 to $17 a month and thereafter experienced no trouble recruiting volunteers. When Congress would not approve funds for establishing navy yards, Stoddert used part of his appropriation for building six 74-gun double-deckers to open facilities at Portsmouth, Boston, New York, Philadelphia, and Norfolk, all of which became naval bases.

Stoddert arrived on the scene at the precise moment when his skills were most needed.

Truxton, *Constellation*; and Samuel Nicholson, *Constitution*. All were veterans of the Revolution.

Adams attempted to mollify the French by sending a three-man delegation to Paris to negotiate a treaty similar to the one Jay signed with Britain. When delegates arrived in France, they discovered that paying bribes to the corsairs had not been a very good idea. The conniving French foreign minister, Charles Maurice de Talleyrand-Périgord, demanded a bribe of $250,000 and a large loan before he would discuss the matter. The delegation flatly refused, and when the American public learned of the insult, the nation embarked on an undeclared quasi-war with France.

The conflict worked wonders on Congress. On April 30, 1798, they voted funds to purchase an additional twenty-four ships armed with eighteen to thirty-two guns. The Treasury Department donated its eight cutters to the cause and the new U.S. Navy was off and running. Not only did the Navy get its ships, it also got its own separate department with a Secretary of the Navy,

Benjamin Stoddert of Georgetown, Maryland.

The French dispatched a flock of frigates, sloops, schooners, and privateers to the American coast. The first Frenchmen had their way, sailing brazenly in sight of the coast and picking off prizes returning from distant voyages. On July 7, 1798, Capt. Stephen Decatur, Sr., an old privateersman himself, sailed out of Egg Harbor, New Jersey, in the 20-gun sloop-of-war *Delaware* and captured the 12-gun schooner *La Croyable*. Others followed, and by the end of the year the new United States Navy had chased the French into the Caribbean. Stoddert organized his force into four squadrons ranging from three to ten ships, placed each squadron under the command of Barry, Truxton, Decatur, or Thomas Tingey, and ordered them "to rid those seas" of the French, adding, "We have nothing to fear but inactivity."

During the Quasi-War with France, American vessels captured eighty ships, mostly lightly armed privateers. In 1780, the undeclared war petered out after seven months of negotiation. By mutual consent the Treaty of Alliance of 1778

THOMAS TRUXTON

Fifty-three-year-old Captain Tom Truxton, commanding the Baltimore-built 36-gun *Constellation*, personified the aggressive spirit of the professional navy officer. At the age of twelve he went to sea, fought with the Royal Navy against the French, and against the British during the Revolution. Returning to the merchant service, he voyaged to China before accepting a captaincy in America's new Navy in 1794. He had a brilliant mind and knew his business, displaying it with valor.

On February 9, *Constellation* fell in with a large vessel flying American colors. Truxton suspected she was French and cleared for action. Sure enough, up went the French tricolor on the 40-gun frigate *L'Insurgente*. When the French captain maneuvered to board *Constellation*, Truxton used her speed to sweep around *L'Insurgente*'s bow and pour a broadside into her hull. Circling around the Frenchman, Truxton raked her from stem to stern. Ninety minutes later *L'Insurgente* was forced to surrender, her decks bloodied with seventy dead or wounded.

A year later Truxton fought his second engagement with a superior French frigate, the 54-gun *La Vengeance*, off Guadaloupe. At first the enemy tried to run, but Truxton caught her at nightfall and opened with a double-shotted broadside. After five hours of battle, the guns on *La Vengeance* fell silent. Truxton, thinking she had struck, laid *Constellation* alongside, only to discover that his mainmast had been severed and was about to fall. He pulled off to rig preventer stays, but the mast toppled into

the sea. In the darkness and confusion, the severely damaged Frenchman crept away with sixty-eight men killed or wounded, her captain reporting that he had been attacked by a two-deck ship of the line. Stoddert would have been quite proud of Tom Truxton and the fighting qualities of the men and frigates he put to sea.

Left: Captain Thomas Truxton (1755-1822), an aggressive and talented naval commander, was best known for his dogged determination against heavy odds in battle.

Below: Congress authorized the Truxton Medal be struck to commemorate the captain's valiant fight with La Vengeance. The medal bears the Latin words: "The fathers of this country to a worthy son."

Right: *One of the few American triumphs of the Quasi-War with France occurred on February 9, 1799, when Tom Truxton, commanding* Constellation *(left), attacked and captured the powerful* L'Insurgente.

▶ **1799**

OCTOBER 2: The Washington Navy Yard is established.

1800

SEPTEMBER 30: The Convention of 1800 ends the Quasi-War.

1801

MAY 14: The Pasha of Tripoli declares war on the United States.

MAY 20: President Thomas Jefferson sends the first American squadron to the Mediterranean.

1803

OCTOBER 12: Commodore Edward Preble negotiates peace with Morocco.

OCTOBER 31: Tripolitans capture the USS *Philadelphia*.

Above right: *Commodore John Rodgers (1772-1838), though too young to fight in the Revolutionary War, served as a lieutenant under Truxton on* Constellation *and learned his tactics from the master. He fought through the wars that soon followed, and won distinction during the Barbary conflict when commanding* John Adams, *28 guns, and capturing the Tripolitan ship* Meshuda.

Right: *On August 1, 1801, Lieutenant Andrew Sterrett (standing), commanding* Enterprise, *12 guns, captured the Tripolitan polarce* Tripoli, *14, after a three-hour fight off Malta without taking a single American casualty. The Tripolitans lost 20 killed and 30 wounded.*

was nullified, and the United States dropped its demand of $20 million as reimbursement for damages done to the American carrying trade.

John Adams lost the presidential election of 1800 because he did not insist upon reparations, and Thomas Jefferson gained the presidency because he had called for an all-out war with France to gain Florida and New Orleans as part of the settlement. On March 1, 1801, one day before Jefferson took office, Congress followed the advice of Adams and Stoddert and provided for a peacetime navy. The act authorized the president to dispose of all but thirteen frigates, those being the *Adams*, *Boston*, *Chesapeake*, *Congress*, *Constellation*, *Constitution*, *Essex*, *General Greene*, *John Adams*, *New York*, *Philadelphia*, *President*, and *United States*. President Jefferson's policy of economy might have abolished the Navy, but supporting a naval force proved prudent. There was still another battle to fight with the Barbary bunch, which had lately taken advantage of America's preoccupation with France.

Jefferson could not find a man interested in becoming Secretary of the Navy. When Robert Smith of Baltimore finally agreed to take the post, Jefferson had a person who would give him no trouble in downsizing the Navy. But in May, 1801, the Pasha of Tripoli thought he could extort more profits by going to war with the United States. Jefferson was restrained by the Constitution from declaring war, but he followed Adams's advice and sent a squadron to the Mediterranean. American vessels could defend themselves and the nation's shipping, but they could not wage war on Tripoli. Forty-five-year-old Captain Richard Dale, who had served under John Paul Jones, drew the assignment, and with the frigates *President*, *Essex*, and *Philadelphia*, and the schooner *Enterprise*, sailed across the Atlantic for the express purpose of blockading the port of Tripoli.

When arriving at Gibraltar, Dale discovered two Tripolitan raiders preparing to dash into the Atlantic and told them that if they tried they would be captured. Dale left *Philadelphia* behind to blockade the corsairs and headed east to make a show of force at Algiers and Tunis. Meanwhile, the two Tripolitan crews ran out of supplies, abandoned their vessels, and rowed across the strait to North Africa. A few days later *Enterprise*, commanded by Lt. Andrew Sterrett, captured the 14-gun *Tripoli* without suffering a casualty, but constitutional shackles prevented him from holding the vessel or its crew hostage, so he turned them loose. Such behavior convinced the pasha that Americans were truly weak-minded amateurs, thereby dashing Dale's hope of negotiating with

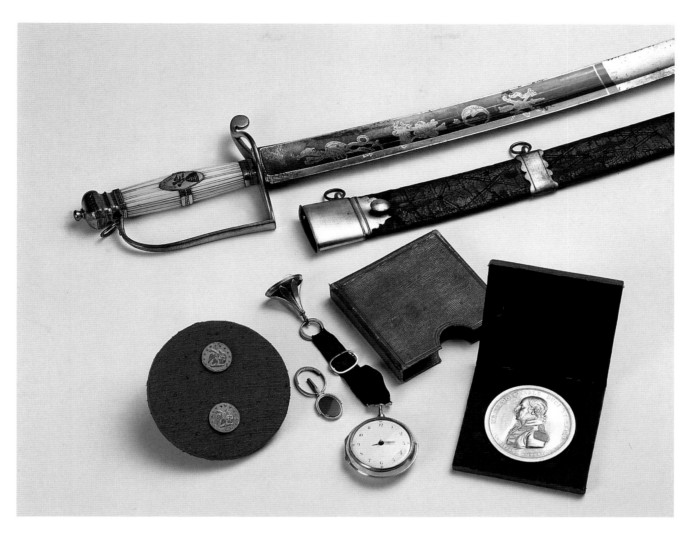

Left: *After a long life of service to his country, Edward Preble left for posterity several artifacts, among them his elegant sword and scabbard. Below them is the Commodore Edward Preble Congressional gold medal, engraved by John Reich. At center is his watch, and to the far left a pair of his buttons.*

Above: *Commodore Edward Preble (1761-1807) fought in the American Revolution, the Quasi-War with France, and the Tripolitan War. In the latter, he concluded a peace with Morocco by a show of force and sent Stephen Decatur on his mission to destroy the captured Philadelphia. He never faltered in his steadfast devotion to the interests and honor of the United States and was a strict but marvelous trainer of young naval officers.*

Tripoli from a show of strength. He now faced the possibility of more serious trouble with all the Barbary States, and since his crews were scheduled for discharge he sailed for home, leaving *Essex*, *Philadelphia*, and *Enterprise* to patrol the Mediterranean.

In early 1802, Jefferson abandoned his plan to liquidate the Navy and dispatched a stronger squadron to the Mediterranean, this time under Captain Richard Morris. With four more frigates and with crews enlisted for two years, Morris had the firepower to subdue Tripoli but neither the will nor the ability to do so. What he did have was $20,000 to secure a lasting settlement with the corsairs, a pittance the enemy would certainly interpret as another demonstration of American weakness. He soon discovered that he could not blockade all the ports of North Africa, nor could he get his vessels into the shallow, fortified harbor of Tripoli. He offered $5,000 to Tripoli to settle differences, holding back $15,000 to placate the other states. The pasha scoffed at the offer, demanding $200,000, plus compensation for Tripoli's costs in the war. Far from being the fighting diplomat needed to resolve the crisis, Morris sulked.

In June, 1803, Captain John Rodgers, commanding *John Adams*, captured the Tripolitan raider *Meshuda*, which turned out to be the *Betsey* of Boston taken in 1784 by the pasha's pirates. A few days later Rodgers fought a Tripolitan blockade-runner and blew it up in sight of Tripoli. Instead of following up on Rodgers's successes, Morris abandoned the blockade and sailed back to Gibraltar. Disheartened by Morris's poor performance, Jefferson and Smith replaced him with Edward Preble, who had commanded *Essex* during the conflict with France.

PHILADELPHIA CAPTURED

Preble dispatched Captain William Bainbridge, commanding *Philadelphia*, and the schooner *Vixen* to renew the blockade of Tripoli. Preble then stopped at Tangiers and intimidated the Emperor of Morocco into a separate, tribute-free peace, but his diplomatic coup was about to unravel when he learned that Tripolitans had captured *Philadelphia*. While chasing a blockade-runner inshore, Bainbridge had put the vessel on the Kaliusa reef and been captured along with his crew. Exalted by their unexpected good fortune, Tripolitans re-floated their trophy and sailed her into the harbor.

Preble tried every diplomatic trick in the book to free the hostages and recapture or destroy *Philadelphia*. Nothing worked until Lt. Stephen Decatur, commanding the schooner *Enterprise*, captured a Tripolitan ketch and gave her the unlikely name *Intrepid*.

Decatur destroyed *Philadelphia*, but Preble still faced the problem of freeing Americans impris-

▶ **1804**

FEBRUARY 16: At nightfall, Lt. Stephen Decatur destroys *Philadelphia*.

1803

JUNE 3: The Pasha of Tripoli signs a peace treaty.

1807

JUNE 22: The British frigate *Leopard* shamelessly attacks the USS *Chesapeake*.

JULY 2: President Jefferson orders all British naval vessels to leave American ports.

Above: *On June 10, 1805, the U.S. consul general at Algiers signed a treaty of peace with Tripoli. The event has been memorialized by the erection of the elegantly detailed Tripoli monument in Washington, D.C.*

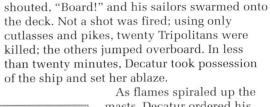

STEPHEN DECATUR

Twenty-five-year-old Stephen Decatur had a plan. Using seventy volunteers as a boarding party, he believed he could disguise *Intrepid* as a friendly vessel, sneak into Tripoli's harbor, and set *Philadelphia* on fire. For support, should he need it, he asked for the two-masted brig *Siren*, whose rig looked identical to a ship recently purchased by Tripolitan agents in Sicily. Preble approved the attack, and on the night of February 16, 1804, *Intrepid* crept into the harbor and passed under the guns of *Philadelphia*, which had been run out in readiness for a surprise attack.

The ketch's Sicilian pilot, Salvatore Catalano, hailed *Philadelphia* in Arabic and asked permission to tie alongside, claiming his ship's anchors had been lost. As lines were being passed, someone hollered, "Americanos!" Decatur

shouted, "Board!" and his sailors swarmed onto the deck. Not a shot was fired; using only cutlasses and pikes, twenty Tripolitans were killed; the others jumped overboard. In less than twenty minutes, Decatur took possession of the ship and set her ablaze.

As flames spiraled up the masts, Decatur ordered his men back to *Intrepid* and shoved off. *Philadelphia*'s loaded guns erupted, scattering projectiles across the water. Harbor guns opened, uncertain what to fire at. *Intrepid*, followed by *Siren*, slid silently out of the harbor as *Philadelphia* burned to the waterline. At home, Decatur became a national hero, giving new life to the fledgling Navy. Smith made him a captain, the youngest man to hold the rank in the U.S. Navy, and Congress awarded the volunteers, only one of whom had been wounded, an extra two months' pay.

Above: *Stephen Decatur (1779-1820) became the youngest man ever to hold the rank of captain in the U.S. Navy (at age twenty-five). His credo became famous: "Our country! In her intercourse with foreign nations, may she always be right, but [I drink to] our country, right or wrong!"*

Left: *On August 3, 1804, Lt. Stephen Decatur's boarding party captured two enemy gunboats in hand-to-hand combat in Tripoli's harbor.*

oned in Tripoli. A bombardment of the city on August 4, 1804, failed to change any minds. Decatur took three gunboats into the harbor to attack the shipping, but the afternoon sea breeze threatened to push the vessels into shoal waters, and forced a withdrawal. Preble lacked the men for an amphibious assault, so on the night of September 4 he packed seven tons of powder onto *Intrepid* and sent her on an attempt to blow up a section of Tripoli's waterfront. Preble never learned the cause, but as *Intrepid* worked into the harbor she suddenly exploded, taking with her all twelve men aboard. Ten days later, after

Commodore Samuel Barron arrived with *President*, *Congress*, *Constellation*, *Constitution*, and *Essex*, Preble sailed for home, smitten by an illness that in 1807 would take his life.

After stationing his squadron off Tripoli, Barron spent most of his time recovering from a liver ailment in Sicily. In the spring of 1805 John Rodgers, the fifth American commodore appointed in as many years, replaced Barron. In the end, it was not the sailors who rescued the prisoners of Yusuf Pasha, but William Eaton, the American consul. He conspired with Hamet Pasha, who yearned to unseat his brother and

Left: *On the night of February 16, 1804, Lt. Decatur with eighty volunteers set the frigate* Philadelphia *on fire. He and his men safely escaped on the previously captured ketch* Mastico, *which the Navy had renamed* Intrepid *(left).*

ascend to the rule of Tripoli. Hamet raised an army of 400 Arabs and turned it over to the consul. Eaton, with a bodyguard of seven Marines, made an arduous march of 500 miles along the coast. Supported at sea by three gunboats, Eaton's force captured Tripoli's outpost of Derna. Yusuf Pasha, fearing a *coup*, immediately sued for peace and released his American hostages. On June 4, 1805, Rodgers signed a new treaty with Yusuf Pasha, giving some credibility to his claim that after five years of war he had defeated the corsairs. Fortunately for Hamet Pasha, Eaton spirited him to sea before Yusuf could hack off his head.

PREPARING FOR WAR

For most of Captain Bainbridge's nineteen-month incarceration, he had been passing messages written in invisible ink back and forth to the American squadron off Tripoli. He had also spent the months conducting a "University in the Prison" – where he and his officers discussed their profession through lectures and debates. Among the young prisoners were men such as Lieutenant David Porter, whose star would rise and fall in the years to come. But without the expansion of the American fleet during the Barbary conflict, the Navy would not have been prepared for its next great contest – the War of 1812.

If Jefferson had succeeded with his plan, he would have put the entire Navy in dry-dock and

Left: *The USS* Constitution *acted as flagship of the squadron during the war with Tripoli. During the bombardment of the city, beginning on August 3, 1804,* Enterprise, Nautilus, Argus, Siren, *and* Vixen *all joined in the affair.*

discharged most of the men. Because of the war with Tripoli, he even agreed to create a navy yard at Washington, convinced that such a facility should be founded near the nation's new capital. But after the Barbary war, he wanted no more expensive frigates built, opting instead for gunboats manned by skeleton crews for coastal defense.

Relations with Great Britain had remained cordial, but in June, 1807, all that suddenly changed when the British frigate HMS *Leopard* shadowed *Chesapeake* out of Norfolk. Commodore James Barron, on a voyage to the Mediterranean, suspected no evil intentions when *Leopard* came alongside off Cape Henry and asked *Chesapeake* to carry some dispatches to Europe. Barron complied because regulations required that the courtesy of carrying dispatches be extended between friendly warships of all nations, but when British officers demanded to come on board to search for

1812

JUNE 18: War with Great Britain begins.

1813

SEPTEMBER 10: Commodore Oliver Hazard Perry defeats the British squadron on Lake Erie.

Above right: *On June 22, 1807, Captain S. P. Humphreys, commanding the HMS* Leopard, *56 guns, opened fire on the U.S. frigate* Chesapeake, *36, killing 4 Americans and wounding 20. Fifteen minutes later Commodore James Barron, without doing battle, struck his flag and the British came on board under the guise of looking for deserters. Barron's abrupt surrender cost him his career.*

Right, above: *On August 19, in the War of 1812's first battle between frigates, Capt. Isaac Hull, commanding the 44-gun* Constitution, *dismasted and captured* Guerrière, *38, commanded by Captain James R. Dacres, in a 40-minute action 700 miles east of Boston.*

and seize deserters, Barron refused. *Leopard* opened fire, and for fifteen minutes pounded the unprepared *Chesapeake* with one broadside after another, killing three, wounding eighteen, and forcing Barron to strike the colors. After a British party came on board and removed four American sailors, the hated *Leopard* moved into Hampton Roads and anchored. The governor of Virginia ordered out the militia, and secretary Smith dispatched as many gunboats as he could marshal to Hampton Roads. The incident brought an end to Barron's career, but it changed Jefferson's mind about diminishing the size of the Navy.

On March 4, 1809, James Madison succeeded Jefferson as president, and Paul Hamilton replaced Smith as Secretary of the Navy. The structure of the Navy changed little under Hamilton, but he added ships, bringing the total number of seagoing vessels to eighteen, ten of which were now close to ten years old, 165 gun-boats built under Jefferson, and a few small brigs carrying an aggregate of 122 guns. By contrast, the British in 1812 had 700 warships, of which 200 were ships of the line.

Impressing American sailors continued, the Navy too weak to stop it, but on May 6, 1811, Commodore John Rodgers took *President* to sea to warn off the HMS *Guerrière*, which had been impressing Americans off New York. He came upon a warship at nightfall and, after an exchange of hails, fired upon her. At daylight he discovered that he had ripped apart not *Guerrière* but the puny 20-gun sloop *Little Belt*. The action angered the British, but after five years of peace, neither wanted a war with the other.

DECLARATION OF WAR

During the days of the American Revolution the British had not been willing to negotiate the colonists' grievances, but in 1811 and 1812 they tried. Because Britain was already locked in a European conflict, the "War Hawks" in Congress, aided and abetted by President Madison, thought the moment ripe for giving the British another "humiliation." On June 12, 1812, Congress declared war on Britain, fastening its eyes upon Canada as a coveted prize. The British, enjoying their naval supremacy after Trafalgar, believed their navy could shatter the American fleet in a few months. This time, there would be no French navy to save the quarrelsome Americans. There

'*Anyone who had predicted such a result of an American war this time last year would have been treated as a madman or a traitor. He would have been told, if his opponents had condescended to argue with him, that long ere seven months had elapsed, the American flag would be swept from the seas, the contemptible navy of the United States annihilated, and their maritime arsenals rendered a heap of ruin.*'

LONDON *TIMES*,
MARCH 14, 1813.

was altogether too much confidence on both sides. In the end, both would pay for a needless war in full measure.

Madison had a problem. He did not know how to fight a naval war with Britain, and he had all of New England, the cradle of American independence, unanimously opposed to it. His idea of naval warfare was to keep all the warships in home waters, using them as floating batteries. Two veteran captains, Bainbridge and Charles Stewart, happened to be in Washington and talked him out of it. At the time, the largest American squadron under Rodgers was at New York – the frigates *President*, *United States*, *Congress*, and *Essex* (which was under repair), the brig *Argus*, and the sloop *Hornet*. The main British squadron, some eight frigates under Vice-Admiral Sawyer, lay at Halifax. Rodgers wanted to get to sea to raid British commerce before Sawyer moved south and blockaded New York.

On June 22, 1812, Hamilton attempted to divide the available warships into two commands, one under Rodgers and the other under Decatur. An hour after learning of the declaration of war, and a day before Hamilton's orders reached New York, Rodgers went to sea, sailing southeastward in search of Britain's richly laden convoy from Jamaica. Instead, he chased the HMS *Belvidera*, engaged her at close quarters, and then let her get away after one of *President*'s bow-chasers exploded, killing nine men and breaking his leg. He then began a 10-week cruise, capturing seven small prizes.

The land war accomplished even less. The triple invasion of Canada planned by the "War Hawks" ended in ruin. Enemy warships commanded the Great Lakes, Tecumseh's Native Americans joined the British, and General William Hull bottled-up his army at Detroit, surrendering it on August 16 to a handful of enemy soldiers.

During the first two months on the high seas, the Royal Navy had its way, capturing *Nautilus*, *Vixen*, and *Viper* while barely firing a shot.

AMERICANS FIGHT BACK

The naval war manifested all the trappings of a regrettable joke on the Americans until Captain David Porter took *Essex* to sea and in July captured nine prizes. Though short of men, he caught up with the British sloop *Alert* on August 13 and smashed her with two broadsides. Five days later Captain Isaac Hull, brother of the general who

HMS *GUERRIÈRE* VS "OLD IRONSIDES"

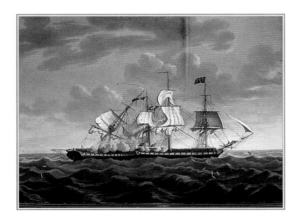

On August 19, 1812, the lookout on *Constitution* sighted a familiar set of topsails. Captain Isaac Hull came to the deck and immediately recognized HMS *Guerrière*, an unfinished piece of business. He knew her captain, James Dacres, since they had once wagered a hat over a glass of wine on who would win in a single-ship action. It was a friendly bet, dating back a year. Now they

would have their answer, but the stakes were higher than a wagered hat.

Dacres believed he had the advantage and depended upon his crew's faster rate of fire, but the first all-important broadside missed completely. Hull's advantage was *Constitution*'s maneuverability and strength. After fifteen minutes of fighting broadside to broadside, Americans noticed that British balls could not penetrate *Constitution*'s hull, giving rise to the frigate's everlasting nickname, "Old Ironsides." While *Guerrière*'s shots caused minor damage aloft, they caused few casualties. *Constitution*'s heavier guns knocked down *Guerrière*'s mizzenmast, enabling Hull to swing his ship across the enemy's bow and, with two devastating broadsides, rake her from stem to stern. Minutes passed as British sailors fought to unsnarl *Guerrière*'s bowsprit from *Constitution*'s mizzen rigging. When the two ships finally separated, the battered British frigate could no longer fight.

Dacres struck his colors and surrendered. Once again the two captains met. When Dacres offered his sword, Hull told him to keep it for putting up so gallant a fight – "but," he growled, "I will trouble you for that hat."

Left: *After the battle between* Constitution *and* Guerrière, *Capt. Hull commissioned artist Michel F. Corné for four paintings, this being the third in the series and titled "Dropping Astern," which is exactly what happened after "Old Ironsides" dismasted the British frigate.*

▶ **1814**

FEBRUARY 2: The frigate HMS *Phoebe* defeats the frigate USS *Essex*, commanded by David Porter, off Valparaiso, Chile.

AUGUST 24-25: Major General Robert Ross routs American forces at Bladensburg, occupies Washington, and burns the White House.

SEPTEMBER 11: Commodore Thomas Macdonough defeats the British on Lake Champlain.

SEPTEMBER 14: Eyewitness to the British bombardment of Fort McHenry, Francis Scott Key composes "The Star-Spangled Banner."

DECEMBER 24: The Treaty of Ghent returns Great Britain and the United Sates to prewar status.

Right: A succession of American victories at sea came to an abrupt end when Capt. James Lawrence, recently appointed to command the USS Chesapeake, *took a disaffected and untrained crew to sea and was badly mauled by the HMS* Shannon.

Below: Capt. Henry Lambert, after surrendering the HMS Java, *went on board* Constitution, *unbuckled his sword and, in a gesture of honor, placed it in the hands of Capt. William Bainbridge.*

surrendered Detroit, went searching in *Constitution* for Rodgers but found instead the 64-gun *Africa* and four British frigates under Captain Philip Broke. After battering the HMS *Guerrière*, *Constitution* became becalmed just out of range of the victim's consorts. Americans won the ensuing three-day chase by kedging. *Constitution* gained headway, found wind, and sailed out of sight, leaving Broke's squadron hull-down over the horizon. *Guerrière*, however, could not be captured, so Hull departed without boarding or sinking her, but it would not be long before they would meet again.

After Rodgers returned from his first cruise, he turned *United States* and the brig *Argus* over to Decatur. Approaching Madeira on October 25,

1812, Decatur sighted the 38-gun frigate HMS *Macedonian*, Captain John Carden, scudding along toward the British West Indies. Though Carden had the wind, he made the mistake of attacking *United States*. He then made the double mistake of trying to close on a frigate having heavier long-range guns. During a short, sharp engagement, *Macedonian* lost her mizzenmast, maintopmast, foretopmast, twelve guns, and a hundred men. Decatur did not want to prolong the slaughter, so he moved to a raking position and ordered Carden to strike. On boarding the stricken frigate, he discovered that though she had been hulled, she could be patched-up, jury-rigged, and kept afloat. He put a prize crew on her and conveyed her back to Newport. Repaired and refitted, *Macedonian* re-entered the war as an American frigate under the command of Captain Jacob Jones, former commander of the sloop *Wasp*.

VICTORY FOR BAINBRIDGE

On October 26, the day after Decatur captured *Macedonian*, William Bainbridge, commanding *Constitution*, sailed from Boston with the sloop *Hornet*, under Master Commandant James Lawrence. He expected to be joined by Captain David Porter and *Essex*, but the frigate was still dockside undergoing repairs. Bainbridge sent

Porter rendezvous instructions and sailed without him. The two frigates would never meet.

After depositing *Hornet* off Bahia, Brazil, to blockade the bullion-laden British sloop *Bonne Citoyenne*, Bainbridge cruised offshore looking for prizes. On December 29 he sighted the 38-gun frigate HMS *Java*, commanded by Captain Henry Lambert. Lambert was not looking for a fight, but he had the wind. *Java* had recently been refitted and was faster and more heavily armed than "Old Ironsides." With such advantages, Lambert decided to fight.

By setting his maincourse and forecourse, which were usually kept clewed up during combat, Bainbridge picked up the wind, outmaneuvered Lambert, and brought his broadside to bear. After losing his jib boom and the use of his headsails, Lambert's only chance was to get alongside and board *Constitution*. Because he was transporting an extra draft of seamen to India, he had the advantage of manpower. *Java*'s lunge missed *Constitution*'s beam, enabling Bainbridge to rake her with two broadsides. Mortally wounded, Lambert ordered the colors struck. Bainbridge rushed men on board before the first officer could destroy the British codebook. After several weeks of trying to keep *Java* afloat, Bainbridge finally burned her and returned to Boston.

A few weeks later Lawrence brought *Hornet* into Martha's Vineyard with $20,000 in bullion. Having been chased away from Bahia by the 74-gun HMS *Montagu*, he captured the bullion brig *Resolution* off Brazil. A few weeks later he shattered the brig *Peacock* off British Guiana. Lawrence's luck ran out when he later took command of the frigate *Chesapeake*. Though the ship was in good fighting trim, having recently been refitted, her disgruntled crew had stayed with her only to collect their pay. In a crushing defeat caused by apathetic American sailors, the HMS *Shannon*, commanded by Philip Broke, boarded *Chesapeake* and captured her in less than fifteen minutes. Lawrence's immortal dying words, "Don't give up the ship," made no impact on the crew, who had wanted only their pay, to go home, and to fight no more.

Essex was to have rendezvoused with Bainbridge off Brazil, but Porter never located the commodore. His alternate orders provided an option – to take *Essex* into the Pacific to prey upon British whalers. Porter battered his way around Cape Horn and soon found the whalers. From February, 1813, to March, 1814, he prowled the islands of the South Pacific and captured fifteen prizes. Renaming one of his prizes *Essex Junior*, he armed her and returned to Valparaiso, Chile, for supplies.

PORTER SURRENDERS

On March 26, 1814, while blockaded by the frigate HMS *Phoebe* and the sloop *Cherub*, Porter made preparations to fight them. As *Essex* sailed from the harbor a sudden gale struck her, bringing down her masts, and crippling her ability to maneuver. Porter anchored her near shore and, using springs, attempted without success to swing her broadside guns into play. In the bloodiest single-ship battle fought during the War of 1812, Porter finally surrendered after losing 89 dead and 66 wounded. Among the survivors was thirteen-year-old Midshipman David Glasgow Farragut, who a half a century later would emerge

Top: *Commodore David Porter won recognition during the War of 1812 with his cruise to the Pacific.*

Above: *Commodore Oliver Hazard Perry built his fleet on Lake Erie and whipped the British squadron.*

Below: *On February 28, 1814, Porter's cruise to the South Pacific came to an abrupt and bloody end when he attempted to fight his ailing frigate* Essex *(center), against two British warships, the frigate* Phoebe *and the sloop* Cherub.

1815

FEBRUARY 7: A Board of Navy Commissioners is established to supervise all naval construction, equipment, and repair.

MARCH 2: War with Algiers resumes.

JUNE 30: Stephen Decatur negotiates an end to the Barbary wars.

1816

APRIL 29: Congress appropriates $8,000,000 to build nine ships-of-the-line and twelve frigates.

1819

FEBRUARY 26: The naval war against Caribbean pirates begins.

MARCH 3: Congress authorizes a slave patrol off West Africa.

1820

MARCH 22: Commodore James Barron mortally wounds Stephen Decatur in a duel.

1822

DECEMBER 21: Commodore David Porter takes command of the pirate-chasing West India Squadron.

Top right: On September 11, 1814, Capt. Thomas Macdonough's flotilla of 86 guns and 850 men battled a British squadron of 95 guns and 1,050 men on narrow Lake Champlain. The fight lasted little more than two hours. Macdonough's victory, more than any other battle, convinced the British to seek peace.

Above right: Perry died quite young, but left many artifacts – a sextant, pocket watch, pistol, an amulet, and other items.

from the Civil War as America's first admiral.

In 1813 the British also dominated the Great Lakes. To meet the threat the Navy Department sent Oliver Hazard Perry to the small backwoods port of Erie, Pennsylvania, to create a freshwater navy. Perry encountered overwhelming obstacles building the squadron, but he did it with the help of a three remarkable people – Daniel Dobbins, Henry Eckford, and Noah Brown. During September, Perry's squadron won the only notable naval victory in 1813, at the western end of Lake Erie, 600 miles from the sea. In a furious fight between square-rigged brigs, armed schooners, and gunboats fashioned from green timber, Perry met the enemy in a stand-up fight. He lost his flagship *Lawrence*, transferred under fire by boat to the brig *Niagara*, and broke through the British line, raking the enemy's largest ships until they all surrendered. In perhaps the sim-

plest of all battle reports, penned on the back of a rumpled letter, Perry sent to General William Henry Harrison, military commander of the Northwest, the message: "We have met the enemy: and they are ours. Two ships, two Brigs, one schooner, and one Sloop."

Not to be outdone by Perry, Master Commandant Thomas Macdonough, who had been with Decatur at Tripoli when he burned *Philadelphia*, built another freshwater navy on Lake Champlain. He, too, used the shipbuilding expertise of Noah Brown to create a squadron, building one 26-gun corvette, one 20-gun brig, two small sailing vessels, and ten armed gondolas. Like Benedict Arnold during the Revolution, Macdonough hid his squadron in Plattsburg Bay off Valcour Island. Captain George Downie, the British commander, made exactly the same mistake as his predecessor, using a fair wind to beat south. In a bloody battle on September 11, 1814, Downie lost his life and the British lost the fight. When the Americans heard the news, they felt partially compensated for the British "hate raid" in August that had swept through Washington and burned the "President's House."

PEACE NEGOTIATIONS

While Macdonough was bloodying the British on Lake Champlain, Anglo-American peace negotiators were at work on a settlement. Both sides had come to the realization that there was nothing to gain from a war that gave their commercial competitors all the profits. On December 24, 1814, both parties signed the Treaty of Ghent and brought the war to a close, but not quite. Without

THE STAR-SPANGLED BANNER

During the War of 1812 the British discovered they could put landing parties ashore at almost any point, and Chesapeake Bay became a major theater of operations because of its proximity to Washington and Baltimore. After attacking Washington, chasing off the militia, torching public buildings, and forcing the navy yard to burn all its ships, the British turned their attention on Baltimore.

Delayed by Baltimore's hurriedly erected defenses, a British force of 5,000 men waited for the Royal Navy to silence Fort McHenry at the harbor's entrance. On September 13, 1814, frigates and bomb vessels opened on the fort and pummeled it throughout the night. At dawn's early light on September 14, Francis Scott Key, who had been on a mission to free a notable Baltimore physician held by the British, and who witnessed the bombardment from a ship in the harbor, observed the tattered stars and stripes still flying over the fort. The sight of Old Glory so inspired him that he wrote "The Star-Spangled Banner," never suspecting that his verse would become America's national anthem.

Stymied by Fort McHenry, the British army re-embarked, and Key returned to the practice of law, never to compose another notable verse.

Above: *Francis Scott Key (1780-1843) stood near the rail of a ship and watched the British bombardment of Fort McHenry, and was inspired to write the poem, "The Star-Spangled Banner," which was later set to music.*

Above: *Key wrote his poem on the back of a letter, and the words were soon adapted to a popular drinking song, "To Anacreon in Heaven." In 1931 Congress adopted both words and music as the national anthem.*

'*Our flag is about as much respected among different nations as an old rag that's hung up on a cornfield to scare crows*'

ANONYMOUS.

a telegraph to flash the welcome news, a British 50-vessel amphibious attack on New Orleans progressed as planned. Two weeks after the war officially ended, British General Sir Edward Pakenham landed his forces at Chalmette Plantation near New Orleans. In the most decisive battle of a war now concluded, Americans under General Andrew Jackson crushed the invaders, killing Pakenham and about 300 men.

BARBARY CORSAIRS

In peacetime, the usual attitude of an economically minded government is to save money by reducing its navy. The United States would have followed this practice had it not been for the Barbary corsairs, who were once again attacking American shipping, this time from Algiers. Who best to send back to the Mediterranean than a man who had been there before? In May, 1815, Stephen Decatur sailed for Algiers with ten powerful warships. He captured the Algerian flagship *Mashuda* and killed its admiral. Sailing into Algiers, he dictated peace terms, demanded a large payment in reparations, and received it one week later. He went on to Tunis and Tripoli and obtained the same terms. By June he was back at sea and heading for home, having fought and been victorious in one of the briefest naval campaigns in American history.

His remarkable success proved a point to a parsimonious Congress. A nation without a navy is a nation without security and vulnerable to acts of war. Not many years would pass before armed vessels would be needed again – this time to protect the shores of the western hemisphere.

From 1815 to the Civil War, the United States Navy became a service of emerging traditions. It maintained its original system for selecting commodores or flag officers from its Captains List, they being senior officers assigned to command a squadron rather than a single ship. But after the conflict with Great Britain ended, quarrels of another nature erupted between the so-called commodores. In 1820 James Barron shot and killed Decatur in a duel. The cause: Decatur's contemptuous testimony towards Barron during an inquiry regarding the *Chesapeake/Leopard* incident in 1807. Barron had not commanded a naval vessel since surrendering *Chesapeake*, and he blamed Decatur for staining his career. Though wounded in the thigh, Barron survived, but the duel brought him only disgrace. Bainbridge also received a career-ending censure for acting as Decatur's second. Among the talented flag officers remaining, Oliver Hazard Perry, hero of Lake Erie, died of yellow fever on the Orinoco River while negotiating for the security of American commerce during Venezuela's fight for independence from Spain.

In 1824 David Porter, one of the few venerable fighters from the War of 1812 and still active in

1823

FEBRUARY 14: The paddle-wheeler *Sea Gull* becomes the first steamer in the world to go to war.

DECEMBER 2: President James Monroe promulgates the "Monroe Doctrine."

1824

NOVEMBER 14: Commodore David Porter invades Puerto Rico, is later court-martialed, and resigns.

1826

SEPTEMBER 3: The sloop *Vincennes* becomes the Navy's first vessel to circumnavigate the world.

Right: *On October 29, 1814, Robert Fulton launched at New York Demologos (Fulton I), the world's first steam-powered warship. Designed for harbor defense, it was propelled by a central paddle wheel and carried 32 cannon.*

Above is the ball that killed Stephen Decatur on March 22, 1820, in a duel with James Barron. Below is Decatur's sword and scabbard, with the comparative size of the ball beneath.

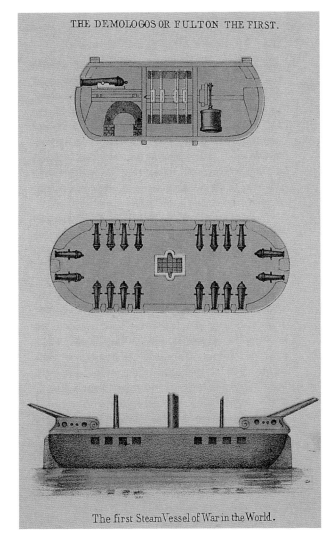

THE DEMOLOGOS OR FULTON THE FIRST.

The first Steam Vessel of War in the World.

the Navy, received a court-martial for doing more than was required of him. Porter had come out of the war as much a hero as Perry for the manner in which he had commanded the frigate *Essex* in the South Pacific. In 1815 he commanded the first experimental steam warship, the paddle-wheeler *Fulton*. With Hull and Rodgers, he became a member of the first Board of Navy Commissioners. But his undoing began in 1823 when Secretary of the Navy Smith Thompson sent him into the Caribbean to rid the sea of pirates.

After circulating through the islands with his West Indies squadron, Porter sent back his deep-draft frigates and replaced them with shallow-draft vessels that could get into the coves where pirates hid. He also persuaded Thompson to buy

the 100-ton steamer *Sea Gull*, which he could use both as a tug and as a weapon. With *Sea Gull*, Porter became the first naval officer in the world to use steam in combat.

Porter did more than chase pirate vessels. If he could not catch them at sea, he followed them into their island hideouts, burned their vessels, dismantled their camps, destroyed their loot, and thoroughly discouraged them from practicing their trade.

One of Porter's more aggressive operations in Puerto Rico got him into trouble with Thompson's successor, Samuel L. Southard. After following the trail of pirates into Fajardo, the captain and first officer of the schooner *Beagle* got thrown into prison. Porter threatened to seize Fajardo and landed 200 Marines on the island to back his threat. Local authorities released the officers, but Spain complained, so Southard launched an inquiry into Porter's behavior. The commodore and Southard did not like each other, and the dispute resulted in a six months' suspension from the service for Porter. In 1826, in an act of pure disgust, Porter resigned. So in five years the Navy lost four of its most respected and celebrated officers, the fourth being Thomas Macdonough (of Lake Champlain fame) who in 1824 had died at sea while commanding the Mediterranean Squadron.

WARSHIPS DETERIORATING

The warships of the Navy deteriorated right along with the fighting officer corps. Of six frigates taken into the War of 1812, *Congress* had rotted and *Constitution* became unseaworthy, but the public outcry against breaking up "Old Ironsides" compelled the Navy to rehabilitate the vessel and use her for seamanship training. Though growing old and obsolete, *Constellation* and *United States* remained in service through the 1850s. It was not until 1854 that Congress appropriated money to replace them with six new steam frigates named after American rivers, the most famous and notorious of which became the USS *Merrimac*. She started her career as a ship of wood and would end it as the first Confederate ironclad.

Other activities besides pirate chasing kept the Navy afloat. In 1808 Congress outlawed the transatlantic slave trade with Africa and twelve years later made slaving punishable by death. In 1817 the American Colonization Society advocated the repatriation of slaves by sending them back to Africa. Two naval officers, Robert Stockton and Matthew C. Perry, agreed with the idea and promoted the creation of Liberia. In 1820, two years before the settlement of Liberia, the Navy maintained a lone frigate off the coast of West Africa to interdict the slave trade, but the vessel represented little more than a show of weak force. Not until 1843 did the United States

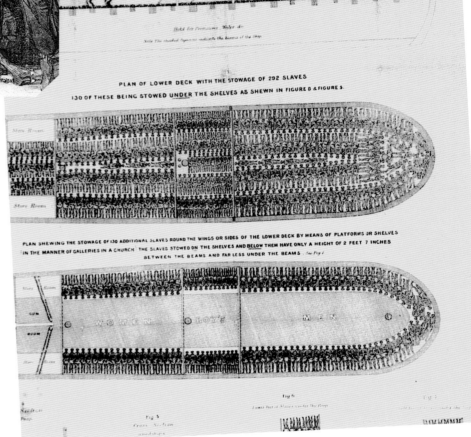

STOWAGE OF THE BRITISH SLAVE SHIP BROOKES UNDER THE
REGULATED SLAVE TRADE
Act of 1788

create a squadron to suppress the trade. By then, trafficking in slaves had become mixed with piracy.

Secretary of the Navy Abel P. Upshur showed no concern about national sovereignty among the tribal countries of Africa. Because several American merchant ships had been captured by natives and their crews barbarously murdered, Upshur's carefully crafted orders to Commodore Perry gave him considerable latitude when dealing with the African problem. Perry anchored his squadron off the Guinea Coast and put a force ashore that destroyed four towns and killed a gigantic native chief, King Crack O. On December 16, 1843, Perry brought the Africans to the table and consummated a treaty at Great Berribee.

CONFLICT WITH SEMINOLES

During the same years, the Navy had its share of trouble in the swampy backwaters of the South. In 1835 the Seminole Indians massacred an army detachment and retreated to their fortress in the swamps of the Everglades. Secretary of the Navy Mahlon Dickerson had allowed the Navy to disintegrate to forty-one ships and 6,000 men. The West Indies Squadron, commanded by Commodore Alexander Dallas, had been patrolling the Gulf of Mexico to interdict the smuggling of slaves into Texas. Dallas suddenly found himself called upon to participate in the Seminole War. He put his Marines ashore in southern Florida and arrested Chief Osceola, but skirmishes continued until 1845, after which the Seminoles were moved west.

In 1836 the Creek Indians extended the war into Georgia and Alabama. In order to quash the trouble, Dallas called up the entire Marine Corps. With them came small steamers to ply the Chattahoochee and other rivers to keep the troops supplied. Sailors called it the brown water "mosquito fleet," because two lieutenants, J. T. McLaughlin and John Rodgers, had to penetrate up hundreds of miles of river and into swamps and tributaries using flat-bottomed barges and

'There is something peculiarly melancholy and impressive in a burial at sea. There is no coffin or hearse, procession or tolling bell; nothing that prepares us for the final separation. The body is wound in the drapery of its couch, much as if the deceased were only in a quiet and temporary sleep…is dropped into the wave, the deep waters close over it, the vessel passes quickly on, and not a solitary trace is left to mark the…resting place of the departed Mariner.'

—JOURNAL OF DANIEL NOBLE JOHNSON,
NOVEMBER 1, 1841,
OFF AFRICA, SMITHSONIAN COLLECTION.

Above: *Slave vessels were ships of untold horror. On the ship Gloria (top left) armed sailors brutalized their cargos of human flesh. On the slave ship Brookes (top right) men and women filled every empty space, lying chained for months. Uprisings on vessels such as Amistad (above) highlighted slave anger that resulted in the death of the ship's captain and all but two of his crew.*

▶ **1830**

DECEMBER 6: The Depot of Charts and Instruments (U.S. Navy Observatory), is established in Washington.

1835

DECEMBER 28: The Seminole War begins.

1836

MAY 23: Marines are sent to quell an uprising of Creek Indians in Georgia and Alabama.

1838

AUGUST 19: Lt. Charles Wilkes begins a four-year expedition to explore Antarctica's polar seas.

1842

MAY 10: The Seminole War ends.

Above right: *George Bancroft established the U.S. Naval Academy and located it at Annapolis, Maryland (right).*

Below: *On February 28, 1844, the 12-inch "Peacemaker" wrought-iron gun exploded during a demonstration for Washington dignitaries, killing eight persons, among them the Secretary of the Navy and the Secretary of State.*

GEORGE BANCROFT AND THE NAVAL ACADEMY

On March 11, 1845, George Bancroft of Massachusetts became President James Knox Polk's Secretary of the Navy. The appointment surprised many people because Bancroft was an historian who knew little about naval affairs, but he did understand the value of an education.

He occupied much of his time with plans to annex Texas, which had led his predecessor to prepare for war with Mexico by dispatching Commodore David Conner's Home Squadron to Veracruz and Commodore John D. Sloat's squadron to the Pacific. In the meantime, Mexico broke diplomatic relations, and in April the administration issued preparatory orders for General Zachary Taylor to march into Texas. Bancroft instructed Conner to consider Texas a part of the United States as soon as the Lone Star Republic accepted annexation.

As the United States and Mexico moved towards war, Bancroft made his greatest contribution to the Navy. In the midst of preparing for a conflict, he founded the United States Naval Academy. For more than ten years Congress had opposed the idea because they doubted whether formal academic training had any value to a naval officer. They believed the country was immune from war and disliked the practice of patronage and preferment associated with appointments at West Point.

Bancroft had two problems: he had not gone to Congress for money, and he had not picked a site for an academy. He solved the site location problem by obtaining Fort Severn at Annapolis, Maryland, from the Army. He then raised $28,200, enough to place eighteen of the Navy's twenty-five professors on waiting orders and transferred them at half-pay to teach at the academy. He named Commander Franklin Buchanan superintendent, and in early 1846, fifty-six students reported for instruction, half being midshipmen returning from sea and the other half new appointees who would eventually be called cadets.

Bancroft remained more interested in improving the quality of the Navy than increasing its size. Even as the nation neared war with Mexico, his parsimonious estimates for ships, guns, and manpower were a third less than those of John Young Mason, his peacetime predecessor. Polk expressed astonishment at his secretary's lack of interest in new construction. Bancroft eventually confessed that he opposed war unless Mexico committed an overt act, so Polk brought Mason back to the post of secretary and had his little war.

Bancroft never fully understood his role, but he did understand the importance of education for naval officers. His stature as Secretary of the Navy rests on one act, the establishment of the U. S. Naval Academy.

dugouts to reach and beat the elusive enemy.

Not until 1845 did the United States take a serious look at its Navy. In many respects, America did not need much of a naval force to defeat Mexico, but President Polk wanted one. Because the Navy performed a secondary role in a contest fought mainly by the Army, Secretary of the Navy George Bancroft wanted no more deep-draft warships built for service in the Gulf of Mexico and purchased instead a number of shallow-draft vessels that became the backbone of Commodore David Conner's "mosquito flotilla."

The Navy's Pacific Squadron needed the larger vessels, and when the vainglorious Commodore Robert F. Stockton arrived on the West Coast with the old frigate *Congress*, he assimilated the overly cautious John D. Sloat's squadron and pressed for action. Landing parties from *Congress* and the sloop-of-war *Cyane* captured Southern California and Los Angeles. On August 14, 1846, Mexican forces in the state surrendered, and Stockton organized and headed a civil government.

In the Gulf of Mexico, Conner experienced problems because of disease and a paucity of steamers needed to bring in supplies. Bancroft sent the side-wheel steamer *Mississippi* – hardly a shallow-draft vessel – to the Gulf with a new commander, Commodore Matthew C. Perry. John Young Mason replaced Bancroft and began building and commissioning steamers, among them *Powhatan*, *Susquehanna*, *Saranac*, and *San Jacinto*. For purposes of comparison, *Saranac* was given side-wheels and *San Jacinto* a screw. None of the vessels ever got into the war. After bombarding the forts protecting the harbor of Veracruz, Perry successfully put General Winfield Scott's army of 12,000 ashore in a single day, after which the Navy mopped up the coast with small amphibious expeditions. During the war, the Marine Corps enjoyed the distinction of acting with the Army in the capture of Mexico City, adding the feat to its spirited hymn – "From the halls of Montezuma to the shores of Tripoli."

From the Mexican War, the United States Navy learned something about the difficulties of maintaining a lengthy blockade in enemy waters. Little did sailors realize that in fifteen short years many of them would be at sea again, watching 3,500 miles of their own coast along a strip of the South called the Confederate States of America.

Above: *On August 15, 1838, Lt. Charles Wilkes began a four-year exploration of the southern polar regions. On January 19, 1840, on board* Vincennes, *he discovered Antarctica. Among his many artifacts are his hat, his sextant, his sword pistol, and a copious 944-page autobiography.*

Left: *Pictured is a passed midshipman in a typical 1840s full dress uniform of the United States Navy.*

Bottom: *On March 4, 1854, Commodore Perry went ashore at Yokohama and negotiated the Treaty of Kanagawa, which opened Japan to the western world.*

MATTHEW C. PERRY

Though Commodore Matthew C. Perry may be most remembered for his actions during the Mexican War, his greatest achievement occurred when he commanded the East India Squadron, operating out of Hong Kong. Secretary of the Navy James C. Dobbin sent him to open trade with Japan. On July 8, 1853, Perry sailed into Tokyo Bay and sent an emissary ashore with a letter from the president to the emperor, promising to stop the following year for an answer.

Perry returned to Japan in February, 1854, with a larger force of ships and entered into negotiations with the Japanese. Amid entertainments and exchanges of gifts, negotiations continued, climaxing on March 31 by the signing of the Treaty of Kanagawa, giving the United States the use of two ports for wood, water, supplies, and refuge. Much of Perry's success was due to the presence of two "Black ships," the steamers *Susquehanna* and *Mississippi*, aboard which Japanese representatives were feasted with food, whiskey, and champagne. Perry used no intimidation during the negotiations and achieved a brilliant success that no career diplomat could have matched.

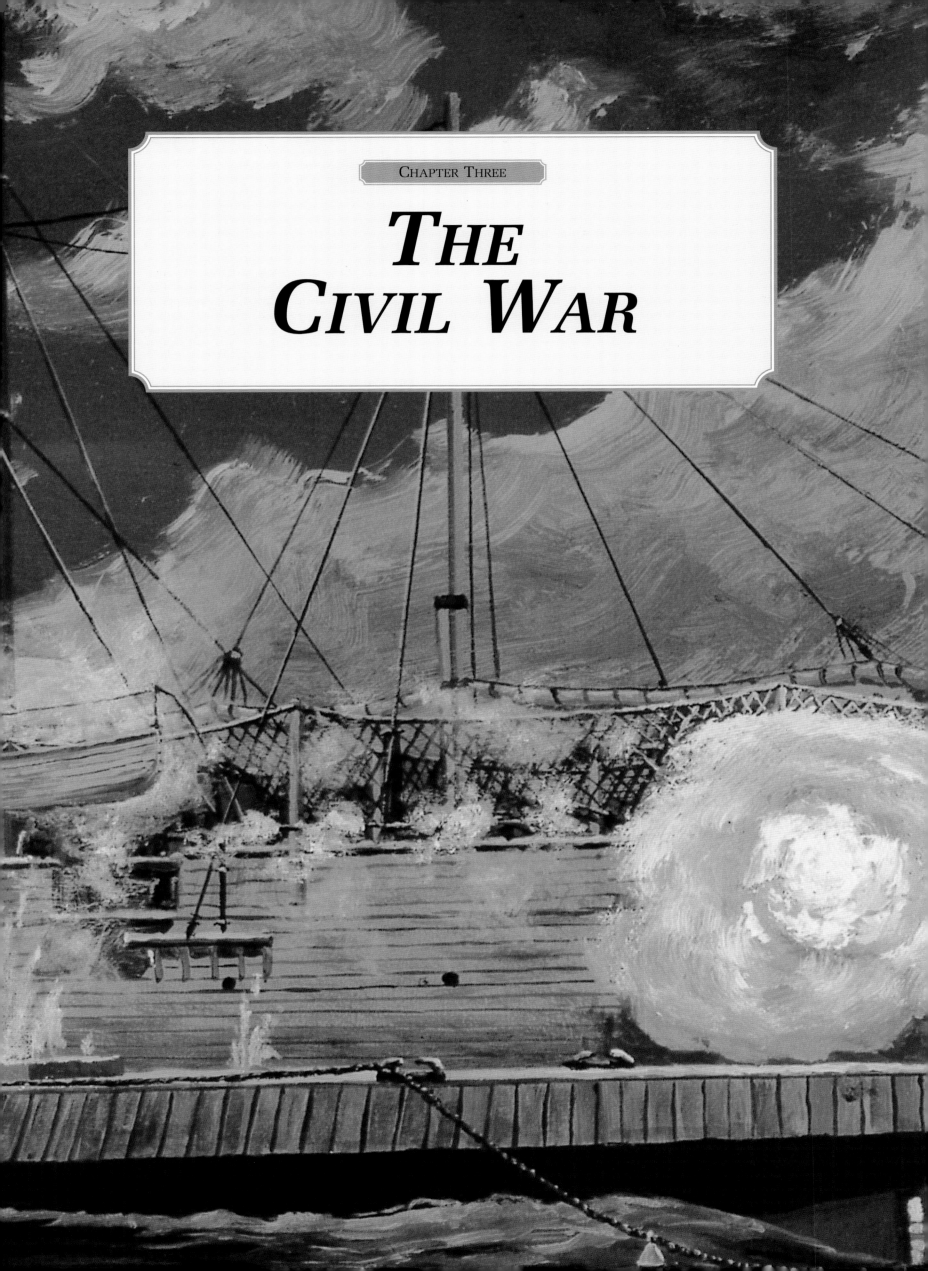

Chapter Three

The Civil War

After the Mexican conflict, the battle shifted to Congress, not because of wars to fight but because a series of laws, debated for seven months, resulted in the Compromise of 1850. The nation was dividing over the issue of American slavery, and though the Compromise of 1850 temporarily ended the debate, it did not end the sectional struggle.

Against this political backdrop William Ballard Preston became Secretary of the Navy. In 1849 he had fifty-two ships in commission, fifteen in ordinary, and ten building. Of those in service, ten were steamers. Seven years earlier a contract had been issued to Robert L. Stevens for an iron war steamer resistant to shot and shell. In July Preston canceled the contract. Over the years large sums of money had been spent to build eight navy yards and stockpile them with wood and other materials should war occur. Preston decided to close some of them, but they were now political plums, so Congress saved the yards. For the next fifteen months Preston pondered over the issue of grog and the abolishment of flogging, issues he never resolved.

In July 1850 President Zachary Taylor died and Millard Fillmore won the next election. Enmeshed in sectional strife, Fillmore made quick changes in his cabinet and on July 18 named William Alexander Graham Secretary of the Navy. Graham banned flogging, and he almost eliminated the Navy. He recommended that the number of captains be reduced from 68 to 26; commanders from 97 to 46; lieutenants from 327 to 300; and that corresponding cutbacks be made in other ranks. He left the question of reductions up to Congress and seemed to take no interest in the outcome.

Before Congress could act, John P. Kennedy took over the reigns of the Navy Department and attempted to raise enlistments from 7,500 men to 15,000 men and increase their pay. He also wanted to confer the rank of rear admiral on two officers and reinstate the rank of commodore. Kennedy also believed the peacetime Navy should become involved in missions of diplomacy and exploration. He sent Matthew Perry to Japan, Commander William F. Lynch to Liberia, and Surgeon Elisha Kent Kane to the Arctic. He also asked Congress for funds to build three first-class screw-propeller frigates and three screw-propeller sloops-of-war, none of which he got. After nine months in office, Kennedy departed when Franklin Pierce became president.

On March 8, 1853, James C. Dobbin became the first Secretary of the Navy to serve a four-year term since 1838. He brought intellect and per-

> '*We want a ship which can not be sunk or penetrated by the shell or shot of the U.S. Navy at a distance at which we could penetrate and sink the ships of the enemy, and which cannot be rereadily carried by boarders.*'
>
> STEPHEN R. MALLORY,
> CONFEDERATE SECRETARY OF THE NAVY,
> MAY 17, 1961

Right: A gun crew on the USS Miami *run through exercises on one of the ship's six 9-inch Dahlgren smoothbore shell guns. Built at the Philadelphia Navy Yard and launched November 16, 1861,* Miami *became one of many double-ended side-wheel steamers built during the Civil War.*

DAHLGREN AND HIS GUNS

John A. B. Dahlgren joined the Navy in 1826, but he never found his niche until 1847 when the Secretary assigned him to the Washington Navy Yard as an ordnance officer. Having the mathematical ability of an engineer, the forty-year-old lieutenant began conducting experiments with cannon and other firearms.

Working tirelessly, he expanded the ordnance department to include laboratories, a foundry, and a test range. In 1850 he introduced his 9-inch smoothbore cannon, nicknamed "soda-water bottles" for their distinctive shape, followed in 1851 by his 11-inch gun. As a class of ordnance, these smoothbores, intended to fire shell against wooden ships of the 1850s, simply became known as "Dahlgrens." In 1853 he added a bronze boat howitzer, one that could also be used on land, and a class of iron rifled cannon. In later years Dahlgren moved toward heavier guns, 15- and 20-inch smoothbores, and 50-, 80-, and 150-pounder rifled cannon, but some of the latter tended to burst.

In 1863 Dahlgren, who wanted sea duty, took command of the South Atlantic Blockading Squadron, where he spent most of his time off Charleston. This experience marked him as a better inventor and engineer than a squadron commander.

Left: *John A. B. Dahlgren (1809-1870) always wanted to be a navy man, and he found his niche in the ordnance department. Like most engineers, he had an irascible side, but the famous guns that bore his name became the mainstay of the U.S. Navy for more than three decades.*

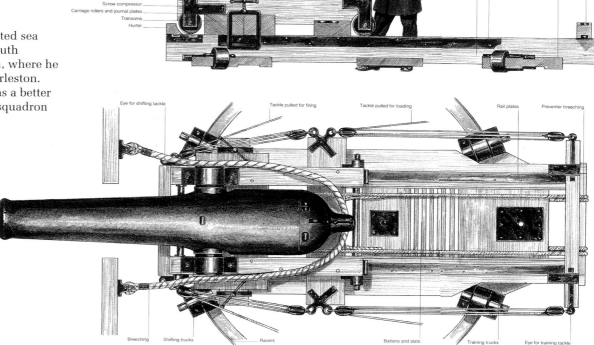

Right: *In 1850, John Dahlgren began designing the 9-inch gun, followed a year later by the 11-incher. He intended his smoothbores to fire shell against wooden ships of the 1850s, but they proved strong enough to fire shot. In 1862, Dahlgren designed both 15- and 20-inch guns, but only one 20-incher was made.*

sonal charm to the office, but he kept the Navy on a seesaw. Congress found merit in Graham's proposal to reduce the size of the Navy, so Senator Stephen R. Mallory, Chairman of the Naval Affairs Committee, established the Navy Retiring Board and waited for three captains, three commanders, and three lieutenants to decide in secret the fate of their brother officers. With an Opium War underway in China, trouble in Paraguay, Perry in Japan, survey vessels in the North Pacific, soundings for laying the first Atlantic Cable, and the launching of six new steam frigates all underway, Dobbin had no reason to reduce the size of the Navy.

Other important work was underway.

Lieutenant Matthew Fontaine Maury, superintendent of the U. S. Navy Observatory, had been tracking the winds and currents of the seas and making sailing faster and safer for the ships of the world. Captain David G. Farragut was building a navy yard on Mare Island in California. Because French General Paixhans had developed an explosive shell, Lieutenant John A. Dahlgren had been hard at work designing and testing his "beer-bottle-guns" with 9- and 11-inch bores. While Dahlgren worked assiduously to perfect his shell gun, Captain Charles Morris, Chief of the Bureau of Ordnance and Hydrography, scotched the program and lost an early opportunity to improve naval gunnery. When Congress approved

▶ **AUGUST 7:** James B. Eads is to build seven shallow-draft ironclad gunboats at St. Louis.

AUGUST 28-29: The first joint Army-Navy expedition captures Hatteras Inlet, North Carolina.

SEPTEMBER 16: Welles recommends construction of three ironclads—*Monitor, New Ironsides*, and *Galena*.

OCTOBER 25: Work begins on the USS *Monitor*.

NOVEMBER 7: A second Union Army-Navy expedition captures Port Royal Sound.

NOVEMBER 8: Captain Charles Wilkes initiates the "Trent Affair."

DECEMBER 21: Congress creates the Navy Medal of Honor.

Above right: *Mathew F. Maury (1806–1873) became one of the true geniuses of the U.S. Navy during the mid-1800s. Many advocates believed that Maury, though a mere lieutenant at the time, should have been made Secretary of the Navy because nobody understood the reforms required by the service better than he. Instead, Maury carved his career in perhaps a more productive way, and for his studies of the sea won international recognition, something that churned up great envy among many of his peers.*

MATHEW FONTAINE MAURY

Lieutenant Mathew Fontaine Maury, a self-trained scientist and astronomer, became disabled when thrown from a stagecoach in the 1830s. The Navy deemed him lame for life and stuffed him away in the Depot of Charts and Instruments, a non-physical assignment having routine duties.

Among boxes of old documents Maury discovered hundreds of musty logbooks, records of voyages going back to the Continental Navy. Having served for nine years at sea and been exposed to navigational problems, he began paging through logs covering voyages like those he had taken. There he began to discover consistencies in wind, weather, and currents. He also discovered that vessels following some courses made faster voyages.

Maury now believed he had found the answers to questions that had baffled sailors for 6,000 years – how to get from one port to another the fastest and safest way. Once he began charting the seas' winds and currents, he now needed more data. He designed a special Abstract Log for the Navy, instructing every commander to return it to the Depot at the conclusion of their voyage. Finding he could not get information fast enough, he recruited commerce carriers. This still did not satisfy him, so he held a conference in Brussels and recruited the sailing nations of the world. Every skipper who participated received a free copy of Maury's charts and *Sailing Directions*.

When the Navy built the National Observatory, they named Maury superintendent. Maury laid out tracks in the sea, and by the late 1850s every sailing vessel in the world followed his oceanic highways. From the information he compiled, he wrote *The Physical Geography of the Sea*, the first comprehensive oceanographic work of the nineteenth century. Maury was just beginning to build a head of steam when Secretary Dobbin advised him that the Navy "plucking board" had removed him from active duty and put him on half pay. The action incensed Maury, and the public outcry at home and abroad made the Navy look like fools.

Maury asked for a court of inquiry and eventually got it. Almost single-handedly, he caused the board to reverse more than half of its rulings, among them that relating to him. Maury's international prominence had attracted many enemies, and those on the board had used an old disability to remove him from active duty. Unfortunately, some deadwood needed to be excised from the service, but Maury's stand against the plucking board aided in upsetting the entire program.

six screw-propelled frigates in 1854, Dahlgren lobbied to have them fitted with his new guns. Dobbin said no, but in January 1856 Morris died, and Dahlgren eventually got his way.

Four years before the outbreak of civil war, James Buchanan became president and appointed Isaac Toucey Secretary of the Navy. In almost every way, Toucey was no more prepared for the post of secretary than Buchanan was for the presidency. Both entered office during the most crucial years for the nation.

'I believe this government cannot endure, permanently half slave and half free….It will become all one thing, or all the other.'

ABRAHAM LINCOLN'S CAMPAIGN SPEECH
FOR THE SENATE,
JUNE 16, 1858.

'The United States of America is hereby dissolved'

SOUTH CAROLINA STATE LEGISLATURE,
DECEMBER 20, 1860.

THE FIRST DAYS OF WAR

Early in his administration Toucey pushed for funds to build seven steam sloops to suppress the slave trade and money to install Dahlgren guns on all fighting ships. He also deserved credit for resolving some of the personnel problems left over from his predecessor's plucking board. Though from Connecticut, Toucey's sympathies were with the South, and his years as secretary were spent as Buchanan's "yes" man. When on January 9, 1861, the merchant ship *Star of the West* attempted to reinforce Fort Sumter and was driven off by South Carolinian artillery, Toucey issued no orders for putting the Navy in a state of readiness to deal with a developing domestic crisis. He stayed on, agreeing with Buchanan that the Executive did not have the authority to suppress secession. By February 1, 1861, seven southern states had seceded and four more would follow.

When Abraham Lincoln took office on March 4, 1861, the Confederate States of America had already been formed with Jefferson Davis as president and Stephen R. Mallory as Secretary of the Navy. Mallory's former post as Chairman of the Naval Affairs Committee made him the most experienced administrator in Davis's cabinet.

Lincoln replaced Toucey with Gideon Welles of Hartford, Connecticut. Though a career publisher and editor of the *Hartford Times*, Welles had spent most of his life espousing the cause of Democrats before becoming a Republican. His brief tenure as the Navy's Chief of the Bureau of Provisions and Clothing during the Mexican War had familiarized him with the routine of naval administration, and he entered the office with more experience in naval affairs than any of his predecessors. While Lincoln's choice of Welles was partly political, he could not have chosen a man with keener insight and ability to manage the Navy thoughtfully, wisely, and energetically in a time of crisis.

When war came Welles had forty-five ships in commission, most of which were obsolete. Of those, thirty were on foreign duty. One-half of the Navy's officer corps, more than 300 officers from captain to midshipman, had resigned or been dismissed because they joined the Confederacy. Much of his department was demoralized, and many of his clerks were in sympathy with the South.

The situation went from bad to worse when on

the morning of April 12, 1861, Brig. Gen. Pierre G. T. Beauregard opened fire on the federal garrison at Fort Sumter and lit the spark that started the Civil War. Lincoln called for 75,000 men and declared a blockade of southern ports. With barely enough ships to operate a peacetime Navy, and with half the number of officers to command them, Welles suddenly had the task of blockading 3,500 miles of Confederate coast.

When war erupted, Lincoln doubted whether Welles could rapidly mobilize a navy, so he decided to give him an assistant. His choice was thirty-nine-year-old Gustavus Vasa Fox, the brother-in-law of politically powerful Montgomery Blair, the Postmaster General.

Above: *On April 12, 1861, South Carolina artillery opened on Fort Sumter and fired the first shots of the Civil War. After twenty-four hours of heavy bombardment, the Union garrison under Major Robert Anderson surrendered, evacuating by ship the following day.*

Above: *Gideon Welles (1802-1878), despite his civilian background, faced the task of war with energy and foresight and built a great navy.*

Left: *The Washington Navy Yard, established in 1799 by John Adams, became a factor in creating the Union's Civil War navy, but most of the deeper draft vessels came from the yards at New York, Boston, Philadelphia, and Portsmouth.*

▶ **1862**

FEBRUARY 4-14: Eads's river ironclads participate in the capture of Forts Henry and Donelson.

FEBRUARY 17: CSS *Virginia*, commanded by Captain Franklin Buchanan, is commissioned.

FEBRUARY 25: USS *Monitor*, commanded by Lt. John L. Worden, is commissioned.

MARCH 9: The *Virginia* and *Monitor* fight the first duel between ironclads.

MARCH 22: The first British-built cruiser, CSS *Florida*, sails from Liverpool.

APRIL 25: Flag Officer David G. Farragut's squadron captures New Orleans.

JUNE 6: Col. Charles Ellet, using unarmed battering rams, captures Memphis.

Above right: *Gustavus Vasa Fox (1821-1883) served as Assistant Secretary of the Navy during the Civil War and rendered valuable service in creating the Union Navy.*

Right: *Stephen R. Mallory (1813-1873), having chaired the Naval Affairs Committee while a member of the U.S. Senate, became Jefferson Davis's choice as Confederate Secretary of the Navy. Among Davis's many appointments to cabinet posts, Mallory's ranked among the best.*

At the age of seventeen, Fox had joined the Navy as a midshipman, advanced to passed midshipman on the eve of the Mexican War, and in 1852 became a lieutenant. Four years later he resigned from the Navy and became an agent for the Bay State Mills. At Blair's urging, President Lincoln had sent Fox to Charleston to seek a solution to mounting tensions, but Fox arrived off the harbor just in time to witness Major Anderson's surrender of Fort Sumter. When Fox returned, Lincoln offered him command of a ship. Fox said he would prefer being the Chief Clerk in the Navy Department.

At first, Welles privately grumbled to his diary about having an assistant imposed upon him by Lincoln, but Fox soon demonstrated his indispensability. Welles possessed a sharp, analytical mind, but he seldom left his office. Fox brought energy, intelligence, and exceptional management skills to the team. He persuaded Welles to use ironclads in battle, improved the curriculum at the Naval Academy, and used his exceptional engineering skills when negotiating with shipbuilders. The two men complemented each other's attributes, and they soon became great friends.

In Richmond, Virginia, Mallory's situation was

even worse than the Union's. He had no ships of war, only a few small steamers and riverboats, but he did have hundreds of skilled officers, sailors, and boatmen looking for work. His years of heading the Naval Affairs Committee had introduced him to the concept of building iron-armored vessels, a recent innovation of Britain and France that senior officers of the U. S. Navy seemed hesitant to adopt. Because of the North's traditional resistance to ironclads, Mallory suspected that Welles might feel the same way. He also believed that if the North built ironclads, they would follow the design of the British *Warrior* or the French *Gloire*, and for several months, Mallory was right.

Mallory also faced another problem. The South had no shipyards, few factories, and little money to build a navy, yet he must find a way to lessen the effect of Welles's blockade and bring harm to the Union. Only through open ports could the South receive the foreign aid it needed to fight a prolonged war, and only through successful military operations could the South hope to achieve foreign recognition. If ironclads could get to sea, they could smash the Union's wooden blockaders. If commerce raiders could be built, they could inflict enough damage on the American carrying trade to discourage

STEPHEN R. MALLORY

Forty-eight-year-old Stephen R. Mallory served as the Confederate Secretary of the Navy, the only member of Jefferson Davis's cabinet to keep his position throughout the war. Growing up in Key West, Mallory studied law, became a customs inspector and a judge, and in 1851 came to Washington as a senator, holding his seat until Florida seceded. Having been since 1855 the powerful chairman of the Naval Affairs Committee, Mallory came well prepared for the Confederate cabinet.

Southerners, however, expected far more from Mallory than he delivered, mainly because the Confederate Congress could not provide him with the necessary funds to build a strong navy. His most successful enterprise was

commerce raiding, using ships built by British shipyards and manned by British sailors. The Laird ironclad rams, being built in Birkenhead, England, to dismantle the Union blockade, were never finished. His domestic ironclads, built along the rivers of the South and configured after the CSS *Virginia* (*Merrimac*), were always more of a threat than an actual menace. Without facilities for manufacturing powerful steam engines, Mallory's ironclads were always underpowered and unseaworthy. None of them ever met the South's expectations, but as the war neared its end, the ironclad CSS *Tennessee* stood alone against Rear Admiral David G. Farragut's squadron in Mobile Bay and stamped an indelible mark on naval history that ended forever the careers of the great steam sloops of the world.

Lincoln from pursuing the war. If both succeeded, the South would win her independence.

Welles and Mallory had different strategies. Welles must build a large enough navy to blockade the South and squeeze her like a coiled anaconda into submission. Mallory must have a small navy, one of impenetrable iron vessels to drive away blockading vessels, and another to prey upon the American merchant fleet. Both strategies made sense, but could either be implemented?

PROBLEMS NORTH AND SOUTH

The economic balance tilted heavily in favor of the North. For every white inhabitant of the South, there were four in the North. For every factory in the South, the North had six. Only one of ten manufactured articles produced in the United States was made in the South. Had it not been for the seizure of Federal arsenals and shipyards by Confederate militia, the South would not have had arms or munitions enough to start a war. And without support from abroad, they would never have been able to sustain a war.

When war severed the American Republic, the North was not without its problems. With an army of 16,000 men, most of who were serving in the West, even Lincoln's first call for 75,000 volunteers could not be mobilized overnight. Welles

'I regard the possession of an iron-armored ship as a matter of the first necessity. Such a vessel at this time could traverse the entire coast of the United States, prevent all blockade, and encounter, with a fair prospect of success, their entire navy.... Naval engagements between wooden frigates, as they are now built and armed, will prove to be the forlorn hopes of the sea, simply contests...of who shall go to the bottom first.'

STEPHEN R. MALLORY
TO THE CHAIRMAN OF THE CONFEDERATE NAVAL
COMMITTEE, MAY 8, 1861.

could not blockade 3,500 miles of Confederate coast with forty vessels any more than he could raise the hundreds he would eventually need to keep blockade-runners from supplying the South. So inept were the early actions of the Union that a small force of Virginia militia captured the navy yards at Gosport and Norfolk, carted away a thousand cannon, and raised the charred hulk of the USS *Merrimac*, which had been mishandled, scuttled, and partially burned.

Raising *Merrimac* marked the beginning of a change in naval warfare that would make obsolete the navies of the world, not because the Confederates raised her and pumped her out, but because of what they afterwards did to alter her. She became not the grand old steam frigate of the United States Navy but an ironclad monolith

Above: *Artifacts of the Civil War have attracted great interest by collectors. A selection of a Confederate naval officers' uniform and equipment include: (above left) lieutenant's frock coat and (below left) jacket; other frock coats (below center and above right); Adams revolver and holster; captains' swords and scabbards (above center); sword from the CSS* Alabama *(top group of three, bottom center); Raphael Semmes's field glass (bottom left); revolver and holster (below right, and cap (top right).*

▶ **JULY 15** The ironclad CSS *Arkansas* attacks the squadrons of Farragut and Charles H. Davis.

JULY 16: Congress creates the rank of rear admiral and bestows it first upon Farragut.

AUGUST 24: The Confederate cruiser *Alabama* begins a 22-month raid on Union commerce.

DECEMBER 12: A Confederate mine sinks the USS *Cairo* in the Yazoo River.

JOHN ERICSSON'S *MONITOR*

Everyone in the Navy Department looked upon fifty-eight-year-old John Ericsson as an eccentric engineer having wild, implausible notions of how to build ships. He was irascible, brilliant, and condemning – a combination of personality traits former Navy appropriations board members found intolerable. Yet Ericsson had used steam to design railway locomotives, fire engines, and screw-driven warships. In the 1840s he built the Navy's first screw-propelled warship, the USS *Princeton*, but he fell out of favor when a gun designed but not built by him exploded during trials and killed two cabinet members.

After Welles gave Cornelius Bushnell of Connecticut a contract to build *Galena*, Bushnell went to Ericsson for advice. Instead of advice, Ericsson showed Bushnell his plan for a monitor. Fascinated by Ericsson's concepts, Bushnell realized that the monitor design was far superior to his own, so he urged Welles to speak with Ericsson. Welles manifested grave doubts because the strange vessel carried only two guns in a rotating pillbox and had no sails. Experts laughed at the design, but Welles gambled, not because he had certain confidence in the vessel but because

Above: *John Ericsson (1803-1889) came to America from Sweden in 1839 and in 1844 built the USS* Princeton, *the first ship with a screw propeller. His innovations in naval engineering changed the world.*

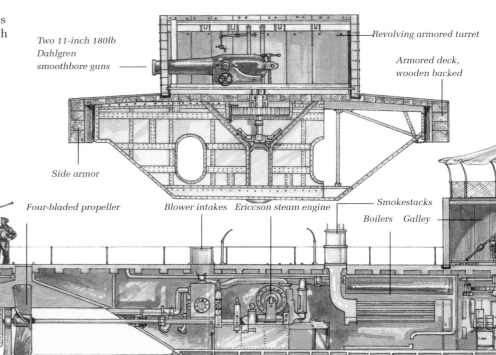

Two 11-inch 180lb Dahlgren smoothbore guns

Revolving armored turret

Armored deck, wooden backed

Side armor

Four-bladed propeller

Blower intakes

Ericcson steam engine

Smokestacks

Boilers   Galley

Rudder

Merrimac had been a handsome, 40-gun, three-masted, square-rigged steam frigate with a screw propeller. When raised off Norfolk, most of her hull and machinery remained undamaged – a gift to the Confederacy. If restored to her original configuration, she would be trapped in the river by the Union blockade. "It has been therefore determined," said Mallory to his colleagues, "to shield her completely with three-inch iron, placed at such angles as to render her ball-proof, to complete her at the earliest moment, to arm her with the heaviest ordnance, and to send her at once against the enemy's fleet. It is believed that thus prepared she will be able to contend successfully against the heaviest of the enemy's ships, and drive them from Hampton Roads and the ports of Virginia."

armed with heavy guns that could sink any Union wooden warship that came in range without suffering more than a small dent. She became Mallory's prototype for his ironclad navy and his one hope of achieving superiority at sea.

Less than 150 miles separated Norfolk from the Federal capital, and soon details of the transformation of *Merrimac* began filtering into Washington. Welles had decided to build two prototypes – *New Ironsides* and *Galena* – but he doubted if they would be ready in time to meet a resurrected *Merrimac*. Union forces had already been drubbed at Bull Run on July 21, 1861, and the last thing the Union needed was to have an enemy ironclad prowling up the Potomac River and laying siege to Washington. In a panicky search to find a weapon to set against *Merrimac*,

Ericsson promised to build her in one hundred days. So in October, 1861, Ericsson began work on the USS *Monitor* and set the stage for making Welles's wooden navy obsolete.

One hundred days was not much time to build an entirely new type of vessel, especially when Ericsson invented and corrected as the work progressed. Welles had written into the contract that *Monitor* must carry sails. The clause gave Ericsson a contemptuous laugh, and he ignored it.

On January 30, 1862, the vessel plunged into the East River, her construction having been subcontracted to separate firms for her hull, engines, turret, armor, a unique ventilation system, and steam donkeys for rotating and orienting the turret. Ericsson combined all the most recent advancements in naval technology,

added to them his own genius, and created *Monitor*. Had it not been for Ericsson, years would have passed before the navies of the world would have incorporated all the new technology into one vessel at the same time.

Monitor, however, had all the trouble one might expect of a prototype. Having so little freeboard, water washed through hatches, down ventilation grates, and into her turret. She had gears everywhere, shaved and fitted to operate with clocklike precision. Not until March 6 was she ready to be towed down to Fort Monroe. By then the hump-backed *Merrimac*, re-christened *Virginia*, was coaling for her revolutionary adventure in Hampton Roads.

Above: *The USS* Monitor *became Ericsson's best-known invention. Since she was a compact and small vessel, her crew aired themselves on the deck or underneath the canopy on the turret, which housed the ship's two 11-inch Dahlgrens.*

Left: *A top and cross-sectional view of* Monitor *illustrates how Ericsson arranged every one of his inventions to fit, from the unique blower intake system, aft, to change the air, and the turret turning machinery with its donkey steam engine, centered topside. Ericsson did not know quite where to position the pilothouse and placed it too far forward.*

Turret turning machinery

Crews' quarters

Officers' quarters

Armored pilot house

Windlass   Anchor

Swedish-born engineer John Ericsson arrived in Washington with an outlandish design of an iron-clad "monitor," an odd creature with a two-gun rotating turret.

While Ericsson worked assiduously on *Monitor* and labors at Norfolk progressed slowly on *Merrimac*, Mallory initiated the second part of his strategy – to buy or build Confederate ships of prey. Commander Raphael Semmes converted the mail packet *Havana* at New Orleans, armed her with five guns, renamed her CSS *Sumter*, and on June 30, 1861, slipped to sea under the nose of the USS *Brooklyn*. Semmes set off on a six-month commerce-raiding cruise through the Caribbean, Atlantic, and Mediterranean. He captured eighteen prizes, signaling to Welles that the Union had more to worry about than blockade-runners.

> '*Take the little thing home and worship it, as it would not be idolatry, because it was in the image of nothing in the heaven above or on earth beneath or in the waters under the earth.*'
>
> CAPTAIN CHARLES HENRY DAVIS TO CORNELIUS BUSHNELL, AT HIS FIRST SIGHT OF ERICSSON'S MODEL OF THE *MONITOR*

While Semmes rampaged through the tropics, Mallory sent James Dunwoody Bulloch to Liverpool, England, as a Confederate purchasing agent, but Bulloch's real purpose was to buy, fit, and arm British sail-rigged screw-steamers for service on the high seas. Because the nations of

▶ 1863

January 31: Two Confederate ironclads – *Chicora* and *Palmetto State* – attack the Union squadron off Charleston harbor.

February 3-March 17: Acting Rear Admiral David D. Porter attempts to flank Vicksburg by moving an expedition of vessels through Yazoo Pass.

March 14-24: Porter's second attempt to flank Vicksburg through Steele's Bayou also fails.

April 2: Porter's squadron passes Vicksburg, enabling the Army to land flanking forces below.

Above right: *Twenty states of the Union fought to reunify the country, and each was represented by a star in the Union flag like the one shown above, and carried by all ships of the U.S. Navy.*

Europe had proclaimed their neutrality, Bulloch was forced to engage in an illegal enterprise. Using various disguises to screen his efforts from local authorities, Bulloch put to sea two of the Confederacy's most powerful commerce raiders, *Florida* and *Alabama*, but neither vessel sailed until 1862.

Kidnap on the High Seas

Britain's neutrality disappointed Jefferson Davis, who had hoped to have her as an ally. Captain Charles Wilkes, prowling off Cuba on November 8, 1861, in search of Semmes, came close to giving Davis his most cherished wish. Wilkes, commanding the USS *San Jacinto*, captured the British mail steamer *Trent* and forcibly removed two Southern commissioners James Mason and John Slidell – from her deck. The nation hailed Wilkes as a hero, but his actions were not unlike those that caused America to go to war with Britain in 1812. On both sides of the Atlantic the press advocated war, but saner minds in Whitehall and Washington allowed the matter to cool. Secretary of State William H. Seward disavowed the kidnapping, and without making an apology explained to British minister Lord John Lyons that Wilkes's act had been unauthorized. Washington released Mason and Slidell, and the incident faded from view. In 1862 the Navy advanced Wilkes to rear admiral and two years later court-martialed him for "disobedience, disrespect, insubordination, and conduct unbecom-

ing an officer." After one year's suspension, he was reinstated, allowing Wilkes to retire in 1866 with the rank of rear admiral.

As early 1862 put its frigid grip on the armies and confined them to winter quarters, work on *Virginia* and *Monitor* progressed toward the most unusual of all coincidences – a showdown in Hampton Roads. The massive Southern ironclad with its 170-foot long "barn roof" waited for her armor plating. She was pierced for ten guns – four in each broadside and one in pivot, fore and aft. She carried a four-foot iron beak beneath her waterline, a spur not found on sailing ships. When Captain Franklin Buchanan, commanding the James River Squadron, took her for a run down the Elizabeth River in early March, she would barely steer.

At New York, Lieutenant John Worden, commanding *Monitor*, took her out for a trial and crashed into a wharf on the other side of the river. For "Ericsson's Folly," it was not a good beginning. She was towed back to her berth, and mechanics made adjustments to her steering. They lifted the turret off its base and mounted two 11-inch Dahlgren shell guns inside, and before reseating the turret they fitted cordage between the gears to seal the teeth during the voyage at sea. Then, on March 6, a towboat passed a hawser to *Monitor* and set a course for Hampton Roads. During the trip *Monitor* became so unweatherly in storms that on two occasions, when continuously swept by heavy seas, she almost foundered.

On March 8, while *Monitor* staggered through the combers, *Virginia* crawled down the Elizabeth

> '*The Merrimac [will] destroy every vessel in the service…lay every city on the coast under contribution…take Fortress Monroe….come up the Potomac and disperse Congress, destroy the Capitol and public buildings; or she might go to New York and destroy those cities, or levy from them contributions sufficient to carry on the war.*'
>
> A PANICKY SECRETARY OF WAR
> EDWIN M. STANTON
> TO LINCOLN'S CABINET MEETING ON
> MARCH 9, 1862.

River and at 1:00 p.m. steamed slowly into Hampton Roads, followed by two small gunboats. An hour later, she came within range of the old 50-gun *Congress* and the 30-gun *Cumberland*. She rammed *Cumberland*, and forced *Congress* aground. *Cumberland* sank and *Congress* surrendered. Buchanan could not board *Congress*, so he pulled away and with hot shot turned the ship into a roaring inferno. Three Union vessels ran aground as they rushed toward the battle. Two floated free with the tide, but the USS *Minnesota* grounded fast on a shoal. Buchanan wanted to finish her off, but a bullet struck him in the thigh and knocked him out of the action. Lt. Catesby ap Rogers Jones took command of the ironclad and withdrew for the night, postponing the destruction of *Minnesota*, *St. Lawrence*, and *Roanoke* until morning.

As night fell, Worden brought *Monitor* into Hampton Roads and anchored her alongside *Minnesota*. In the morning, as Jones approached *Minnesota*, he sighted what looked like a "cheese

box on a raft" and at first believed that the Yankees had brought down a small floating battery. He soon discovered that the "cheese box" would not let *Virginia* get within range of *Minnesota*, so he decided to deal with her first. To Jones's surprise, *Monitor* outmaneuvered *Virginia*, but neither vessel could inflict serious damage upon the other. About noon, a shot from *Virginia* struck the pilothouse of *Monitor* and blinded Worden. Both vessels withdrew and spent the balance of the afternoon watching each other from a distance. The battle, though indecisive, relieved Washington, for *Virginia* would never get out of Hampton Roads.

Two months later Maj. Gen. George B. McClellan brought the Army of the Potomac to the James River, forcing the Confederates to evacuate Norfolk and destroy *Virginia*, their now-

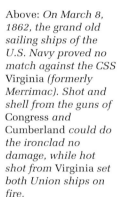

Above: *On March 8, 1862, the grand old sailing ships of the U.S. Navy proved no match against the CSS* Virginia *(formerly* Merrimac*). Shot and shell from the guns of* Congress *and* Cumberland *could do the ironclad no damage, while hot shot from* Virginia *set both Union ships on fire.*

Left: *After ramming the USS* Cumberland, Virginia *pulled free, and her crew stood by to watch the Union sloop-of-war slowly sink. In the distance to the left USS* Minnesota *waited, aground in the river. Her crew watched the devastation wrought by the first Rebel ironclad and wondered whether they would be next.*

APRIL 7: Rear Admiral Samuel F. Du Pont's ironclads are repulsed at Charleston.

JULY 4: Vicksburg surrenders.

OCTOBER 5: The CSS *David*, the first torpedo-boat, damages the USS *New Ironsides*.

Above right: *On March 9, 1862, Ericsson's* Monitor *made her debut and attacked the CSS* Virginia. Monitor's *skipper maneuvered to keep* Virginia *away from the grounded* Minnesota. *Both ironclads circled, often in their own smoke, each determined to destroy the other, but whenever they could,* Virginia's *gunners would lob a shell in* Minnesota's *direction.*

Below: *In the first major naval engagement on the Tennessee River, the Union flotilla under Flag Officer Andrew H. Foote bombarded Fort Henry into submission.*

famous ironclad. On December 31, 1862, the unseaworthy *Monitor* foundered in a gale off Cape Hatteras. Both vessels, rough prototypes of Yankee ingenuity, fought a drawn battle that raised the curtain on a new era in naval technology and changed the design of warships forever.

With help from millionaire shipbuilder James B. Eads, Welles put a squadron of seven new ironclad gunboats on the Mississippi in the remarkable time of sixty-five days. Samuel M. Pook designed them and Eads built the boats in timber yards, foundries, and machine shops scattered through eight northern states. All were broad-beamed, flat-bottomed, stern-wheelers, and because of their humped shape, sailors called them "Pook's Turtles." Named for some of the cities of their origin, they became *Cairo, Carondelet, Cincinnati, Louisville, Mound City,* *Pittsburgh,* and *St. Louis.* Eads later added two more ironclad gunboats – *Benton* and *Essex* – *Benton* converted from a river salvage boat and *Essex* from a ferry. To limit their drafts to six feet, none of the river ironclads was thickly plated. They were slow in the water, traveling upstream at four knots, but they carried a battery with a punch, usually six 32-pounders, three 8-inch Dahlgrens, and a scattering of army rifles and howitzers.

FLOTILLA ON THE TENNESSEE

Commanded by Flag Officer Andrew Hull Foote, the squadron got off to a good start. Early in 1862 Foote brought his flotilla into the Tennessee River. On February 6, in a combined attack with forces under Brig. Gen. Ulysses S. Grant, Foote's gunboats bombarded Fort Henry, shattered the shore batteries, and forced its surrender. On February 11, as Grant's army crossed by land to attack Fort Donelson, Foote brought his gunboats around to the Cumberland River and on February 14 opened on the fort's shore batteries. After a short engagement Foote sustained a serious wound, one he tried to ignore. He also discovered that his vessels' iron plating was not impervious to shot and pulled out of the action. This time the Army saved the day, but it took two days to force the Confederates to surrender.

Foote should have rested, but he took his squadron back to the naval base at Cairo for repairs and prepared to attack Island No. 10, the first Confederate bastion on the upper Mississippi River. Heavily fortified, Island No. 10

Left: *Union river ironclads resembled their Confederate counterparts. They had sloped casemates but were thinly iron-plated vessels driven by paddlewheels mounted aft. They carried a mixture of batteries ranging from howitzers to 8- and 9-inch Dahlgrens.*

lay dead center in a horseshoe bend in the river and was supported by fortifications along the Tennessee shore. To reach Memphis, Island No. 10 had to be conquered, but Foote now realized that Confederate rifled artillery could punch holes through his thin-skinned ironclads. Not until the night of April 4, during the height of a raging thunderstorm, was the USS *Carondelet* able to slip by the island and hurl shells into the fort's undefended rear, setting the stage for its capture. It would be Foote's last battle. Replaced by Capt. Charles Henry Davis, Foote took leave to heal, but on June 26 blood poisoning took his life.

While river ironclads operated on the upper Mississippi, sixty-one-year-old David Farragut tried to do the impossible – capture New Orleans with a squadron of seventeen wooden vessels ranging from old side-wheelers to the newer sloop-rigged screw steamers *Hartford*, *Richmond*, and *Pensacola*. Welles augmented Farragut's squadron with Comdr. David D. Porter's mortar flotilla, which consisted of twenty-two schooners refitted to carry 13-inch mortars, and a half-dozen gunboats to serve as towboats. Lincoln asked General McClellen to provide 20,000 infantry troops for the expedition. Under duress, McClellan eventually parted with about 12,000 soldiers and placed them under the command of Maj. Gen. Benjamin F. Butler.

RUNNING THE GAUNTLET

Farragut planned a surprise attack upon Forts Jackson and St. Philip. He believed that to pass such heavily armed forts with minimal damage the enemy must not be given time to improve his defenses. He did not put much faith in Porter's mortar bombardment, but he believed it might do

some good and agreed to try it. When Farragut found that he could not get his heavy steamers over the Mississippi bars he lost four weeks along with the element of surprise.

The delay caused another concern. The two forts mounted 126 guns which together covered three and one-half miles of the river. Above the forts were other obstacles – a small Confederate navy of ten gunboats, dozens of prepared fire rafts, and the ram CSS *Manassas*. Then, as Farragut prepared to run the gauntlet, the Confederates dispatched the ironclad *Louisiana* from New Orleans, adding another unknown element to the tension building in the Union fleet. Having recently received news about the ease with which the CSS *Virginia* destroyed *Congress* and *Cumberland*, some of the commanders of Farragut's wooden steamers envisioned an early end to their fighting careers if attacked by *Louisiana*.

On April 18 Porter's mortar squadron opened

Above: Sh*ipbuilder Cornelius Bushnell did the Navy a great service by recognizing that Ericsson's design of* Monitor *was far superior to his own, the ironclad* Galena, *for which he had a contract. Nonetheless, Bushnell finished* Galena, *and the Navy sent her to Hampton Roads. When the Army of the Potomac invaded Virginia, both* Monitor *and* Galena *went up the James River. Struck 43 times,* Galena's *4-inch armor shattered, and she returned a complete wreck after fighting shore batteries.* Monitor *came through the same fight unscathed, but she could not elevate her guns to bear upon the enemy's batteries.*

1864

FEBRUARY 17: The Confederate submarine *H.L. Hunley* sinks the USS *Housatonic*.

MARCH 12: Admiral Porter takes his squadron up the shallow Red River and on May 13 withdraws with loss after the Army retreats.

Left: *The men who manned Comdr. David Dixon Porter's schooners called the 13-inch mortars mounted aft "chowder pots." They could loft a 200-pound shell two miles, but there is no record of any sailor using them for cooking.*

Below: *As Hartford passes Fort St.Philip, she is confronted by the CSS* Louisiana, *and in a quick exchange of fire, steams safely up the river without suffering serious damage.*

Below: *Vessels displacing 3,000 tons like Hartford did no more cruising in the river than necessary. On calm, sunny days, sailors dried out the sails and pinned their wash to the rigging.*

on Fort Jackson. Six days later, though moderately battered, the fort still stood defiant and, with the undamaged Fort St. Philip, fully prepared to resist a Union attack. In the early hours of April 24, Farragut pushed through the broken chain barrier below Jackson and began his attack with seventeen vessels. In the smoke of battle, some of his commanders became confused, running all about the river while firing wildly at the forts. Three became entangled in the chain barrier or with each other and were forced back downstream after daylight flooded the river. The USS *Varuna*, Commander Charles S. Boggs, sank upriver after a heated fight with enemy gunboats. When Farragut assembled his ships above the forts at daylight he had lost *Varuna*, but thirteen ships had come through the battle with only slight damage. During the passage they all but swept the enemy squadron from the river, leaving

Louisiana behind to be destroyed by her crew a few days later.

On the afternoon of April 25, the Union squadron appeared off the defenseless city of New Orleans and held it captive until General Butler arrived with his army of occupation. Farragut had accomplished what Confederates believed impossible and what many in Washington believed would result in a useless loss of ships and sailors. In one bold move, Farragut dashed asunder the old navy axiom that wooden vessels could not pass heavily armed forts, and two of the strongest forts in North America were those below New Orleans, Forts Jackson and St. Philip. For Farragut, there would be many forts to pass before the war ground to a close.

REAR ADMIRAL DAVID GLASGOW FARRAGUT & COMDR. DAVID DIXON PORTER

David Glasgow Farragut had been in the Navy since the age of nine having become, after his mother died, a ward of Commodore David Porter. Porter obtained for Farragut a midshipman's warrant and in 1812 put him on board the frigate *Essex*. When Porter took *Essex* into the South Pacific during the War of 1812, Farragut went with him. At the age of twelve Midshipman Farragut became one of Porter's prize masters. Off Valparaiso he fought the HMS *Cherub* and *Phoebe*, and with Porter became a British prisoner. After that, like every other naval officer, he never saw much fighting. When Welles chose him to lead the New Orleans expedition, many of the old salts questioned the decision because Farragut had been born in the South, lived in Norfolk, had relatives in New Orleans, and had married a Virginian.

Being a ward brought him into the family that twelve years later gave birth to David Dixon Porter. For the New Orleans expedition, it was Porter's idea to form a mortar flotilla. He assured Welles and Fox that such a force could destroy Forts Jackson and St. Philip in forty-eight hours and thereby enable Farragut to reach New Orleans without serious injury. Porter also took credit for introducing the idea of naming Farragut flag officer, but beneath all the scheming was Porter's own ambition to command a squadron. While claiming to have recommended Farragut for squadron command, he also warned Fox that Farragut must be watched, and if his foster brother needed to be pressed to take action, Porter would be there to force it. Fox encouraged Porter to report on Farragut's activities. This played directly into Porter's hands, so much so that Porter seldom had anything good to say about his foster brother.

Farragut never needed prompting from anyone. He was among the most audacious commanders in the Civil War and its first rear admiral, not only dominating the naval war on the Mississippi and the Gulf of Mexico but also capturing Mobile Bay in 1864. He was to the Navy what General Grant became to the Army – its outstanding leader. Porter, however, did not suffer from his education under Farragut, becoming in September, 1862, acting rear admiral in command of the Mississippi Squadron. There he worked hard and performed well. After the war, Farragut became the Navy's first full admiral. Porter coveted the distinction, but he had to wait until Farragut died in 1870 to become the Navy's second admiral.

Left: David Glasgow Farragut (1801-1870) went into the Civil War as a captain with untested combat qualifications. Given an opportunity to prove himself under the most difficult assignment concocted by the navy – the capture of New Orleans – Farragut not only proved himself in the Mississippi but went on to become the most admired admiral of his century.

Above: While running Fort St. Philip, Hartford ran into a dose of trouble. The Confederate tug Mosher laid a fire raft beside the flagship and set her on fire. The signal officer on Hartford dropped a few shells onto the fire raft and blew it up. Hosed down, Hartford steered upriver with her port beam still smoldering.

On the upper sector of the Mississippi, another drama was being staged by Charles Ellet, a civil engineer who believed that fast, unarmed steamers fitted with iron bows could smash Confederate ironclads by ramming them abeam. Welles showed no interest in such a force, but Secretary of War Edwin M. Stanton did. He financed the scheme and Ellet went to war using several members of his family to prove his theory. When his boats made their appearance among Flag Officer Davis's Mississippi flotilla, they were scorned as trash vessels having no business mingling among the powerful river ironclads of the U.S. Navy.

Davis, however, suffered from a rash of timidity; so on the morning of June 6, 1862, Ellet took matters into his own hands. Standing off Memphis were eight gunboat-rams of the Confederate River Defense Fleet, commanded by Captain James E. Montgomery. When Davis steamed down to Memphis, Ellet followed, and when Davis anchored his fleet upriver and dined on breakfast, Ellet passed through the Union squadron with two of his battering rams. With his brother commanding the ram *Monarch* and he the *Queen of the West*, they struck two enemy vessels and initiated what became the annihilation of the Confederate squadron. Davis then entered the fight and chased the remnants of the River Defense Fleet downriver. Wounded during the action, Ellet sent his nineteen-year-old son into Memphis to demand its surrender. Ellet lost his life proving that all kinds of vessels could win the war on the waters, but it was the resolution of the

▶ **JUNE 19:** *Kearsarge* sinks the CSS *Alabama* in the English Channel.

AUGUST 5: Rear Admiral Farragut captures Mobile Bay. Comdr. Napoleon Collins, commanding the USS *Wachusetts*, illegally captures the CSS *Florida* in Brazil.

Bottom: *An array of Union naval officers' uniforms and equipment include: (top l to r) engineer's blue wool frock coat; surgeon's white linen sack coat, wool vest, frock coat, foul-weather rubberized leggings and canvas sea bag; lying across them, monocular glass, naval ordnance instruction manual, Model 1852 sword plus regulation Model 1841 Eaglehead sword (bottom right), sword belt and plate, octant (below left), wool vest (center); shoulder straps of 1st Asst. Engineer, non-regulation sword (bottom); medical case; and medal for service aboard USS Brooklyn (bottom right)*

Left: *On February 2, 1863, 19-year-old Col. Charles Rivers Ellet, commanding the ram* Queen of the West, *took the lightly armed vessel through a cordon of fire, struck the Confederate transport* City of Vicksburg, *and mortally wounded her.*

Below: *Brig. Gen. Alfred W. Ellet commanded the ram* Monarch *during the Battle of Memphis, and after the death of his brother, Col. Charles Ellet, Jr., he assumed command of the Ram Fleet and formed the Mississippi Marine Brigade.*

person in charge that won battles.

Welles eventually realized that Davis was not much of a fighter and replaced him, raising David Dixon Porter from commander to acting rear admiral. Porter had the better temperament and skills for command of the Mississippi Squadron and distinguished himself during the Vicksburg and Red River campaigns. Welles never placed full confidence in the unpredictable Porter, but if there was a tough task that involved the Navy, Porter, like Farragut, always topped the list of men to lead it.

While the Union Navy of 1862 was winning the war on the Mississippi, Confederate armies in the east were routing Federal forces in the Shenandoah Valley and on the peninsula of Virginia. And as General Robert E. Lee took his Army of Northern Virginia across the Potomac and into Maryland, another drama unfolded on the high seas.

Left: Kearsarge's Acting Master Eben M. Stoddard displays a shell and a charge of grape beside an 11-inch Dahlgren. Chief Engineer William H. Cushman (right), having no duties below, came topside to join Stoddard for the photograph.

Below: The USS Kearsarge spent much of her career chasing Rebel cruisers, and in June 1864 she defeated the CSS Alabama in one of the most famous duels of the war.

In September, Captain Raphael Semmes struck west across the Atlantic in the British built CSS *Alabama* and captured ten prizes in fourteen days. In January, 1863, Lt. John Newland Maffitt escaped with the CSS *Florida*, and a second Confederate raider sprang loose. Over a span of eighteen months, *Alabama* and *Florida* captured 124 prizes, driving much of America's commerce from the seas. Through poor vigilance on the part of Charles Morris, *Florida*'s second commander, she was seized by the Union Navy in the neutral port of Bahia, Brazil, and on Porter's orders, "mysteriously sunk" in Hampton Roads. *Alabama* suffered a more glorious fate in a duel with the USS *Kearsarge*, under Captain John A. Winslow, off the port of Cherbourg, France.

THE FIRST SUBMARINES

While Farragut controlled the western Gulf waters and Porter the Mississippi, Rear-Admiral Samuel F. Du Pont, victor at Hatteras Inlet in November 1861, attempted to take Charleston in a bold frontal assault using nine ironclads, seven of them being turreted monitors. Among his squadron was the 4,120-ton *New Ironsides*, the first American armored steamer to be shaped like the warships of the future, though she still carried short masts and rigging. Like all the early ironclads, she was difficult to handle at sea. Armed with fourteen 11-inch Dahlgrens and two 150-pounders, she packed a punch, but not enough to help Du Pont breach Charleston harbor defenses. After two hours of battle, during which the Union squadron fired only 139 shots, Du Pont ordered a humiliating withdrawal. A fortress too strong for the Navy to penetrate, Charleston had also become a base for submarine experimentation.

At Charleston, two ironclads had been built – *Chicora* and *Palmetto State* – but like all

Confederate monoliths, they were unseaworthy and could barely stem the tide. Frustrated by the slothfulness of Mallory's ironclads, General Beauregard sought a weapon that could dismantle the Union blockade and re-open Charleston to foreign trade. After several failed attempts to design a submersible vessel armed with a torpedo, he sent for a submarine designed at Mobile by Horace L. Hunley. Hunley came with his creation and lost his life during a demonstration. So

Above: In one of the strangest clashes of the war, two of Ellet's unarmed rams, Monarch (M) and Queen of the West, attack and punish the Confederate River Defense Fleet off Memphis, after which four members of the Ram Fleet land on the levee and occupy the defenseless city.

▶ **OCTOBER 27:** Lt. William B. Cushing, using a spar torpedo fitted to a steam launch, sinks the CSS *Albemarle*.

DECEMBER 23-27: The first Fort Fisher expedition of fifty-five warships fails.

1865

Sixty warships under Admiral Porter and 8,500 infantry under Brig. Gen. Alfred H. Terry capture Fort Fisher.

FEBRUARY 17-18: Charleston, long under siege by the Union Navy, surrenders.

Above right: *Capt. Raphael Semmes (1809-1877) took the first Confederate raider, the CSS Sumter, to sea and commanded the greatest marauder of them all, the CSS Alabama. He left an indelible mark on the art of commerce raiding, and evaded his Union pursuers until June 19, 1864.*

Below: *No Confederate commerce raider gave the U.S. Navy more grief or the American carrying trade more hysteria than the CSS Alabama. She began her life in a British shipyard and ended it in a famous battle with the USS Kearsarge in the English Channel.*

SEMMES OF THE *ALABAMA*

No commander of a Confederate vessel was never more hunted than Raphael Semmes of the CSS *Alabama*. He took her on an eighteen-month cruise that began in the Atlantic, swept through the Far East, and ended in the English Channel. He left behind a torched trail of sixty-six prizes. He even found time to slip into the Gulf of Mexico and sink the USS *Hatteras*. Welles called him a pirate and dispatched more than a dozen warships to destroy him. Semmes out-witted them all until finally, after fatiguing *Alabama*'s bottom and boilers, he sought refuge in the French port of Cherbourg.

The Union hunter USS *Kearsarge*, commanded by Capt. John A. Winslow, lay in the Scheldt off Flushing in the Netherlands. *Kearsarge* had been searching for Confederate raiders for more than a year and had not caught one. Now with Winslow at her helm she had her chance, so he ordered her to Cherbourg and stood off the harbor.

Winslow knew as much about *Alabama* as Semmes knew about *Kearsarge*, and both believed their vessel outmatched the other. There were differences. *Alabama* carried a pair of heavy long-range guns; *Kearsarge* carried a pair of short-range 11-inch Dahlgrens; otherwise their batteries were equal. *Kearsarge*, however, had a decided advantage. Her gunners were better trained, her hull was chain-armored, and she was in fine sailing trim. *Alabama* needed repairs, had lost her speed, and her powder showed decay after months in the tropics. Nevertheless, Semmes wanted to fight his way out.

On June 19,1864, he took her into the English Channel and opened on *Kearsarge*, firing wildly. As the two vessels closed, they circled. Winslow's Dahlgrens began ripping the raider to pieces. Fifteen minutes into the action a lucky shell from *Alabama* lodged in *Kearsarge*'s sternpost. Had it exploded, *Kearsarge* would have gone to the bottom, but during the battle two-thirds of Semmes's shells failed to burst. Blood covered *Alabama*'s deck, and men began to fall, but Semmes remained hopeful. He watched a shell from the 110-pounder plunge through *Kearsarge*'s engine room skylight. He counted off seconds, waiting for a grand explosion that never came.

An hour into the fight, Semmes knew his ship was hopelessly crippled. In a final desperate effort he ordered sail set and tried to escape to the safety of the marine league, but Winslow laid *Kearsarge* in her way and continued firing. Semmes struck his colors, ordered his men off the sinking ship, and barely escaped with his life. But Winslow's victory would never be complete. Semmes and most of his officers were picked up by the English yacht *Deerhound* and carried off to England.

The fight with *Kearsarge* marked the end of Semmes's career as a commerce raider, but he returned to Virginia as an admiral and took command of the James River Squadron. Forced to scuttle his ironclads when Grant's army threatened Richmond, Semmes retreated overland. President Jefferson Davis made him a brigadier general, and Semmes became the only man in the Civil War to become both an admiral and a general.

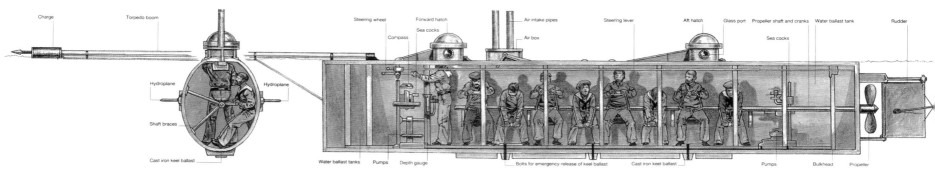

many crews had drowned in earlier experiments that the vessel became known as the "peripatetic coffin." Men raised her from the harbor, removed the bodies, cleaned out the vessel, and renamed her *H. L. Hunley*. Months later, a thoroughly trained crew took her outside the harbor and blew up the USS *Housatonic*, but disaster struck again as *Hunley* ran afoul of her victim and followed *Housatonic* to the bottom.

"DAMN THE TORPEDOES"

The torpedo menace continued to play a role in the Civil War, no more so than at the strategically important Mobile Bay, Alabama. In August, 1864, as Farragut planned his attack, he faced several obstacles. The guns of Forts Morgan and Gaines covered the channel, obstructions and mines stretched into the channel, and the most powerful ironclad built by the Confederacy, the CSS *Tennessee*, lay inside. Because of the presence of *Tennessee*, commanded by Admiral Franklin Buchanan, Farragut waited for four monitors to join his squadron before attempting the attack. Buchanan had commanded CSS *Virginia* at Hampton Roads, and Farragut correctly surmised that his old shipmate would put up a stiff fight.

On the morning of August 5, 1864, Farragut headed his squadron toward Mobile Bay with fourteen wooden warships, two single-turreted monitors, and two double-turreted river monitors. The minefield lay along the western side of the channel, which forced the Union vessels to enter the bay directly under the guns of Fort Morgan. Farragut had carefully explained to his commanders that the starboard division of monitors must lead the attack and engage the fort while the port division of wooden vessels skirted the edge of the minefield. When Commander Tunis A. M. Craven in the lead monitor *Tecumseh* decided to chase after *Tennessee*, he conned the vessel too far to port, crossed in front of the division of wooden vessels, struck a mine, and minutes later went to the bottom. The shock of seeing *Tecumseh* sink shattered the nerves of Capt.

James Allen, commanding the lead steam sloop *Brooklyn*, so he stopped, forcing Farragut to voice those famous words to his helmsman on the USS *Hartford*, "Damn the torpedoes, full speed ahead!" As *Hartford* led the column through the minefield, men on the vessels that followed could hear mines scraping against the hulls of their ships and fuses snapping, but the only mine still working seemed to have been the one that had sunk *Tecumseh*.

Once inside the bay the real battle began. If any old salt in the Navy believed that wooden warships still had a future, the fight that began at 9:00 a.m. would end the argument. The lone *Tennessee* fended off Farragut's entire squadron for ninety minutes. The big wooden sloops-of-war rammed *Tennessee* and hammered her with shot, doing more damage to themselves than to the ironclad. Not until the double-turreted USS *Chickasaw* began battering *Tennessee*'s casemate with 11-inch projectiles did her plates begin to crack. By 11:00 a.m. *Tennessee* could no longer make way. Buchanan's leg had been severely fractured, and Captain James D. Johnston surren-

Top: *Since the beginning of the Civil War, southern investors experimented with submarines. After a dozen failures, only the H. L. Hunley succeeded in sinking a Union warship, the USS* Housatonic.

Above: *James R. McClintock, one of Horace Hunley's partners, finally improved the submarine, renamed it* H. L. Hunley, *and trained the crew that sank the USS* Housatonic.

Left: *The Union used a variety of projectiles during the Civil War. Top left is the 7-inch Schenkl for a 7-inch rifled cnnon. Below left is a stand of 6.4-inch grape. In the background, top right, is a 5-inch Whitworth shell for an 80-pounder. Right center is a 5.1-inch Stafford shell for a 50-pounder Dahlgren, while below right is a 5.8-inch shell grooved to fit the gun's barrel.*

"INFERNAL MACHINES"

With the Civil War came the torpedo menace, popularly known among sailors as "infernal machines." Most of the explosives were various types of underwater or floating mines. Cables running to galvanic batteries manned along shore activated some mines; others were anchored in waterways and exploded upon impact. A third type, such as the device used by experimental submarines, were either fixed to the end of a spar and driven into the enemy vessel, or towed by a cable and floated, exploding against the hull after the submarine dove under the ship.

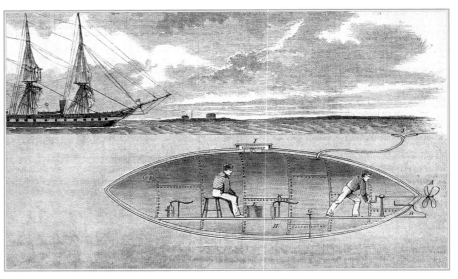

Above: *Experimenters soon abandoned the idea of towing the charge when on one occasion a combination of wind and tide pushed the torpedo directly toward the submarine towing it.*

dered the crippled ironclad. As a testament to the durability of *Tennessee*, the victorious Farragut fitted her with a new smokestack, made a few repairs, and used her a few days later to force the surrender of Fort Morgan.

CUTTING OFF WILMINGTON

In the aftermath of Mobile Bay, Welles attempted to give command of the North Atlantic Blockading Squadron to Farragut, but the gouty old admiral had fallen ill, so Welles gave the task to Porter. The mission — to force the surrender of Fort Fisher at the mouth of the Cape Fear River,

Below: *After Farragut's squadron captured the CSS* Tennessee, *the admiral had her repaired and manned, and few a days later she was back in action, firing shot and shell at Fort Morgan.*

thereby eliminating Wilmington, North Carolina, as one of the two remaining ports of supply for the Confederacy. During the latter months of 1864, blockade-runners into Wilmington had delivered 750 tons of lead, 100 tons of powder, 69,000 muskets, 43 cannon, and thousands of tons of food and clothing. Without supplies flowing through Wilmington, the Confederacy could not survive.

Using the huge North Atlantic Blockading Squadron, Porter took two cracks at Fort Fisher. The first assault failed because Major General Benjamin F. Butler refused to disembark his entire force and abandoned those he had landed. The second attempt, under a different Army commander, included a landing party of marines, sailors, and infantry. Without monitors, Fort Fisher may have never been taken, but the ironclad ships could get inshore and pulverize the palisades of the giant earthwork with 11- and 15-inch shells. The attack on Fort Fisher was the last great amphibious operation of the war. It was not as well coordinated as Farragut's amphibious operations in Mobile Bay, but it did the job and led to the capture of Wilmington.

At war's end, the United States had the most powerful and technologically advanced navy in the world. When Great Britain stonewalled demands by Americans for reparations caused by Confederate commerce raiders built in Britain, Welles sent the twin-screw, double-turreted *Miantonomoh* abroad as a gentle show of force. A correspondent for the London *Times* observed that, "There was not one [British warship] that the foreigner could not have sent to the bottom in

five minutes, had his errand not been peaceful...not one of these big ships...could have avenged the loss of its companion, or saved itself from sharing its fate. In fact, the wolf was in fold, and the whole flock was at its mercy."

Great Britain eventually paid the United States $15.5 million in gold because of her complicity in damaging the American carrying trade. But the cost was small compared with the capital Queen Victoria had to raise to replace her Royal Navy – which had been made obsolete by rambunctious Yankees who had once been colonists of the English crown.

Above: Farragut's squadron pushes its way into Mobile Bay, passing Fort Morgan as Rebel ships wait to attack.

Above left: From Farragut's perch in Hartford's tops, he shouted down to the officers on the deck, "Damn the torpedoes, full speed ahead!"

LT. WILLIAM B. CUSHING

The CSS *Albemarle*, known as the ironclad built in a cornfield, had supported the Confederate recapture of Plymouth, Virginia. She severely damaged the Union squadron in Albemarle Sound, and as long as she remained near the mouth of the muddy Roanoke River, Federal forces could not regain lost ground. The Navy Department wanted her removed, but wooden gunboats could not damage her, and the water was too shallow for monitors.

When Lt. William B. Cushing learned of *Albemarle* he proposed a plan so audacious that it just might work. Cushing had already established a reputation for executing daredevil missions, so people listened. He suggested using a spar torpedo – a tactical weapon originated by the Confederacy – connected to the bow of a steam launch. He made such a strong case for leading the mission that the Navy approved it.

Cushing got his steam launch and spar. By using an intricate arrangement of small ropes attached to the assembly, he could lower the spar below the waterline and arm the torpedo. At the time, he did not know that *Albemarle* had been surrounded by a log-boom to ward off night attacks. In the dark, Cushing did not see the boom until reaching it, forcing him to sheer off and circle to the opposite shore. By then,

sentinels discovered the attack and opened fire. To get at *Albemarle*, Cushing realized he must hurdle the boom. Steaming at full speed, the bow of the launch mounted the logs, enabling Cushing to lower the spar under the ironclad and trigger the torpedo. A sharp explosion lifted *Albemarle* far enough out of the water for the first fire from her guns to whiz over Cushing's head. Then she settled, and in the morning only part of her casemate showed above the river.

Cushing dove into the river, swam to shore, and three days later made it back to the squadron. Elevated to lieutenant commander, he also received the thanks of Congress. Ten years later, while commanding *Monticello*, he became insane and died.

Left: Comdr. William B. Cushing (1842-1874) distinguished himself as one of the Civil War's heroic daredevils. He attacked and sank the CSS Albemarle by using a small steam launch rigged to carry a spar torpedo.

Below: Of the Confederate ironclads, the 2-gun Albemarle, at 150-feet in length, was among the smallest put to sea by the Confederacy.

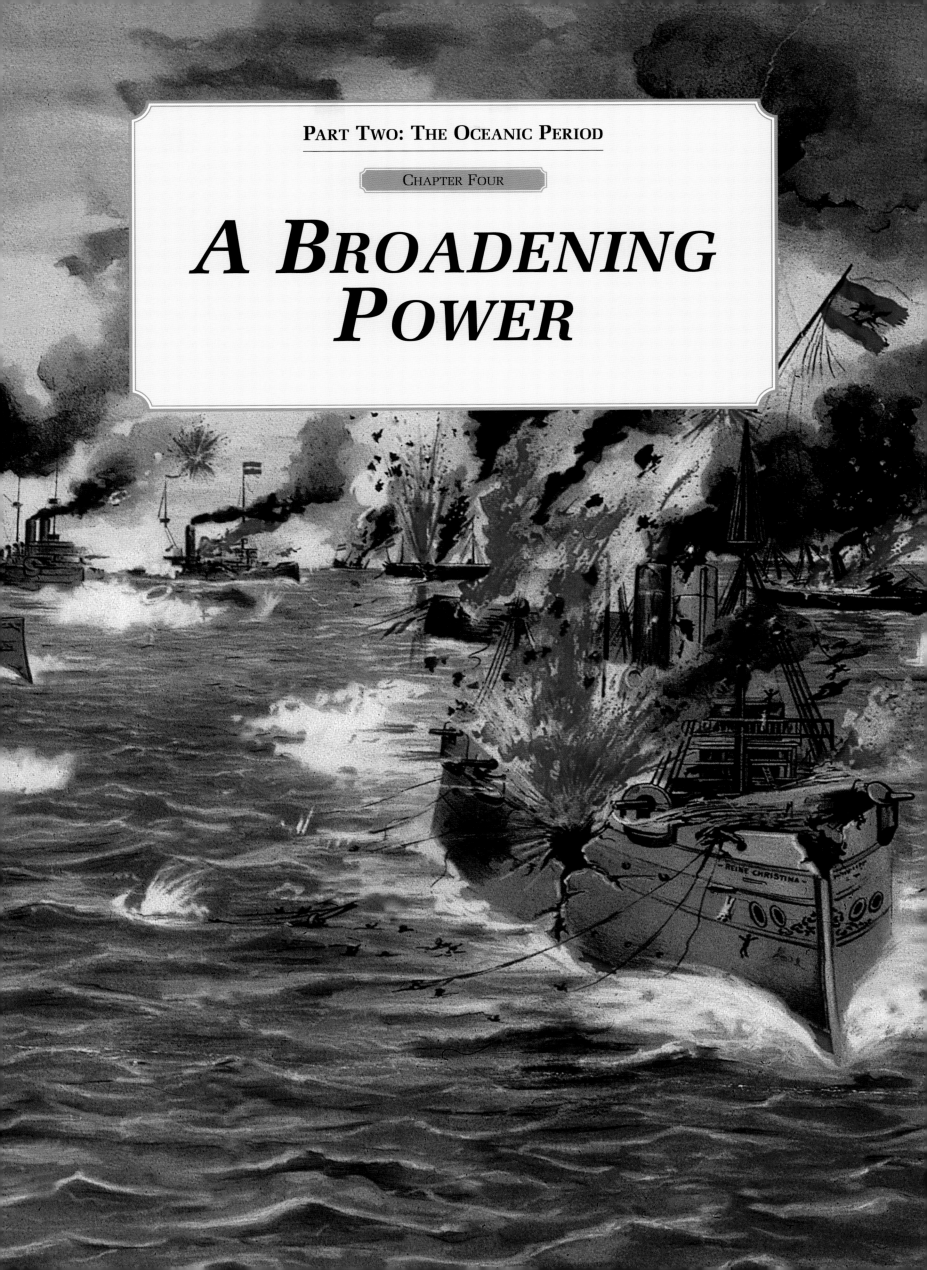

PART TWO: THE OCEANIC PERIOD

CHAPTER FOUR

A BROADENING POWER

In the aftermath of the Civil War, Gideon Welles gazed upon one of the most rapid buildups of naval strength ever accomplished in so short time by any nation of the world, and he wondered what to do with it. During the war he had contemplated a powerful peacetime navy that could defend the nation's coasts, its shipping and foreign interests, and its expansion of overseas trade. But the public's mood pressed him in opposite directions. By the end of 1865 he reported to President Andrew Johnson that the Navy had been reduced from 700 to 120 vessels of all types. When he departed from office in 1868, he had trimmed to eighty-one the number of commissioned vessels, but his Navy had led the world in the development of armored steam warships carrying turreted guns. Mine warfare took on new meaning among quarreling nations, as did the torpedo-launch William Cushing employed to sink the CSS *Albemarle*.

There were other lessons to be learned beyond the rivers and coastal waters where America fought her Civil War. Confederate commerce raiders served as a reminder that the Navy must maintain an oceanic cruiser force to keep her sea-lanes open, and that those protecting ships must be among the most modern and best-armed vessels afloat. When in 1864 Welles issued a contract for the USS *Dunderberg*, he had naval superiority in mind. She was a 5,090-ton ironclad goliath 376 feet long with 15-inch Dahlgrens in two revolving gun casemates and eight 11-inch Dahlgrens in broadside. The heaviest battleship in the world could not match her in strength. The cost-conscious administration, struggling with internal problems, sold her to the French. Thirty years later French warship design still bore the unmistakable stamp of the old *Dunderberg*.

Though an economic conservative himself, Welles recognized the need for coaling stations abroad. In 1867 the Navy occupied Midway, established a coaling base there, and the Pacific Mail Steamship Company began monthly service between San Francisco and Hong Kong. Also in 1867 Secretary of State William H. Seward bought Alaska from Russia and secured the Aleutians, raising America's stake in the North Pacific.

INCURSION INTO KOREA

Like Japan in the 1850s, Korea, the "Hermit Kingdom," cherished its isolation. Rear Adm. John Rodgers did not have the finesse Matthew Perry had demonstrated when entering Japan. In May, 1871, he arrived at the mouth of the Salee River and sent a mission ashore to craft a treaty with Korea. Several American vessels had been wrecked off the coast and their crews murdered, so Rodgers demanded reparations. While waiting for an answer, he sent details ahead to sound the channel. When shore batteries fired upon the intruders, Rodgers demanded an apology. When none came, he put 650 sailors and marines ashore to square accounts. Leaving several hundred dead Koreans behind, Rodgers hastily departed to avoid a typhoon. Having not accomplished his mission, he returned to Washington and suggested that the Army send a force of 5,000 men to

Right: *On May 30, 1871, an American squadron under Rear Adm. John Rodgers entered Korea's Salee River. After being fired upon, Rodgers sent a force ashore to assault Fort Duconde. On June 10 the defenders fled, leaving behind 481 cannon of various calibers, one of which is pictured with some of the men who captured the fort.*

occupy Seoul. The Navy accepted Rodgers's account and awarded the Medal of Honor to two marines for capturing a Korean flag. Ten years later Commodore Robert W. Shufeldt returned to Seoul and quietly negotiated a treaty – the first signed by Korea with a Western nation. In 1876, during the years between Rodgers's failure and Shufeldt's success, the Navy negotiated a treaty with Samoa for an American naval base at Pago Pago without spilling a drop of native blood.

When the nations of Europe began competing for naval bases in the Pacific and Indian Oceans, Congress feared that the United States would become embroiled in another conflict. Instead of authorizing funds for building better warships, Congress cut expenditures, suggesting that the United States should maintain its sailing navy because it was cheaper to operate than steamers. In 1869 Admiral Porter issued a general order under the auspices of the Navy Department stipulating that all new naval vessels have "full sail power." So frugal had Congress become that the department warned commanders of steamers that if they used excessive coal they might be charged personally for it.

First Conflict With Spain

Even the USS *Wampanoag*, a fast cruiser designed by Benjamin F. Isherwood and built during Welles's administration, was mothballed because old line officers under Porter did not like Isherwood and feared that steam engineers rather than sailors would begin to control the Navy. *Wampanoag* made 17.7 knots during her trials, but to improve her sailing qualities under canvas the Navy removed a number of her boilers. She never went to sea again and slowly rotted. Twenty years elapsed before another American warship could match her speed.

In 1873 the Navy barely averted its first crisis close to home when a Spanish warship captured the Cuban-owned steamer *Virginius*. The Spaniards caught her under American colors while carrying arms to Cuban insurgents fighting for independence. Taken into Santiago, *Virginius* was impounded and fifty-three passengers and crew, including Americans and Britons, were executed after a summary trial. The press clamored for war, and Secretary of the Navy George Robeson recalled the European Squadron. While five frigates, six monitors, and fourteen small wooden gunboats demonstrated off Key West, Spain paid indemnities to the families of those shot, released 102 prisoners, and postponed war for another twenty-five years.

The delay worked to the advantage of the United States. One newspaper correspondent witnessing the combined squadrons exercising off the Keys found them "almost useless for military purposes. They belong to a class of ships which

other governments have sold or are selling for firewood." A future admiral, Robeley D. Evans agreed, writing, "two modern vessels of war would have done us up in thirty minutes." The Navy was not to blame because, he said. "We did the best we could with what Congress gave us."

In 1879, when Chile went to war against Peru and Bolivia, Secretary of the Navy Richard W. Thompson sent a naval mission to Valparaiso to protect American interests and induce Chile to stop fighting. When the old wooden vessels of the Pacific Squadron arrived off the coast, it became apparent to every member of the mission that the navy of either warring side could have blown the Americans out of the water. Chile had two new British-built battleships with 12-inch armor, breech-loading guns, speeds of 18 knots, and no sails. *Esmeralda*, the first of the protected cruisers built for Chile, became the modern cruiser's prototype and completely outclassed any ship in

Above: *On the USS Colorado, Cpl. Charles Brown and Pvt. Hugh Purvis stand with (left) Capt. McLane Tilton, USMC, before the Korean military flag captured in the June 1, 1871, attack on Fort McKee. For capturing the flag, Brown and Purvis won the Medal of Honor.*

'*The American Republic has no more need for its burlesque of a Navy than a peaceful giant would have for a stuffed club or a tin sword.*'

Henry George,
social commentator,
1882.

▶ **1882**

MARCH 23: The Office of Naval Intelligence is established.

1883

MARCH 3: Congress authorizes the construction of the first four steel warships.

1884

OCTOBER 6: Secretary of the Navy William E. Chandler establishes the Naval War College.

1886

AUGUST 6: Congress authorizes the construction of the first American battleships, *Maine* and *Texas*.

1888

MAY 17: The naval reserve originates in Massachusetts.

Above right: Chicago, *flagship of the Squadron of Evolution, leads the flotilla to sea, followed by (right to left)* Atlanta, Boston, *and* Yorktown.

Right: *One of the first protected cruisers, the USS* Chicago *lays in drydock at the Brooklyn Navy Yard.*

Far right: *The USS* Boston, *one of the ABCD cruisers, carried a full set of square sails but, unlike* Chicago, *no bowsprit.*

the U.S. Navy. The Chileans dispensed with the American admiral by telling him to "mind his own business [or] they would send him and his fleet to the bottom of the ocean."

The Chilean incident had its impact at home. In 1881, after Chester A. Arthur became president, the future of the Navy began to look brighter. William E. Chandler, who had a son in the Navy, became the new secretary and created a board of naval officers to study and make recommendations for modernizing the service. Meanwhile,

Congress made an important but unintended step to revitalize the Navy when it refused to repair a ship if the cost exceeded 30 percent (later 20 percent) of its replacement cost, thereby hastening the retirement of all the relics from the Civil War.

The new fifteen-man Navy Board barely knew where to start. European navies operated cruisers and battleships ranging from 6,000 to 9,000 tons. They were armed with 8- to 16-inch breech-loading guns and protected by thick belts of armor. Some members of the board, prompted by a parsimonious Congress, agreed with the argument that the United States did not need a blue-water navy for offensive operations, and that the nation's needs could met by building fast, protected cruisers best suited for commerce raiding.

On March 3, 1883, Congress approved the board's request, appropriated $1.3 million, and authorized construction of four new ships to be built of steel (not iron) to the most modern design. The protected cruisers *Atlanta* and

Left: *On August 15, 1895, the United States launched its first battleship, the USS* Texas. *By then, sails were falling out of favor, and* Texas *went to sea with only two stubby masts.*

Below: *The cruiser USS* Charleston, *tied to the dock at San Francisco, prepares to cross the Pacific. On June 21, 1898, under the command of Capt. Henry Glass, she captures Guam.*

Boston of 3,000 tons, *Chicago* of 4,500 tons, and the gunboat *Dolphin* of 1,500 tons marked the beginning of what became known as the New Navy, but the steamers, popularly known as the "ABCDs," still carried a pair of masts, three tiers of brig-rigged sails, and a jib.

THE NAVY GAINS PEARL HARBOR

What the Navy needed was a man like John Ericsson to design its cruisers, but by then the Swede was in his mid-eighties. What the Navy settled for was an odd mixture of the old and the new. Part of the problem can be traced to Chandler, who was so anxious to start construction that he issued contracts before specifications had been finalized. The new cruisers were completely electrified with double bottoms and watertight compartments, but they still carried sails. *Chicago*, with twin screws, was still powered by Civil War engine technology. She did carry four 8-inch, eight 6-inch, and two 5-inch breach-loading rifles – heavy arms for a ship her size. The guns had great range, but aiming them still required that a man look down the barrel through an open sight.

The four vessels, despite their experimental nature and their jumbled design, provided good service. Having an improved Navy made it easier to negotiate a trade reciprocity treaty with Hawaii, which rapidly reduced the islands to economic dependence upon the United States. The treaty, extended in 1887, gave the United States the use of Pearl Harbor. Building a naval station with coaling facilities quickly followed. When

► **1890**

APRIL 23: *Cushing*, the first torpedo boat, is commissioned.

MAY: Alfred Thayer Mahan becomes America's first naval strategist.

JUNE 30: Congress authorizes three Indiana-class battleships of 10,000 tons displacement.

1893

JANUARY 16 : The U.S. Navy intervenes during a revolt in Hawaii.

Right: *In 1899 a group of sailors practice sewing skills whilerepairing uniforms on board the protected cruiser USS* Olympia.

Below: *Two 18-inch diameter Whitehead torpedoes undergo maintenance on the cruiser* Olympia. *The 836-pound missiles were 11 feet long, had a range of 1,000 yards, carried a 110-pound warhead, traveled at 26 knots, and could disable a battleship.*

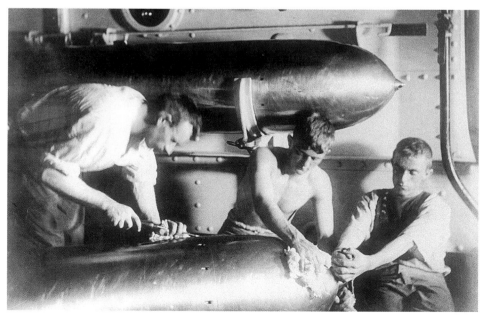

constitutional unrest erupted on the islands, U.S. Marines landed in January, 1893, to protect American residents. Four years later Hawaii signed a treaty of annexation with the United States.

In 1885 the Navy began work on two more cruisers. This time they used British plans and built *Charleston*, the first American warship to exceed the speed of 17.7 knots established by the discarded *Wampanoag*. Another yard built *Newark*, which steamed into history as the last American cruiser rigged with sails.

By 1886 a retooled steel industry began producing armor thick enough to build larger ships. William C. Whitney took over the reigns of the Navy Department and added thirty more vessels to the fleet. All were products of contradictory planning by naval officers who understood the tactical significance of firepower and mobility but failed to understand the strategic advantage of having a unified battle fleet with offensive capability. When Whitney ordered *Maine* and *Texas* – two 6,500-ton cruisers later reclassified as America's first second-class battleships – they were intended to be the strongest warships ever built by the Navy. They could cruise at 17 knots and carried the heaviest weapons yet mounted on American men-of-war, 12-inch guns on *Texas* and 10-inchers for *Maine*. As work progressed, Whitney purchased another set of plans from the British and began building the protected cruiser *Baltimore*, with a top speed of 20 knots.

NAVAL WAR COLLEGE

In 1887-1888, Congress provided funds for seven more men-of-war, among them the 8,150-ton armored cruiser *New York* and the 5,865-ton protected cruiser *Olympia*. A long-awaited change occurred during Whitney's administration. *Charleston* shed her canvas, setting a precedent her sisters soon followed.

Almost thirty years earlier, English inventor Robert Whitehead had designed for the Austrian government the "automobile torpedo," which Europe soon improved to operating status and created a new tactical weapon. With technology advancing so rapidly, Commodore Stephen B. Luce, who twenty years earlier had commanded a monitor off Charleston, lobbied for a Naval War College. In 1884 Secretary Chandler signed the order and established the school. Luce took charge of the college and brought Comdr. Alfred Thayer Mahan home from the Pacific Station to instruct it. Whitney did not like Mahan, but Mahan persevered, became president of the school, and eventually demonstrated his value to even those in the Navy who opposed his academic approach to warfare.

On March 6, 1889, Benjamin F. Tracy became Benjamin Harrison's Secretary of the Navy. Both had fought in the Civil War, both became generals, and Tracy had won the Medal of Honor for heroism during the Wilderness campaign. To define the requirements of the Navy, Tracy turned to Mahan, and in the secretary's first annual report to Congress in 1889 he gave all the reasons why "The country needs a navy that will exempt it from war but the only navy that will accomplish this is a navy that can wage war." He presented a revolutionary plan for the construction of twenty armored battleships, twelve for the Atlantic and eight for the Pacific. He urged Congress to regard the expenditure as a "practical business question of insuring our property and our trade." Harrison supported the request, asking Congress to authorize eight battleships immediately. Political bickering ensued, and the hotly debated topic resulted in the Navy Act of 1890, providing for only three battleships — *Indiana*, *Massachusetts*, and *Oregon* – each of 10,288 tons. Though somewhat smaller than European battleships, these superbly designed

AFRED THAYER MAHAN

By all rights, Alfred Thayer Mahan should have been a West Point man. His father taught strategy at the Military Academy and imbued his son with the science of warfare. Instead, Mahan went to Columbia College and two years later obtained an appointment to the Naval Academy, entering as a third-year man. Graduating in 1859, he drifted with the naval tide, writing a small book on naval operations during the Civil War titled *The Gulf and Inland Waters*. Commodore Luce read the book, found it fascinating, and offered Mahan a post as lecturer at the Naval Academy.

Before Mahan could report to the school, the Navy forced him to complete his tour in the Pacific. Marking time on the old *Wachusetts*, Mahan immersed himself in a study of warfare and concluded that command of the sea was the decisive factor in the rise and fall of empires.

When in 1886 Mahan became president of the Navy War College, he struggled to keep it open. Old salts scoffed at the institution, one feisty admiral grumbling, "Teach the art of war? Well, I'll be damned! You have Cooper's *Naval History* and Parker's *Fleet Tactics*; what more do you want?" But for Mahan those works applied to old thinking. In 1890 he published *The Influence of Sea Power Upon History, 1660-1783*, and three years later, *The Influence of Sea Power Upon the French Revolution and Empire, 1793-1812*. While writing, Mahan suddenly became what he had never been before, an imperialist. He argued that foreign trade was essential to national prosperity. He believed in a powerful fleet, arguing that small coast-defense vessels and commerce-raiders, America's traditional weapons, were useless. Ninety years had passed since Benjamin Stoddert, America's first Secretary of the Navy, advocated a strong battle fleet to protect the nation's ports. Now, after nine decades of technological advancements, Mahan proposed a fleet of armored battleships and cruisers.

Naval Secretary Whitney attempted to close the college, but his predecessor, Benjamin F. Tracy, fully endorsed Mahan's doctrine and sought his advice on building capital ships. The next secretary, Hilary A. Herbert, tried to abolish the school by sending Mahan to sea as captain of the USS *Chicago*. Mahan fought to avoid a seagoing billet, but the cruise proved beneficial for the embattled strategist. The British extolled his books as the greatest contribution to naval tactics ever written. Queen Victoria entertained him, and the universities of Cambridge and Oxford honored him with degrees. Kaiser Wilhelm II began building battleships and placed copies of Mahan's books on every vessel in the German Navy.

When Mahan returned home, he had become "the high priest of a rising imperialism." Latent vestiges of manifest destiny again swept the country. But as Mahan's doctrine so aptly articulated, expansion meant more than exploiting the commerce of the world. It meant building capital ships and bases to protect trade and then settle any conflicts growing from American expansion with power.

In six years Mahan went from a struggling instructor at a Naval War College having few admirers to an international strategist driving the United States and its Navy toward acts of imperialism.

Above: *On October 6, 1884, Rear Adm. Stephen B. Luce (1827-1917) became the first president of the Naval War College at Newport, Rhode Island, and had the foresight to invite Mahan as a professor.*

Left: *Alfred Thayer Mahan (1840-1914), though he yearned for the vanquished days of sail, probably did more to eliminate them on fighting vessels than any other member of the Navy.*

▶ **1898**

FEBRUARY 15: An unexplained detonation sinks the USS *Maine* at Havana.

APRIL 11, 19: President McKinley asks and receives approval from Congress to intervene in Cuba.

APRIL 22: The U.S. Navy blockades Cuba.

APRIL 27: Commodore George Dewey sails for the Philippines.

MAY 1: Dewey captures Manila Bay.

MAY 26: Commodore Winfield Scott Schley's squadron arrives off Santiago, Cuba.

Above right: *Built in 1898, the fifth American battleship, the USS* Kearsarge, *is launched at Newport News.*

Below: *On June 16, 1897, the Navy commissioned the USS* Iowa, *the nation's fourth battleship. After action at Santiago in July 1898, she is photographed going into drydock.*

nickel-steel armored vessels packed a punch, mounting four 13-inch, eight 8-inch, and four 6-inch breech-loading guns.

In 1892 Congress began grudgingly to yield to Mahan's philosophy and Tracy's urging, providing funds for the larger *Iowa*. A financial panic in the early 1890s slowed progress, but in 1895 the building program resumed with the battleships *Kearsarge* and *Kentucky*, followed in 1896 by *Alabama*, *Illinois*, and *Wisconsin*. The capital ships all carried four 13-inch guns with slightly different secondary batteries.

> '...ultimately those who wish to see this country at peace with foreign nations will be wise if they place reliance upon a first-class fleet of first-class battleships...'
>
> THEODORE ROOSEVELT,
> 1897.

British imperialism, which earlier American administrations had condemned, now infected the United States. The government looked to the North Pacific as the place to expand and to San Francisco as a permanent base for the Pacific Squadron. By the mid-1890s the Navy had established bases from Puget Sound in the north to San Diego in the south, creating for the first time a "two-ocean" navy. America now had coaling stations, and she could stop building brig-rigged warships and furl those sails forever.

On three prior occasions the United States had attempted to buy Cuba from Spain. With discussions brewing about building a canal through Central America, the island became even more important. When in 1880 Cubans revolted against the mother country, Americans had already invested $50 million in island property. Spain met the insurrection with swift, brutal repression, and over a span of eighteen years thousands of Cubans died of starvation or execution.

In January, 1898, while Congress ruminated over the trouble in Cuba, Capt. Charles D. Sigsbee, commanding *Maine*, steamed into Havana to protect the lives and property of Americans during another uprising. On the evening of February 15, as he closed a letter to his wife and listened to the bugler sound taps, an explosion rocked the vessel, pitching the ship partly out of the water, listing her to port, knocking out the lights, and blanketing her in smoke. Sigsbee bolted from his cabin and felt his way along the deck. Finding the forward section shattered, he ordered the survivors – 88 of 354 officers and men – off the sinking ship. She settled in the mud, leaving little more than her upper works exposed to mark her grave.

WAR WITH SPAIN

National press "jingoists" such as powerful William Randolph Hearst, whose main interest was improving his paper's circulation, accused Spain of sabotage and whipped up the public, using the disaster as good reason to declare war. That Spain apologized and offered numerous remedies for resolving the crisis only made her look more culpable. What caused the explosion had not been determined, but with "Remember the *Maine*! To hell with Spain!" resonating in the halls of the Capitol, Congress passed a joint resolution on April 19, 1898, promoting war with Spain and formally declared it six days later. The American goal was not Cuba but securing the Spanish Philippines, which lay on China's doorstep.

During weeks of congressional debate over the

issue of war, Secretary of the Navy John D. Long took a day off on February 25, 1898, and left the department in the hands of his assistant secretary, Theodore Roosevelt. Without authorization, Roosevelt arranged for Commodore George Dewey to become commander of the Asiatic Squadron. He intended to make the Spanish empire vulnerable in more places than Cuba. He transferred the Pacific Squadron from Hawaii to Hong Kong and told Dewey to move upon the

Above: *The USS* Maine *enters the port of Havana on January 25, 1898, for her appointment with destiny which could not have been foreseen by her captain.*

Left: *On February 15, 1898, an explosion on the USS* Maine *(probably caused by a fire in the coal bunker that set off an adjacent magazine) sent the vessel to the bottom and the United States to a war with Spain.*

JUNE 1: Rear Admiral William T. Sampson takes command of Santiago.

JUNE 10: Marines, the first Americans on Cuban soil, land at Guantánamo.

JUNE 21: Captain Henry Glass captures Guam.

JULY 3: The Navy destroys the Spanish fleet at Santiago.

JULY 7: The United States annexes Hawaii.

AUGUST 12: The United States and Spain sign an armistice.

AUGUST 13: Manila surrenders to Commodore Dewey.

Above right: *Among the artifacts rescued from* Maine *were items such as binoculars, a light fixture, a barnacle-encrusted light bulb, inkwell, sailor's hatband, keys to the powder room, a bugle, and the ship's pennant.*

Right: *After the explosion,* Maine *sank rapidly, leaving only her mast and top hamper above the waters of Havana's harbor.*

Philippines the moment war was declared. While Americans focused on a limited war in the Caribbean, Roosevelt formulated plans to intervene not only in Cuba but also in the Philippines.

Roosevelt knew Dewey as a man whose temperament and imperialistic proclivities were much like his own. Neither man feared responsibility. Roosevelt called Dewey a man "who meets the needs of the situation in whatever way is necessary." During the Civil War, Dewey served under Farragut in the Mississippi River. In 1862, he ran batteries at Forts Jackson and St. Philip and aided in the capture of New Orleans. He had few reservations about running Spanish batteries in Manila Bay.

Closer to home, the Navy mustered four first-class battleships – *Indiana*, *Iowa*, *Massachusetts*, and *Oregon* – the armored cruisers *Brooklyn* and *New York*, and, with several lighter vessels, sta-

tioned them in the western Atlantic and the Caribbean. To protect Cuba and Puerto Rico, Spain responded and sent four armored cruisers and several smaller ships under the command of Admiral Pascual Cervera y Topete. Though on paper the Spanish warships were equal to their American counterparts, the vessels were in poor condition and manned by disgruntled crews. After inspecting his squadron, Admiral Cervera predicted the "total destruction of the fleet or its hasty and demoralized return."

A SHORT, SHARP CONFLICT

European authorities, unaware of either America's new naval strength or Spain's deteriorating assets, predicted a long war. Though having retired from active service, Mahan declared that the Navy would dispose of the Spaniards in three months. Roosevelt, who began preparing for the conflict months in advance, had become the embodiment of Mahan's doctrine of sea power. There was no better way for Roosevelt to demonstrate the value of a navy and justify the addition of more warships than by employing the squadrons supervised by his boss to annihilate an enemy reputed to have an equal or superior force.

On April 27, when Dewey received word that war had been declared, he stood out for the South China Sea in his flagship, the cruiser *Olympia*, and set a 600-mile course for Manila Bay. With him went three cruisers, *Baltimore*, *Boston*, and *Raleigh*; two gunboats, *Concord* and *Petrel*; and the revenue cutter *McCulloch*, together mounting thirty-three guns of six inches or more. Dewey

Left: *Two armored cruisers, the USS* New York, *the second of its type to go into service, and* Brooklyn, *the third, both played a role in the attack on Santiago, Cuba.*

knew he would be up against seven cruisers (one of them wooden) and three gunboats, but informants had told him that some of the Spanish ships were unfit to fight a Chinese junk. Even the hull of Admiral Patricio Montojo y Pasarón's flagship, the cruiser *Reina Cristina*, leaked and could not be taken to sea.

A DAWN RAID

In the early morning hours of May 1, 1898, *Olympia* crept through the passage between the fortified islands of Corregidor and El Fraile and entered Manila Bay. The squadron followed, every light extinguished except for carefully hooded stern lanterns. Half the vessels were in the bay before sentinels at the forts spotted sparks flowing from *McCulloch*'s smokestack. Flares soared over the misty, dead-calm bay, illuminating the dull gray shapes of warships crawling at four knots. Guns boomed and projectiles splashed into the water, but the column slithered by undamaged and steamed for Manila, twenty-two miles away.

As dawn streaked the sky, Dewey rounded off Manila and came in sight of the Spanish squadron lying off the naval station at Cavite, five miles south of Manila. At long range the Spaniards opened from ship and shore batteries, but Dewey's force plunged ahead in perfect formation. The Spanish vessels lay in line, anchored haphazardly east to west. As *Olympia* came in range, Dewey signaled the column to starboard, putting it on a course parallel to the enemy's largest cruisers, *Reina Cristina* and *Castilla*. From

the bridge he called into the conning tower below him and said, "You may fire when you are ready, Gridley." Charles V. Gridley, the flagship's captain, passed the word down the line, and the forward 8-inch guns opened, punctuating a new era of American sea power.

Barely a mile separated the two columns, and after the battle opened a thick cloud of smoke engulfed both squadrons. For Dewey, the scene

Below: *Adm. George Dewey (1837-1917) is on board the USS* Olympia *in Manila Bay. Behind him are the turrets for 8-inch and 5-inch guns.*

► **1889**

JANUARY 17: The Navy seizes Wake Island.

1899

FEBRUARY 4: The two-year Philippine insurrection begins.

MARCH 2: George Dewey is elevated to Admiral of the Navy.

MAY 23: Marines are sent to the Philippines.

1900

MAY 13: The General Board of the Navy is formed to provide professional advice on Navy matters.

MAY 18: The Boxer Rebellion begins.

Right: *Medals awarded Adm. George Dewey, including those for the Civil War, Manila Bay, Spanish Campaign, and the Philippine Campaign.*

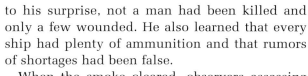
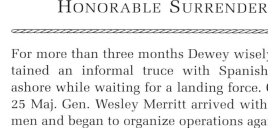

Below: *On June 10, 1898, Marines commanded by Lt. Col. R. W. Huntington become the first American soldiers to land on Cuban soil and the first to hoist the American flag over Camp McCalla, Guantánamo, Cuba.*

was reminiscent of the Civil War, where the only targets that could be seen were muzzle flashes from enemy guns. Off Cavite, the peninsula at Sangley Point jutted into the bay, forcing Dewey's column to come hard to starboard and inscribe an oval that put the squadron back in range of the Spaniards. After making three loops, Dewey still could not see whether any of the Spanish ships had been disabled. At 7:30 a.m. he decided to pause for breakfast, let the smoke clear, and hold a short conference with his commanders. Much

to his surprise, not a man had been killed and only a few wounded. He also learned that every ship had plenty of ammunition and that rumors of shortages had been false.

When the smoke cleared, observers assessing the damage through telescopes reported the Spanish fleet in ruins. Ships were on fire, *Reina Cristina* and *Castilla* had sunk, and others listed badly as they limped toward the shallows. Spanish crews could be seen abandoning ship, but Admiral Montojo had not lowered his flag. Shortly after 11:00 a.m. Dewey put the squadron underway to finish the job. A half-hour later Montojo surrendered all his vessels, and Dewey moved his squadron up to Manila.

HONORABLE SURRENDER

For more than three months Dewey wisely maintained an informal truce with Spanish forces ashore while waiting for a landing force. On July 25 Maj. Gen. Wesley Merritt arrived with 10,000 men and began to organize operations against the Philippine capital. Then, on August 13, with the mutual consent of the enemy, Merritt put a small force ashore and Dewey bombarded an abandoned fort, promoting a ruse that enabled the Spaniards to claim an honorable surrender. By prearrangement the Spanish struck their colors, and Dewey sent Lt. Thomas N. Brumby ashore to raise the American flag. When word reached President William McKinley of the surrender, he

Left: *After sailing from San Francisco to join the fight, the battleship USS* Oregon, *commanded by Capt. Robeley D. Evans, opens on the batteries at Santiago, Cuba.*

Above: *Rear Adm. William T. Sampson (1840-1902) served as an officer on Patapsco during the Civil War and became commander of the North Atlantic Squadron during the Spanish-American War. Though he was not present for most of the Cuban battles, his plans were responsible for the destruction of the Spanish fleet at Santiago.*

declared laconically that he "could not have told where those darned islands were within two thousand miles." Dewey became a hero and the first full admiral since Porter. Whether McKinley ever learned of the location of the Philippines is not recorded.

During the time that Dewey was sweltering in Manila Bay and waiting for forces under General Merritt, Long and Roosevelt initiated operations against Cuba. Admiral Cervera's squadron had crossed the Atlantic but not been sighted. Newspapers spread rumors implying that Cervera intended to bombard America's eastern ports, and demands cascaded upon the government for protection. To placate the public, the Navy Department divided the fleet being marshaled for operations against Cuba and Puerto Rico into three squadrons. To Commodore Winfield Scott Schley at Hampton Roads the Navy assigned a "Flying Squadron" of fast ships to go wherever they were needed. A smaller squadron operated north of the Delaware Capes to calm the nerves of jittery New Yorkers. The third squadron, under Acting Rear Admiral William T. Sampson, moved south and blockaded Havana. Sampson wanted to bombard the Cuban port, but the War Board conferred with Mahan, who had been recalled to active duty, and he advised against it.

Sampson believed that Cervera would head for Puerto Rico and, having nothing better to do, sent three cruisers to the Windward Islands to watch for him. He deposited a few vessels off Havana and sailed with the rest of his squadron for San Juan. Cervera expected to find Sampson at San Juan and took elusive measures. After stopping first at Martinique, he then steamed to Curaçao for coal.

After Sampson returned to Havana, the Navy Department dispatched Schley's squadron to blockade Cienfuegos on the southern side of Cuba. When Schley arrived with the "Flying Squadron," he could not ascertain whether Cervera had moved inside Cienfuegos harbor or not. Meanwhile, Sampson learned that Cervera had entered the port of Santiago, near the southeastern tip of Cuba, and had anchored his squadron behind the minefields and shore batteries guarding the narrow passage into the harbor. Schley, instead of running over to Santiago to blockade the port, sailed back to Key West for coal.

BLOCKING THE CHANNEL

On May 29 Schley returned and spotted Cervera's squadron in Santiago harbor and wasted a few shells firing upon *Cristóbal Colón* from an ineffectual range. On June 1 Sampson arrived with the battleships *Indiana*, *Iowa*, *Massachusetts*, *Oregon*, and *Texas*, two armored cruisers and several smaller vessels. Cervera manifested no appetite for fighting, so Sampson looked for ways to bottle-up the Spanish squadron. Lt. Richmond P. Hobson volunteered to sail the collier *Merrimac* into the harbor and block the channel by sinking his vessel at the narrowest point. Sampson approved the mission. Spotted by shore batteries and under fire, Hobson and his seven volunteers stopped *Merrimac*'s engines and let her drift, and when reaching a good spot in the channel, they tripped the charges. As the vessel settled, Hobson's men pushed off in a raft, drifted

Right: On June 22, 1898, the auxiliary cruiser St. Paul, *commanded by Capt. Charles D. Sigsbee, disables the Spanish destroyer* Terror *when she advances, with support from the light cruiser* Isabel II, *during an exchange of fire off San Juan, Puerto Rico.*

into the harbor, and were rescued by none other than Admiral Cervera. Later, all seven sailors received the Medal of Honor, but Hobson, being an officer, needed a special Act of Congress in 1933 to receive his.

While waiting for Army transports to bring a landing force, Sampson took a battalion of Marines forty miles east of Santiago and put them ashore at Guantánamo Bay. Sampson wanted the site as a base for coal and supplies, and the quick little sortie under Lt. Col. R. W. Huntington marked the first assault of American troops on Cuban soil.

On June 14, thirty-two transports carrying the V Army Corps, commanded by 300-pound Civil War veteran Maj. Gen. William T. Shafter, sailed under naval escort from Tampa Bay. On June 22, surfboats began landing the 17,000-man expedi-

tionary force at Dauquirí, sixteen miles east of Santiago, and by the 25th every man was ashore. Spaniards who observed the landing quickly fled and scrambled into blockhouses that formed the outer defenses of Santiago.

CONFUSION IN CUBA

On June 20 Sampson and Shafter discussed tactics, and each came away from the conference with a slightly different version of what the other would do. Sampson expected Shafter to come to the aid of the Navy and capture Santiago, thereby avoiding the necessity of running his ships through a minefield. After carrying two strong Spanish positions – El Caney and San Juan Hill – by frontal attacks and losing 1,572 men, Shafter dispatched a message to Sampson urging him to attack Santiago from the sea. On July 3 Sampson departed from the blockade to confer with Shafter, leaving Schley in charge. During the same interval of time, the governor general of Cuba ordered Cervera, over the admiral's objection, to escape from the harbor.

At 9:51 a.m. lookouts on *Brooklyn* reported *Infante Maria Teresa*, Cervera's flagship, coming down the channel. Schley unaccountably turned *Brooklyn* away from *Maria Teresa* in a maneuver for which he was later criticized because it enabled the Spanish squadron to reach deep water and turn west along the Cuban coast. Schley did not have too many choices because only one ship in the squadron had all her boilers lit, Captain Charles Clark's *Oregon*. After recognizing his mistake, Schley signaled the squadron and went in chase. By the time Sampson reached

Below: During the action off Santiago in July, 1898, men on board the USS Iowa *wait under the battleship's 13-inch guns as American cruisers and destroyers fire into the harbor.*

Watching the Battle, on the U.S.S. Iowa.

the running battle, all the Spanish cruisers had been damaged and run aground except for *Vizcaya* and *Cristóbal Colón. Oregon* and *Brooklyn* continued the chase, forcing *Vizcaya* into the shallows. Sampson came up and ordered *Iowa* to finish her. *Oregon*, at maximum range, fired a shell that landed close enough to *Cristóbal Colón* to send her fleeing into Rio Tarquino, where she grounded off the mouth. Two Spanish destroyers, *Furor* and *Plutón*, fared no better. *Indiana* sank *Plutón*, and, in a close action, Lt. Comdr. Richard Wainwright's auxiliary gunboat *Gloucester* sank *Furor*. That afternoon Sampson dispatched his battle report, writing, "The fleet under my command offers the nation as a Fourth of July present the whole of Cervera's fleet."

The lopsided battle spanned little more than three hours. Only one American was killed and another seriously wounded. Sampson's ships rescued Admiral Cervera and 1,800 survivors, but the Spaniards lost 323 dead and 151 wounded. Though it was a celebrated victory, Mahan put the battle in perspective, warning that Americans might never again fight an adversary so weak as Spain. He also condemned the marksmanship. American vessels had fired 8,000 shells but scored only 120 hits. The July 4th celebration had barely ended before a battle of another nature erupted, this one between Schley and Sampson. Each took credit for the victory at the expense of the other, and because each had his advocates and detractors, a bitter factional dispute erupted in the Navy and lasted for many years.

After the destruction of the Spanish fleet, the war ended quickly. On July 17, after a short siege and a long-range naval bombardment, Santiago surrendered. Nine days later the Navy landed an expeditionary force on Puerto Rico under Maj. Gen. Nelson A. Miles. On August 12, all resistance ended. The United States and Spain signed an armistice, ending the Spanish-American War. As part of the settlement Spain agreed to cede Puerto Rico and Guam to the United States and to free Cuba, but the Navy would eventually retain possession of its base at Guantánamo. The following day, on the other side of the globe, Spanish authorities at Manila surrendered the Philippines to Commodore Dewey, giving the United States another possession in the Far East. Mahan had predicted a three-month war; it had taken four.

On December 10 the United States and Spain signed a definitive treaty in Paris. For all the newly acquired territories, the United States paid Spain $20,000,000. President McKinley never intended to keep the Philippines, arguing that such far distant territories could only be defended by a battle fleet. The public disagreed with McKinley. Because men like Mahan and Roosevelt prevailed, the American empire was born, clinching forever the new nation's commitment to sea power. Now that America had her empire would she be ready, as McKinley feared, for the far-reaching foreign and domestic consequences that would span the next half-century?

The ink had barely dried on the new treaty when on February 4, 1899, General Emiliano Aguinaldo, who disavowed the annexation of the Philippines, led an army of insurrectionists against American forces at Manila. For two years the Navy, using mainly gunboats, skipped from one island to another bombarding guerrilla positions. Marines landed on the islands and got a good taste of jungle fighting. When it became

▶ **OCTOBER 12, 1900:** The USS *Holland*, the Navy's first submarine, is commissioned.

NOVEMBER 24, 1902: The Navy commissions *Bainbridge*, the first torpedo-boat destroyer.

NOVEMBER 18, 1903: A treaty is signed with Panama for building the Panama Canal.

DECEMBER 16, 1907: The cruise of the Great White Fleet begins.

APRIL 6, 1909: Comdr. Robert E. Peary claims to have reached the North Pole.

Left: *Army soldiers from Nebraska embark for the trip home at Pasig, Manila, on June 23, 1899, after being relieved by Col. Percival C. Pope's 1st Battalion, USMC, during the Philippine insurrection.*

1910

JANUARY 4: The U.S. Navy commissions its first dreadnought, the USS *Michigan*.

NOVEMBER 14: Eugene B. Ely becomes the first pilot to fly off a ship.

1911

APRIL 12: Lt. T. Gordon Ellison becomes the Navy's first trained pilot.

MAY 8: The first naval airplane contracts are awarded to Glenn Curtiss.

JULY 1: Curtiss successfully demonstrates his first "hydroaeroplane" to the Navy.

SEPTEMBER: The Navy establishes its first air station at Annapolis.

Below: *The first Marine detachments arrive at Peiping, China, on May 31, 1900, to protect American interests during the Boxer Rebellion.*

apparent to men like Roosevelt that Japan was building a powerful fleet, maintaining possession of the Philippines became even more important.

While skirmishes continued in the Philippines, inter-tribal warfare broke out in the Samoan Islands. The United States, Britain, and Germany each operated bases there and jointly administered the islands. To protect their consulates, American Marines joined forces with the British, and in the early months of 1899 launched punitive expeditions into the interior and suppressed the fighting. As McKinley predicted, having interests in the Far East would keep the Navy busy.

When on May 18, 1900, the Western penetration of China finally provoked a mass rebellion by the Righteous Society of Heavenly Fists, or Boxers, the United States suddenly became embroiled in another little war. As the Boxers approached Peking, U.S. Minister Edwin Conger called upon the Asiatic Squadron to send a force to guard the American legation. On May 31 warships from the United States, Britain, France, Italy, Japan, and Russia assembled off the mouth of the Pei-Ho River and pieced together an international force of 337 men to protect their respective legations. The forty-eight Marines and five bluejackets who joined the guard soon found themselves overwhelmed by thousands of screaming Chinese, so 140 Marines had to be rushed over from the fighting in the Philippines. When this force proved inadequate, the Navy landed 482 Marines and 2,000 soldiers under Maj. Gen. Adna R. Chaffee. By then the International Relief Expedition had

> TEDDY ROOSEVELT WROTE:
>
> *'I grew so excited [over Japan's victory at Tsushima] that I myself became almost like the Japanese, and I could not attend to official duties. I spent the whole day talking with visitors about the battle." But as a strategist he later remarked, "I am well aware that if they [the Japanese] win out, it may possibly mean a struggle between them and us in the future; but I hope and believe not." A year later in 1905 he guardedly admitted that Japan and its navy had become a "formidable new power – a power jealous, sensitive, and war-like, and which if irritated could at once take the Philippines and Hawaii from us, if she obtained the upper hand on the seas.'*
>
> TO SHINING SEA, BY STEPHEN HOWARD.

grown to 18,600 men, mostly Europeans. The Navy eventually withdrew the Marines and left the task to the Army.

CHILL RELATIONS WITH JAPAN

Being latecomers, Americans never expected to have a free hand in the exploitation of China, but it was also becoming clear that Japan, a new entrant in the race to dominate China, had been copying the latest models of European warships and building a powerful navy of her own. After Commodore Perry's visit during the 1850s, relations between the United States and Japan had gradually chilled. Japan resented the exploitation of the Far East by Western nations, making it increasingly important for the United States to maintain its grip on the Philippines. After more than two years of fighting, American forces finally captured General Aguinaldo, the leader of the resistance, on March 23, 1901. Fighting continued with the Moslem Moros inhabiting the southern islands, but by July 4 the islands were secured and the military government replaced by a civil government under future U.S. president, William Howard Taft.

Relations with Japan remained guardedly cordial until President Theodore Roosevelt stepped in to settle the Russo-Japanese War, which had culminated in the Battle of Tsushima and the destruction of the Russian Baltic Fleet. When Japan failed to win all its demands, the negotiators accused the United States of thwarting their objectives. Roosevelt wanted to avoid a break with Japan, mainly because America was not prepared for war in the Far East. Because of chronic uprisings in the Philippines, the Army-Navy board had drafted the Orange Plan, which stipulated that the Philippines would be abandoned and the Asiatic Fleet withdrawn to the West Coast should war with Japan occur.

Roosevelt, who had worked so assiduously to gain a foothold in the Far East, now looked for a way to stabilize relations before Japan became any stronger. He decided upon a show of strength, a demonstration couched in peace that Japan would be certain to understand. With work on the Panama Canal slowly progressing, Roosevelt wanted to know what would happen if the nation had to go to war with Japan before the canal was completed. Russia had lost its navy partly because it had to travel 18,000 miles to meet the

THE NAVY'S GUNS

By 1901, Lieutenant William S. Sims had become a leader among the Navy's outspoken officers, commonly known as "Young Turks." He had a keen, inquisitive mind and exercised it on naval gunnery, a subject of great concern to Roosevelt. While carrying out his duties in the Far East he met British Capt. Percy Scott, commanding HMS *Terrible*, another maverick much like himself. Scott demonstrated a gunnery system of his own design called "continuous aim," which had the remarkable success of achieving 80 percent hits. Sims concluded that *Terrible*'s firepower was as effective as any three-dozen similar American ships put together and that *Terrible* alone could out-fire the combined U.S. Navy.

When Roosevelt became president, Sims had been hammering away at the Navy Department to adopt the system. Having made no progress, he took a step that could have ended his career – he wrote directly to the president. Sims understood that a single accurate shot was worth more to a commander than a fusillade of a hundred misses. Roosevelt happened to be a man who thought the same way. Instead of dismissing Sims for effrontery, he made arrangements for the Young Turk to become inspector of target practice for the Asiatic Squadron. Roosevelt then brought him home, appointed him to the same post for the entire Navy, and made him fleet intelligence officer as well.

Sims adopted and refined Scott's continuous-aim firing system, a process that made it possible for a gunner to keep his sights fixed on a target despite the rolling of the ship. He also developed a "dotter," a device that enabled gun crews to practice continuous-aim firing without expending ammunition. He established gunnery drill competition, presented trophies and small cash awards to the winners, and in eighteen months had surpassed the Royal

Navy's performance in both accuracy and rapidity of fire.

Roosevelt spoke often with Sims, listened with interest to his ideas, and soon made him a naval aide. From Sims's perspective, Roosevelt's Great White Fleet had serious defects in design and construction. Freeboards were too low to fight in stormy seas. Transfer conditions between powder rooms and turrets lay open, vulnerable to sparks that could accidentally ignite the charges. Turrets, though heavily armored, had ports too wide to protect the guns or their crews. Sims not only complained to the president, but he also complained to the press, infuriating bureau chiefs and old salts responsible for designing the ships. Resentment against so-called "Simian Theories" became so strong among the bureaucrats that Roosevelt probably saved Sims's career by giving him command of the battleship *Minnesota*. But the Navy took note and design improvements followed.

Above: Two officers stand under a pair of 12-inch guns on the quarterdeck of USS Connecticut, the Navy's 18th battleship, commissioned on September 29, 1905.

---

enemy. Roosevelt wanted no such surprises, so he decided to send the entire battle fleet around the world. To ensure that the Navy understood its mission, he ordered "all failures, blunders and shortcomings...be made apparent in time of peace and not in time of war."

EUROPEAN RIVALS

Roosevelt did not demonstrate his Great White Fleet solely for the purpose of impressing the Japanese. America had other rivals on the oceans. Great Britain and Germany had entered a building race measured primarily by each other's number of new battleships. The U.S. Navy, faced with challenges both East and West, could no longer withdraw from its costly "two-ocean" commitment. When the Great White Fleet steamed into Yokohama, the Japanese govern-

ment seemed sincere in dispelling its growing bitterness. Fourteen months and 46,000 miles later, after stopping briefly at the ports of the world, the fleet returned to Hampton Roads, just in time to usher out Teddy Roosevelt's administration. Looking back on his years in politics, Roosevelt credited his "big stick" diplomacy as "the most important service I rendered to peace." But the fleet that returned from its "big stick" mission had already become obsolete.

In 1906 Britain commissioned the enormous, revolutionary battleship *Dreadnought*. Nothing could match her. She displaced 17,900 tons, cruised at 21.6 knots, carried eleven inches of armor, and was propelled by a new system of steam turbines. While American battleships carried a range of guns from 3-pounders to 12-inchers, *Dreadnought* carried ten 12-inch guns in twin turrets, three on the centerline, one on each beam, and a few 12-pounders to defend against torpedo-boats. The Germans acknowledged that

▶ **1912**

JULY 16: Rear Admiral Bradley A. Fiske patents the first aerial torpedo.

JULY 27: The Navy establishes the first radio communication between ship and aircraft.

NOVEMBER 12: Using a catapult, Lt. Ellison lifts a Curtiss A-1 hydroaeroplane into flight.

NOVEMBER 30: Lt. Ellison successfully tests the Navy's first flying boat, a Curtiss C-1.

Right: *On April 4, 1906, following the Russo-Japanese War, President Theodore Roosevelt speaks at an armament conference at Annapolis, Maryland.*

Dreadnought had reduced every battleship in the world to second-class status and set to work to outmatch her.

Before Roosevelt left office, work had been started on America's own dreadnoughts. First came the 16,000-ton *Michigan* and *South Carolina*. They carried two fewer 12-inch guns than HMS *Dreadnought*, but because they were all turreted and on centerline, they could match *Dreadnought*'s broadside. About the time *Dreadnought* came off the line, America started work on the 20,000-ton *Delaware* and *North Dakota*. The new turbine-driven battleships could fire a broadside 25 percent greater than any vessel afloat. All four vessels mounted piggybacked turrets, one on top of the other. European designers first scoffed at the arrangement but later adopted it.

In 1909 William H. Taft became president, and though less enthused about the Navy than Roosevelt he continued building dreadnoughts. By 1912 the Navy had six large battleships in commission, including the two newest, the 26,000-ton *Arkansas* and *Wyoming*. Both vessels carried improved 12-inch guns mounted in stacked turrets.

In a vain attempt to keep pace with Britain, Germany, and Japan, Roosevelt and Taft dedi-

---

JOHN P. HOLLAND'S SUBMARINE

Though America's Civil War developed the use of spar torpedoes, the design of the "automobile torpedo" in 1864 attracted little interest in the United States for thirty years. While the Navy concentrated on methods to deliver the device from surface vessels such as the destroyer *Bainbridge*, Irish-born inventor John P. Holland looked for ways of firing the torpedo from a submerged vessel. Since the days of David Bushnell, entrepreneurs having no government support had built every American submarine. Holland's efforts fell into the same category, Holland having produced a number of practical submarines before winning in 1888 the Navy Department's competition for

design. Seven years passed before the Navy awarded him a contract, to which he caustically remarked, "The Navy does not like submarines because there is no deck to strut on."

Holland went to work on an 85-foot submarine with two torpedo tubes, and in 1897 launched *Plunger*. When submerged, she drew her power from storage batteries, but when on the surface, the Navy wanted a running speed of fifteen knots, an impossible task for the engines available. Holland abandoned the design and began work on a craft that would carry his name.

The 64-ton *Holland*, at 53ft 10in in length, carried a single torpedo tube, three Whitehead torpedoes, and received power from a gasoline engine when on the surface. She had a crew of seven, a surface speed of seven knots, and a range of 1,500 miles. She operated at a maximum depth of seventy-five feet, but because she had no periscope her commander had to surface frequently to get his bearings through small glass ports in the conning tower. Roosevelt, then Assistant Secretary of the Navy, recommended she be purchased. In 1900 the Navy bought her for $150,000, about half of Holland's cost. Admiral Dewey, among those who assessed her performance, remarked that if the Spaniards "had two of these things in Manila, I could never have held it with the squadron I had."

The Germans did not adopt the submarine until 1906, but with the perfection of the gyrocompass in 1908 submarines would become the commerce raiders of World War I.

Above: *John Philip Holland (1840-1914) stands in the conning tower of a submarine he designed and built for the Navy.*

Right: *After several attempts to interest the Navy in a fleet of submarines, John P. Holland's* Plunger *finally proved successful.*

BRADLEY ALLEN FISKE

Teddy Roosevelt had a marvelous aptitude for finding talent among Navy personnel. As one senior officer observed, Roosevelt "took his duties as commander in chief of the Army and Navy more conscientiously than any other president than George Washington," and one of Roosevelt's rare finds was Bradley Allen Fiske.

Fiske was both a reformer and an inventor. As a lieutenant, his constant flow of ideas agitated his less imaginative superiors. In 1891 naval gunners still aimed by sighting down the barrel, so Fiske invented a telescopic gun sight. Since this solved only a small part of the problem, he then invented the optical range finder and a stadimeter for estimating ranges. The inventions were timely because the range of naval guns leapt from 6,000 yards in 1898 to 20,000 yards by 1918. This led to the development of "director firing," which enabled an officer in an elevated control platform to orient a ship's big guns on a target and discharge them by pressing a button. The director would evaluate the pattern and communicate hits and misses to a gun-battery plot where alterations in elevation and range were calculated and relayed to the turrets.

When in 1898 Roosevelt became aware of "flying machines," he immediately initiated a study to determine whether they had a practical application in warfare. Not until 1903, however, did the Wright brothers get a powered flyable contraption airborne. Five years later Roosevelt was still waiting for an answer when an improved version of Wright's aircraft took to the sky for a test flight, crashed, and killed its

occupants. The Army continued the experiments, but Roosevelt wanted to know if such a plane could fly off a naval vessel. In 1910 Eugene Ely, a civilian pilot, took off from an inclined platform hastily erected on the bow of the cruiser *Birmingham*. Five minutes later, after first dropping out of sight, the aircraft landed safely on a nearby beach.

Fiske, now an admiral, took a serious interest in the project and in 1911 crawled into the cockpit of a biplane, flew it off the platform, circled, and landed it back on the ship. Sold on the tactical importance of aircraft, he designed and patented a device that would allow an airplane to carry a torpedo. He also recommended that four air bases be built on Luzon, each equipped with 100 planes to defend the Philippines if attacked by Japan.

Fiske's inventions were only a small part of the man. His most enduring and important contribution to the Navy was his persistent demand to create the office of Chief of Naval Operations, a position well suited to himself. In 1915 he finally got his wish but not the post. Fiske believed the nation must prepare for war, but Secretary of the Navy Josephus Daniels found the idea of national involvement unpalatable. In 1942 Fiske died at the age of eighty-eight, having patented more than sixty naval inventions. He served as president of the U.S. Naval Institute for twelve years and wrote five books on naval tactics.

Left: *Bradley Allen Fiske (1854-1942) served at Manila Bay and afterwards distinguished himself as the Navy's leading inventor of electric communications devices.*

Below: *On November 14, 1910, Eugene B. Ely, a civilian barnstormer, proved to the navy that a Curtiss pusher biplane could take off from the deck of the scout cruiser USS Birmingham.*

Below: *The blue winter enlisted man's uniform worn on the USS Ohio during the years 1904-1918.*

> '*Unless all signs deceive, the American Republic breaks from her old moorings, and sails out to be a world power*'
>
> BLACKWOOD'S EDINBURGH MAGAZINE.

cated most of the funds appropriated to the Navy to build battleships. But for battleships to succeed in war, fast cruisers and destroyers were needed for reconnaissance and to screen the dreadnoughts. Not until 1902 did the Navy begin to commission destroyers. They evolved from torpedo boats and were primarily intended as a counter-weapon to be used against them. The USS *Bainbridge*, the first American destroyer, displaced 420 tons, cruised at 29 knots, and carried a pair of 3-inch guns and had two 18-inch torpedo tubes. The vessel became obsolete the day it was commissioned. Destroyers that followed, such as *Smith*, were twice as large and

propelled by turbines instead of reciprocating engines. *Paulding*, commissioned in 1910, was the first to burn oil instead of coal.

Without Teddy Roosevelt and his turn-of-the-century Navy, the United States would have been far less prepared for world war. And had it not been for a handful of Navy aviators who had the opportunity to test their flying machines during the Mexican revolution in 1914, the aerial wing of the Navy may have paused in its development for years to come. While U.S. naval forces were protecting American lives and investments along the Mexican coast, Austria declared war on Serbia, beginning a chain reaction that would

WORLD WAR I

In August 1914, the outbreak of war in Europe caused little consternation among Americans. President Woodrow Wilson cautioned against direct involvement and practiced a doctrine of pacifism. Experienced observers, among them the president, believed the war would be short. Wilson appointed Josephus Daniels to the post of Secretary of the Navy. He was another pacifist who knew more about planting cotton and raising hogs than the difference between fore and aft. Senior naval officers lamented Wilson's choice and steeled themselves for tempestuous battles with the new secretary. Daniels surprised them all when he chose thirty-one-year-old Franklin Delano Roosevelt, a cousin of the former president, as assistant secretary. Daniels had probably never heard of Mahan, who died in 1914, but young Roosevelt knew the man by his work and had became a disciple.

When Daniels took office, the Navy already had eight dreadnoughts afloat and two New Mexico-class battleships, displacing 32,000 tons and mounting twelve 14-inch guns, under construction. This gave the United States a clear lead over Japan, but the British Grand Fleet contained 29 dreadnoughts and the German High Seas Fleet 20 battle-cruisers. As long as America remained neutral, the U.S. Navy could handle the situation developing in the Pacific, but Japan's rapid occupation of Germany's Pacific islands gave everyone reason to worry. To be better prepared for a crisis, should one come, the Navy asked for

FRANKLIN DELANO ROOSEVELT

Secretary of the Navy Josephus Daniels admitted knowing nothing about the Navy. His department contained a Council of Aides, with whom he rarely spoke, a General Board whose plans and advice he seldom understood, and a Joint Army and Navy Board that President Wilson in 1913 had prohibited from meeting. Into this picture stepped thirty-one-year-old Franklin Delano Roosevelt, whom Daniels picked as his assistant. When war erupted in Europe, Daniels moved too slowly to suit Roosevelt, who found his boss bewildered and unable to grasp the situation. In a letter to his wife on August, 2, 1914, Roosevelt wrote, "I am running the real work."

Roosevelt enjoyed getting out of Washington and going to sea. Once while on a destroyer to inspect naval facilities in Maine, he turned to Lt. William F. Halsey, Jr., the ship's commander, and asked to take her into Frenchmen's Bay. Roosevelt asserted that he was familiar with the narrow strait between Campobello Island and the mainland, but the idea of a civilian putting the destroyer on the rocks gave Halsey a jolt of consternation. With trepidation he yielded the conn to Roosevelt and watched as the assistant secretary took the vessel through the narrow channel as slickly as a seasoned pilot, amazed that Roosevelt actually "knew his business."

In 1917, when German U-boats threatened to starve the British into submission, Woodrow Wilson made a casual observation, remarking that it might be easier for "the British to shut up the hornets in their nests" rather than hunt them "all over the farm." Wilson had no plan in mind, but Roosevelt conceived the idea of running a cordon of mines 240 miles across the North Sea from Scotland to Norway. The project drew little interest from the Admiralty when it was learned that 400,000 mines would be required. Meanwhile, Ralph C. Browne of Massachusetts designed an antenna mine, which did not have to touch a ship to detonate its 300 pounds of TNT. Suddenly closing the North Sea required only 100,000 mines. America mobilized mass production of the devices, and in June, 1918, Rear Admiral Joseph Strauss began mining the North Sea. By the end of the war, 70,000 mines had been laid and six U-boats sunk. The barrier contributed to the deteriorating morale in the German Navy and its eventual mutiny and defeat.

As historian Edward L. Beach observed, "Roosevelt is variously said either to have 'inherited' or to have 'built' a navy. Both judgments are in fact correct, for the fleet he inherited from the war with Spain was not the same fleet as the one he 'built.'"

Above: Assistant Secretary of the Navy Franklin D. Roosevelt (right) poses with Admirals Sims (center) and Burrage (left) in front of the painting "The Return of the Mayflower."

Both Roosevelt and Admiral Fiske pressed Daniels to prepare for war, but in 1916 the secretary found himself caught in a cross fire between those who favored and those who opposed preparedness. Being politically cautious, Daniels followed the president's defensive posture and let his young assistant carry the load.

Left: *A mine-laying crew, supervised by an officer, begins to lay mines off the stern of one of dozens of ships assigned to the task.*

Below: *Hundreds of mines lay at Invergordon, Scotland, waiting for placement in the North Sea as part of Franklin Roosevelt's 1918 Mine Barrage.*

another 20,000 men. Daniels caused an internal furor by rejecting the request, but Roosevelt shifted among the Navy's squabblers and established himself as the department's "good guy" while his boss retained the role of "bad guy."

GERMANY'S U-BOATS

In 1914 every world power, belligerent and neutral alike, underestimated the impact about to be made on naval tactics by German U-boats. The war started sublimely enough, giving rise to the belief that it would end quickly. The European belligerents threw up blockades and attempted to starve each other as they had done in every previous war. The Royal Navy swept German commerce from the seas and shut down her trade with neutral countries. Without bothering to inspect American cargos at sea, British warships hauled the vessels into British ports on the pretense of suspecting them of being laden with contraband for Germany. This infuriated Americans, but Wilson ignored the static, mainly because he favored the Allied cause and knew that British and French purchases of war material were lifting the United States out of an economic depression. Germany struck back with her newly developed naval weapon, the U-boat.

While trench warfare on the Western Front settled into a weary combat of attrition, war on the high seas became a cat and mouse game of dynamic proportions. Unlike the commerce raiders of times long past, German submarines could neither disembark prize crews nor give fair warning to intended victims without exposure on the surface to detection and destruction. The war

took on a new dangerous character when in February, 1915 Germany declared the waters around Great Britain a war zone and that any shipping in the area would be sunk without warning. The declaration defied international law, but Germany brushed away complaints by attributing the law to the age of sail, not modern warfare. The United States warned the German government that if American lives were lost, repercussions would follow. But Americans continued to travel through the war zone on Allied vessels carrying munitions, lives were lost, and nothing happened.

While Wilson's stand on neutrality renewed America economically, it worked against the Navy. After Eugene B. Ely flew off a warship fitted with a flight deck, and months later proved

▶ **1915**

MAY 7: A U-boat sinks the Cunard liner *Lusitania*.

OCTOBER 19: A submarine base is established at New London, Connecticut.

OCTOBER 28: Parris Island is opened as a Marine training base.

1916

MAY 5: Marines land to quell a rebellion in the Dominican Republic.

AUGUST 29: Congress approves President Wilson's request to "build a navy second to none."

1917

FEBRUARY 1: Germany declares "unrestricted submarine warfare."

Above right: *During the first years of the war, U-boats ravaged transports, such as the unlucky British steamer* Dalton.

Below: *The* Lusitiana, *carrying 128 American passengers, gives a blast from her steam whistle as she leaves from New York for England. She never completed the trip, sunk by a German U-boat off the British Isles.*

that a similar platform could be used for landing an aircraft, America proclaimed her neutrality, and experiments with naval aviation stopped. The British went on to design aircraft carriers, leaving the United States five years behind. A neutral America also prevented the Navy from accumulating the important combat experience pilots would need when drawn into the war. A country on peacetime footing would never keep pace with the rapid technological advances being made by combatants.

LUSITANIA SUNK

On May 7, 1915, a wake-up call stirred the sleeping giant when the *U-20* sank the Cunard liner *Lusitania*, taking 1,198 men, women, and children to the bottom, among them 128 American passengers. Because the ship carried a small amount of arms, Germany tried to justify the sinking. Wilson protested to Berlin. The Germans,

'*Clean bow shot from 700 meters range. Shot hits starboard side right behind bridge. An unusually heavy detonation follows with a very strong explosion cloud. She has the appearance of being about to capsize. Great confusion on board.... In the bow appears the name 96.*'

U-20 KAPITÄNLEUTNANT WALTER SCHWEIGER, MAY 7, 1915.

unwilling to provoke the United States into war, agreed to pay reparations and ordered U-boat commanders to allow passenger liners to pass.

Prodded by Congress, Wilson asked Daniels to prepare a five-year building program. Admiral Dewey's General Board came back with a proposal for building 156 ships – 10 battleships, 6 battle-cruisers, 10 scout cruisers, 50 destroyers, and 67 submarines. The cost – $500 million. Wilson backed the proposal, but Congress seemed dazed by the request. Midway through the debate the British and German fleets fought the Battle of Jutland. In the greatest and most confused naval engagement of the war, the Royal Navy lost heavily while driving the Germans back to Heligoland. Spurred by concern over British naval losses, Congress acted and on August 29 passed the Naval Act of 1916, accelerating the building program from five to three years. Work soon began on four battleships – *Colorado*, *Maryland*, *Washington*, and *West Virginia* – each displacing 32,600 tons and armed with eight of the Navy's new 16-inch guns.

Despite urging from Congress and senior naval officers for haste, Daniels still had no intention of entering the conflict and refused to prepare for antisubmarine warfare. While Daniels temporized over combat readiness, the German High Command increased its efforts to starve Britain into submission by ordering the resumption of unrestricted submarine warfare against all ship-

THE RETURN OF THE *MAYFLOWER*

On May 4, 1917, the inhabitants of Queenstown, Ireland, witnessed "the return of the *Mayflower*" in the form of six American destroyers of Commander Joseph K. Taussig's Destroyer Division 8 that came steaming up the swept channel. Hundreds of harbor craft tooted whistles and thousands of townsfolk converged along the shore to stare at the strange vessels that looked so unlike their British counterparts. American vessels were slender and graceful in comparison to the sturdy-looking British vessels. Though they carried more fuel, these first American destroyers to reach Europe were not as fast and maneuverable as the British version, and everything on their decks from funnels to guns, torpedo tubes, and depth charges were arranged differently. Taussig had departed from Boston on April 24 in response to a cabled summons from Admiral Sims and arrived at Queenstown exactly on the day expected.

After receiving hearty greetings from the city, Taussig and his officers trudged up a hill to the Admiralty House to meet their new commander, Vice Admiral Sir Lewis Bayly. Britain's official history describes the admiral as "the father of destroyer tactics and organization." Taussig described him as energetic, taut, taciturn, and exacting. Bayly

intended to lose no time utilizing the Americans and asked Taussig, "When will you be ready to go to sea?" Instead of the expected answer, Taussug replied, "We are ready now, sir, that is, as soon as we finish refueling." Pleased with the response, Bayly nevertheless gave Taussig and his sailors four days for rest and repairs and a few words of sage advice: "No lights of any kind at night, no steaming below 13 knots, constant zigzagging, only short signals, no fixed system of patrol, careful watching of all fishing vessels lest they be disguised submarines, and above all no underrating of an enemy who has shown skill, perseverance and cleverness in the art of irregularity." Bayly's orders on the duties of destroyers were plain and simple – to destroy submarines, convoy and protect shipping, and save the lives of people from torpedoed ships.

As more ships became available, Taussig's command under Bayly grew to eighteen destroyers.

Above: Comdr. Joseph K. Taussig, USN, arrives with his six destroyers at Queenstown, Ireland, and reports to Vice Adm. Sir Lewis Bayly.

Below: In Bernard Gribble's famous painting "The Return of the Mayflower," Irish sailors (left) extend an enthusiastic welcome to the first American destroyer squadron as it heads into Queenstown.

▶ **MARCH 17:** The Navy is authorized to enlist "Yeomanettes."

APRIL 6: Congress approves war with Germany.

MAY 4: The first American destroyers arrive at Queenstown, Ireland.

MAY 24: The first American convoy sails from Hampton Roads.

JUNE 6: The first naval aviation unit reaches France.

AUGUST 14: A Navy plane launches the first torpedo.

NOVEMBER 17: Destroyers based at Queenstown sink the first U-boat to be sunk by a U.S. ship.

DECEMBER 7: Five American dreadnoughts arrive at Scapa Flow.

Right: In 1918, American convoys with escorts steam for Great Britain, this one led by George Washington *with* America *and* DeKalb *following. The photographer shot the image from the deck of the USS* Whipple.

ping – merchant and passenger – found in the war zone. The German High Command expected the action would draw the United States into the war, but the Kaiser's strategists gambled on defeating the Allies before America could mobilize its forces. U-boats went to work and sank several American merchantmen. Wilson had just been re-elected for keeping the country "out of war," but upon taking office for another four years he promptly asked Congress for a declaration of war. On April 6, 1917, America declared war on Germany and two days later on Austria-Hungary.

William S. Sims was no longer a Young Turk, but he had become a rear admiral. Daniels pulled him from the presidency of the Naval War College and the sent him to London to confer with the First Sea Lord. Admiral Sir John Jellicoe shocked Sims by dourly admitting that Britain was approaching the brink of starvation and that German U-boats were winning the war. Sims asked the admiral why merchant vessels were not escorted through the war zone by destroyers. Jellicoe replied that destroyers could not be spared from the important task of screening the Grand Fleet. Sims took immediate action, cabling Daniels to send every available destroyer to Europe. On May 4 Destroyer Division 8 of six ships under Comdr. Joseph K. Taussig sailed into Queenstown, Ireland, and reported to Vice Admiral Sir Lewis Bayly as ready for duty. In time, Bayly grew to love his Americans. On the anniversary of their arrival at Queenstown, he told Taussig, "To command you is an honor, to work with you is a pleasure, to know you is to know the best traits of the Anglo-Saxon race."

Sims found that younger officers in the Royal Navy agreed with his concept of deploying destroyers to guard massed convoys. With the concurrence and urging of Prime Minister Lloyd

George, two experimental convoys with destroyer escorts pushed off for Britain, one from Gibraltar and one from Hampton Roads. Sims had found the solution. U-boats sank only one straggler. Allied shipping losses in April of 900,000 tons fell in November to 300,000 tons. Never again did U-boats threaten to win the war.

CONVOY TACTICS

Convoys leaving North America consisted of twenty to thirty ships guarded by cruisers, and together they zig-zagged across the Atlantic to the danger zone, about 200 miles west of the British Isles. Off the danger zone Taussig's Queenstown destroyers fitted with antisubmarine devices met the convoys. For the crossing, the transports were arranged in several parallel columns, each containing about four ships in a single file, the whole covering several square miles. Its slowest ship determined the speed of the convoy. When the destroyers arrived they covered the flanks while one or more followed behind to protect any stragglers.

Any sighting or indication of the presence of a submarine brought swift destroyers to the area. Depth charges, better known as "ash cans" and loaded with 300 pounds of TNT, were set to explode at certain depths. They were either run off the stern or pitched over the side from "Y" guns. The underwater explosions created an unnerving effect on U-boat crews. American escorts operating in European waters participated in more than 200 attacks, sinking or damaging at least twenty-three submarines.

Convoy duty in the cold, foggy northeastern Atlantic was dreary, bone-chilling work with

Left: *An officer on board an escort destroyer stands with his watch and scans the sea, searching for signs of a plume from a U-boat's periscope.*

Below left: *On November 17, 1917, the destroyers* Fanning *and* Nicholson *depth-charge the U-58, bringing her to the surface and forcing her surrender.*

Above: The crew manning a Y-gun on an escort destroyer load a depth-charge and adjust the setting to the depth they want the charge to detonate.

little to relieve the constant monotony of peering through glasses onto a storm-lathered sea. There were sudden moments of excitement when the plume of a U-boat's periscope was seen skimming along the surface, or when the enemy surrendered and came to the surface. In 1918, the USS *Fanning* brought the *U-58* to the surface in the danger zone. The German commander scuttled the sub, and *Fanning* pulled off the survivors. Admiral Sims praised *Fanning*'s crew for their success, adding, "Go out and do it again."

Sims argued against keeping destroyers in the western Atlantic. Only five or six German U-boats, whose missions were primarily diversion-ary, had the range to make the trip across the Atlantic. They sank the old cruiser *San Diego* off Long Island, planted a few mines, torpedoed a few small ships, and created more alarm and anxiety than their presence justified.

Sims became Commander of the US Naval Forces Operating in European Waters and served the early weeks of the war under Admiral Bayly. By July, 1917, Daniels had sent thirty-five American destroyers to Queenstown, and before the war ended the U.S. Navy had eighty-five destroyers operating out of Queenstown, Brest, and Gibraltar. Promoted to vice admiral, Sims moved to London as a member of the Allied

▶ **1918**

MARCH 19: Ensign Stephen Potter becomes the first American naval officer to shoot down an enemy aircraft.

MAY 12: The first six wooden subchasers of the "splinter fleet" reach Europe.

MAY 25: U-boats appear off the American coast.

JUNE 8: The Navy begins laying the North Sea "Mine Barrage."

Below: *Sailors scramble up the barrel of a turreted battery to frolic for a photographer during a rare playful moment at sea.*

Naval Council but retained command of his Queenstown destroyers. When Sims first arrived in London, he had one aide; at the armistice his administrative and technical staff had grown to 1,200 officers, enlisted men, and clerks.

Daniels centralized overall control of American naval activities in two places. From Washington, Daniels, Roosevelt, and Chief of Naval Operations Admiral William S. Benson established American policy and strategy, and, with greatly expanded staffs, supervised the furnishing of personnel, supplies, munitions, and other necessities for off-shore operations. In London, Vice Admiral Sims served as central staff for the European theater, guiding the expansion of American naval forces in Europe from the first six destroyers steaming into Queenstown in May, 1917, to 370 vessels, 5,000 officers, 75,000 enlisted men, and, by war's end, 45 bases.

In December, 1917, Rear Admiral Hugh Rodman reinforced Admiral Sir David Beatty's British Grand Fleet with five coal-burning battle-ships – *Delaware*, *Florida*, *Texas*, *Wyoming*, and the flagship *New York*. The coal burners were a welcome addition because Britain had no oil to spare. Beatty incorporated the American battle-ships into the Grand Fleet as Battle Squadron Six,

but it took a few weeks to achieve solidarity. As one British officer noted, "Nothing could have been easier than a clash of ideas, of principles of fighting, of routine methods between two Services which had never been at sea together and had been trained in completely different environments." But in quick order Rodman adopted the British signals, tactics, and fire con-trol, and soon had the squadron cooperating in patrols, commerce protection, and the ceaseless vigil in the North Sea.

TROOPSHIPS IN THE ATLANTIC

A sailor's life in World War I lacked the drama of fighting great battles or, for most bluejackets, any battle at all. As the United States mobilized, the task of the Navy fell to transporting hundreds of thousands of troops with their equipment and supplies safely across the Atlantic to France. The American merchant marine had declined to the point where not enough ships were available to handle the demand for transports. The United States had only 1,000,000 tons available to replace more than 7,000,000 tons of Allied ship-ping destroyed by the Germans. The Army oper-ated no troopships, and the Navy had but two, *Hancock* and *Henderson*.

On April 26, 1917, Congress created the Emergency Fleet Corporation to purchase, requi-sition, or construct ships of steel, wood, or even concrete. The corporation impressed 300,000 tons of idle Dutch ships, 600,000 tons of interned German shipping, and during the next eighteen months built or bought another 9,000,000 tons. By the end of the war Rear Admiral Albert Gleaves's forty-five troopships together with twenty-four cruisers and other escort craft carried the American Expeditionary Force to Europe, while supply ships operated by the Naval Overseas Transportation Service grew from 72 vessels in 1917 to a fleet of 453 ships with 5,000 naval officers and 45,000 men. So effective had Gleaves's convoy tactics become that of 2,000,000 men transported to France, not a single American ship under escort was torpedoed or a man aboard injured.

On the day President Wilson declared war, the Navy mustered 269,000 officers and men. At war's end, the number had grown to a half million men and women – marking the first time that the Navy had accepted women into the service. About 11,000 women served as "Yeomanettes" in the Navy and 300 more enlisted as "Marinettes" in the Marine Corps.

Obtaining manpower proved to be far easier than training them. Annapolis could not handle the flow of officers and branched into colleges and universities around the nation. The four Navy "Boot Camps" at Norfolk, Great Lakes, Newport News, and San Francisco could not

Left: *Troops of the 105th Regiment, Field Artillery, crowd the decks of the transport* Mercury *as she departs for her voyage to France on June 30, 1918.*

expand their facilities fast enough to assimilate the 48,000 recruits going through training all at the same time. During the early months of the war, experienced men were needed at sea, but instructors and cadre had to be pulled from warships to train the flood of volunteers.

While training problems were being solved, the naval construction program experienced a sudden shift in emphasis. Battleships gave way to the mass production of 273 destroyers, all displacing 1,200 tons and having a design speed of thirty-five knots. Their common design made it barely possible to distinguish one from another. They all carried four 4-inch guns, a 3-inch anti-aircraft gun, twelve 21-inch torpedo tubes, and

two depth-charge racks. The fast, slender, four-funneled destroyers became the backbone of the Navy. Most of them were never finished in time for World War I but twenty-two years later became an important factor in preserving Great Britain in the early years of World War II.

"SPLINTER FLEET"

To augment the destroyers, the Navy built 400 submarine-chasers: 100-foot, 60-ton, wooden craft armed with 3-inch guns, a "Y" for launching depth charges off the beam, and a depth-charge rack aft. A rookie ensign usually commanded the boats of the so-called "splinter fleet," and his crew of twenty-five officers and men were composed of reservists and volunteers drawn from colleges across the nation. Only five percent of the men were experienced sailors, but they all learned enough about seamanship to navigate the tiny gasoline-engine-driven boats across the icy, storm-swept Atlantic during the winter of 1917-1918.

The "splinter fleet" operated mainly out of Queenstown, Plymouth, Portsmouth, Gibraltar, Brest, Corfu, the Azores, and as far north as Murmansk. Patrolling in trios at fifteen knots, the chasers used their hydrophones — a primitive underwater listening device — to locate their prey by a "triangulation fix." Once bracketed, the boats quickly converged on the U-boat and bombed it with depth charges. During the summer of 1918,

Above: *In 1918 Navy recruiting posters flooded the United States, relying on slogans that would induce young men to call upon their patriotism and join the fight against the Axis powers.*

Left: *A Yeoman First Class, capitalizing on a rare opportunity to boost the country's Victory Loan campaign, is joined by a bevy of "Yeomanettes," the forerunner of the WAVES.*

Above right: The SC405 submarine chaser of "the splinter fleet" slips by a freighter as she returns from a patrol and heads into port at Brest, France.

Below: Two new destroyers are under construction on the ways at Fore River shipyards where workmen begin to fabricate the decks.

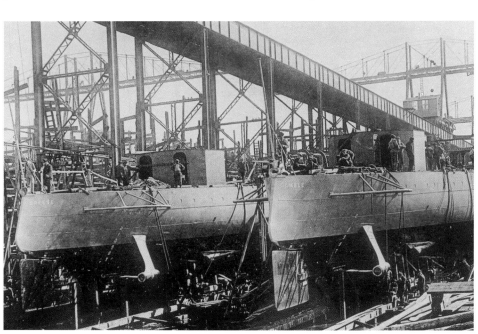

thirty-six American sub-chasers operating out of Corfu shut down German and Austrian submarine operations in the Mediterranean by blockading the 40-mile-wide Straits of Otranto with 24-hour Adriatic patrols. When U-boat commanders learned they could be heard underwater, they simply shut down their engines. British and Italian destroyers, drifters, kite balloons, and net barrier defenses all participated with the "splinter fleet" in the Adriatic operation.

CONDITIONS IN THE ATLANTIC

Sailors on escort duty or submarine patrol in the North Atlantic suffered almost as much as the infantryman who lived out each day in a cold trench filled ankle-deep with mud. As the slender destroyers pitched through housetop-high seas, sheets of seawater cascaded across the decks, streamed down companionways, and sloshed into living compartments. Men dressed in foul-weather gear staggered about the decks, clutching railings to keep from being hurled against steel bulkheads. Few hot meals were served in the gale-swept North Atlantic. The constant pounding of the sea broke the spirits of men almost as fast as it broke down the vessels' equipment, and when the ocean raged through the night, sending snow, sleet, and spray into the eyes of men on watch, collision with the ships of the unlit convoy became a constant concern.

For submarine destroyers such as the USS *Cassin*, the hunter sometimes became the prey. On October 15, 1917, while patrolling off the coast of Ireland, *Cassin*'s watch spotted a U-boat on the surface. As she sheered to close range, the U-boat submerged. After several minutes passed, the sub came to periscope depth, took a mark on the destroyer, and fired a torpedo.

Gunner's Mate Osmond K. Ingram spotted a milky plume streaking for the ship's stern, and after giving a hoop and a holler, he ran aft to jettison the depth charges. The helmsman conned the ship hard to port, and for several critical seconds it appeared that the torpedo might slither by, but as Ingram reached the depth charge rack, the torpedo struck, killing him and wounding nine others. Shattered, *Cassin* limped into port. Awarded the Medal of Honor posthumously, Ingram was further honored by having a destroyer (DD-255) named after him.

Allied submarines also entered the war against the U-boats, and duty off Bantry Bay in Ireland ranked among the worst. American submarines went on eight-day patrols along southeastern coast of Ireland to help protect incoming convoys. Crews constantly worried that they would strike a mine or be attacked by a friendly surface vessel. Submarines on patrol remained submerged as long as possible, but they still came frequently to the surface in every kind of rotten weather to recharge their batteries. Engagements with U-boats were sudden and short, the issue determined either by a well-aimed torpedo or by ramming.

As one captured U-boat commander glumly admitted, "We got used to your depth charges and did not fear them: but we lived in constant dread of your submarines. We never knew what moment a torpedo was going to hit us."

U-boats avoided areas where Allied submarines operated, but still got a dose of the same medicine they dished out to helpless merchant vessels. The Allies never deployed more than 100 submarines, but those few destroyed 20 U-boats. Allied destroyers, about 500 in number, sank another 34 enemy submarines, and some 3,000 other types of surface craft sent another 31 U-boats to the bottom.

NAVAL AVIATION

Without World War I, America's naval aviation arm would have fallen desperately behind the powers of the world. On January 18, 1911, men like Eugene Ely proved that crude airplanes could fly off the decks of warships and return to land on the same platform. Marc A. Mitscher, who during World War II became commander of a carrier task

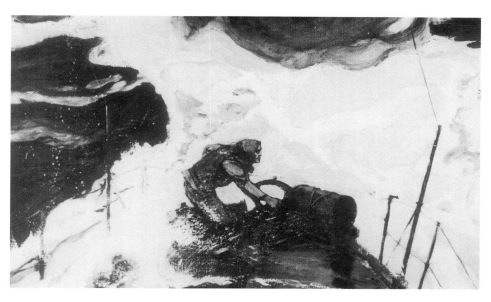

force in the Pacific, learned in 1916 to fly a Curtiss and Wright "hydroaeroplane" and became the Navy's "Aviator No. 33." When the United States entered the war, the Navy had thirty-nine qualified pilots, the Marine Corps five, and there were fifty-four planes suitable only for limited training exercises. During the war the Naval Air Corps grew to 2,500 officers – of which 1,656 were pilots – and 22,000 enlisted men. America built 2,127 aircraft, most of which were stationed at twenty-seven bases in Europe. The aviation units of the Marine Corps grew to 282 officers and 1,180 enlisted men.

On June 7, 1917, the first American force to reach France, other than medical units, were seven officers and 122 men of the United States Flying Corps, Foreign Service, which originated

Above: *On October 15, 1917, sailor O. K. Ingram, USN, makes a gallant effort to release the ship's depth charges moments before a torpedo strikes the USS* Cassin. *Ingram is blown overboard, becomes the first Navy man to be killed in World War I, and is awarded the Medal of Honor posthumously.*

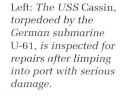

Left: *The USS* Cassin, *torpedoed by the German submarine U-61, is inspected for repairs after limping into port with serious damage.*

▶ **1919**

FEBRUARY 4: The Navy Cross and Navy Distinguished Service Medal are created.

MAY 8-31: A Navy Curtiss flying boat makes the first trans-Atlantic flight.

DECEMBER 25: American gunboats operating in China are organized into the Yangtze Patrol.

1920

MAY 19: Marines crush a long uprising in Haiti.

1921

JULY 23: In the event of war with Japan, the Navy and Marine Corps prepare the "Orange Plan."

Above right: *It took the United States many years before adopting the submarine as a weapon of war. On June 29, 1916 the* MI *(SS47) sets a heading for sea.*

Right: *The USS R-21, built at Bridgeport, Conn., features four torpedo tubes positioned in the forward section of the submarine.*

from the Naval Reserve Flying Corps. Most of the bases established in Great Britain, Ireland, France, and Italy were for seaplanes, which over the course of nineteen months grew from small, single-seated aircraft built mainly in Britain and France to huge flying boats powered by Liberty engines built in America. On the east coast of England a large American seaplane base at Killingholme escorted convoys to Scandinavian countries, flew reconnaissance missions, and made war against German U-boats. Seaplanes operating out of two Italian bases and piloted by Americans bombed Austrian naval bases at Pola with good success. In France, the Northern Bombing Group at Dunkirk struck German submarine bases at Zeebrugge and Ostend. During the last year of the war, no convoy guarded by seaplanes or blimps suffered a single loss.

On August 21, 1918, five floatplanes – two bombers and three fighters – under the command of Ensign George H. Ludlow departed from their base in Italy to drop propaganda leaflets over the Austrian naval base at Pola. Attacked by seven enemy aircraft, Ludlow shot down one plane before a bullet struck his fuel system. With smoke and flames spewing from his engine, Ludlow shoved the aircraft into a steep spin and extinguished the blaze. He steadied the plane and leveled her off, but with his engine dead he force-landed on the water five miles from Pola. Ensign George H. Hammann spotted Ludlow's plane sinking and landed beside it, hollering to Ludlow to swim over and grab a strut. Overloaded with Ludlow clinging to the struts, Hammann conned his plane just high enough over the water to fly it back to base. For gallantry, Hammann received the first Medal of Honor won by a Navy flier.

MEDALS OF HONOR

On October 8, 1918, eight German aircraft suddenly attacked two Marine aviators, Lt. Ralph Talbot and his gunner, Cpl. Robert G. Robinson, who were flying a reconnaissance mission over France. They shot down two enemy planes and escaped from the others by flying over German trenches at an altitude of fifty feet. For their most unusual feat, both men received the first Medals of Honor awarded to Marines.

Some Navy fliers cooperated with the infantry and flew missions over the battlefield. Nineteen-year-old David S. Ingalls, flying Sopwith Camels with the Royal Air Force, shot down five German planes in short order and became the Navy's only ace of the war.

The first full-fledged American unit to land in France was not the U.S. Army but a regiment of

'When you lunch with a man, talk to him, see him
go out and get into his plane in the prime of his
youth and the next day someone tells you he is
dead – it just doesn't sink in and you can't believe
it. And the oftener it happens the harder it is to
believe. I've lost over a hundred friends, so they tell
me – I've seen only seven or eight killed – but to me
they aren't dead yet. They are just around the
corner, I think, and I'm still expecting to run into
them at any time. I dream about them at night
when I do sleep a little and sometimes I dream that
someone is killed who really isn't. Then I don't
know who is and who isn't....'

JOHN MACGAVOCK GRIDER IN *WAR BIRDS*.

Marines. By May, 1918, two full regiments of 8,000 Marines were assimilated into the Army's Second Infantry Division. At Château-Thierry and Belleau Wood, they participated in some of the most desperate fighting of the war, gaining ground measured in feet rather than miles.

When French and British guns could not reach German long-range artillery, the Navy sent ashore five 14-inch rifles with bluejacket crews to serve them. The 14-inchers did not have the range of Germany's "Paris gun," which could hurl a shell seventy-five miles, but the naval guns could fire 1,400-pound shells twenty-four miles. Navy gunners lobbed 742 rounds into German-controlled railway centers, supply dumps, and bridges during the final months of the war, the final shot landing three minutes before the 11:00 a.m. armistice took effect on

November 18, 1918. Airplanes acted as spotters, enabling gun crews to make corrections on the target. The big shells were so devastating that one landing on a rail line could open a crater twelve feet deep and destroy one hundred yards of triple-tracked roadbed.

The last shot fired by the Navy's 14-incher punctuated the end of the war. Calm descended upon the battlefield, and for the first time in more than four years the war at sea also came to an end. Consistent with the terms of the armistice, Germany surrendered her navy, which had been bottled-up in

Top: *In 1918, Ensigns Theodore F. Dillon and Robert S. Waters make a reconnaissance mission over Nas Treguier, France, soaring overhead in their Curtiss HS-1 flying boat.*

Lt. G. H. Ludlow (lower left) sits in his Italian Macchi M.5 flying boat. After his plane was disabled by enemy fire, Ensign C. H. Hammann (inset, left), in another flying boat, came to his rescue. Lt. David S. Ingalls (below) became the first American naval ace.

1922

FEBRUARY 6:
The Washington Naval Treaty is signed to limit naval construction.

MARCH 20:
The Navy's first aircraft carrier Langley is launched.

OCTOBER 17:
The first Vought VE-7SF takes off from Langley.

1923

SEPTEMBER 8: Seven ships of Destroyer Squadron 11 go aground off Santa Barbara.

1925

MARCH 4: Congress establishes the Naval Reserve Officers Training Corps (NROTC).

Right: *Assistant Secretary of the Navy David S. Ingalls, a World War I ace, flew his own plane when attending inspections at different naval airfields. Here he stands before his official pursuit plane at the Naval Air Station at Washington, D.C.*

Below: *Like most American naval pilots in World War I, Ingalls flew British fighters that in the latter stages of the war also carried bombs.*

her North Sea and Baltic harbors since the Battle of Jutland.

On November 21, 1918, thirty-three dreadnoughts of the Anglo-American fleet steamed out of the Firth of Forth and formed two parallel columns six miles apart with an open lane in between. It was the day set by the armistice for the surrender of the German fleet, but rumors ran rampant that the enemy might fight one last great battle. Men of the U.S. Navy's Sixth Battle

'It's something that grows on you, day by day, that eats into your constitution and undermines your sanity....Here I am, twenty-four years old. I look forty and I feel ninety. I've lost all interest in life beyond the next patrol....Last week I actually got frightened in the air and lost my head. Then I found ten Huns and took them all on and I got one of them down out of control. I got my nerve back by that time and came back home and slept like a baby for the first time in two months. What a blessing sleep is!...I know now how men laugh at death and welcome it.'

FROM THE JOURNAL OF
JOHN MACGAVOCK GRIDER,
OF THE AMERICAN NAVAL FLYING CORPS, IN *WAR BIRDS*.

Squadron, standing in line with the Royal Navy, scanned the North Sea for the first smudges of smoke against the eastern horizon. Early in the afternoon the enemy column loomed ahead, nine battleships and five battle-cruisers slithering through a light mist hanging over a choppy sea. In a solemn ceremony reminiscent of mourners proceeding to a burial ground, the German fleet entered Scotland's Scapa Flow, there to be interned while the Allies determined its disposition. German Vice Admiral Ludwig von Reuter did not wait for the Allies' decree. On June 21, 1919, seven days before the signing of the Treaty of Versailles, von Reuter ordered the fleet scuttled, and a few hours later only smokestacks and masts marked the graves of the once powerful German Navy.

Before World War I, Japan bought the Imperial

Left: *On the night of November 10/11, 1918, Marines of the 5th and 6th Regiments, 4th Brigade, led the advance of the 2nd Infantry Division and seized a bridgehead on the Meuse River in France.*

Navy's capital ships from Great Britain. In 1911 Japan ordered the battle-cruiser *Kongo*, specifying that she carry 14-inch guns, be protected by 10 inches of armor, and cruise at 27 knots. She was a true battleship, the first to move up to a 14-inch gun, and superior to anything the British had ordered for the Royal Navy. British shipbuilders expected more contracts but none came. The Japanese copied *Kongo* and proceeded to build three sister ships – *Hiei*, *Haruna*, and *Kirishima* – in their own shipyards. The Japanese battle fleet continued to grow with four more 14-inch and two of the world's first 16-inch gun battleships, *Nagato* and *Mutsu*.

THE RISING SUN

While Western nations grappled on one front, Japan used her new navy to seize German interests in China and German bases among islands of the Marianas, Marshalls, Palaus, and Carolines. Every conquest increased Japan's ability to intrude upon American communications in the Pacific. Since Japan had already captured Germany's possessions in the Pacific, the Treaty of Versailles officially ceded them, giving the empire of the Rising Sun an enormous fortified bastion extending from her island homeland to the equator. American holdings at Guam, Marcus, Midway, and Wake now lay among or near Japanese possessions while the Philippines and Hawaii became more vulnerable should Japan wish to continue her expansion. Of equal concern, Japan was bullying China into closing her

Left: *Rear Adm. Charles P. Plunkett, USN, moved five of the Navy's 14-inch guns ashore and mounted them on railway cars, making it possible for naval gun crews to deliver a long-range bombardment of German positions north of Soissons, France.*

'*Without the cooperation of the American Navy, the Allies could not have won the war.*'

ADMIRAL WILLIAM S. SIMS.

long-standing Open Door policy with the trading nations of the world. In effect, the postwar settlement in the Pacific strengthened Japan at the expense of the United States.

During the war in Europe, Japan had been busy building its fleet while work in the United States had stopped on the battleships *Colorado*, *Maryland*, *Washington*, and *West Virginia* to divert capacity for building destroyers. Wilson viewed the sprouting empire of Japan with cau-

1926

AUGUST 27: New fighting in Nicaragua brings the Navy and Marines into another conflict.

1929

JANUARY 23-27: The Navy begins war maneuvers.

1930

APRIL 22: The London Naval Treaty establishes new five-year ratios for building capital ships

MAY 15: The Navy commissions the USS *Narwhal*, the first large streamlined submarine.

1933

JUNE 16: President Roosevelt begins rebuilding the Navy.

Above right: *While members of the 4th Marine Brigade served ashore, a traditional Marine force remained on the ships of the Navy. Here they stand inspection on the USS New Mexico.*

tious trepidation. He urged that the battleships be finished and the naval construction plan of 1916 be resumed and expanded. Because four years of war had worn down the Royal Navy and created an enormous public debt, Wilson believed that by 1925 the United States could have the most powerful navy in the world. He envisioned an unparalleled battle fleet crowned with thirty-nine dreadnoughts and twelve battle-cruisers. For a two-ocean navy, however, he believed the United States would have to build two capital ships for every one built by Japan because one would have to be be kept in the Atlantic and another in the Pacific. The opening of the Panama Canal in 1914 made crossing into the Pacific much faster but did not quell growing concerns over the expansion of Japanese imperialism.

While haggling with Congress for funds, Wilson also attempted to coerce Britain into supporting the League of Nations, through which he hoped the leaders of the world would peacefully settle future disputes. But Wilson's term in office was coming to an end. Congress approved funds to resume the 1916 building program, but in 1920, after Warren G. Harding won the presidential election by a landslide, the Senate rejected America's membership in the League of Nations.

The British had planned extensive fleet reductions during the 1920s, but with the United States building six 16-inch gun battle-cruisers (Lexington class) and Japan intent on outpacing America with more capital ships, the Royal Navy nervously placed orders for a new class of super-battle-cruiser. By 1921 another global warship-building race, much like the prewar race between Britain and Germany, gathered steam.

President Harding believed that the best way to reduce military expenditures was to derail the growing conflict between China and Japan by drafting separate treaties and then hammering out

details with the latter to limit battleship construction for a period of ten years. Harding mistakenly believed that the size and power of battleships had reached maximum displacements at 35,000 tons and 16-inch guns. Such misconceptions proved to be more political than realistic.

While battleship mania preoccupied the contestants for naval supremacy, one of the many wartime innovations provoking the interest of the U.S. Navy was Britain's introduction of the aircraft carrier. The new-fangled ship featured a floating hangar and workshops fitted under a long flight deck having none of the later, modern superstructures that towered off one side. In 1919 the United States added four such carriers to their appropriations bill, which would bring the Navy into parity with the British and outright superiority over Japan, which had *Hosho*, a single small carrier under construction. Congress voted funds for the new Lexington- and South Carolina-class battleships but denied funds for the aircraft carriers, although it did finally authorize enough money to convert the old collier *Jupiter* into an experimental carrier.

THE WASHINGTON TREATY

In the meantime, Harding's Washington Treaty attempted to establish parity by limiting the building race to maximum tonnage totals on an assigned ratio of: United States 5, Britain 5, Japan 3, France and Italy each 1.75. The three principal powers agreed to scrap sixty capital ships and provide a ten-year moratorium on laying down more than the agreed number of capital ships. New aircraft carrier construction could proceed, however, provided that hulls intended for or taken from decommissioned battleships or cruis-

USS LANGLEY AIRCRAFT CARRIER

In 1898, Professor Samuel P. Langley tinkered with a model of a steam-powered "aerodrome," a device the Bureau of Construction and Repair shoved aside as belonging "strictly to the land service and not the Navy." The Army then built a platformed houseboat on the Potomac River and told Langley to go ahead and launch a full-sized airplane. The test failed not because the idea was bad but because a reliable flying machine had not been invented. Ten years later Teddy Roosevelt promoted the same idea, and in 1910 Eugene Ely proved that an airship could take off from a platform on a cruiser and land on shore. The following winter he took off from shore and landed on a platform built on the stern of the cruiser *Pennsylvania*. Congress grudgingly gave the Navy $25,000 to perform further experiments in naval aviation.

Congress was even more grudging in 1919 when the Navy asked for money to build four aircraft carriers using the British design, which had worked effectively during World War I. Instead of four carriers, Congress told the Navy Board that, if they wanted a carrier, they would have to make one out of ships in service. In March, 1920, the collier *Jupiter* steamed into the Norfolk Navy Yard for revisions. Workmen stripped down her decks, revised her structure topside, and twenty-four months later converted her into the USS *Langley*, Carrier Number 1, named in honor of the American who conceived the idea. With a flight deck 534 feet long and 64 feet wide, she was about the same size as escort cruisers built during World War II. Borrowing from the British the nickname of the HMS *Furious*, a carrier of the same vintage, the Navy dubbed her "The Old Covered Wagon." Admiral William A. Moffett could only see the carrier's inadequacies, but she proved a point. Fighter aircraft could land on her and take off, ushering in a new era of naval tactics.

Left: *The Navy refitted the old collier* Jupiter, *gave her a deck, and transformed her into the USS* Langley, *the first United States aircraft carrier. The Navy affectionately called her "The Old Covered Wagon."*

Right: *To prove a carrier's viability, a Vought VE-7SF, flown by Lt. Comdr. Virgil C. Griffin, takes off from the deck of* Langley.

ers were used. The United States, Britain, and Japan were each given the prerogative of converting two of their uncompleted hulls into 33,000-ton carriers. Instead of slowing the naval race, the Washington Treaty actually stimulated carrier building, again giving the United States and Britain each 5 (135,000 tons), Japan 3 (81,000 tons), and France and Italy 2.2 (60,000 tons). The major problem for the U.S. Navy was the unwillingness of Congress to fund the program, but on March 20, 1922, the Navy launched and commissioned the USS *Langley*, its first American aircraft carrier.

The second problem for the Navy was developing a clear tactical concept of the carrier's role in warfare. Most senior naval officers believed a carrier should serve as an adjunct to the traditional reconnaissance role of cruisers, making the job of battleships easier. Barely anyone thought of using the carrier as a separate strike force working independently or as part of a task group composed of battleships, cruisers, and destroyers. But tacticians could see the value of having a ship in the fleet from which planes could be detached to bomb enemy ships sheltered in anchorages too far into a harbor to be reached by the guns of an offshore battle fleet.

INDEPENDENT AIR FORCE

Carrier proponents found both a critic and an ally from an unexpected source, Brig. Gen. William Mitchell, chief of the Army Air Service in Europe during the war. Mitchell had a vision — an independent air force similar to the Royal Air Force and equal in stature to the Army and the Navy. "Air power," he said, "has completely superseded sea power or land power as our first line of defense." As World War II would prove, Mitchell's prediction was way ahead of its time, but one statement upset naval proponents when he glibly suggested that battleships would become "as obsolete as knights in armor after gunpowder was invented."

The ink had barely dried on the Washington Naval Treaty when the U.S. Navy began work on the carriers *Lexington* and *Saratoga*, and Japan began building *Kaga* and *Akagi*, all four from capital ship hulls. To all observers it became obvious that no way existed for enforcing the spirit of the treaty's provisions short of war. All four of the heavy carriers surpassed the 33,000-ton limit allowed for conversions. Using old hulls seemed to be the easiest way to circumvent treaty restrictions without inviting international censure. By the time of the London Naval Conference in 1930, whose purpose was to extend the treaty for another ten years, delegates instead agreed upon a five-year term and established a new ratio 10:10:7 of cruiser tonnage for the United States, Great Britain, and Japan.

The negotiators gave little thought to Germany, which in 1933 withdrew from the Geneva Disarmament Conference and followed Japan out of the League of Nations. The Japanese believed that they should be entitled to the same number of capital ships as the United States and Britain. Had anyone been listening they would have heard General Sasao Araki, Japan's army minister, advise his government that "in order to have enough of the raw materials…which will be lacking in wartime, we should plan to acquire and use foreign resources existing in our expected sphere of influence, such as Sakhalin, China, and the Southern Pacific." Yet in 1937, the United States naval attaché in Tokyo calmly reported, "Japan has no intention of constructing a Navy which will be a menace to other nations."

Meanwhile, on January 23, 1929, the carriers *Lexington* and *Saratoga* participated in their first

> *'It is all a question as to whether the airplane carrier, equipped with 80 planes, is not the capital ship of the future.'*
>
> ADMIRAL WILLIAM S. SIMS TO
> SENATOR HENRY CABOT LODGE,
> FEBRUARY 14, 1914.

combat exercises with a battle fleet. Rear Admiral Joseph M. Reeves, commanding the aircraft squadrons, demonstrated the carrier's potential by sending *Saratoga* on an end-run around the defending force, which included *Lexington*, and launched a mock attack that "destroyed" the Panama Canal. The action raised the possibility of aircraft carriers acting independently of the main battle force.

In 1933 the Navy experimented with *Ranger*, the first carrier to be built from the keel up – a lightweight ship that fell well below the tonnage proscribed in the treaty. Disappointed with her performance, the Navy forged ahead with heavy carriers, commissioning in 1936 *Yorktown* and *Enterprise*. In 1939 the Navy launched another lightweight, the carrier *Wasp*, and after that settled upon the medium-heavy 27,000-ton "Essex" class, the first of which was ordered in 1940.

In 1937 the United States Navy awoke to a new reality — that despite the Depression, they were in a race with Japan to build capital ships. When orders were cut to build the first of the fast "North Carolina" and "South Dakota" class battleships, the Navy had finally solved the problem of getting a full battery of 16-inch guns into a vessel of 35,000 tons displacement by triple-stacking the turret mountings.

When Great Britain went to war in 1939, the U.S. Navy benefited enormously by borrowing British technology. Americans improved radar for

Right: Carriers rapidly grew from the old Langley *design to the powerful* Lexington, *converted in 1922 along with* Saratoga *from a pair of unfinished battle-cruisers.* Lexington *earned high marks early in World War II.*

surface and air surveillance, and sonar for detecting submerged submarines. The British experience also became a laboratory for naval tactics, showing that no number of rapid-firing anti-aircraft guns could beat off a well-organized enemy air attack, nor could carriers escape U-boat attacks without heavy destroyer support. To extend cover over convoys, the British designed the escort carrier, whose flight deck was not all that different from the old USS *Langley*. In June, 1941, the U.S. Navy launched *Long Island*, an escort carrier design that in 1942 would go into mass production.

When Franklin Delano Roosevelt became president on March 4, 1933, he faced the worst depression in American history. The nation could be grateful that during World War I he had come to understand the needs of the Navy while serving as the department's assistant secretary. In 1931, President Herbert Hoover had halved the Navy's destroyer production for 1932 and canceled all shipbuilding for 1933, causing horrified naval experts to accuse the president of trying "at every turn to restrict, to reduce, to starve the Navy." On June 16, 1933, with marvelous foresight and determination, Roosevelt scrounged $238,000,000 from the National Industrial Recovery Act at a time when Congress could barely find any money at all. The program called for 32 vessels to be laid down during a three-year period, among them the carriers *Yorktown* and *Enterprise*.

During the six years between taking office and

the outbreak of war in Europe on September 1, 1939, the Navy built 4 carriers, 6 battleships, 3 heavy cruisers, 13 light cruisers, 83 destroyers, and 38 submarines. Then, as Adolph Hitler's war enveloped all of Europe, America began crawling out of its depression. Roosevelt went to Congress demanding more funds for warships. In 1940 the Navy ordered 9 battleships, 17 carriers, 8 heavy carriers, 38 light cruisers, 196 destroyers, and 73 submarines. Without Roosevelt campaigning for the Navy, the Japanese might still have control of the Pacific.

Above: *In 1934 the 14,500-ton USS Ranger became the Navy's fourth carrier, and the first to be built from the keel up. Pictured here in 1938, she still carried a deck full of obsolete biplanes.*

BILLY MITCHELL

In 1919, Brig. Gen. William "Billy" Mitchell launched a one-man campaign to demonstrate why fighting aircraft should be organized under an independent service. He used every publicity stunt to make his point, including a series of testimonials before a doubting Congress.

In 1921 Mitchell began using aircraft to sink decommissioned ships, among them the 22,800-ton ex-German Navy dreadnought *Ostfriesland*. Because naval personnel wanted to go on board and assess the damage inflicted by each bomb, they instructed Mitchell to drop only one bomb at a time. Mitchell agreed to the rules, but when his aircraft arrived over the target, they dropped sixty-seven 2,000-pound bombs on the ship, scoring three near misses and sixteen direct hits. Naval observers were furious. They never had a chance to board the old dreadnought and glumly watched as *Ostfriesland* sank. The press corps did exactly as Mitchell expected and made the "death of dreadnoughts" headline news. Though Mitchell's demonstration did little to induce the Army or Navy to establish an independent air corps, it gave emphasis to the value of air power.

Despite being court-martialed in 1925 for accusing the War and Navy Departments of "incompetency, criminal negligence, and almost treasonable administration," Mitchell continued to fervently preach that in the next war air power would displace sea power. World War II proved him wrong, but in 1924 he predicted what could happen if Japanese aircraft attacked the naval base at Honolulu, and after December 7, 1941, one might wonder whether the Japanese had been listening.

In the end, Mitchell lobbied so hard for his independent air force that he could not admit the value of carriers, though he could certainly envision their future. Admiral Sims, when head of the Naval War College, contemplated what might happen if two battle fleets, equal except in carriers, should fight. Even before Mitchell's bombers sank *Ostfriesland*, Sims had decided that the force having the most carriers would "sweep the enemy fleet clean of its airplanes, and proceed to bomb the battleships, and torpedo them with torpedo planes." But from Mitchell's perspective, carrier planes would remain the property of the Navy, a matter he found inconsistent with his concept of a unified force.

Above: *Billy Mitchell, America's foremost advocate of air power, tries to explain his position during his court-martial for insubordination.*

CHAPTER SIX

WORLD WAR II
REGAINING THE PACIFIC

For the United States Navy of 1940, the price tag for preparedness continued to climb. President Franklin D. Roosevelt sensed danger when during the summer of 1940 the German *blitzkrieg* overran France and created new problems for America. Ever since the mid-1920s the Royal Navy had dominated the Atlantic, enabling the United States to maintain a close watch on Japan by keeping its strongest fleet in the Pacific. Should Britain fall, America would be thrust into either fighting a two-ocean war or subordinating its interests to those of Germany and Japan. Abandoning Great Britain was not an acceptable option, so on June 17, 1940 – three days after the fall of France – Admiral Harold R. Stark, Chief of Naval Operations, appeared before Congress and asked for $4 billion. The funds would triple the size of the existing combat fleet, adding 257 ships and 15,000 naval aircraft. Included in the proposal were several fast battleships and twenty-seven Essex-class carriers. Congress approved the package, and on July 19 Roosevelt signed the new Naval Expansion Act into law. Six weeks later he sent fifty World War I destroyers to Great Britain in exchange for the use of British bases, but he had still not solved a festering problem in the Far East.

Japan had taken the first step toward World War II when in 1931 the Imperial Army invaded Manchuria. Six years later Japan broke the arms limitations treaty and in secret began constructing the largest battleships ever built, the 68,000-ton *Yamato* and *Musashi*, each mounting 18.1-inch guns. Observing that the United States still adhered to the 35,000-ton limit for battleships, Japan felt quite comfortable about her own military buildup and in 1937 invaded Mainland China. After four years of fighting the multitudes of China, Japan needed to find new sources to replenish its rapidly diminishing supplies of oil and minerals. During the summer of 1941 Imperial forces began driving south and in July occupied Indochina, which served as a stepping-stone to the rich resources of Malaya and the Netherlands East Indies.

As Japan flexed her muscles, ranking military and naval officers from the United States, Britain, and Canada designed the ABC-1 Plan, stipulating that if America became drawn into a two-ocean war, the defeat of Germany would hold the highest priority. Japan may have learned of this agreement because Admiral Osami Nagano, chief of the Imperial Navy's general staff, designed a strategy that worked against America's commitment to defeat the Germans first. Nagano planned to attack American bases in the Philippines while driving toward the Dutch Indies. If the U.S. Pacific Fleet attempted to protect the islands, Nagano would destroy it with aircraft and submarines operating from Japanese island bases in the Marshalls and Carolines. Admiral Isoroko Yamamoto, commander in chief of the Combined Fleet, proposed a better idea. Instead of pursuing the Americans, why not send a carrier force to

> *'If you attack us, we will break your empire before we are through with you...we shall crush you.'*
>
> ADMIRAL STARK TO AMBASSADOR NOMURA, NOVEMBER 26, 1941.

Right: In November, 1941, while President Roosevelt temporized about declaring war on Germany, cruisers of the Japanese Navy were already taking war stations to perpetrate General Hideki Tojo's acts of great treachery.

destroy the Pacific Fleet where it lay at Pearl Harbor? "If we are to have war with America," he cautioned, "we will have no hope of winning unless the U.S. fleet in Hawaiian waters can be destroyed." Having eliminated the fleet, Yamamoto believed Japan would face few obstacles for six months to a year as they executed their strategy to seize a vast section of the Far East and the Central Pacific.

Yamamoto expressed concerns about the wisdom of attacking the United States, but he doubted whether Americans had the resolve to sustain a two-ocean war. So on November 26, 1941, an Imperial strike force under the command of Vice Admiral Chuichi Nagumo set sail from the Kurile Islands for Oahu with two battleships, three cruisers, sixteen destroyers, and six carriers jammed with 425 aircraft. Nagumo planned his armaments carefully, right down to torpedoes fitted with wooden fins to ensure shallow running in Pearl Harbor.

AMERICAN CARRIERS ABSENT

On November 7 Admiral Husband E. Kimmel, commanding the U.S. Pacific Fleet, received a war warning from Admiral Stark, which read, "Japan is expected to make an aggressive move within the next few days." The message mentioned "the Philippines, Thai or Kra Peninsula, or possibly Borneo." Because the warning excluded Hawaii, Kimmel failed to put his force on alert. By dumb luck, two of the carriers – *Lexington* and *Enterprise* – were ferrying aircraft to Wake and Midway, and a third, the USS *Saratoga*, was on the West Coast for repairs. The rest of the Pacific Fleet, eighty-six combat and service ships, lay in Pearl Harbor basking in the warm Hawaiian sun when at 7:55 a.m. a swarm of Japanese bombers droned over the island. The first force peeled off to strike the air bases. Torpedo planes flying forty feet above the water followed. Dive-bombers, swooping down from 2,000 feet, dropped their loads on the row of veteran battleships off Ford Island, the newest being eighteen years old.

Japanese aircraft attacked in two waves, the second coming at 8:40 a.m.. Sixty minutes later they were gone. The once proud Pacific Fleet lay in ruins. Of eight battleships in the harbor, five sank. Only three, *Maryland*, *Pennsylvania*, and *Tennessee*, were able to limp to the U.S. West Coast under their own power for repair. Destroyed by a bomb that detonated her forward magazine, *Arizona* blew up, killing 1,103 of 1,400 men aboard. *Oklahoma* capsized, taking with her 415 of her 1,354 officers and men. *California*, *West Virginia*, and *Nevada* – the only battleship to get underway – settled to their superstructures. Of 202 serviceable naval planes on Oahu, only 52 could still fly. Altogether, 2,403 American ser-

vicemen were killed and 1,178 wounded, with naval personnel suffering the greatest loss.

Vice Admiral William F. Halsey, two hundred miles at sea and returning with *Enterprise* after depositing twelve Grumman Wildcats at Wake Island, knew nothing of the attack when he sent a group of unarmed dive-bombers into Pearl Harbor. Friendly antiaircraft guns shot down four of the planes, and the enemy knocked down several more. During the melée above the airfields, the B-17s arrived from the mainland.

While the Navy assessed its damages at Pearl Harbor, the Japanese captured Guam and landed forces on Luzon in the Philippines. On December

Above: *As Vice Adm. Chuichi Nagumo's strike force converged on Hawaii, Japanese pilots huddle around their charts to pinpoint their targets at Pearl Harbor.*

Left: *Admiral Isoroku Yamamoto, the mastermind of Japanese naval strategy, studies one more time the tactical plan for attacking and destroying the U.S. Pacific Fleet, key airfields, and supply depots on Honolulu.*

The Day of Infamy

The morning of December 7, 1941, which President Roosevelt aptly coined "a day that will live in infamy," evolved from the president's edict on July 26, 1941, to freeze Japanese assets in the United States and halt the sale of oil. Japan's Achilles heel was her utter dependence on foreign oil, and Roosevelt's decree forced Minister of War General Hideki Tojo to seek it by conquest.

After three months of inconclusive negotiations, Japanese Special Envoy Saburo Kurusu presented Secretary of State Cordell Hull with Japan's final terms, demanding a free hand in the Far East. Six days later, November 26, Hull replied to Ambassador Kichisaburo Nomura with a counterproposal, agreeing to sign a non-aggression pact if Japan withdrew from China and Indochina. On that day the Japanese strike force under Vice Admiral Chuichi Nagumo secretly sailed from Hitokappu Bay with orders to strike Honolulu if by December 5 an agreement had not been reached with the United States. On the 5th Roosevelt appealed directly to the Emperor of Japan, promising that, "A withdrawal of the Japanese forces from Indo-China would result in the assurance of peace throughout the whole of the South Pacific area."

Early Sunday morning, December 7, American cryptologists, who had broken the Japanese diplomatic code, learned that Kurusu and Nomura intended to seek a meeting with Hull at 1:00 p.m. (7:00 a.m. Pearl Harbor time). The 14-part message contained a statement that Japan "cannot but consider that it is impossible to reach an agreement through further negotiations." As the message was being decoded in Washington, the Japanese carrier force paused 230 miles off Oahu, turned into the wind, and launched the first wave of 183 torpedo planes, dive-bombers, and fighter planes. At 7:00 a.m. on Oahu, Private Joseph Lockard, a radar operator, detected a swarm of aircraft bearing toward the island and notified his superior. The sleepy lieutenant brushed off the observation as a flight of B-17 Flying Fortresses due from the West Coast.

Meanwhile in Washington, Kurusu and Nomura completed their decoding and presented the message to Hull, not at 1:00 p.m. but at 2:20 p.m. Cryptologists had already informed Hull of the contents, and General George C. Marshall had asked Admiral Stark to send warnings to commanders in the Pacific. Unfortunately, General Douglas MacArthur in the Phillipines got top priority, and the message to Pearl Harbor went by commercial radio, arriving there seven hours after the attack. Kurusu and Nomura delivered their declaration to Hull a full hour after Japanese aircraft had struck Pearl Harbor. When receiving the Japanese envoys, Hull looked them squarely in the eye and, exploding with hot indignation, fumed, "In all my 50 years of public service, I have never seen a document that was more crowded with infamous falsehoods and distortions – infamous falsehoods and distortions on a scale so huge that I never imagined until today that any government on this planet was capable of uttering them."

The two emissaries departed without comment, hurried back to the Japanese embassy, and burned their papers.

Left: *On December 7, 1941, Japanese bombers strike the naval airfield on Ford Island. Stunned airmen and mechanics roam about in shock as they watch explosions erupting on the battleship* Arizona. *Enemy dive-bombers destroyed 33 planes on the field.*

Left: *Japanese aircraft strike Battleship Row. The USS* Arizona, *mortally wounded, pours clouds of black smoke skyward as she settles in the harbor. Behind her lies the USS* Tennessee, *badly damaged, but three weeks later she sailed to the West Coast for repairs. On the far left, the USS* West Virginia *rests on the bottom.*

Below: *Although she is still burning after the attack, the crew of* Nevada *work frantically and succeed in getting her to sea and out of harm's way.*

11 they attacked the Marines on Wake Island and suffered their first reversal. The Marines held out for twelve days, waging a stubborn defense against repeated air and amphibious attacks before exhausting their artillery and losing their Wildcats.

REPAIRING THE BATTLESHIPS

Early on Christmas morning, 1941, a Navy flying boat landed on the oil-smudged waters of Pearl Harbor. Admiral Nimitz disembarked and stepped onto a whaleboat. He had read reports and seen pictures of the devastation, but nothing compared to the actual sight of the capsized hull of *Oklahoma*, the tilted masts marking the watery grave of *Arizona*, and the solemn boats fishing bloated corpses of sailors and Marines from harbor waters. Nimitz could not find the words to express his grief, muttering to himself, "This is a terrible sight." But he also observed that Admiral Nagumo had failed to finish the job. Six of the injured battleships could be repaired, and he wasted no time getting work started on *California*, *Maryland*, *Nevada*, *Pennsylvania*, *Tennessee*, and *West Virginia*. Plan Orange, the carefully crafted defense against Japanese attack, had suddenly lost its relevance. Now, and for the time being, he must depend upon his carriers.

Admiral King urged Nimitz to hold at all costs the line running from Midway through the Marshalls and Gilberts to Australia. In his usual terse, adamant manner, he told the Pacific commander to "hold what you've got and hit them where you can." Nimitz had just the man to make a demonstration, Admiral Halsey, who had been chomping at the braces to strike back. Taking a carrier task force, led by his flagship *Enterprise*, Halsey launched his planes and struck Wake and Marcus islands, and Kwajalein in the Marshalls. Another task force, built around *Yorktown* hit the

1942

JANUARY 3: The ABDA (American, British, Dutch, and Australian) fleets are unified.

FEBRUARY 1: First carrier strike – Admiral Halsey bombs Gilbert and Marshall Islands.

FEBRUARY 27: The ABDA Fleet is defeated in the Java Sea.

MARCH 11: A Navy torpedo boat rescues MacArthur from Corregidor.

APRIL 18: Colonel Doolittle's B-25s bomb Tokyo.

MAY 7-8: The Battle of the Coral Sea begins.

Above right: *Listing heavily just before she sinks, the USS Arizona, engulfed in blazing oil, settles to the bottom with most of her crew.*

Right: *On December 8, 1941, President Roosevelt signs the bill officially declaring war against Japan. Secretary of State Cordell Hull watches from over the president's left shoulder. To his left is Secretary of the Navy Frank Knox. Before the week ends, the United States joins Great Britain in the war against Germany and Italy.*

Gilberts. On February 20, a third task force consisting of the carriers *Lexington* and *Yorktown* and a multi-national fleet under Vice Admiral Wilson Brown fought the first large air battle of the war. Lieutenant Edward H. O'Hare shot down five enemy planes, became the Navy's first World War II ace, and earned the Medal of Honor.

In December Admiral Thomas C. Hart, commanding the U.S. Asiatic Squadron, lost his bases when the Japanese invaded the Philippines. Hart withdrew to the Dutch East Indies and on January 15 became for a short time the commander of the ABDA (American, British, Dutch, and Australian) Fleet, whose mission was to stop the Japanese at the "Malay barrier" and prevent them from penetrating into the Netherlands East Indies. The combined fleet contained a motley array of old vessels – nine cruisers, twenty-six destroyers, and thirty-nine submarines based at Batavia and Surabaya. Before the fleet could run through its paces as a united force, two powerful Japanese squadrons entered the area and began landing troops on Borneo.

MORALE-BOOSTING ATTACK

On the night of January 24, 1941, the commanders on four old American destroyers – *John D. Ford*, *Parrott*, *Paul Jones*, and *Pope* – sighted a large enemy force about to put troops ashore at Balikpapan. Silhouetted by burning oil tanks on shore, the Japanese vessels lying in Macassar Strait made good targets. Swooping out of the dark, the four-pipers dashed through the transports, launched torpedoes, fired guns, and scurried away after sinking four armed ships, three transports, and a patrol boat. The action did nothing to curb the Japanese invasion of the Netherlands East Indies, but it was the first surface action fought by the United States since 1898, and it bolstered American morale.

For the ABDAs, the action off Balikpapan served as the beginning of the end. On February 27-28 Admiral Karel Doorman, after a seven-hour battle, lost most of the squadron in the Java Sea. Two cruisers, the USS *Houston* and the MHAS (Australian) *Perth*, escaped to Sunda Strait and fell upon a Japanese landing force in Banten Bay.

After a confused battle during which six enemy transports were sunk or damaged, both cruisers ran afoul of the Japanese covering force and were sent to the bottom. In eight weeks the Japanese Navy had annihilated the ABDA fleet and captured the rich resources of the East Indies.

With the Imperial Navy having its way on all fronts, President Roosevelt looked for a way to strike at Japan. He found a willing volunteer in Lieutenant Colonel James H. Doolittle, a test pilot who had experimented with short takeoffs but not deck landings. After several weeks of training in modified twin-engine, long-range B-25 bombers, Doolittle loaded sixteen aircraft onto Captain Marc A. Mitscher's carrier *Hornet* and with Halsey's Task Force 16 headed for Tokyo. The B-25s were to be launched 400-500 miles from the Japanese mainland and, after bombing selected targets, fly to fields in China. Because of concerns over discovery, Halsey cut Doolittle's squadron loose 668 miles from Japan. The inhabitants of Tokyo had just completed a mock air raid drill when the B-25s swept over the city at 500 feet and scattered their four-bomb payloads on Tokyo, Yokohama, Kobe, and Nagoya. Doolittle lost most of his planes, ditching them in China and Russia, and two of his crews.

The psychological impact of the raid overshadowed the small amount of damage done. It boosted American morale and embarrassed the Imperial Navy, which had promised but failed to keep the Home Islands safe from attack. The Japanese searched in vain to find the B-25 base. Roosevelt intimated that the attack emanated from "Shangri-La," the fictional Tibetan hideaway in James Hilton's novel *Lost Horizons*.

Flushed with victory in the Dutch East Indies, Japanese strategists looked south and gambled on a campaign that would extend their conquests to New Guinea, the Solomon Islands, and the Coral Sea. Surprise attacks had worked well for Imperial forces, but Americans had broken the Japanese naval code and knew the enemy had designs on northern Australia.

Nimitz worked fast, using all the ships he could muster to meet the enemy. Early in May 1942 he ordered Rear Admiral Frank J. Fletcher to bring *Yorktown* into the Coral Sea. He then dispatched Rear Admiral Aubrey W. Fitch and the *Lexington* task force to join Fletcher and summoned Halsey to hurry down to the Coral Sea as soon as *Hornet* and *Enterprise* launched the Doolittle raid. On May 4, before the carriers could be assembled, aircraft from *Yorktown* struck a Japanese landing force at Tulagi, marking the first naval action in history where surface ships never exchanged a single shot.

For two days Fletcher looked in vain for a Japanese landing force that Navy code-breakers at Honolulu warned was en route to attack Port

Left: Lt. Edward H. "Butch" O'Hare accounted for 5 of 18 enemy planes shot down on the on the raid on Rabaul, February 20, 1942. He became the first Navy ace of World War II and earned the Medal of Honor. He was further honored by having Chicago's international airport named after him.

Left: On April 18, 1942, a squadron of modified B-25 bombers line up for take-off from the pitching deck of the USS Hornet in their desperate raid on the Japanese homeland, later made famous by the book Thirty Seconds Over Tokyo.

► **JUNE 4:** Admirals Spruance and Fletcher defeat the Japanese at Midway.

JULY 30: The Navy establishes the WAVES.

AUGUST 7: The Guadalcanal campaign begins.

AUGUST 8-9: The Navy suffers its worst defeat during the Battle of Savo Island.

OCTOBER 26-27: The Navy wins a victory off the Santa Cruz Islands.

Above right: *On May 7-8, 1942, during the Battle of the Coral Sea, an American torpedo bomber sends a "fish" into the Japanese light carrier* Shoho *and leaves her burning.*

Below: *During the same action, a Japanese air attack destroys the USS* Lexington, *forcing Capt. Frederick C. Sherman to abandon ship after a number of explosions occur between decks.*

Moresby. On May 7 scout planes made contact. Aircraft from *Yorktown* and *Lexington* sank the carrier *Shoho*, losing only one dive-bomber. In another part of the Coral Sea Japanese planes from the carriers *Shokaku* and *Zuikaku* bombed the American fleet oiler *Neosho* and the destroyer *Sims*, mistaking them for a carrier and a cruiser. The day had been confusing for both sides, with B-17s attacking Allied surface ships, and Japanese aircraft attempting to land on the carrier *Yorktown*.

Early on May 8 opposing carriers again launched their aircraft. Navy dive-bombers damaged *Shokaku*'s flight deck, forcing many of her planes to ditch, but *Zuikaku* became hidden by a

rain squall. Bombs damaged *Yorktown* and *Lexington*, and later two torpedoes shot from a Japanese submarine ended the career of the battle-scarred *Lexington*. Captain Frederick C. Sherman ordered her abandoned, saving most of her crew of 3,000 men.

SET-BACK FOR JAPANESE

The Japanese had destroyed the greater tonnage, but the Battle of the Coral Sea scored as an American victory because it stopped the enemy invasion of Port Moresby. Startled by the sinking of *Shoho*, damage to *Shokaku*, and the loss of ninety-seven planes, Japanese commander Vice Admiral Takeo Takagi no longer had air support and ordered the invasion fleet to turn back until American warships could be eliminated from the area.

The repulse worried Admiral Yamamoto, who had hoped for one great naval battle that would remove the menace of the U.S. Navy from the Pacific and bring the war to a victorious conclusion. Already the dreaded industrial strength of America had pumped up production, commissioning three new battleships, *South Dakota* on March 7, *Indiana* on April 30, *Massachusetts* on May 12, and dozens of smaller warships. Yamamoto called for a strike, one that would provide him with air bases from which he could lure American vessels into a final showdown in the central Pacific.

Honolulu's code-breakers went to work and

Left: *Destroyers rush to the aid of sailors from the USS* Lexington *and pull 2,735 men to safety.*

through skullduggery and deception learned that Yamamoto planned to strike Midway in early June. Nimitz reacted with speed, ordering Fletcher's *Yorktown* and Halsey's *Enterprise* and *Hornet* to Midway, along with eight cruisers, fourteen destroyers, and twenty submarines. Rear Admiral Raymond A. Spruance, an exceptional strategist, took over Task Force 16 from Halsey, who had been hospitalized with a skin rash. Fletcher, commanding Task Force 17, took the other half of the American fleet. On June 2, both squadrons began moving into position northeast of Midway and out of Yamamoto's direct line of attack. The Navy knew that Yamamoto intended to make a diversionary attack on the Aleutians. Nimitz spared a few cruisers for the Aleutians operation, but for all the good they did he may as well have left them in port.

Numerically, the Imperial fleet enjoyed an insurmountable advantage, having eight carriers, seven battleships, and fifty-five cruisers and destroyers. Yamamoto divided his strike force into three divisions: four carriers under Admiral Nagumo (the same that had struck Pearl Harbor); a dozen troopships escorted by battleships, cruisers, and destroyers; and the main body of seven battleships, including *Yamato*, Yamamoto's flagship. The battle did not start at Midway but on June 3 at Dutch Harbor in the Aleutians, where Yamamoto hoped to sidetrack the American fleet. As bombs fell on Dutch Harbor, Ensign Jewell H. Reid, piloting a Navy PBY 700 miles west of Midway, peered through a small break in the clouds and looked below. Turning to his co-pilot, he said, "Do you see what I see?" Because of

cloud cover, not much could be seen of the Japanese ships below, but enough for the co-pilot to reply, "You're damn right I do." B-17s based at Midway took to the air but accomplished nothing.

At sun-up on June 4, another PBY reported the Japanese carrier force 200 miles northwest of Midway. The carriers *Akagi*, *Hiryu*, *Kaga*, and *Soryu* had already launched bombers and fighters against the airfields of Midway. Fletcher counterattacked, sending every plane on Midway to strike the flattops, holding back a few old F2A fighters flown by Marines to protect the airfields. Spruance ordered *Enterprise* and *Hornet* to be swung into the wind and waited for Fletcher to communicate a positive fix on the enemy's position. The Midway aircraft stumbled into a hail of anti-aircraft fire, suffered heavy damage, and failed to injure Nagumo's carriers.

DISASTER FOR IMPERIAL NAVY

The turning point of the war in the Pacific occurred when a Japanese reconnaissance plane radioed that a single American carrier had been sighted to the northeast. The report surprised Nagumo because no enemy carriers had been expected in the area. Having a second wave of ninety-three aircraft on deck being armed with bombs designed for use against ground targets, Nagumo faced a dilemma — should he attack Midway as planned or go after the American carrier? He chose the latter, ordering the payloads

▶ **1943**

FEBRUARY 9:
Marines secure
Guadalcanal.

MARCH 1-4: Navy
planes win the Battle
of the Bismarck Sea.

APRIL 18: Lockheed
P-38s shoot down
Yamamoto.

JUNE 30: MacArthur
begins his advance
along the north coast
of New Guinea.

JULY 28: The
Japanese evacuate the
Aleutians.

Above right: *On June
4, 1942, Japanese
aerial torpedoes
breach the USS*
Yorktown's *port side
during the Battle of
Midway. Already
damaged by bombs,
the carrier could not
dodge the swarm of
"fish."*

'*I could see a huge fleet, so many ships that I
knew it was their main body. I wanted to keep
looking at it but I was obliged to make sure we kept
close formation…and also keep an eye out for
enemy planes. We made a slight change in course
that would bring us ahead of the enemy.
Consequently, within a few minutes, off to my right
I had an intoxicating view of the whole Japanese
fleet. This was the culmination of our hopes and
dreams. Among those ships I could see two long,
narrow, yellow rectangles, the flight decks of
carriers…. Then farther off I saw a third carrier. I
had expected to see only two and when I saw the
third my heart went lower. The southwest corner of
the fleet's position was obscured by a storm area.
Suddenly another long yellow rectangle came
sliding out of obscurity. A fourth carrier!
I could not understand why we had come this far
without having fighters swarming over and around
us like hornets. But we hadn't seen a single fighter
in the air and not a shot had been fired at us.* '

LIEUTENANT CLARENCE E. DICKINSON,
JUNE 4, 1942,
A THREE-TIME NAVY CROSS WINNER, WHO FLEW ONE OF
ENTERPRISE'S DIVE-BOMBERS THAT ATTACKED AND STRUCK
THE CARRIER *KAGA*.

changed over to torpedoes and armor-piercing
bombs.

The delay proved fatal. Planes returning from
the first attack on Midway could not land on the
carriers' crowded decks. Confusion on board the
carriers intensified when the first wave of fifteen
old TBD Devastator torpedo planes from *Hornet*
were sighted droning in over the water. The
Devastators could not breach the cordon of
enemy fire, and all were shot down. The Japanese

were just beginning to celebrate their good marksmanship when fifty-four SBD Dauntless dive-
bombers swooped down upon the crowded decks
of *Akagi*, *Kaga*, and *Soryu*. Planes, torpedoes,
bombs, and gas hoses cluttered the decks of the
carriers, touching off secondary explosions as
bombs fell from the sky. By nightfall, all three carriers were sinking.

YORKTOWN SUNK

Hiryu, the last carrier to be sighted, had launched
eighteen dive-bombers against *Yorktown*.
Antiaircraft guns shot down most of *Hiryu*'s
planes, but three bombs struck *Yorktown*, causing
an internal explosion that rocked the ship. A pair
of torpedoes struck her, but she still remained
afloat. Two days later a Japanese submarine
picked her off while she was being towed, and the
gallant old carrier finally sank. *Enterprise*
avenged *Yorktown* and destroyed the defenseless
Hiryu, which had lost all of her planes.

Having lost four carriers, 250 planes, and a
number of other vessels, Yamamoto turned
solemnly away and headed for Japan. The
Imperial Japanese Navy had not been decisively
defeated since 1592, and Yamamoto understood
the consequences of having not succeeded at
Midway. The U.S. Navy had prevailed. As
Yamamoto had predicted in September, 1940, if
America could not be driven out of the Pacific in
six to twelve months, the war for Japan would
become one of attrition, not of victory.

On June 2, while Fletcher and Spruance were tackling the Imperial Navy at Midway, Admiral King decided to stop the further penetration of Japanese forces in the Solomon Islands. He called for aggressive action, ordering the 1st Marine Division under Major General Alexander A. Vandergrift to assault Tulagi, Gavutu, and Guadalcanal, where the enemy was building airfields. General MacArthur had intended to launch an offensive against Rabaul, but before his attack could be organized the Japanese forces landed on the northeastern coast of New Guinea and threatened Port Moresby, forcing the Army to reinforce Papua.

HENDERSON FIELD

On August 7, 1942, the 1st Marine Division, supported by planes from *Enterprise*, *Saratoga*, *Wasp*, and eight cruisers, landed 19,000 men on Tulagi and Guadalcanal. Finding enemy resistance light, Marines quickly secured the airfield on Guadalcanal. Construction battalions went to work to finish building what soon became Henderson Field. Ten days later the first Marine Hellcats touched down on the airfield.

The American attack on Guadalcanal took Yamamoto by surprise. Having been recently embarrassed at Midway, he ordered Vice Admiral Gunichi Mikawa at Rabaul to break up the invasion. This time no word of an impending attack came from code-breakers at Hawaii. Admiral Fletcher had chosen the wrong moment to withdraw his carriers for refueling. During broad daylight on August 8, Admiral Mikawa's five heavy cruisers, two light cruisers, and a destroyer steamed down New Georgia Sound, a passage through the central Solomons called "the Slot." Early on August 9, off Savo Island, the Japanese squadron inflicted one of the worst defeats in the history of the U.S. Navy, sinking four cruisers and severely injuring a fifth in thirty minutes without losing a ship. Mikawa's attack failed to liberate Guadalcanal, but it drastically weakened the American naval force protecting the island from invasion. Six more naval battles were to be fought off Guadalcanal, eventually rendering Savo Sound so littered with sunken vessels it became known as "Ironbottom Sound."

Yamamoto organized a complicated plan to rid the Solomons once and for all of American ships and recapture Guadalcanal. Using three squadrons coming from different locations, he sent three carriers, three battleships, a cruiser-destroyer force, and three transports carrying 1,500 troops around the Slot. On August 24, in the Battle of the Eastern Solomons 150 miles east of Guadalcanal, Admiral Fletcher's Task Force 61, composed of the carriers *Enterprise*, *Saratoga*, and *Wasp*, and the battleship *North Carolina*, met the attack and turned it back, sinking the

Japanese carrier *Ryujo*. Fletcher lost the services of *Enterprise* for a few weeks, and on September 15, he also lost *Wasp* when she was torpedoed by a submarine.

In October, Nimitz became annoyed with Admiral Robert L. Ghormley's management of the Solomons campaign and on the 18th replaced him with pugnacious "Bull" Halsey, who had already established a reputation for hitting the enemy hard with whatever ships and planes Ghormley gave him. The news of Halsey's appointment as commander of the South Pacific Area and South Pacific Force produced a wave of

Above: After taking two more torpedoes on July 6, Yorktown's salvage crew walk her deck in life preservers as preparations are made to abandon ship.

Left: Adm. Ernest J. King (center) became Commander-in-Chief, U.S. Fleet, on December 20, 1941. Eleven days later he placed Adm. Chester W. Nimitz (right) in charge of the Pacific Fleet. Here they meet with Vice Adm. William F. "Bull" Halsey to discuss strategy for recapturing the Solomon Islands.

AUGUST 15: The island-hopping campaign begins with the occupation of Vella Lavella.

NOVEMBER 1: Marines land on Bougainville.

NOVEMBER 20: The Tarawa offensive begins.

DECEMBER 17: Rabaul is neutralized by air attack.

DECEMBER 26: The 1st Marine Division lands on New Britain.

Above right: *During the Battle of Santa Cruz, on October 26, 1942, men of the USS* Enterprise *converge on deck to get the carrier's planes into the air.*

Right: *The battleship USS* South Dakota *survived the fighting in the Pacific, but as she neared the end of her career, some thoughtful soul preserved a section of her 16-inch belt armor, which can be seen at the Washington Navy Yard.*

'*Before we finish with 'em, the Japanese language will only be spoken in hell.*'

ADMIRAL WILLIAM F. HALSEY, JR.

jubilation throughout the theater. Halsey had commanded destroyer squadrons in World War I, and his keen interest in early development of naval aviation had led to his command of one of the Navy's first carriers.

Still frustrated by an inferior but stubborn American naval force, Yamamoto marshaled Japan's Combined Fleet of four carriers, four battleships, fourteen cruisers, and forty-four destroyers to settle the naval issue in the South Pacific. On October 26, eight days after his promotion, Halsey met the attack north of Santa Cruz Islands with the carriers *Enterprise* and *Hornet*, the battleship *South Dakota*, six cruisers, and fourteen destroyers. By brute strength the Japanese won a tactical battle, sinking *Hornet* and damaging

South Dakota, but Yamamoto lost a hundred planes and the services of the severely damaged carriers *Zuiho* and *Shokaku*.

On November 12 Yamamoto tried again, this time sending Admiral Hiroaki Abe's two battleships, a light cruiser, and fourteen destroyers to soften up Guadalcanal, while Admiral Raizo Tanaka's Tokyo Express landed the 38th Division near Henderson Field. At 1:50 a.m. on the 13th, Rear Admiral Daniel J. Callaghan's force, composed of two heavy cruisers, three light cruisers, and eight destroyers, spotted the enemy squadron off Lunga Point. In what Admiral King described as "one of the most furious sea battles ever fought," though it lasted exactly twenty-four minutes, the American force steamed line ahead and cut through the wedge-shaped Japanese formation. Callaghan, after telling his captains, "We want the big ones," lost his life pitting the cruiser *San Francisco* against the battleship *Hiei*. The only other American flag officer present, Rear Admiral Norman Scott, also lost his life while directing the fight from the bridge of the cruiser *Atlanta*. Once again the Japanese brought over-

> '*If I am told to fight regardless of consequence, I shall run wild considerably for the first six months or a year, but I have utterly no confidence for the second or third years.* '
>
> FLEET ADMIRAL ISOROKU YAMAMOTO
> TO PRINCE KANOYE,
> SEPTEMBER, 1941.

whelming firepower, but Callaghan's stubborn resistance forced the Imperial Navy to turn away without shelling Guadalcanal. At daylight, aircraft from *Enterprise* found *Hiei* northeast of Savo Island and sank her. Doing so provided little consolation. Callaghan's squadron left two cruisers and three destroyers on Ironbottom Sound.

On November 14 Yamamoto once again attempted to get the 38th Division's 10,000 men ashore on Guadalcanal, this time using Admiral Nobutake Kondo's battleship *Kirishima*, three cruisers and six destroyers in one squadron, and Admiral's Tanaka's eleven destroyers of the Tokyo Express in another. American aircraft sank six of Tanaka's transports, and only 2,000 Japanese infantry reached shore. Rear Admiral Willis A. Lee intercepted Kondo's squadron off Savo Island and at the cost of three American destroyers added *Kirishima* and the destroyer *Ayanami* to Ironbottom Sound. Six weeks later Japanese Imperial General Headquarters conceded defeat and issued orders to evacuate Guadalcanal.

As Yamamoto had predicted, Japan would "run wild considerably for the first six months or a

year," but after that, the mighty American war machine would be reaching full mobilization. Yamamoto, a Harvard graduate and ex-naval attaché in Washington, had studied the American people well. A year had elapsed since the outbreak of war and the turning point had been reached. On December 31, 1942, the U.S. Navy commissioned the 27,100-ton carrier *Essex*. Nine of her class would follow, and each would carry one hundred planes. On January 14, 1943, the carrier *Independence* joined her, followed in February by the light carrier *Princeton* and the new *Lexington*; in March, by *Belleau Wood*; in April, the new *Yorktown*; and in May, *Bunker*

Above: *During the Battle of Santa Cruz on October 26, 1942, a Japanese torpedo bomber makes a glide-run at the battleship USS* South Dakota.

Left: *The Battle of Santa Cruz became a fight involving aircraft against ships rather than ships against ships. In the ensuing battle, men from the USS* Pensacola *watch as enemy torpedo planes and dive-bombers win a tactical victory by hammering the USS* Hornet *until she sank.*

▶ **1944**

JANUARY 31: The Marshall Islands offensive begins.

FEBRUARY 17: Admiral Spruance's carrier planes strike Truk.

FEBRUARY 18-23: Marines capture Eniwetok.

FEBRUARY 23: Admiral Mitscher's carrier planes attack the Marianas.

APRIL 22: Marines land behind Japanese lines at Hollandia, Dutch New Guinea.

JUNE 15: Spruance lands Marines on Saipan.

Above right: *During the early stages of the war in the Pacific, the Navy could barely muster enough ships to supply the Marines on Guadalcanal. By the end of 1943, battleships arrived in bunches as the island-hopping campaign began.*

Below: *With the battleships came the carriers. Seen from the deck of the new* Wasp *are (l to r) the* Hornet, Hancock *and* Yorktown, *all replacements for the old rugged carriers of the same name lost in 1942.*

Hill, Cowpens, and *Monterey*. All would go to the Pacific Fleet.

In early 1943, battleships came off the line almost as fast as carriers – *Iowa* in February, *New Jersey* in May. They, too, joined the Pacific Fleet, bringing with them new cruisers and destroyers bristling with antiaircraft guns, making it possible for Nimitz to form larger, more powerful task forces. Instead of a task group limping along with one or two old battered carriers, perhaps a single battleship and a dozen cruisers and destroyers, Nimitz reached the point where he could combine a dozen carriers with a half-dozen battleships supported by a large complement of cruisers and destroyers. By mid-1943 the Navy operated 18,000 aircraft, better planes to match the

swift, maneuverable, but thin-clad Zeroes. The Grumman TBF Avenger replaced the lumbering old Devastator torpedo plane. Japanese fighters lost their edge to the new Vought F4U Corsairs and Grumman F6F Hellcats. The new Curtiss SB2C Helldiver replaced the old reliable Douglas Dauntless, which some pilots still preferred to fly and did.

It took millions of men and women to supply the needs of the Navy. From 325,000 officers and men in 1941, the Navy rapidly expanded to a force of 3.4 million, including 100,000 enlistees from the Women Accepted for Voluntary Emergency Service, a designation carefully crafted to spell WAVES when the unit was organized on June 30, 1942. Seven boot camps were established to absorb the influx of young men, many of whom had never shipped on so much as a rowboat. To train such enormous numbers, the Navy opened nearly a thousand schools to daily instruct 300,000 men and women.

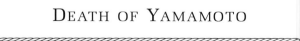

DEATH OF YAMAMOTO

Yamamoto never lived to witness the fulfillment of his prediction. Navy code-breakers learned that the admiral planned a tour of inspection and would fly into Kahili, Buin. Nimitz asked Admiral Mitscher to arrange a reception. Sixteen Lockheed P-38 Lightnings from Henderson Field met two Japanese bombers approaching Kahili and shot them down, taking the life of Japan's greatest admiral.

WOMEN IN SERVICE

The WAVES (Women Accepted for Voluntary Emergency Service) began with the creation of the Women's Reserve, organized as a part of the U.S. Naval Reserve under Captain Mildred H. McAffee. Though originally intended for continental service, their tours were extended to shore stations on Hawaii, Alaska, and bases in the Western Hemisphere. They carried the rank and rating according to their qualifications and performed such services as radio operators, motor vehicle drivers, medical and laboratory technicians, supply clerks, interpreters, and also served many other roles according to administrative needs.

On February 13, 1943, women Marines became a valued branch of the U.S. Marine Corps. They were originally organized as Marinettes during World War I, but Colonel Ruth Cheney Streeter discarded the appellation and proudly called her 18,000 girls simply Marines. They served on more than 50 bases, mainly in the Western Hemisphere, and filled 125 job classifications, including parachute riggers, gunnery instructors, trainer operators, celestial navigators, and machinists. Their rank and pay were the same as for men and their pride in the Corps as strong.

Ten thousand women served as SPARS in the Coast Guard Reserve. Organized in November, 1942, under Lieutenant Commander Dorothy C. Stratton, the unit's name came from the Coast Guard motto: "Semper Paratus" (Always Ready). Because so many of the men of the Coast Guard had been assigned convoy or amphibious duties,

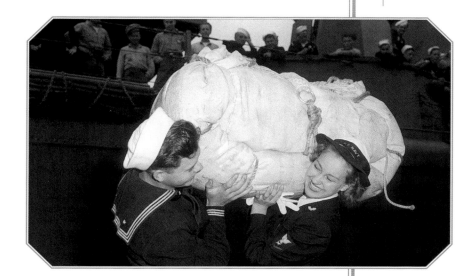

Above: Sailors gawk at WAVES sent to replace men on shore duty, releasing males for the nastier duties associated with fighting a war.

the SPARS filled the openings created, serving as yeomen, seamen, radio operators, and storekeepers.

The American Red Cross formed the largest of all the non-military service organizations during World War II, comprising nearly 30 million senior members and 18 million junior members. The Red Cross recruited 60,000 war nurses who served actively in the Army and Navy Nurse Corps. During World War II, the organization collected 10 million pints of blood, issued 762,000 first aid certificates, and at home and abroad operated 2,382 first aid stations and 11,479 mobile first aid stations.

In 1942, Japan's possessions in the Pacific inscribed a crude circle about 5,000 miles in diameter with a 15,000-mile perimeter. Of the thousands of islands inside the perimeter, the Japanese had chosen several on which to build strongholds – Rabaul in the Solomons, Truk in the Carolines, Tarawa in the Gilberts, and islands here and there all the way up to Kiska in the Aleutians. By the end of 1942, Admirals King and Nimitz designed a strategy to isolate certain of the Japanese strongholds by hopping around them to other islands where air and naval bases could be established, thereby leaving the strongholds behind and rendering them ineffectual. While fighting raged in the Solomons and on New Guinea, Nimitz kept pressure on the enemy elsewhere, using the fleet in the central Pacific to prowl among the Marshalls and the Gilberts, while bombing islands such as Tarawa, Makin, and Kwajalein.

The war in the Pacific became one of logistics, and in 1942 Japan had the edge, being able to run supplies to the Solomons through a network of bases stretching in nearly a straight line from Toyko through Iwo Jima and Saipan to New Guinea and Rabaul. For the United States it meant crossing thousands of miles of ocean. Ever since World War I, when the oiler *Maumee* first refueled destroyers crossing the Atlantic to

> '*One of the many mysteries on the Navy is 'Where do they come up with the food?' I remember the first day out [on the troopship USS W. A. Mann] we ate fried rabbit! I mean fried rabbit for 1,000 to 1,500 men is one hell of a lot of rabbit. This was a little strange, but not half as much as eating it two more times that month.* '
>
> LANCE CORPORAL K. C. LIPPARD.

Below: The logistic aspects of war involve the replenishment of supplies and machinery at sea. During November/December 1943, the battleship USS Minneapolis *takes on supplies as she prepares for duty in the Gilbert and Marshall Islands.*

PT-BOATS

PT boats (patrol, torpedo), sometimes called "Pete's," were used for both combat and rescue work. During the war they shot up many barges and damaged a few larger ships, such as the old Japanese cruiser *Abukuma*, which was afterwards sunk by bombers. The 77-foot boats usually carried two officers, nine enlisted men, four torpedoes, five machine guns and, later in the war, rockets. They normally traveled together, skimmed along at 45 knots, churned up an enormous wake, and lent credence to their motto (from John Paul Jones): "Give me a fast ship, for I intend to go in harm's way."

Were it not for the PT boat, General Douglas MacArthur may have served out the war in a Japanese prison camp on Luzon. The task of evacuating the general, his family, and his entourage from Corregidor fell upon Lt. John D. "Buck" Bulkeley and his "Philippine Expendables," a squadron of four PT boats. At nightfall, March 11, 1942, MacArthur stepped on board *PT-41*, turned to Bulkeley, and said, "You may cast off, Buck, when you are ready."

Bulkeley gave the signal, and the engines of the battle-scarred boat roared to life. At 8:00 p.m. the small squadron, consisting of *PT-41, -32, -34*, and −35, rendezvoused at Turning Bay just outside the minefield. *PT-34* carried Admiral Francis W. Rockwell, who had been the commander of the Cavite Navy Yard, but for this mission it was "Buck" Bulkeley who called the shots.

Left: *PT-boats performed a multitude of duties from missions of attack to missions of mercy. Here, this picture taken on November 11, 1944, from the Hancock shows a PT crew rescuing a Japanese survivor in the Surigao Strait.*

During the squadron's run to Cabra Island, the enemy on shore signaled to the blockaders that boats were making a break. As Bulkeley began closing on the Japanese fleet offshore, the sea became choppy and heavy rollers slapped against the thin-skinned hulls. "We waited, hardly breathing," recalled MacArthur, "for the first burst of shell that would summon us to identify ourselves." No challenge came and Bulkeley changed course, again and again, as the weary, blacked-out boats drove south into the towering waves of a storm.

By 3:30 a.m. the four boats could no longer keep formation and separated, rendezvousing at dawn off uninhabited Cuyo Island. It had been a

Queenstown, the Navy had been developing faster methods to transfer fuel at sea. When World War II came, the Navy had the technology but not the ships. Until specialized vessels could be built, shipyards adapted civilian vessels to the task. No vessels burned fuel faster or demanded more food and supplies than carriers and battleships. As the Pacific Fleet expanded, Nimitz provided a ratio of oilers, ammunition ships, tenders, and freighters, adding a new page to the logistics of war.

On June 30, 1943, Rear Admiral Turner, supported by Halsey's Third Fleet, landed an amphibious force on New Georgia on the same day that General MacArthur began moving his army along the northern coast of New Guinea. The action marked the beginning of the island-hopping campaign, forcing the Japanese to muster more reserves from Rabaul, rushing them down "the Slot" to islands under attack. So many transports had been lost that the Japanese had to use destroyers to move troops. In mid-August, faced with unacceptable losses in aircraft and destroyers, Imperial Headquarters decided to stop reinforcing the Solomons. On the other end of the

spectrum the Japanese secretly evacuated the Aleutians, ending a ruse that never worked during their grab for Midway.

During the summer and fall of 1943, while attrition nibbled away at the Imperial Navy, the U.S. Navy commissioned the Essex-class carriers *Intrepid*, *Wasp*, and *Hornet*, and three light carriers, *Cabot*, *Langley*, and *Bataan*. During the same period Rear Admiral Theodore S. Wilkinson bypassed the Japanese stronghold on Kolombangara and landed a small force on Vella Lavella and the 3rd Marine Division on Bougainville.

JAPANESE FRUSTRATED

Ordered to stop the American invasion of Bougainville, Rear Admiral Sentaro Omori sent all the ships he could muster — four cruisers and six destroyers — to break up Wilkinson's landing. Rear Admiral A. Stanton Merrill met the enemy at the mouth of Empress Augusta Bay and repulsed the attack, sinking a cruiser and a destroyer with-

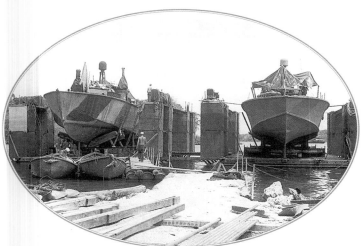

Above: PT-41 *became famous for evacuating General MacArthur and his family from Corregidor.*

Left: *At Rendova in the Solomons, a number of PT-boats go into drydock for repair.*

rough night. At one point the commander of *PT-32*, mistaking *PT-41* for a Japanese destroyer, had taken her in his torpedo sights.

A submarine had been ordered to rendezvous with the boats at Cuyo, but when it failed to appear, Bulkeley took *PT-41* and Rockwell's boat into the Sulu Sea and headed for Cagayan de Oro on the northern coast of Mindanao. Arriving there at 7:00 a.m. on March 13, MacArthur disembarked and awarded every member of the crew a Silver Star "for gallantry and fortitude in the face of heavy odds." For transporting the general and his family to safety, Bulkeley received the Medal of Honor.

On August 2 the following year, a sailor destined for even greater fame, Lt. John F. Kennedy, commanded PT-109 when she was rammed by the Japanese destroyer *Amagiri*, part of the "Tokyo Express" force disembarking troops and supplies off Kolombangara Island. Kennedy assisted in the rescue of the PT boat's crew, including swimming to Olasana Island while towing a badly injured man. He carved a message on a coconut shell and coaxed a native to take it to an Australian Coastwatcher on another island. Five days later a rescue party arrived. Later, Kennedy received the Purple Heart and the Navy and Marine Corps Medals.

Everywhere Marines landed, Seabees followed to build airfields, and when men got wounded "... the biggest job was to get them clean. That's one thing about being a Seabee. Aboard ship you bathe, wash down with antiseptic, and put on clean clothing before an action. In the Air Force you can take a bath before you take off. But when a Seabee gets hit, he's usually on the beach in the mud. Mud seems to be our element. When we die we die in the mud."

WILLIAM BRADFORD HUIE,
WAR CORRESPONDENT

Left: *During mid-December, 1943, Seabees moved their equipment onto Bougainville to level a bomb-pitted airfield and lay the steel mats needed to support the landing and take-off of heavy bombers.*

out losing a ship. On November 5 Admiral Mineichi Koga, Yamamoto's replacement, demanded another Bougainville sortie and sent eight cruisers and four destroyers from Truk. Helped by Navy code-breakers, Halsey detached Admiral Sherman's carrier force. When Koga's reinforcements stopped at Rabaul, ninety-seven planes from the carriers *Saratoga* and *Princeton* severely damaged five heavy cruisers and ended the Imperial Navy's efforts to recover

▶ **OCTOBER 26:** The first *kamikaze* attacks begin.

DECEMBER 15: The five-star rank of Fleet Admiral is authorized.

DECEMBER 18: A Philippine typhoon damages part of Halsey's fleet.

1945

JANAURY 10-20: Halsey smashes the Japanese fleet in the South China Sea.

FEBRUARY 19: The Iwo Jima campaign begins.

MARCH 18: Admiral Mitscher launches raids on Japan.

Above right: *Navy guns pound Tarawa Atoll as Marines prepare to assault the beaches.*

Below: *In the War Room aboard* Maryland, *officers assess progress on Tarawa. Seated (l to r) are Edson and Bourke (USMC), Hill (USN), and Julien C. Smith (USMC). At back (l to r) are Thomas J. Ryan and Jackson R. Tate.*

Bougainville. In mid-December, Navy bombers using airfields prepared on Bougainville neutralized Rabaul as a useful base. Two months later Japan abandoned it.

With the Solomons under control, Nimitz laid plans for the next island hop. On September 18 carrier planes from Rear Admiral C. A. Pownall's task force dropped bombs on Tarawa Atoll. In mid-November carrier planes began flying daily sorties over enemy installations in the Gilbert and Marshall Islands. Fighting still raged on Bougainville and New Guinea when on November 23 Vice Admiral Spruance's Fifth Fleet launched the main attack on Tarawa, reviving a strategy first conceived in 1921 – Plan Orange. Admiral Mitscher commanded the carriers, Rear Admiral Richmond Kelly Turner the assault force, and Major General Holland M. Smith the newly formed V Amphibious Corps. Lightly defended Makin and Apamama quickly fell, but Major General Julien C. Smith's 2nd Marine Division encountered stiff resistance on Betio, losing 990 killed and 2,391 wounded during 76 hours of bitter fighting.

JOINT OPERATIONS

On January 29, 1944, Mitscher's Task Force 58 began bombarding Japanese positions on Eniwetok and Kwajalein in the Marshalls while naval aircraft from Midway attacked Wake Island. Operations in the Marshalls were joint efforts between Spruance's Fifth Fleet, Turner's assault force, Smith's Amphibious Corps, Major General Harry Schmidt's 4th Marine Division, and the Army's 7th Infantry Division under Major General Charles H. Corlett. On Kwajalein the Japanese fought to the death, but the Marines, having learned harsh lessons on Tarawa, used vastly improved landing techniques and suffered far fewer casualties than previously.

As with Rabaul, Nimitz decided to flank the island fortress of Truk in the Carolines and strike directly at Saipan, Tinian, and Guam in the Marianas – a 1,000-mile leap across the Pacific that would bring B-29 Superfortresses within 1,500 miles of Japan. Nimitz did not intend to entirely ignore Truk. On February 17-18, Admiral Spruance's Fifth Fleet carrier planes flew more than 1,200 sorties, destroying one light cruiser, three destroyers, and 265 enemy aircraft.

On February 23, 1944, Mitscher moved his carrier group into the Marianas to begin softening up Japanese positions. Nimitz wanted the Marianas because they would provide bases for long-range bomber and submarine attacks on Japan. On June 15 the 2nd and 4th Marine Divisions went ashore on Saipan, where 29,622 Japanese defended the island. The Imperial High Command could not afford to lose the Marianas. In desperation they assembled a massive fleet containing nine carriers and five battleships to drive off the invaders. When submarines reported the approach of the Japanese flotilla, Spruance postponed the June 18 landing on Guam and deployed Mitscher's task force of fifteen carriers and seven battleships to meet the enemy west of Saipan.

Japanese Admiral Jisaburo Ozawa enjoyed an advantage over Spruance, who had to protect the thousands of men ashore, their transports, and supply ships. Spruance had the edge in carrier aircraft, but Ozawa expected to be supported by land-based planes. He also intended to use airfields on nearby islands from which to shuttle-bomb the invading American forces. What Ozawa did not know was that many of those airfields had been bombed, the planes destroyed, and the runways rendered unusable. Mitscher wanted to attack Ozawa's fleet before it came within reach of the islands, but Spruance felt obliged to hang back to protect the invasion force.

MARIANAS "TURKEY SHOOT"

The Battle of the Philippine Sea – which Mitscher called The Great Marianas Turkey Shoot – began on the morning of June 19 with a battle in the sky. When it ended, Navy aviators had shot down 346 Japanese planes, losing only thirty of their own. While all eyes were on the skies, two American submarines slipped among the Japanese fleet. *Albacore*, Commander James W. Blanchard, sank the carrier *Taiho*, Ozawa's flagship. The USS *Cavalla*, commanded by Lieutenant Commander Herbert J. Kossler, sank the carrier *Shokaku*, one of the two survivors from the Pearl Harbor strike.

Shocked by enormous losses, Ozawa turned the fleet about and vanished at nightfall. On the 20th Spruance pursued Ozawa, sending scouting planes searching far to the west. Late in the afternoon aircraft sighted the enemy fleet steaming

across the Philippine Sea and just in range of Mitscher's planes. If Mitscher launched, his planes would return after dark with empty tanks, but it would be his last chance to strike the enemy. So he launched, his orders plain and simple – "Get the carriers!"

Mitcher's pilots followed orders. Early in the evening they sighted Ozawa's fleet and in the face of heavy antiaircraft fire sank the carrier *Hiyo* and two oilers, damaged the carrier *Zuikaku*, and destroyed sixty-five planes, leaving the Japanese carrier fleet with only thirty-five aircraft. As American pilots returned to their carriers after nightfall, Mitscher did the unthinkable. He turned to his chief of staff and said, "Turn on the lights."

On July 21 the 3rd Marine Division landed on

Above: Officers on board the USS Birmingham *enjoy the rare opportunity of watching a dogfight during the Marianas Turkey Shoot.*

Left: Navy and Marine pilots were generally better trained and ultimately flew better planes than their Japanese counterparts, and they proudly displayed their "kills" below their cockpits. Commander David McCampbell flew a Grumman F6F Hellcat during most of the dogfights in the Pacific. He knocked down seven Japanese planes during the Marianas Turkey Shoot. During the forthcoming Battle of Leyte, he shot down nine more in a single day. At war's end, he had become the Navy's leading ace with thirty-four confirmed kills and received the Medal of Honor.

MARCH 24: Iwo Jima falls.

MARCH 26: The Okinawa campaign begins.

APRIL 6: The Japanese launch massed *kamikaze* attacks on the U.S. naval force off Okinawa.

APRIL 7: Admiral Mitscher destroys the last Japanese naval sortie.

Above right: *The diving officer on the USS* Batfish *oversees two enlisted men as they man the stern planes and the bow planes.*

Right: *Prior to the landings on June 15, 1944, an Iowa-class battleship opens the Marianas campaign by hurling shells at enemy positions on Saipan, the first of the islands to be assaulted during Operation Forager.*

AMERICA'S SUBMARINES

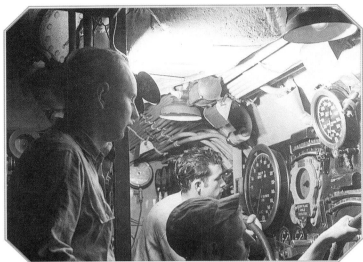

Since January 27, 1942, when the submarine *Gudgeon* scored the first kill on the Japanese submarine *I-173* west of Midway, the undersea wing of the U.S. Navy had been a struggling service. In the early stages of the war little more than a dozen submarines were on patrol at any one time. Shortage of other vessels made it necessary for submarines to take on rescue and supply missions in the Philippines. This did not upset many commanders because their torpedoes were unreliable, often failed to explode, and sometimes fatally circled back to the vessels that launched them because of defective gyroscopes.

When in 1943 Vice Admiral Charles A. Lockwood took command of the Pacific Fleet's submarines, he fixed the problems and built the squadron into an aggressive strike force. Defective torpedoes were replaced, and boats were fitted with radar capable of operating at night. With Navy code-breakers at work, convoys could be monitored. Soon the toll on Japanese merchant vessels began to mount, often eclipsing 200,000 tons a month.

Convoys leaving the oil-rich Dutch East Indies made spectacular targets. By 1944 three or four submarines working as teams destroyed tankers faster than they could be replaced. During October, sixty-eight U.S. submarines operated off Japan and sent 320,00 tons of shipping to the bottom, but tankers were not the only prey. On the night of November 21 *Sealion*, cruising in Formosa Strait, torpedoed *Kongo*, the first Japanese battleship to be sunk by an American submarine. Six days later *Archerfish* put four torpedoes into the largest aircraft carrier in the world, the 59,000-ton *Shinano*, which sank off Honshu.

By the end of the war, Lockwood had 288 submarines operating in the Pacific. Notwithstanding other manifold duties performed, American submarines sank 4,861,000 tons of Japanese shipping, including one battleship and six carriers.

Guam, and three days later the 2nd Marine Division waded ashore at Tinian. The Seabees moved ashore with heavy equipment and began to expand the airfields to accommodate B-29 Superfortresses. Island by island, the Japanese domination of the Pacific began to wither.

GREATEST NAVAL BATTLE

With the Marianas in American control, Nimitz accelerated his timetable by two months, setting October 20 for a landing on Leyte in the Philippines. Halsey, having succeeded Spruance in command of the Fifth Fleet (now the Third Fleet), and Vice Admiral Thomas C. Kincaid, commanding the Seventh Fleet, both converged on the Philippines to put MacArthur's army safely ashore on Leyte.

Once again the Japanese High Command designed a clever but complicated plan called SHO-1 to eliminate the American naval threat and smash MacArthur's landing. Having little choice in the matter, the Imperial Navy staked everything on one decisive battle. Losing the Philippines would deprive Japan of the resources she needed to continue the war.

Left: *The fighting had barely ended on Saipan when the battleships and cruisers of Task Force 58, commanded by Rear Adm. Richard L. Connolly, opened on Guam. This picture was shot from the lookout's position on the forward superstructure of the USS* New Mexico.

The Imperial High Command divided the Japanese fleet into three squadrons. Admiral Ozawa commanded the "Northern Force" consisting of four carriers, two hybrid battleship-carriers, three light cruisers, and eight destroyers. Ozawa would be the decoy, using his carriers to lure Halsey's Third Fleet hundreds of miles north of the Leyte beachhead. As Halsey fell for the bait, Vice Admiral Takeo Kurita's "Center Force" of five battleships, twelve cruisers, and fifteen destroyers would attack through San Bernardino Strait. Simultaneously, a third "Southern Force," divided between Vice Admirals Shoji Nishimura and Kiyohide Shima, consisting of two battleships, three carriers, four cruisers, and eleven destroyers, would enter through Surigao Strait and with Kurita's squadron converge on Kincaid's Seventh Fleet and MacArthur's landing force. The ensuing four actions in terms of men, planes, ships, and distances traveled, stands today as the greatest naval battle in history.

CONFUSION, BUT SUCCESS

On October 24 the Imperial Navy's complicated strategy incurred its first setback when planes from Halsey's Third Fleet discovered Kurita's Center Force coming through the Sibuyan Sea and sank the battleship *Musashi*, and the destroyer *Wakabe*, and disabled the cruiser *Myoko*. On the following afternoon Halsey's planes spotted Ozawa's Northern Force off Luzon. Thinking that his bombers had stopped

Kurita in the Sibuyan Sea, Halsey took the bait and chased after Ozawa.

Because of miscommunications, Admiral Kincaid believed that Halsey had left part of the Third Fleet at San Bernardino Strait, so he made no effort to cover it with the Seventh Fleet. As a consequence, Kurita's Center Force steamed uncontested through the strait on the morning of October 25 and fell upon six little escort carriers under Rear Admiral Clifton F. Sprague, who immediately launched his planes and called for help. Aside from his few planes, Sprague had only three destroyers and four destroyer escorts to pit against Kurita's battleships and cruisers.

Below: *On November 25, 1944, the signalman on the deck of the aircraft carrier* Hancock *gives the go-ahead to the pilot of a Helldiver taking off to strike Japanese positions in Manila bay.*

JUNE 21: Okinawa is secured.

JULY 1: Naval operations begin against the Japanese home islands.

AUGUST 6-9: The first atomic bombs fall on Hiroshima and Nagasaki.

AUGUST 15: V-J Day – the Japanese surrender.

AUGUST 28: The occupation of Japan begins.

Right: *During the Marianas Turkey Shoot, a Japanese bomber goes down in flames as it attempts to strike the American carrier shown in the distance.*

Right: *Most Japanese committed suicide rather than face capture. On October 24, 1944, a few prisoners taken in Leyte Gulf are brought aboard* New Jersey *for questioning by a Third Fleet intelligence officer.*

Though Americans suffered heavy losses during the battle off Samar, Sprague's aircraft sank three of Kurita's heavy cruisers. Having lost two flagships, and rattled by Sprague's fierce attack, Kurita imagined that he was facing heavy combat carriers and withdrew.

Later in the day off Cape Engaño, planes from Halsey's Third Fleet located Ozawa's Northern Force and attacked. Soon after launch, Halsey received a curt message from Nimitz ordering him to send his fast battleships back to San Bernardino Strait. Halsey came about but left most of Mitscher's carriers with a cruiser-destroyer screen to pursue Ozawa. Mitscher's force sank all four of Ozawa's carriers and two destroyers.

Forewarned that Nishimura's Southern Force was heading for the Surigao Strait, Admiral Kincaid ordered Rear Admiral Jesse B. Oldendorf to deploy six old battleships salvaged from Pearl Harbor across the northern end of the strait. Nishimura started through the strait shortly after midnight on October 24, only to run into a hornet's nest of PT-boats and destroyers that promptly sank the battleship *Fuso*, damaged *Yamashiro*, and sank two destroyers. Oldendorf's battleships opened with radar-directed 14- and 16-inch shells on the remnants of Nishimura's fleet and sent the battered survivors across the Mindanao Sea. At that moment, Shima's cruiser and destroyer column came in sight and, upon seeing the remains of Nishimura's fleet, turned tail without ever firing a shot. For Oldendorf, it was a heartwarming victory won in part by the grand old battleships resurrected after being put out of action at Pearl Harbor.

KAMIKAZE ATTACKS

After fighting four battles on October 24-25, the Imperial Japanese Navy no longer existed as a cohesive fighting force, but a new desperation became manifest in the Leyte Gulf when Japan launched its first *kamikaze* attacks. On October 26, suicide planes flown by young, inexperienced pilots crashed into five escort carriers, sinking *St. Lo. Kamikazes*, the enemy's "Heavenly Wind,"

would soon become the most deadly anti-ship weapon of the war.

While MacArthur's forces mopped up the Philippines, Mitscher took his eleven fleet carriers north and on February 16 began striking installations around Tokyo. Three days later he was back at Iwo Jima to support the landing of Marines on that eight-square-mile volcanic island. The bombardment became the heaviest of the Pacific war. Nimitz wanted Iwo because the island lay midway between Saipan and Tokyo and would provide an airbase 660 miles from Japan's capital. The month-long battle took the lives of 5,981 Marines, and wounded 19,920 more, the Corps' costliest campaign of the war.

COSTLY OKINAWA CAMPAIGN

On March 26, two days after securing Iwo Jima, 10 battleships, 7 heavy and 3 light cruisers, and 32 destroyer and destroyer escorts opened on Okinawa, augmented later by Spruance's entire Fifth Fleet. On April 1 the Marines waded ashore with slight resistance. Five days later a storm of *kamikazes* filled the sky in a massive suicide attack on the American fleet. Admiral Soemu Toyoda, commander of the Japanese Combined Fleet, hoped to have 4,500 aircraft to repel the attack, but all he could muster were 699, including 355 *kamikazes*. In the first attack, Navy planes knocked down 400 enemy aircraft. While weathering six *kamikaze* attacks, the Okinawa campaign cost the Navy dearly, losing 34 ships, 368 damaged, with a butcher's bill of 4,900 sailors killed or missing and another 4,800 wounded.

In the last sortie by the Imperial Navy, the Japanese turned their dwindling Navy loose as surface *kamikazes*, sending ships to Okinawa with only enough oil for a one-way trip. In little more than two hours, Mitscher's carrier aircraft sank the 68,000-ton super-battleship *Yamato*, a light cruiser, and four destroyers.

After the conquest of Okinawa on June 21, American carriers ranged almost at will off the Japanese coast, launching sorties to bomb airfields, supply dumps, and railroads. After having penned themselves inside a cordon of mines and submarines to await the American invasion, all last-ditch efforts ended when on August 6 the "Enola Gay" flattened the city of Hiroshima by dropping the first atomic bomb. Three days later a second atomic bomb leveled Nagasaki.

Above: *On September 2, 1945, officers and enlisted men congregate on the deck of the USS Missouri to witness the Japanese surrender ceremony in Tokyo Bay.*

Left: *On April 6, 1945, the Japanese begin their kamikaze attacks against the U.S. fleet engaged in shelling Okinawa. The attacks continued through April and into May. On April 28 a kamikaze Zero is caught as it maneuvers in an effort to strike the deck of the USS Missouri.*

CHAPTER SEVEN

WORLD WAR II
CONQUERING THE ATLANTIC

Admiral Harold R. Stark's reference to the United States entry into the war being "when," not "whether," stemmed from two diplomatic actions occurring in March, 1941, both having been urged by British Prime Minister Winston Churchill in conversations with President Roosevelt. On March 11 Congress passed the Lend-Lease Act, enabling the United States to supply the Allied Powers with war materials on credit or loan. Sixteen days later military representatives of the United States and Great Britain signed the ABC-1 Staff Agreement, stating that if America entered the war both countries would first concentrate their resources on the defeat of Germany. ABC-1 also provided that British and American chiefs of staff would work together as combined chiefs of staff, and that the U.S. Atlantic Fleet would assist the Royal Navy in Atlantic convoy escort, and for all practical purposes, immediately. The two actions marked the end of America's fictitious neutrality and the beginning of an undeclared war on Germany. At the time, Adolph Hitler was too busy preparing to attack the Soviet Union to digest these unneutral acts.

> '*It is not believed that Germany, government or people, want war. The building up of the armed forces is primarily for a show of German strength at diplomatic conferences...*'
>
> NAVAL ATTACHÉ, BERLIN, JUNE 22, 1938.

Such pacts with Great Britain were bound to draw the United States into war with Germany. U-boats operating in the Atlantic had been ripping apart convoys and sinking the escorts. With American destroyers already actively aiding the Royal Navy in the hunt for U-boats, encounters were bound to occur. On September 4 the destroyer USS *Greer* located *U-652* on sonar and tracked her for nine hours, guiding British aircraft to the spot. *U-652* fired a torpedo, which missed, and *Greer* replied with a spread of depth charges. Neither vessel harmed the other, but three days later in the Gulf of Suez, German aircraft sank *Steel Seafarer*, an unarmed American merchant ship.

On the sinking of *Steel Seafarer*, Roosevelt announced, "We have sought no shooting war with Hitler. We do not seek it now. But neither do we seek peace so much that we are willing to pay for it by permitting him to attack our naval and merchant ships. Let this warning be clear. From now on, if German or Italian vessels of war enter the waters the protection of which is necessary for American defense, they do so at their own peril."

NAVY PILOTS ASSIST ALLIES

In addition to destroyers, the U.S. Navy also lent its pilots. When the 50,000-ton German battleship *Bismarck* and the cruiser *Prinz Eugen* slipped through the British blockade and escaped into the Atlantic, the battle-cruiser HMS *Hood* and the battleship HMS *Prince of Wales* caught up with them on May 24, 1941, between Iceland and Greenland in the Denmark Strait. In a sharp battle, *Bismarck* sank *Hood*, severely damaged *Prince of Wales*, and disappeared into the ocean.

On May 26, Ensign Leonard B. Smith, on loan from the U.S. Navy and flying co-pilot on an American-built PBY reconnaissance plane, spotted *Bismarck* 750 miles west of Brest, France, and radioed her location to the Royal Navy. The British dispatched ships and planes and on the following day sent *Bismarck* to the bottom after one of the most desperate pursuits during the Battle of the Atlantic.

Right: Survivors from the sinking Bismarck struggle *in the water as they reach for ropes dropped to them from an Allied warship.*

Left: *Enormous convoys, often containing a hundred ships, plow through the U-boat infested waters of the North Atlantic, zigzagging in an effort to escape from torpedo attacks.*

After publicly announcing his position, Roosevelt turned to the Navy with orders to "shoot on sight" any intruder that threatened American or foreign shipping under escort. The warning did nothing to dissuade Hitler's U-boats. On October 17 *U-586* torpedoed the USS *Kearny* and sent the destroyer limping into Iceland. On October 31, *U-562* fired a torpedo into the old destroyer *Reuben Jones* and split her in half, killing 115 officers and men, many of whom burned to death or suffocated in blazing oil as they jumped into the ocean. On November 7 Admiral Stark, CNO, grimly observed that, "The Navy is already at war in the Atlantic, but the country doesn't seem to realize it."

"WAR WARNING"

Eighteen days later – one day before the Imperial Japanese Navy's carrier force departed for Pearl Harbor – Stark observed that neither the president nor Cordell Hull "would be surprised over a Japanese surprise attack." Without waiting for events to unravel further, on November 27 Stark sent a "war warning" message to the commanders of the Atlantic, Pacific, and Asiatic fleets. Ten days later, while Stark waited for the war to erupt in the Atlantic, all hell broke loose over Honolulu.

Roosevelt declared war on Germany, Italy, and Japan. After some reflective thought regarding the impact of America's entry into World War I, Germany and Italy declared war on the United States on December 11.

> '*The question as to our entry into the war now seems to be when, not whether.*'
>
> ADMIRAL STARK TO ADMIRAL KIMMEL,
> APRIL 3, 1941.

Technology had radically improved since World War I. Twenty-four years earlier, U-boats operated independently and without guidance. In World War II, that all changed. Admiral Karl Dönitz organized wolf packs of up to twenty submarines and sent them into the North Atlantic to wait for radioed instructions on the tracks of con-

Below: *Standing watch in the cold, storm-lashed North Atlantic, sailors on board the USS* Greer *maintain a constant vigil for the telltale signs of an enemy periscope.*

1941

MARCH 11: Congress passes the Lend-Lease program.

MARCH 27: The ABC-1 Staff Agreement is signed, giving the war against Germany top priority.

MAY 21: The freighter *Robin Moore* becomes the first U.S. merchant vessel sunk by a U-boat.

JUNE 12: The U.S. Naval Reserve is mobilized.

voys. U-boat commanders surfaced at dark, received directions, and set their courses, using faster surface speeds to intercept a convoy. After the attack, they submerged to avoid surface detection but kept on the heels of the convoy. After escort vessels gave up the hunt, U-boats struck again, sometimes covering a thousand miles of ocean in repeated raids.

Once Germany declared war, Dönitz wasted no time initiating an offensive in American coastal waters. On January 12, 1942, the same day that Congress authorized 500,000 men for the U.S. Navy, one of Germany's six Type IX long-range submarines sank the 10,000-ton merchant carrier *Cyclops* off Cape Sable, Nova Scotia. Six days later two torpedoes from another U-boat sank the Standard Oil tanker *Allan Jackson* off Cape Hatteras, sending 72,870 barrels of Columbian crude to the bottom. Dönitz soon solved the prob-

> '*The conditions have to be described as almost of peacetime standards…. [One] Commander found such an abundance of opportunities for attack in the sea south of New York to Cape Hatteras that he could not possibly use them all. At the time up to ten ships were in sight sailing with lights on peacetime courses.*'
>
> DÖNITZ REPORT,
> FEBRUARY 20, 1942.

lem of distance, sending 1,700-ton "milch cow" submarines with fresh supplies of fuel and torpedoes to U-boats operating off the American coast. He promised the Fuehrer that by April 1, 1942, his U-boats would sink no less than one million tons of Allied shipping.

"AMERICAN SHOOTING SEASON"

During what U-boat commanders called the "American Shooting Season," ordinary seaman Robert Peck came into a Delaware port and related how a big American liner had been torpedoed one hundred miles off the coast as she bucked a head gale and waves that topped twenty feet. After the explosion, only one of four lifeboats crammed with twenty passengers cleared the doomed vessel. The survivors included a three-year-old girl, her mother, and several other women. Within ten days half the men had died, and with no weights to sink the bodies the corpses drifted on the surf near the boat. When the child's mother died from exposure, the girl flew into hysterics, screaming over and over again, "Please don't throw my Mummy in the water. Please don't." Dönitz's commanders were out to get their tonnage, regardless of whether the targeted vessel carried oil or young mothers with helpless children.

Right: *In November 1943, a lookout on a submarine ranging off the coast of New England keeps a sharp eye on the sky for approaching aircraft.*

'Without warning of any kind the ship was suddenly struck by a torpedo on her starboard side, forward of the bridge, at her number No. 3 tank, setting the oil afire. At that time the vessel was proceeding generally in a northeasterly direction, about 80 miles off the Delaware Capes. The sea was bad, with a strong northeasterly wind. It was snowing hard, making the visibility two miles at best....The master ordered me to get the two amidships boats ready for lowering.
Weather conditions were fierce, with the snowstorm and dangerous northwest seas running. Everyone in the boat was suffering from cold, due mostly to lack of clothes. The men in lifeboat No. 2 died one after another until February 5, when Chief mate Einar A. Nilsson and myself were the only ones alive.
On the morning of February 6, Nilsson showed signs of weakness and extreme fatigue. At about 9:30 a.m. I sighted a steamer coming close to us and made every effort, waving and hailing, to get her attention, as she seemed to go past, but finally she hove around, headed for us and picked us up.'

FROM SECOND MATE SYDNEY WAYLAND'S REPORT, FEBRUARY 28, 1942.
(Nilsson died on February 10. Second Mate Sydney Wayland, the only survivor, left the Halifax hospital on February 28.)

The United States had never prepared for U-boat attacks in coastal waters. The Navy had spent too much money building carriers, battleships, and cruisers, and too little on building sub-chasers. On November 1, 1941, the U.S. Coast Guard became part of the Navy, but it was too small to pick up the slack. Cutters were few and not equipped for war. The Navy mounted the larger vessels with Spencer depth charges and attached the cutters to trans-oceanic convoys.

U-BOATS OFF THE EAST COAST

To stop coastal attacks, the Navy refitted derelicts from World War I – wooden Eagle boats, auxiliary craft, and even private yachts for inshore convoy service. Old World War I sub-chasers were no match for 770-ton German Type VIIC U-boats, which at 220 feet were twice as long, could cruise on the surface at 17 knots, and make 8 knots submerged. They carried four bow torpedo tubes, one stern tube, a 20mm antiaircraft cannon, Twin Flak on deck, and had a cruising range of 8,500 miles. The Navy put top priority on building a fleet of destroyer escorts and escort carriers using freighter hulls, but months passed before the ships were ready with trained crews.

U-boats prowled thirty miles offshore, where at night commanders could find their victims silhouetted against the glow of city lights. When struck, a torpedoed tanker erupted in a fireball, pitching thick, black smoke into the sky, setting the sea ablaze, and cluttering Atlantic beaches with oil, refuse, smashed boats, and charred

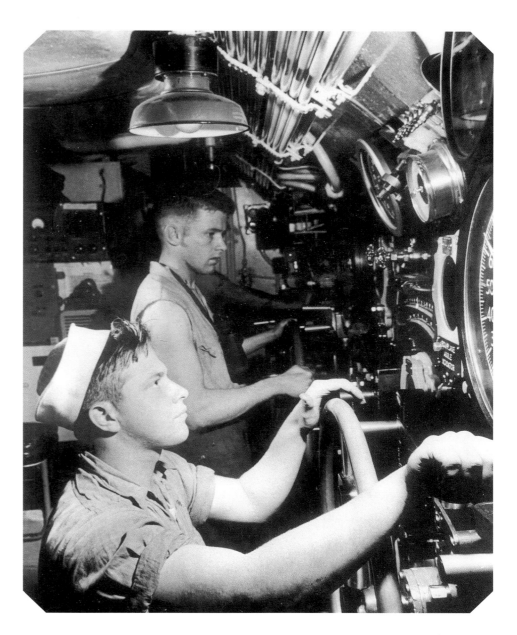

pieces of human remains.

Survivors plucked from the sea came into port oil-smeared, half-naked, badly burned, and exhausted. "Give us guns!" they hollered, adding with grim determination, "I'm shipping out again." In ordinary times many of these men were drifters, drunks, and brawlers. Being torpedoed rejuvenated a fierce pride, for they had found a common enemy, one that had destroyed all their earthly possessions. Out of misery, anger, and hatred came a new patriotism. When posters began appearing on waterfront grog shops, reading, "A SLIP OF THE LIP MAY SINK A SHIP," the sailor who made his living on the sea echoed, "Amen."

By tuning into certain wave bands, U-boats could pick up information being transmitted from coastal defense stations to ships at sea. Allied air patrols announced not only the route of their planes but also their time schedule. Where rescue work was in process following an attack, passing freighters freely announced their positions. After eighty freighters went to the bottom off the United States' East Coast during the month of February, the Navy borrowed bombers and blimps from the Army and began more extensive patrols. Not until March 1, 1942, did the Navy

Above: A pair of young sailors man controls on the USS Capelin (SS-289), adjusting the diving planes on orders from the captain.

SEPTEMBER 11: Roosevelt issues orders to "shoot on sight" any ship that threatens American vessels.

SEPTEMBER 16: The first American-led escorts begin.

SEPTEMBER 27: The first Liberty ship is launched.

NOVEMBER 1: The Coast Guard is placed under the Navy.

NOVEMBER 17: Congress authorizes the arming of merchant ships.

Right: *During late 1942 the Germans produced about twenty U-boats a month, among them the utilitarian Type VIIC. Most of the VIIC class U-boats were manned by new recruits, not the seasoned veterans from earlier in the war. Though the VIICs performed as well as the longer range U-boats, their commanders preferred the older models.*

> '*Coming topside for the dawn watch, it is a recurring wonder to see the same ships day after day, each in her appointed station, each with her characteristic top-hamper, bow-wave, lift and dip; the inevitable straggler, the inveterate smoker, the vessel with an old shellback master who 'knew more about shipping forty years ago than any goddam gold-braid in a tin can,' and whose sullen fury at being convoyed translates itself into belated turns, unanswered signals and insolent comebacks.* '
>
> LIEUTENANT COMMANDER SAMUEL ELIOT MORISON,
> *THE TWO-OCEAN WAR.*

report its first U-boat kill when Patrol Wing 82 sank *U-656* south of Newfoundland.

The Navy was slow to respond to the flurry of disasters. Not until mid-May did daylight coastal navigation rules came into play. Ships sailing between Maine and Delaware Bay spent the night in Boston or New York. Farther south, where no such convenient stopping places existed, the government built artificial ports — huge pens consisting of booms and submarine nets spaced 125 miles apart. As night approached, the Navy's old 1918 destroyers herded freighters and tankers through the minefields and into the pens, and in the morning escorted them back to sea. Soon after the Navy turned up the heat on U-boats off the East Coast, Dönitz sent them south. A few submarines with a "milch cow" concentrated in the Gulf of Mexico, and in May, using charts supplied by the German consul at New Orleans, sank

220,000 tons of shipping. The toll continued, and America faced a new crisis — replacing the freighters and tankers lost during the first months of the war.

On September 27, 1941, *Patrick Henry*, the first of America's Liberty ships, went into commission. In 1938 the Maritime Commission had begun replacing obsolete merchant vessels with faster ships, but the program called for only fifty new vessels a year. After the United States officially entered the war, the program of replacement — this time for sunken vessels — mushroomed to 300 tankers and 2,000 Liberty or Victory ships, a total of 24,000,000 tons to be delivered in 1942 and 1943. Creating the new construction took time, but by the end of the war shipyards had produced 30,000,000 tons of merchant shipping for transporting men, arms, and supplies across the oceans.

DESTROYER ESCORTS

The once elegant Cunard liners like *Queen Mary* and *Queen Elizabeth*, which Britain converted to transports, could sprint across the Atlantic at 26 knots and did not need escort vessels, but Liberty ships did. Shore-based air patrols discouraged U-boat attacks along America's coast but could do nothing once convoys reached the mid-Atlantic. Here U-boat wolf packs congregated and continued their attacks on shipping. The Navy answered with the destroyer escort, a fast ship averaging 1,300 tons that could release conventional destroyers from convoy duty, and the escort carrier, which could bring planes into waters beyond the reach of shore-based aircraft.

In 1942, between August and December, U-boats sank 500,000 tons of shipping a month. In March, 1943, they reached high tide, sinking 567,000 tons of Allied shipping, losing only six U-boats. As one British Admiralty officer observed, "The Germans never came so near disrupting communications between the Old World and the New as in the first twenty days of March 1943."

But then the escort carriers became available and began patrolling the danger zone. They intercepted convoys on the edge of one protected zone and conducted them to an air umbrella covering the next protected area. When not engaged in convoy duty, escort carrier planes flew independent hunter-killer missions, and in the first six months of 1943 sank 150 U-boats.

Armed merchant ships, sailing on their own without the protection of destroyers, were always at risk. On September 27, 1942, the Liberty Ship *Stephen Hopkins*, commanded by Captain Paul Buck, fell in with two German surface ships in the South Atlantic – *Stier*, armed with six 5.9-inchers, and *Tannenfels*, a blockade runner. *Hopkins*, armed with only a 4-inch gun served by a Navy detachment under Lieutenant Kenneth M. Willett, fought a furious battle. Both ships went down. Of *Hopkins*'s survivors, only 15 men reached Brazil after thirty-one days in a lifeboat.

The Battle of the Atlantic became more than a cat and mouse game between escorts and U-boats;

it became a race between rival technologies. German scientists developed an acoustical torpedo which, when fired into a convoy, headed for the screws of the noisiest vessel. Admiral King's so-called Tenth Fleet, a Scientific Council made up of America's distinguished civilian scientists, responded with noisemakers that could be towed so that they attracted enemy torpedoes away from a ship's propellers.

SONAR AND RADAR

The chief battle became one of detection. The Navy entered the war with two submarine detectors they constantly improved – sonar, which bounced supersonic waves against hulls of submerged U-boats, and radar, which bounced radio waves off hulls when U-boats surfaced to charge their batteries. German scientists responded with rubber-coated submarines and other devices, none of which worked well. Radar became the terror of the U-boat commander. After the German surrender, Dönitz admitted that plane-directing radar, "next to the atomic bomb, was the most decisive weapon of the war." Germany found a partial answer to radar detection when her scientists developed the *schnorkel*, a breathing mechanism that allowed U-boats to charge their batteries without surfacing, but the device came too late in the war.

In 1943 U.S. Navy destroyer escorts, fitted with

Left: *The Type IXC U-boat, such as the captured* U-505, *was among the largest models produced by the Germans but was still too small to take on survivors of its victims. In June 1944, sailors on board the escort carrier USS* Guadalcanal *(CVE-60) watch as the captured* U-505 *is taken in tow. The submarine later entered service in the U.S. Navy as* Nemo, *and is now preserved in Chicago.*

▶ **1942**

JANUARY 14:
Roosevelt authorizes
the invasion of French
North Africa.

MARCH 1: The Navy
sinks its first U-boat,
U-656.

MARCH 25: Task
Force 39 is sent to
reinforce the Royal
Navy.

JUNE 26: Germany
announces
unrestricted
submarine warfare off
the American coast.

*Right: Across the
dungaree work
uniform of the regular
sailor are earphones,
microphone, and
(right) steel talker's
helmet used by the
gun crew. The M1
helmet (top left) is
adorned with folk art.
Below the helmets are
the regulation belt
with knife, scabbard
and canteen and a
pair of M1938 pattern
leggings issued to the
Seabees.*

the new forward-firing "hedgehogs," were equipped with high-frequency direction finders. The device enabled the ship to pick up radio transmissions between Dönitz's headquarters and the wolf pack, thereby pinpointing a U-boat's position. Allied engineers also developed the sonobuoy. Dropped in the water where a U-boat had submerged, the sonobuoy communicated signals to any nearby aircraft, its automatic radio-sender broadcasting sonar sounds directly into the cockpit of the prowling aircraft.

Convoys bore the brunt of the war at sea. As the ships crossed the storm-beaten tracks of the North Atlantic, officers and sailors on escort vessels suffered right along with the men of the Merchant Marine. Brutal weather, constant vigilance, cold food, little sleep, and the steady pinging of sonar gear kept everyone on edge. Surviving the tension and fatigue brought sailors to the verge of nervous breakdowns.

The turning point came in late April, 1943, after a forty-two-ship convoy, west-bound

The number of Allied ships sunk for each U-boat destroyed rapidly dropped.			
1940	26	1943	2
1941	16	1944	0.8
1942	13	1945	0.4

across the North Atlantic, encountered fifty-six U-boats stretched in four groups across the middle of the ocean. The wolf packs sank twelve merchant ships but lost ten U-boats, five from depth charges, three by patrol planes, two by accidental self-inflicted collision. Forty-one of 120 U-boats at sea failed to return home. Dönitz later admitted that at this point he realized that Germany had lost the Battle of the Atlantic.

Minimizing the U-boat threat made the transfer

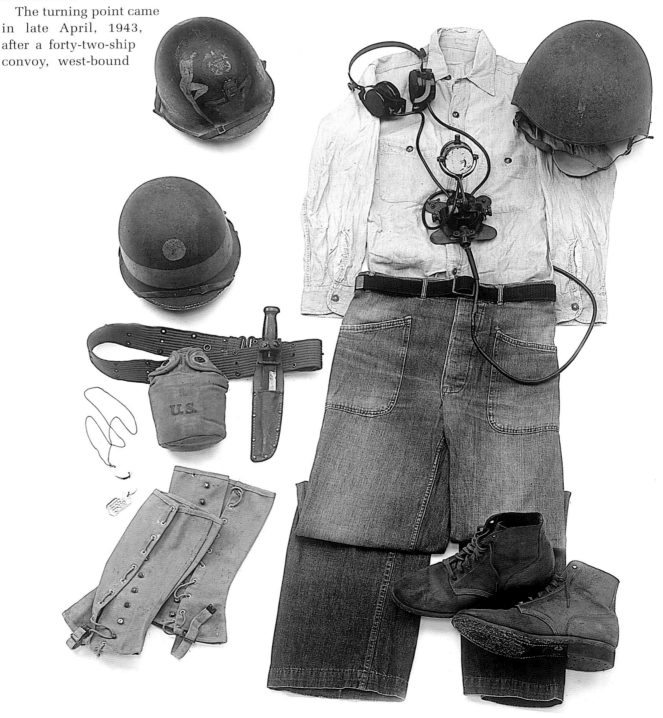

of troops from the United States to Africa and Europe less risky. It was the Navy's job to make these passages safe for transports, landing craft, and supply vessels, and then get the men ashore by providing an accurate cover of gunfire.

INVASION OF NORTH AFRICA

Long before the United States entered the war, British troops had been fighting in Egypt and Libya. In 1941 Britain laid plans for an invasion of French North Africa in order to keep the Axis out of the area. With America's entry into the war, these plans were expanded to include the naval and ground forces of the United States with simultaneous landings on Morocco and the Mediterranean coast of Algeria. The combined chiefs of staff projected the invasion for the summer of 1942 and considered it essential as a prelude to opening a second front on continental Europe. North Africa could provide bases for operations in the Mediterranean and reopen the sea to Allied shipping. The expedition would also reveal any shortcomings in amphibious landings that needed to be corrected before more massive campaigns could be tackled.

Uncertainty surrounded the North African invasion because of the unpredictability of the Vichy French. Would they resist an Allied landing or welcome it? Admiral Jean Darlan, commanding the French Navy, posed a major concern because he had notoriously collaborated with the Axis. Would he fight or contribute his warships to the common cause? Britain and the United States were also concerned about the French generals, each of whom aspired for control of the government through the military. The United States sent secret operatives into Algeria to strike a deal, but neither party trusted the other.

The combined chiefs of staff named Lieutenant General Dwight D. Eisenhower the United States commander in chief of the Allied force with British Admiral Sir Andrew Cunningham as his chief naval subordinate. The plan called for assaults on Casablanca on the Atlantic coast and on Oran and Algiers on the Mediterranean coast. At French Morocco, Admiral H. Kent Hewitt would put ashore troops under Major General George S. Patton at points north and south of Casablanca, while battleships and cruisers would contain the French fleet in the harbor. In the Mediterranean, British naval units would support landings of American and British troops at Oran and Algiers.

In late October, 1942, the Western Task Force of ninety-nine vessels and the first wave of 37,000 troops set out from Hampton Roads. On November 7, after taking a circuitous route to the south, the battleships *Massachusetts*, *New York*, and *Texas,* the carrier *Ranger*, four escort carriers, seven cruisers, twenty-eight transports and cargo

vessels, along with destroyers, mine-sweepers, and auxiliary craft, appeared off the coast of French Morocco. On the same day the Center and Eastern Task Forces – 170 vessels carrying 49,000 Americans and 23,000 British troops – passed through the Straits of Gibraltar and approached Oran and Algiers.

Above: Off St. Tropez on August 17, 1944, sailors aboard a U.S. Navy supply ship tackle the job of lowering a tank destroyer into an LST tied alongside.

ALLIED TROOPS ASHORE

At dawn, November 8, landing operations began at Fedala, Lyautey, and Safi in French Morocco. At Fedala cruisers and destroyers covered the landings, and rocket boats moved in with the first wave to silence shore batteries. Early that afternoon the French garrison surrendered. By November 10 the Navy had put 160,000 troops and 70 tanks ashore, all of which moved toward Casablanca.

Near Lyautey, eighteen waves of small, flat-bottomed landing boats got ashore before being discovered. When French artillery opened on the landing party, *Texas*, *Savannah*, and three destroyers replied with heavy salvoes. A few French planes attempted to strafe the American positions but were driven away by twenty Wildcat fighters. Troops from the French Foreign

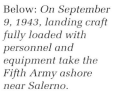

▶ **July 20:** Admiral William D. Leahy becomes Roosevelt's chief of staff and Chairman of the Joint Chiefs of Staff.

November 8-10: American ground forces land in French North Africa.

Right: *In Bagnoli Harbor, the 3rd Infantry Division prepares for the invasion of southern France. With backpacks fully loaded, the troops file on board waiting landing craft for another practice landing exercise.*

Below: *On September 9, 1943, landing craft fully loaded with personnel and equipment take the Fifth Army ashore near Salerno.*

Legion supported by tanks attacked but were driven off by Navy planes. After Army Rangers seized the airfield near Lyautey, all resistance ended.

To the south, destroyer escorts covered by *New York*, *Philadelphia*, and three destroyers led landing craft right into the harbor at Safi. By nightfall November 8, Americans had possession of the city and its docks. Two days later a column supported by tanks began moving north along the

coast, with *Philadelphia* and two destroyers following to provide protection.

The most serious problem for the U.S. Navy was the unpredictability of the French fleet at Casablanca. American battleships, cruisers, and destroyers had been detached to cover landings, leaving *Massachusetts*, *Wichita*, *Tuscaloosa*, and four destroyers with the considerable task of covering a French fleet composed of the battleship *Jean Bart*, a cruiser, ten destroyers, eleven submarines, and three sloops. At daybreak on November, French planes attacked half-heartedly and were driven off by antiaircraft fire. When shore batteries and ships in the harbor opened, Admiral Hewitt responded with a furious bombardment that sank three submarines, damaged a destroyer, knocked out a battery on *Jean Bart*, and left the battleship resting on the bottom.

French Surrender

During the bombardment, French submarines, seven destroyers, and a cruiser sortied from the harbor, ran into the supporting Navy group at Fedala and, in an action dominated by American carrier planes, lost every surface ship except for one destroyer. On November 11 the French naval commander at Casablanca surrendered the remnants of this fleet. Two nights later unidentified submarines torpedoed seven American transports in the Casablanca-Fedala area, and, for reasons of diplomacy, the attacks were credited at the time to the Axis and not the French.

In the Mediterranean the prize was the heavily fortified port of Oran, where Admiral Darlan kept the bulk of the French Navy. On the morning of November 8 the Center Naval Task Force, composed mainly of British ships, drew the task of putting 39,000 American troops ashore in flanking positions around the harbor. The French resisted at Oran without much enthusiasm and most fortified positions fell with little loss to either side. The Eastern Task Force encountered trouble at Algiers, mainly from Germans. On November 10 Admiral Darlan surrendered all French forces, and a few days later the admiral of the French fleet at Toulon ordered his naval commanders to scuttle their ships rather than have them fall into German hands.

LANDINGS MISTAKES

French troops not wanting to fight led to an easy victory for the Allies, but the U.S. Navy made mistakes. In many instances assault waves landed far away from the designated beaches. In the Algiers assault, 94 percent of the landing craft were lost or damaged by mishandling, giving rise to the development of the LST (Landing Ship Tank), a vessel uniquely designed to put rapidly ashore any combination of troops, artillery, and tanks. While the Army fought in the desert, the Navy went back to the drawing board, established new training techniques, and formulated plans for moving the war into Europe.

Operation Husky, the invasion of Sicily, had to wait. In mid-February, 1943, the German Afrika Korps struck untried American troops at Kasserine Pass and almost split the Allied forces in two. Two fresh divisions raced to the rescue from Oran and helped push 238,000 Germans and Italians into the Cape Bon Peninsula of Tunisia, where on May 11 they surrendered. The delay gave the Navy time to move 2,500 vessels, 4,000 aircraft, and 250,000 troops into the newly established North African bases.

For the first time, the Navy planned to use LSTs, LCIs, and LCTs to put an amphibious force ashore on Sicily. The new craft represented a valuable addition, for they could move directly to the beach and land troops without first loading them into boats. Admiral Hewitt's formation stretched for 60 miles across the Mediterranean and was more than a mile wide. Rounding Cape Bon off Tunis, the long line of vessels feinted south before turning north. On the night of July 8 the flotilla crossed the Mediterranean to Malta and sub-divided into three attack forces. Meanwhile, Army Special Forces personnel parachuted into Sicily, and Allied planes bombed enemy airfields and fortified positions in an effort to disrupt communications between Sicily

and Italy across the Straits of Messina.

On D-Day, July 10, the largest amphibious assault in history, in terms of the number of troops put ashore at one time and the extent of coastline under assault, began shortly after midnight. Fourteen hundred ships and landing craft spread across 100 miles put three Seventh Army divisions under General Patton ashore at Licata, Gela, and Scoglitti on Sicily's southwestern coast. Cruisers laid down a heavy barrage on coastal batteries and smashed an armored attack by the Hermann Goering Division as it rumbled toward Gela. On the Sicilian east coast, a British task

Above: During the invasion of southern France in August 1944, two Vought OS2U Kingfisher floatplanes warm-up as they prepare to be launched from the USS Quincy (CA-71).

Left: On August 15, 1944, D-Day for Operation Dragoon, a Navy F6F Hellcat returning from an air support mission over southern France is waved off during an attempted landing on the USS Tulagi (CVE-72).

▶ **1943**

MARCH 1-20: U-boats in the Atlantic reach the high water mark of their depredations against Allied shipping.

MARCH 5: The escort carrier *Bogue* becomes the first of its type exclusively assigned to antisubmarine operations.

MAY 13: The German Army in North Africa surrenders.

Right: *On August 15, 1944, the cruiser USS* Philadelphia *opens fire on the targeted landing sites for Operation Dragoon, the invasion of southern France.*

NAVY BOMBARDMENT AT SALERNO

On D-Day at Salerno, General Mark Clark thought he could get his troops ashore with little trouble, but after landing discovered German 88mm artillery "Looking down our throat" and a herd of enemy tanks cranking toward the infantry's freshly dug foxholes. Out to Rear Admiral Lyal A. Davidson's First Support Group went a belatedly desperate call for fire support. Davidson, a tall, lanky flag officer, firm in decision and quiet of speech, had provided fire support at Safi and again at Palermo. He was said to never lose his temper, but he became privately irked at General Clark for waiting so long to call for help from the Navy.

With his flagship *Philadelphia*, the cruiser *Savannah*, and four destroyers, he moved close inshore and opened on enemy positions, sharpshooting as well as possible while communicating with the few shore fire-control parties still operational. For spotting, he used his own SOC float planes and Mustangs from Sicily airfields. Salvo after salvo began landing on German machine-gun emplacements. When two SOC planes spotted a covey of German tanks hiding in a thicket, *Philadelphia*'s 6-inch guns flushed thirty-five of them, following the tanks with salvos as they fled to the rear. The destroyers *Bristol*, *Edison*, *Ludlow*, and *Woolsey* steamed inshore through minefields. Their accurate fire toppled mobile artillery off their wheels, knocked out heavy artillery units, and devastated bridges. About the time that Admiral Davidson began to wonder whether his ships were actually doing any damage, he received a message from General Lange (Fifth Army): "THANK GOD FOR THE FIRE OF THE NAVY SHIPS X PROBABLY COULD NOT HAVE STUCK IT OUT AT BLUE AND YELLOW BEACHES X BRAVE FELLOWS X PLEASE TELL THEM SO."

force under General Sir Bernard L. Montgomery's Eighth Army landed and made rapid progress, capturing Augusta and Syracuse. Axis losses in Sicily led to the overthrow of Benito Mussolini, and on July 25, King Victor Emanuel III began restoring a non-Fascist Italy.

As Allied forces pushed inland, cruisers and destroyers roved offshore and provided supporting fire. At dawn, enemy aircraft attacked at thirty-minute intervals, sinking the destroyer *Maddox*, plus a minelayer and an ammunition ship, and damaging others. Fighter plane support from Malta and North Africa combined with accurate antiaircraft fire prevented heavier losses. PT-boats patrolled the north coast, preventing the enemy from landing reinforcements and supplies. Six weeks later, August 17, the Sicilian campaign ended with the fall of Messina.

The assault on mainland Italy began on September 3, 1943, when two divisions of the British Eighth Army crossed the Straits of Messina, established a beachhead against light Italian resistance, and began pushing up the Italian boot towards Taranto and the Adriatic.

On the evening of September 8, as an Anglo-American force under Rear Admiral Frank J. Lowry moved towards the Gulf of Salerno, General Eisenhower hoped to throw the Germans into confusion by announcing the surrender of Italy. The armistice had been signed in secret on September 3, not to become effective for five days so as to coincide with the attack at Salerno. The Germans were not surprised. They had already taken over key communication and defense points and stripped the Italians of arms. They also anticipated where Lieutenant General Mark W. Clark's Fifth Army would be put ashore and hunkered into a strong defensive position on the ridges overlooking Salerno Gulf.

At 2:45 a.m. on September 9, Lowry's battleships and cruisers lay off Salerno with guns quiet. The Army protested against a bombardment, thinking it would destroy the element of surprise. Lowry wanted to pulverize hill positions before

Left: *The USS Savannah (CL-42) had her share of trouble. On June 16, 1943, she caught fire in the harbor off Algiers. After being repaired, a radio-controlled glide bomb launched from German aircraft off the Salerno beachhead penetrated three decks and exploded in her lower handling room, killing 197 men and wounding 15 others.*

the Army went ashore, arguing that to attack otherwise would be madness, but the Army would not listen. When the first assault waves moved ashore – the British to the north, the Americans to the south – the Germans let them come. After the beaches became congested with men, material, and equipment, the Germans opened with a deadly crossfire from pillboxes, batteries, and tanks. As the beachhead began to crumble, cruisers and destroyers came inshore and hurled salvo after salvo at enemy positions. Using the barrage as a shield, the assault force moved tentatively toward the ridges and dug in for the night. Early in the morning *Luftwaffe* bombers swooped over the beachhead and began blasting it to pieces. Allied carrier planes and fighters from Sicily threw back the aerial attack while the Allied fleet, directed by spotter planes, bombarded enemy coastal and hill positions. Landing craft rushed more troops and tanks ashore, and by the evening of September 10, Allied forces secured their beachhead and in the morning went on to seize the port of Salerno.

LUFTWAFFE ATTACKS THE NAVY

By September 13 the assault forces had pushed seven miles inland, but the Germans, reinforced by fresh troops under Field Marshal Albert Kesselring, launched a counteroffensive that threatened to drive the invaders into the bay. The Allied lines held through the night, giving the Navy time to come inshore and pound German

positions with a furious bombardment. At this critical stage the *Luftwaffe* made a sudden appearance with their new radio-directed glider bombs and heavily damaged the cruiser *Savannah*. Supported by swarms of planes from Sicily, the Navy held on, and by the end of the day had helped to crush the counteroffensive, forcing the enemy to withdraw to the north. On September 14 General von Vietinghoff, commanding German forces at Salerno, reported to Field Marshal Kesselring, "The attack this morning...had to endure naval gunfire from at least 16 to 18 battleships, cruisers, and large destroyers....With astonishing precision and freedom of maneuver, these ships shot at every recognizable

Below: *On 22 January 1944, DUKWs of the Fifth Army waddle inland to secure the Anzio beachhead while LSTs unload equipment and personnel in the background.*

▶ **MAY 24:** Admiral Karl Dönitz recalls his U-boats from the North Atlantic.

Admiral Ernest J. King establishes the "Tenth Fleet," Washington headquarters for the finest scientific minds in America.

JULY 10: Operation Husky, the invasion of Sicily, begins.

SEPTEMBER 3: Italian government secretly signs an armistice.

SEPTEMBER 9: The Navy lands troops at Salerno.

Right: *As they prepare to assault the coast of Normandy, U.S. troops board LCVPs at Torpoint, Plymouth, in southern England, where they will later transfer to LCTs.*

Below: *On June 1, 1944, as D-Day draws near, men load vehicles and artillery aboard LCTs at Brixham, Devon, in England.*

target with overwhelming effect." On October 13, bolstered by Allied gains, the new Italian government declared war on Germany.

The U.S. Navy followed the Army as it fought north towards the Italian port of Naples. Three weeks later the Germans abandoned the port but left the harbor a wreck, blowing up wharves, warehouses, drydocks, and obstructing the channel with sunken ships, sometimes dropping one on top of the other. Commodore William A. Sullivan of the U.S. Navy went to work clearing the port. His crews blasted most of the sunken vessels out of the way and built causeways over the others, but four months elapsed before Naples became fully operational.

On January 22, 1944, after the enemy stopped the Allied advance at the Gustav Line – a heavily fortified mountainous barrier south of Rome – the combined navies landed a flanking force of three divisions at Anzio, fifty-five miles behind the German front. Taken by surprise, the enemy at first offered little resistance, but soon heavy shells began dropping among the Allied fleet and on the beaches. When the *Luftwaffe* appeared with glider bombs, Allied aircraft from Naples drove them away. Bad weather stopped the offensive and the fight for Anzio settled into a standoff until May, when Cassino fell. The Fifth and Eighth Armies moved forward, made contact with the forces at Anzio, and on June 4 they entered Rome.

NORMANDY LANDINGS

During the months while Allied forces worked through Italy, the greatest invasion force in history came together on the British Isles to assault the French beaches at Normandy. The decision had been made at Casablanca, the plans formulated by the combined chiefs of staff, and in August 1943 were accepted by Roosevelt and Churchill at the Quebec conference. Allotted the southwest quarter of England to prepare for a massive amphibious assault, Americans went through rigorous training as the force continued to multiply in men, equipment, and landing craft.

The Germans had heard about an operation called Overlord and another called Neptune but lacked verifiable details. Admiral Sir Bertram H. Ramsey commanded Neptune, the naval phase of

Left: *Beginning in late May 1944, the great arsenal stored in southern England began moving from camouflaged shore positions onto landing craft. Here M4 Sherman tanks and other gear are loaded onto an LCT, while in the background a gathering of LSTs wait at anchor.*

Overlord. Moving the Americans to the beaches designated Utah and Omaha became the task of the Western Naval Force, 911 ships under Rear Admiral Alan G. Kirk. Admiral Sir Philip Vian, commanding 1,796 ships of the Eastern Naval Task, had the job of moving two British and one Canadian division to beaches designated Gold, Juno, and Sword. Such vast preparations could not be concealed from the Germans, who had built a formidable line of defenses along the French coast facing the English Channel. Reasoning that an invasion of such great magnitude could not be sustained without the use of harbors, the Germans gave particular attention to fortifying Calais. Hitler promised his countrymen that if the enemy should breach the unassailable "Atlantic Wall" and make landings on the French coast, they would stay "exactly nine hours."

General Eisenhower intended to stay much longer, and to guarantee that his forces did, he put emphasis on weakening the *Luftwaffe*. In 1943 American and British air forces began destroying the enemy's aircraft factories. In April, 1944, Eisenhower turned the air arm on German communications in France, blasting airfields, railroads, trains, bridges, and roadways. By D-Day, June 6, 1944, not a bridge remained intact over the Seine between the English Channel and Paris.

While the *Wehrmacht* envisioned Calais as the most likely site for an Allied invasion, the combined chiefs of staff chose Normandy. A drive across the Cotentin Peninsula would seal off the port of Cherbourg, which could be taken later. With beachheads secured on Normandy, a temporary supply line could be established using "Mulberries," artificial harbors prepared in England. The amphibious assault on Europe embodied all the tactical knowledge gleaned from all the preceding invasions in the Atlantic, Pacific, and Mediterranean.

On June 5, after several days' delay because of strong winds and low clouds, General Eisenhower, Supreme Commander of the Allied Expeditionary Force, gave the order that put in motion the assault. Four thousand ships bearing a million men prepared to leave port. A part of the armada had already reached the Channel when storms strong enough to imperil the landings struck, forcing Eisenhower to postpone the invasion. Twenty-four hours later the weather, though far from perfect, had improved enough for the immense operation to get underway.

Before dawn on D-Day, Operation Neptune, the greatest invasion fleet ever assembled, sprang into motion. The American task force under Admiral Kirk sailed for the beaches of Omaha and Utah. Kirk's heavy ships of the American fire support group had already come down from Belfast,

Left: *General Dwight David Eisenhower (1890-1969) had much on his mind during those frantic days of bad weather in the English Channel. As Supreme Commander of the Allied Expeditionary Force for Operation Overlord, he still had much to prove to the Allies. After the war his reward as a capable military strategist, sound tactician, and able administrator earned him two terms as the American president.*

▶ **1944**

JANUARY 22:
Operation Shingle, the
assault at Anzio
begins.

APRIL 28: Secretary
of the Navy Frank
Knox dies in
Washington, D.C.

MAY 19: James V.
Forrestal becomes the
48th Secretary of the
Navy.

Right: *During the war,
the U.S. Coast Guard
had many busy
assignments abroad.
Here members of the
Coast Guard guide a
landing barge ashore
at Normandy.*

Right: *On D-Day,
American troops from
the 9th Infantry
Division clamber from
an LCI to an LCA for
transit to Utah Beach
at Normandy.*

Northern Ireland, and headed for the assembly point off the Isle of Wight, off England's south coast. Further west along the coast, from Falmouth to Poole, ships as far as the eye could see began crossing the Channel to Normandy. From Southampton, Portsmouth, and Newhaven came the British and Canadian forces that would assault the beaches to the east. Landing craft bound for the French coast pounded through the Channel chop under the watchful protection of the Allied navies.

As dawn broke, the guns of 800 ships opened on forty miles of the Normandy coast. One of the ships was the USS *Nevada*, resurrected from the mud at Pearl Harbor, and others were the venerable *Texas* and *Arkansas*, all of them relics from World War I. Thousands of bombers and fighters roared overhead, a thundering prelude to the assault. Veteran battleships, old in age but not technology, fired methodically at targets spotted by fighter planes, an innovation introduced during the Sicilian campaign. Cruisers worked close inshore, their guns illuminating the sky with arcs of light as tracer projectiles streaked toward shore. Here and there scattering flashes from enemy artillery winked along the dim coast. Destroyers moved in closer, replying to enemy fire while keeping a careful watch on the sky for the *Luftwaffe*'s planes. Landing craft specially fitted with rocket launchers opened up near shore, hurling banks of shrieking missiles with flaming tails zooming toward the enemy's fortifications behind the beach.

On cue, two hundred thousand Americans began crowding into cramped landing craft. The men peered occasionally toward a dark shore as the boats bobbed about in the rollers. Destroyers cut through the flanks, keeping the wallowing landing craft bunched together. An officer from the U.S. Coast Guard steered the LSTs and LCTs, keeping in formation with the first wave to hit the beach. One ensign studied the infantrymen packed between the bulwarks and wrote, "A few men quipped jokes that drew a few nervous laughs. Some smoked in quiet, contemplating a

UTAH BEACH

On June 5, 1944, Vice Admiral Morton L. Deyo began bringing his fire support group through the Irish Sea, rounding the light on Land's End, south-west England, and coming parallel with the coast of Cornwall. Changing course to a single column, Deyo's squadron fell in behind the HMS *Enterprise*. At 10:45 a.m. the fleet picked up the 4th Army Division off Plymouth. During the afternoon the battle squadron passed hundreds of five-knotters – a heterogeneous assortment of cutters, corvettes, trawlers, sub-chasers, and blunt-nosed LSTs, all waiting for squalls to slacken off. "For an invasion of this size we had to have a plan," declared Admiral Kirk. "You have to have a plan, and we had a *beautiful* one!" – all but for the weather.

For men packed into LCTs and LSTs, the wait seemed interminable. As dusk gathered, thousands of men rolled, lurched, vomited, and then rolled and lurched some more. Rain sputtered from low clouds, keeping the cramped open decks cold and wet. Robert J. Casey, a Chicago *News* correspondent sitting in an LST off Southampton, overheard a major ask the captain what action station to take. "If you can work an Oerlikon gun you might try that."

"In that case," asked the major, "I might as well know where my abandon ship station is, too."

The captain shrugged, replying, "Stand on the deck, and when the water gets up to your navel, get off."

As darkness fell, Casey recalled hearing "a lot of conversation…about such things as our prospects. I don't think anybody put much value on them." He somehow fell asleep, but at 1:30 a.m. was snapped awake by "an infernal row with the engines, which seemed to be starting and stopping every few minutes." He looked outside and saw dark shapes all around, all seemingly bearing down upon him. "The world seemed filled with ships, ahead of us, behind us, abreast of us…all charging without any more purpose of direction than logs suddenly released from a jam." Landing craft squeezed together so close that at times they bumped. A combination of rollers and wake sent seawater crashing over the bow and beams, so much so that soldiers began to wonder whether the vessel would fill before it reached the coast. The lieutenant merely smiled. "We're crossing a great minefield," he said. "And these ships have to be made to head into it properly. There's a swept channel, of course, if we can get them to take it."

At 4:45 a.m., June 6, fire support ships filed into predetermined positions and opened communications with spotter planes over Normandy beaches. Forty-five minutes later enemy shore batteries opened on the fleet silhouetted against the horizon. Six minutes later Deyo signaled, "Commence counter battery bombardment." From *Tuscaloosa*'s forecastle inside No. 2 turret came the shrill, ascending whirr of an ammunition car traveling upward from the magazines. A metallic thump followed as an 8-inch shell dropped into the loading tray. The clatter of the shell in the breech reverberated through the gun barrel; a blow rammed it against its seat. Nine long, powerful 8-inch rifles moved to the desired elevation. Two buzzes for "Stand by" were followed by one. The entire ship shook as nine 8-inch shells spouted forth in a blaze of fire and smoke.

On the LST the captain cheerfully announced, "D-Day! And we're all here. And we're here on time."

Above: *In one of the first pictures taken of D-Day landings, U.S. infantrymen wade ashore under a screen of protective naval shellfire from cruisers and destroyers that worked so close to shore that their bows kissed the bottom.*

Left: *An LCVP bursts into flame when German machine gun fire explodes hand grenades carried on the vessel, but men of the U.S. Coast Guard pilot the craft safely onto a Normandy beach*

JUNE 6: D-Day for Operation Overlord/Neptune, the Allied landings on Normandy.

JUNE 25: The Navy shells German positions at Cherbourg.

AUGUST 15: Vice Admiral Hewitt lands Allied forces in southern France.

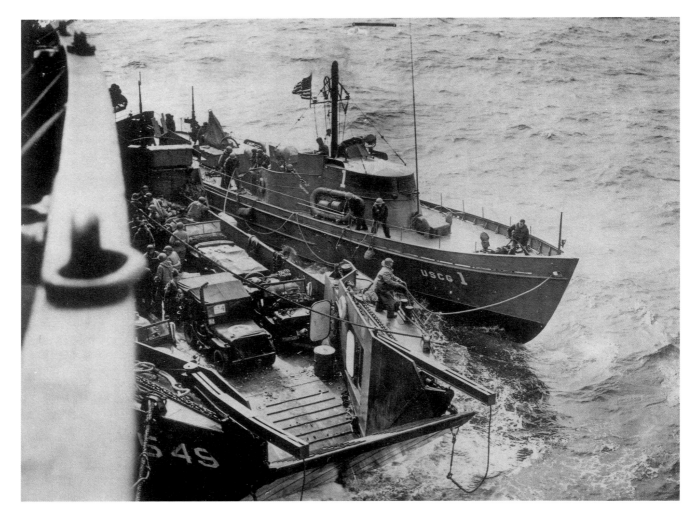

Right: *The Coast Guard brought their cutters across the Atlantic to be used as rescue craft. During the Normandy invasion, they are used to bring the wounded to a waiting LCV.*

Right: *Working from the rail of a cutter, men of the Coast Guard rescue a sailor after his ship had been hit during the landings.*

life that had brought them to this horrific moment in time. Others bent their heads, some in prayer, but most because a queasiness had worked its way to the stomach and minute by minute increased its grip on the landlubbers." The first wave continued to circle the transports until all were loaded. Three thousand yards offshore, they moved to the point of departure. As one observer recalled, "Lights on the control vessels went on – five minutes to go. Then the lights went off and the boats started in."

At Utah Beach on the right flank of the American assault, Navy demolition teams going in with the first wave cleared wide passages through a network of mined underwater obstructions. Fire from cruisers and destroyers using VT-ammunition – deadly to personnel – kept opposition from a completely surprised enemy to a minimum. With only light resistance, the Navy put 21,000 troops from General Omar Bradley's First Army ashore in twelve hours, along with 1,700 vehicles and 1,700 tons of supplies.

MAIN ASSAULT POINT

With the British and Canadian landings farther to the east, Omaha Beach in the center became the main assault point and encountered the stiffest enemy resistance. Demolition teams, under constant fire, lost half their men and were barely able to cut a few narrow passages through an unusually thick maze of offshore hedgehogs and tetrahedrons meshed together with barbed wire. Landing craft were blown up by mines, snagged by underwater obstacles, and blasted out of the water by shore batteries. *Texas* and *Arkansas* continued to pour a hail of shells at casemated gun positions, but the enemy remained resolute inside their pillboxes. A 20-knot southwest wind whipped up the sea off Omaha and made it impossible to get tanks ashore. Lowering clouds and light rain hampered air operations. By

Left: *On June 7 two artificial harbors, nicknamed "Mulberries," were started off the Normandy beaches by sinking concrete caissons. An LST, which took 12 hours to unload on a beach could be unloaded on a Mulberry in an hour. The Normandy coast's lack of port facilities was one reason why the Germans believed the Allies would land near Calais. By the great storm that scoured the channel on June 18-22, Mulberry A off Omaha Beach was rendered unusable.*

chance, an entire German army division happened to be nearby and rushed to the defense.

Bradley's troops continued to wade ashore, but at 4:00 p.m. it seemed that the entire force might be thrown back. Admiral Kirk sent his destroyers so close inshore that "they had their bows against the bottom." From point-blank range the destroyers blasted away at gun positions near the beach and then stepped their fire inland as the Army began to advance. Sailors used fire hoses to cool the barrels of the big guns. Battleships and cruisers offshore, aided by air spotters and Navy fire control units attached to the Army, hit enemy tanks and support vehicles rushing forward to support the battle on the beach.

A MILLION MEN

By early evening, bolstered by tanks and artillery, American troops secured the Omaha beachhead and moved inland. German Marshal Karl von Rundstedt later lamented, "the power of the Allies' naval guns…reached deep inland in the time of the Normandy invasion, making impossible the bringing up of reserves needed to hurl the Allied invasion forces into the Channel." As D-Day ended, follow-up forces arrived and waded ashore with barely any opposition. In less than a month, the Navy poured a million men into France, plus 650,000 tons of supplies, and nearly 200,000 vehicles.

U.S. naval losses on D-Day were light. During the battle for the beachhead three destroyers struck mines and settled offshore, joining the scattered wrecks of a destroyer escort, two transports, two minesweepers, a submarine chaser, and eleven landing craft. A few days later, just as "Mulberries" were being set in place, the worst

three-day storm to strike the English Channel in forty years destroyed or beached more than 300 small craft and wiped out one of the crucial artificial harbors.

The loss of the harbor escalated the importance of securing Cherbourg, further west along the coast. When Bradley's First Army reached the outskirts of the city on June 25, Admiral Deyo's naval support force ranged offshore with three battleships, four cruisers, and eleven destroyers to reduce the enemy's coastal defenses. The Germans answered with 280mm casemated guns and began scoring hits. Allied destroyers laid down a smoke screen, enabling the ships to scatter and maneuver independently. Using spotter planes and fire directed from shore, the squadron hammered the enemy's defenses for more than three hours. Enemy artillery damaged four destroyers and the battleship *Texas*, but only one destroyer suffered serious damage. On June 27 Bradley's infantry captured the city, and in early July Cherbourg became operational as a major Allied port.

In conjunction with the Normandy invasion, the combined chiefs of staff decided to open another front in southern France. Code-named

▶ **1945**

MARCH 11: Four Navy boat units carry the Army across the Rhine.

APRIL 12: President Roosevelt dies and is succeeded by Harry S. Truman.

MAY 7: Germany surrenders unconditionally.

MAY 8: V-E Day

AUGUST 15: V-J Day. World War II ends.

Below: *On June 6 Omaha Beach becomes a melée of snarled traffic as men and equipment flood ashore. In front of the landing craft nosing toward shore is a beached DUKW and a half-track. In the background smoke from naval support gunfire spreads in a pattern a few hundred yards ahead of the advancing infantry.*

Operation Dragoon, the plan had two objectives: to gain the important port of Marseille and to attack German divisions which might otherwise move north and flank General Patton's Third Army. Admiral Hewitt once again drew the naval phase of the mission, this time getting three American and two French divisions ashore between St. Tropez and Cannes. The original plan called for Operation Dragoon to coincide with the invasion of Normandy, but Hewitt could not obtain enough landing craft to make the attack. He scrounged for boats from wherever they could be found, including an odd assortment of craft seized by the Free French at Naples and Corsica. His fire support group included battleships and cruisers brought from the Atlantic after the bombardment of Cherbourg. The Allied force bore all the characteristics of a United Nations navy, comprising 515 American, 283 British, 12 French, and 7 Greek ships, together with 63 various merchant vessels.

For three months prior to the invasion, Allied planes had been bombing targets in southern France, isolating the area of attack by destroying bridges and railroad lines. On August 15, the day set for the assault, 1,300 aircraft bombed and strafed a 40-mile section of coast. Destroyers and small craft staged mock attacks at points east and west of the target area, drawing enemy forces away from the beaches. At daybreak, guns of the fire support group opened on shore defenses. Planes from nine escort destroyers covered the assault and provided the dual role of spotting for

the Navy. The only hotly contested landing occurred on the east flank at Saint-Raphael, compelling the assault force to pick another beach.

At most points the Germans abandoned their elaborate shore defenses and fled inland. Hewitt's fire support group, aided by aircraft, kept pressure on the fleeing enemy, enabling Major General Alexander M. Patch's Seventh Army to get swiftly ashore. General de Gaulle's French Forces of the Interior, the underground resistance movement that for four years had harassed the Germans, engaged in open warfare. Using weapons dropped from Allied aircraft, they laid siege to Toulon and Marseille while the Navy bombarded enemy strongholds. Allied forces in hot pursuit of the enemy up the Rhône Valley soon made contact with Patton's Third Army tanks at Sombernon and Epinal. On August 25, 1944, Paris fell.

CROSSING THE RHINE

After a difficult winter along Germany's Siegfried Line, where American forces had been temporarily repulsed during the Battle of the Bulge, the spring campaign opened in March, 1945, and Allied forces reached the Rhine. After the crucial bridge at Remagen collapsed into the river, finding other means of crossing became extremely urgent. Since October, 1944, naval landing craft units had been training in England, and later in France and Belgium, for the task of getting the Army across the river. As the American First, Third, and Ninth Armies approached the Rhine, four U.S. Navy boat units under Commander William J. Whiteside began hauling 37- and 50-foot craft overland to carry out river crossings. Each unit contained 218 officers and men with 24 LCVPs (Landing Craft, Vehicle Personnel). During March 11-27, Boat Unit 1 ferried 14,000 troops and 400 vehicles across the river at Bad Neuenahr. Similar crossings occurred at Boppard, Oberwesel, Oppenheim, and Mainz. When not ferrying troops, the Navy worked with engineers laying pontoon bridges. German artillery continuously harassed the crossings, destroying shuttlecraft and taking lives. The task could not have been accomplished by any other means, and the Navy was there to do it.

On May 7, representatives of the German High Command met with General Eisenhower at his headquarters in Rheims, France, and signed the instrument of surrender, a ceremony repeated on the following day in Berlin. "We the undersigned, acting on behalf of the German Supreme Command, agree to unconditional surrender of all our armed forces on land, on sea, and in the air, as well as all forces which at present are under German command...." Four months later, on September 2, 1945, the war officially ended in the Far East when the Japanese Foreign Minister

Above: *D-Day at Normandy, and the hard-fought drive inland, made big news in the world's press, both of the Allies and enemies. Every paper from* The New York Times *to the German-language* MZamAbend *fashioned its own report on the news that made history.*

Below: *On August 28, 1944, the Germans attempted to block the harbor of Marseille in southern France by scuttling vessels. Here the French steamer* Cap Corse *sits on the bottom at the entrance to Port St. Jean, shown in the background.*

and the Chief of the Imperial General Staff signed the instrument of surrender on behalf of the Emperor and the Imperial General Headquarters.

LAND, AIR, SEA POWER

Victory over the European Axis and Japan had been the work of armies, fleets, and aircraft, tri-elemental forces working in close cooperation with each other. While operations in the Pacific were largely Navy-controlled, operations in Europe were mainly Army-controlled. The strength of the Allied powers lay in the balance of their land, sea, and air forces and their ability to merge the three together into cohesive units. In the typical tri-elemental advance, ships and planes opened the way by gaining command of the sea and the air, and under their protection ground forces went ashore to take control of the land. As each conquest was achieved, new bases were created for staging the next advance. Balanced power provided the means that in earlier times would have been considered extremely dangerous and risky ventures. In Europe, Allied ships used air cover and new techniques in fire control to engage heavily fortified land positions, fighting it out with coastal batteries. In the Pacific, dominance on the sea and in the air made it possible to make great leaps across the ocean, bypassing and rendering ineffectual the enemy's powerful island bases.

In the concluding months of the war, advances in devastating explosives and the means of deliv-

ering them to a target added another dimension to future military operations. Armed might, in terms of its old meaning in previous conflicts, had been redefined by technology.

The Soviet Union emerged from World War II as the world's greatest land power. The United States emerged as the world's greatest sea power. With the sudden debut of the atomic age, both became as vulnerable to nuclear holocaust as weaker nations. As never before, the hope of civilization lay in the creation of permanent peace. Until then, the United States could not turn away from the basic concepts of sea power. Five years later that power would be needed again.

CHAPTER EIGHT

COMMUNISM & THE COLD WAR

After Secretary of the Navy Frank Knox died on April 28, 1944, three weeks passed before James V. Forrestal entered office as the Navy's 48th Secretary. The *New York Times* spoke for the nation when it said that the appointment was "the best thing for the Navy, for the War, and for the country." No civilian in the United States understood the importance of a powerful Navy better than Forrestal.

As the war ground to an end in Europe, Ambassador Averell Harriman's pleas from Moscow for a firm policy against Soviet expansion and possible domination of Central Europe drew Forrestal's indignation. When Congress asked him to explain his bellicose attitude toward communism, Forrestal replied, "We are going to fight any international ruffian who attempts to impose his will on the world by force. We should make that determination clear – by deeds as well as words." When asked in 1945 to explain the Navy's mission, Forrestal replied, "Control of the sea by whatever weapons…necessary." Without realizing it at the time, Forrestal articulated what would become the policy of the United States, but not always with the same firm determination expressed by the secretary.

For the postwar Navy, Forrestal asked for 400 ships and 8,000 aircraft – about one-third of the wartime peak. His request included a number of mobile carrier task forces, each with a complement of Marines. Under pressure from Congress, Forrestal promised to complete the transition to a peacetime Navy in twelve months, but he warned of the consequences, emphasizing that there was "no better way to ensure a third world war" than by demobilizing too quickly. After asking for $5.1 billion for fiscal year 1947, he responded to critics' questions by replying vehemently, "I cannot help but feel that if this country, in the present state of the world, goes back to bed, we don't deserve to survive."

CUTS IN NAVY BUDGET

He watched as the Soviet Union flexed its muscles in the Black Sea and Central Europe, planting the seeds of a Cold War. Too few men in government understood Forrestal's philosophy, including those in later administrations. "It is well that we remind ourselves that the weight of American influence at the peace tables is in almost direct proportion to the strength and readiness of our armed forces." For fiscal 1947, Congress gave the Navy $4.1 billion, so Forrestal cut the force to 319 combat ships, 724 lesser vessels, 1,461 combat aircraft, 491,663 naval personnel, and 108,798 Marines. A year later Congress knocked nearly another billion off the Navy bill. The timing could not have been worse. To keep the Soviets out of the Mediterranean, Forrestal needed ships. In 1948 he created a task force that would eventually become the Sixth Fleet, the first Mediterranean squadron since the nineteenth century, and he did it just in time to discourage communists from overthrowing the Italian government.

With more than a hundred out-of-date ships on his hands, Forrestal sent some of them to the

Right: Secretary of the Navy Forrestal found a handy source for disposing of his surplus warships. When in 1946 the government decided to learn more about the power of A-bombs, Forrestal sent his discards to Bikini Atoll to assess the effect of underwater atomic explosions on surface vessels.

other side of the globe as fodder for atomic tests at Bikini Atoll. He went there in person to see whether capital ships could survive atomic power. Forrestal considered the tests inconclusive, but he agreed with scientists that the "Navy of the future, if there is any such, will consist of submarines which will travel a thousand feet below the ocean" surface. In this regard he had strong support from Admiral Nimitz, who believed that the defense of the United States against atomic bombardment depended upon having submarines capable of "carrying atomic weapons to within short distances of coastal targets and for insuring accuracy in the use of...missiles." Conclusions drawn from these studies led to the development of the Polaris missiles, and eventually to the nuclear submarine.

Forrestal's biggest fight came over the unification of the armed services under one titular head, an idea promoted and strongly advocated by the Army. When President Truman decided to support the Army position, he left the Navy department in a quandary. Forrestal worked with Secretary of War Robert P. Patterson to reach a compromise, while trying to avoid a rift with Truman. He had opposed the president's sloppy handling of the Potsdam Conference, but unification of the services was a different matter. A measure of Truman's stature was his ability to tolerate Forrestal's eccentricities while using the latter's exceptional skills. As long as Forrestal balked, no settlement could be reached on unification. On July 26, 1947, Truman solved the problem by signing a bill creating the new Department of Defense and nominated Forrestal as its first secretary, a position he held until his death in May 1949. The Cold War became hotter in Greece, Turkey, Czechoslovakia, and Berlin during Forrestal's two years as Secretary of Defense.

BERLIN AIRLIFT

On March 31, 1948, the Soviet Union began impeding the flow of traffic into West Berlin, and on June 24 Joseph Stalin, who wanted to drive out the Allies, halted all land transportation to the city. General Lucius Clay, the military governor and commander of occupation forces in the American sector, directed Major General Curtis LeMay to employ all available transport aircraft to supply the city by air. Clay informed the National Security Council that he would need to airlift into Berlin 3,500 tons of supplies a day, and an extra 1,000 tons of coal when winter came. The U.S. Air Force could not supply all the aircraft without disrupting worldwide operations, so President Truman called upon the Navy.

Navy tankers had been delivering huge quantities of aviation gas to Bremerhaven, Germany, since the beginning of the blockade, but naval aircraft had not been directly involved in transport-

ing supplies to Berlin. Using the Navy's C-54 transport squadrons would seriously reduce the country's operational inventory needed to implement the nation's emergency war plans. Nonetheless, on October 27 Navy Secretary John L. Sullivan transferred two transport squadrons, VR-6 and VR-8, to Operation Vittles for 180 days. and added a third Navy squadron of fifteen planes, VR-3, to provide transatlantic support for the two squadrons assigned to the airlift.

Navy fliers soon made themselves known to their Air Force counterparts. Being more accustomed to making instrument landings, they managed to cope with the cold winter fogs that frequently blanketed Berlin's Tempelhof Airport and which grounded Air Force planes. While Air Force pilots averaged six flight hours a day, the Navy squadrons, having brought their own mechanics, averaged more than eight. During the first two weeks of flying the air route from Rhein-Main to Tempelhof, the two squadrons delivered 6,526 tons of cargo. By the end of December VR-8 led all squadrons in the airlift on aircraft utilization, total cargo carried, payload efficiency, and tons per plane. By February, 1949, VR-6 matched and sometimes exceeded VR-8 in operational achievements. Each C-54 flew about thirteen

Above: *Deployed in 1960 as a sea-based strategic deterrent weapon, the Polaris became the primary weapon for the first three Polaris fleet ballistic-missile submarines, the first of those being USS* George Washington *(SSBN 598).*

Above right: On rare occasions, the Navy parades its arsenal of power. The task group flagship USS Valley Forge (CV 45) is flanked by destroyers and submarines, and covered by search and patrol aircraft, and ASW helicopters.

hours a day, and during the month of April the two squadrons delivered 23,550 tons of supplies to Berlin.

The Soviet Union agreed to lift the blockade on May 12, 1949, but the two Navy squadrons were not released from Operation Vittles until mid-August. As one historian observed, "It was a masterful achievement."

THE KOREAN WAR

The Korean surprise fell like a thunderclap upon Louis A. Johnson, the new Secretary of Defense. Truman appointed Johnson to the post not because of the man's superior qualifications but because the lawyer-politician had been a successful fund-raiser during the 1948 presidential campaign. A few weeks after taking office Johnson displayed such a tactless, overbearing nature that he threw the entire defense establishment into chaos, which led to what became known as the "admirals' revolt."

The "revolt" started in April, 1949, while the Secretary of the Navy was out of town. Johnson halted work on the 60,000-ton supercarrier *United States*, which was fully funded and under construction at Newport News. Funds saved by the cancelation of work on *United States* were being diverted to build a greater number of B-36s, the Air Force's new 5,000-mile intercontinental bomber. Admiral Arthur W. Radford, commander in chief of the Pacific Fleet, and Adm. Louis E.

Denfeld attacked Johnson's budget manipulations and the B-36 program itself, calling it "a billion dollar blunder." The admirals had a valid complaint. The B-36 had been designed in 1940, was driven by piston engines, had a top speed of only 375 miles an hour, a ceiling of 40,000 feet, and would be a sitting duck for the new Russian MiG-15 jet fighters. Congress called for hearings, and just as discussions began Russia exploded a nuclear device, ending America's sole control of the atom bomb.

The political war between the Air Force and the Navy had been waging for several years over prestige and appropriations. When Congress opened testimony on the issue, it responded in characteristic fashion, retaining the Navy's budget cuts while reducing the number of B-36s authorized. Despite Johnson's grudging stand against the Navy, the admirals articulated the importance of being prepared for fighting limited wars, such as the Cold War, as well as nuclear wars. Their logic fell upon deaf ears. Johnson took the Air Force position that the only war of the future would be nuclear, and the one likely enemy would be Russia. He was not oblivious to conditions in China, where communists had taken control of the country, but he was completely surprised by the news that North Korean troops had assaulted their southern neighbor. By then Congress and Johnson had nearly cut the heart out of the American military machine.

The roots leading to the Korean conflict began in 1945 when the Russian Army accepted the Japanese surrender of Korea north of the 38th

Parallel, and the United States accepted the surrender of the southern half. Plans for the country's future government collapsed when Russia refused to allow free elections in North Korea. The peninsula became two countries, one free and the other ruled by a Russian-backed communist regime. The Soviet Union would not settle for half and wanted it all.

NORTH KOREAN ADVANCE

Early in the morning on June 25, 1950, the North Korean army crossed the 38th Parallel using the fictional ploy of being compelled to drive back an invasion. Reminiscent of the Nazi *blitzkrieg*, the communist war machine drove rapidly south, capturing Seoul and overrunning the country until stopped at a perimeter formed around Pusan in the southeastern corner of the Korean peninsula.

The United States, branding the invasion a violation of international peace, put the armed intrusion before the United Nations Security Council and demanded a resolution that North Korea withdraw. Because the Soviet Union refused to attend the meeting, the resolution passed. Two days later the Security Council voted a second resolution inviting members of the United Nations to provide forces for repelling the invasion. Without waiting for other countries to respond, President Truman authorized General Douglas A. MacArthur, commander in chief in the Far East, to use all available naval, air, and ground forces to check the invasion. Because one communist assault in the Far East might encourage the Chinese to attack Taiwan, or vice versa, Truman ordered the Seventh Fleet to the Formosa Strait to prevent Communist and Nationalist Chinese from using the Korean conflict as an excuse to initiate war upon each other.

MACARTHUR BELIEVED THAT IF THE WAR IN KOREA WERE LOST TO COMMUNISM, THE FATE OF EUROPE WOULD BE JEOPARDIZED. IN A CHARACTERISTIC FLARE OF FLAMBOYANCE THAT PERSONIFIED THE GENERAL'S STYLE, HE SAID,

'*I can almost hear the ticking sound of destiny. We must act now or we will die....We shall land at Inchon, and I shall crush them.*'

Below: *The battleship USS* Iowa *(BB 61) first made her appearance in 1943. After World War II she returned to the Pacific and on September 10, 1952, bombarded enemy installations on Korea with her 16-inch guns.*

1952

JULY 11: Carrier aircraft strike Pyongyang.

SEPTEMBER 1: The first Sidewinder air-to-air missile is fired.

NOVEMBER 1: The first shipboard firing of a Regulus I missile is made from USS. *Norton Sound.*

1953

JANUARY 18: Landing tests begin on the first angled-deck carrier *Antietam.*

JANUARY 28: The first shipboard launching of a Terrier surface-to-air missile is made.

JULY 27: A Korean cease-fire armistice is signed.

1954

SEPTEMBER 30: *Nautilus*, America's first nuclear-powered vessel, is commissioned.

Below: *Marines had barely settled into peacetime vocations before being recalled to fight in Korea. Within weeks after the outbreak of the war, they were back in landing craft and going ashore at Pusan.*

Secretary of Defense Johnson had performed wonders by first thinning the U.S. Navy to alarmingly low levels and then deploying most of the ships and resources in the Atlantic. Vice Admiral Arthur D. Struble commanded the once great Seventh Fleet, now reduced to the carrier *Valley Forge*, the heavy cruiser *Rochester*, and eight destroyers. Vice Admiral C. Turner Joy's Task Force 96 based in Japan consisted of the antiaircraft cruiser *Juneau* and four destroyers. He also had a few minesweepers and auxiliary craft that were far better vessels than the small craft and Russian-built torpedo boats used by the enemy.

While Gen. MacArthur poured troops and supplies into the Pusan perimeter, aircraft from *Valley Forge* and the British light carrier *Triumph* struck the North Korean Army and its lines of supply. Carrier fighter-bombers, both piston planes and jets, carried the workload because Air Force jets based in Japan did not have the range to reach and return from targets in Korea. Long-range bombers were of little value because of the scarcity of strategic targets. Using bombs and rockets, carrier planes hit the main airbase at Pyongyang, the capital of North Korea, and wiped out most of the enemy's Air Force. Cruisers and destroyers roamed the coast, knocking out enemy shore batteries, destroying bridges, and harassing columns of infantry and vehicles traveling along coastal roads.

On July 2, the North Korean Navy made one sortie using Russian torpedo boats to attack two Allied cruisers, the USS *Juneau* and the HMS

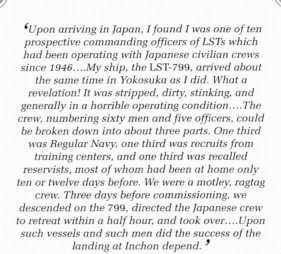

'Upon arriving in Japan, I found I was one of ten prospective commanding officers of LSTs which had been operating with Japanese civilian crews since 1946....My ship, the LST-799, arrived about the same time in Yokosuka as I did. What a revelation! It was stripped, dirty, stinking, and generally in a horrible operating condition....The crew, numbering sixty men and five officers, could be broken down into about three parts. One third was Regular Navy, one third was recruits from training centers, and one third was recalled reservists, most of whom had been at home only ten or twelve days before. We were a motley, ragtag crew. Three days before commissioning, we descended on the 799, directed the Japanese crew to retreat within a half hour, and took over....Upon such vessels and such men did the success of the landing at Inchon depend.'

LIEUTENANT TRUMOND E. HOUSTON.

Jamaica. The cruisers sank the torpedo boats, destroying in one brief engagement the enemy's entire navy.

So far, all of Defense Secretary Johnson's predictions of future wars had been repudiated by the end of summer. There had been no nuclear attacks, and the Air Force had been unable to participate in a helpful manner. Johnson's other pronouncement that "amphibious operations are a thing of the past. We'll never have any more amphibious operations," was also about to be shattered when MacArthur decided that conditions were right to launch a decisive blow on the enemy's rear. For strategic as well as tactical reasons, MacArthur chose to land an amphibious force at Inchon, a port city near Seoul and close to Korea's largest airfield. He planned to crush the North Korean Army between two pincers. When U.S. Marines landed on Inchon, the Eighth Army was to break out of the Pusan perimeter and push the enemy into the jaws of the 1st Marine Division. The plan looked good on paper, but there were many obstacles to overcome for the assault to succeed.

Preparations for landing Marines on Inchon began on June 30, five days after the war started in Korea. At the time, the 1st Marine Division at Camp Pendleton had no specific orders and only 641 officers and 7,148 enlisted men on the muster rolls. By September 15 the division had ballooned to 26,000 men and officers, an expansion, augmentation, and movement unparalleled in Marine Corps history.

LANDING PROBLEMS AT INCHON

Of all the possible landing sites along the coast of Korea, none was less promising than Inchon. Tides reaching a height of thirty-three feet created a current of five knots and, when ebbing, exposed mud banks that stretched more than three miles seaward. The main channel approach to Inchon, poetically called "Flying Fish Channel," was narrow, winding, and difficult to follow even during daylight. Without navigation lights to guide the way, combined with the likelihood of mines and enemy gunfire, to bring an invasion fleet through this treacherous channel created grave problems for the Navy. If a ship foundered or ran off course during the final approach, the vessels ahead of it would be trapped on mud flats

INCHON

Rear Admiral Doyle brought up the rear in the command ship *Mount McKinley*. With him were General MacArthur and "a star-studded galaxy of admirals and generals, whom the staff officers irreverently called "VIKs" – Very Important Kibitzers.

At 6:33 a.m. the 5th Marine Regiment, supported by the Gunfire Support Group, went ashore at Wolmi-do, overran the 400-man garrison in less than thirty minutes, and raised the Stars and Stripes. MacArthur said to his VIKs, "That's it. Let's get a cup of coffee." By noon Marines had secured the surrounding area, reporting only seventeen casualties.

The invasion force moved up the Narrows on the afternoon tide and at 2:30 p.m. cruisers and destroyers opened on Inchon. At 4:45 the first wave of the 1st Marine Regiment went ashore, climbed ladders onto the seawall, and by sunset had established a lodgment. Matters went slightly awry when the second wave, caught in the ebb tide, grounded on mud flats and had to wade ashore. Eight LSTs specially loaded with jeeps, trucks, tanks, and supplies disgorged them at the seawall. On September 17 Marines took possession of the Kimpo airfield and by the 19th were in control of Inchon, the Han River, and most of the surrounding area.

Satisfied with the Marines' progress, MacArthur put the 7th Infantry Division ashore at Inchon to meet up with General Wallton H. Walker's Eighth Army, which had broken out of Pusan. The Inchon and Pusan forces made contact on September 26 at Osan, a site that became America's first disastrous land battle of the war. The 5th Marines raised the flag over Seoul on September 27, two days behind the timetable set by MacArthur.

The badly beaten North Korean Army never became a serious factor in the remaining years of the war. Effusing praise, MacArthur declared, "The Navy and the Marines have never shone more brightly." Though the general referred to Inchon as his "master stroke," he

never seriously anticipated Chinese communist intervention into the conflict until November, when his forces approached the Yalu River on the border of Manchuria and were suddenly struck by 300,000 troops from the Chinese regular army.

Above: *Because of high tides, Koreans had built a seawall at Inchon. Marines, taking no chances, loaded ladders on their landing craft. On September 15, 1950, General MacArthur's surprise attack went off with few hitches. Marines took few casualties as they scaled the walls and two days later captured Seoul's important Kimpo airfield.*

at low tide, and those behind would stack up and ground as well. In the final analysis, the tides determined the invasion date. At least twenty-nine feet of water would be required to ensure that the LSTs would have enough clearance beneath their keels to reach the designated landing beach. Unlike amphibious landings made on the sandy beaches of World War II, the one at Inchon required that assault troops scale high sea walls and piers while under constant enemy fire.

MacArthur set September 15 as D-Day for the Inchon assault, but Typhoon Jane packing 110-mile-an-hour winds almost delayed the attack until October. On September 10 the softening-up process began. Carrier planes from Task Force 7 launched a series of strikes against Wolmi-do, an island fortress connected to Inchon by a cause-way. By baiting the enemy to show themselves, three of the squadron's six destroyers suffered damage when they moved close inshore to draw fire. Spotters relayed coordinates of the enemy's positions, and four cruisers waiting farther off-shore began pulverizing the fortifications. On September 13, with the expedition's transports now at sea, 60-mile-an-hour winds from Typhoon Kezia struck and scattered some of the vessels. The ships wallowed through heavy seas and arrived off the marshaling area just in time.

In the pre-dawn murk breaking over Inchon Narrows on September 15, the shadowy shapes of 230 ships carrying 70,000 men worked in from the Yellow Sea. Compared with landings in 1944-45 the invasion force was small, but considering the horrendous cutbacks in ships and service-

▶ **1955**

JANUARY 17:
Nautilus makes its first successful trial run.

Forrestal, the first of a new class of six carriers is commissioned at Norfolk.

1956

JANUARY 10: The Navy's first nuclear power school is established at New London, Connecticut.

DECEMBER 3: The Polaris missile is approved for development.

1958

Grayback, the first submarine designed to fire missiles, is commissioned.

JULY 15: Marines land on Lebanon.

AUGUST 3: *Nautilus* passes below the Arctic icecap and crosses the North Pole.

AUGUST 23: Communist China bombards the islands of Quemoy and Matsu.

1959

DECEMBER 31: *George Washington*, the first ballistic-missile submarine, is commissioned.

Above right: *On July 3-4, 1950, the Navy's new F9F-2 Panthers were the first fighter jets in combat. Operating from the carrier* Valley Forge *(CV 45), they struck the North Korean capital of Pyongyang and scored the first jet victories, knocking down two propeller-driven Yak-9 fighters.*

men, the assemblage had been organized in phenomenally short time. For the assault, Admiral Forrest P. Sherman, CNO, had pressed every naval vessel in the Pacific into service, as well as American and Japanese merchant ships (manned by Japanese sailors), and turned them all over to Admiral Struble. Rear Admiral James H. Doyle, second in command, worried because no time had been allotted for rehearsal. He called his commanding officers together and told them "to personally instruct boat crews and coxswains what they were to do, why they were to do it, and how their individual tasks fitted into the overall picture."

POOR PREPARATION

On October 10, MacArthur's luck began running out at Wonsan, 115 miles northeast of Seoul on the Sea of Japan. Disregarding warnings that an invasion of North Korea could bring China into the war, the general rushed ahead with his plans without proper preparation. Truman had authorized an invasion of North Korea provided that "there was no action by major Soviet or Chinese communist forces." Wonsan's channel contained 3,000 enemy mines, and the Navy had few sweepers available to clear it. As a consequence, 200 transports and supply vessels lay off Wonsan for more than a week waiting for the channel to be swept. Meanwhile, South Korean forces captured the port from the rear, leaving Admiral Sherman grumbling that, "Those damn mines cost us eight days' delay in getting the troops ashore and more than two hundred casualties." After landing

> *'One of my toughest jobs was the constant battle to keep pilots' morale up. Day after day, for weeks on end, pilots had to fly over the same area of Korea, bombing bridges and punching holes in the same roadbeds. The antiaircraft fire over Korea grew steadily heavier, more accurate, and more intense....A pilot would go out one day, do a first-rate bombing job on a bridge and leave several craters in a roadbed, and come back the next day and find everything repaired overnight. It was hard for him to see how his efforts were having any effect on the course of the fighting.'*
>
> COMMANDER M. U. BEEBE,
> ESSEX AIR GROUP FIVE.

Marines at Wonsan, he picked up the remaining transports, ran them up the coast, and finding no mines put the 7th Infantry Division ashore at Iwon.

On November 8 aircraft from Admiral Struble's carrier force began destroying bridges across the Yalu, but by presidential decree, only the bridge-ends on the Korean side of the river were to be bombed. The bombing had little deterrent effect because the river could be waded, but it did invite a whole swarm of Russian-built MiG-15 jet fighters to cross the Yalu and pitch into the bombers. On November 9, Lieutenant Commander W. T. Amen, flying an F-9F2 Panther jet from the carrier *Philippine Sea,* became the first Navy pilot to shoot down an enemy jet fighter. The Navy's fighters could not match the agile MiG in speed, maneuverability, or rate of climb, but superior training and gunnery worked to outweigh the Russian aircraft's advantages.

MacArthur's two-pronged advance to the Yalu River encountered little resistance, but on the night of November 25, 1950, the Chinese regular army began crossing the shallow Yalu and attacked widely separated United Nations outposts south of the river. The western force beat a hasty retreat to the 38th Parallel, leaving behind thousands of men and tons of supplies. Eight Chinese divisions struck at U.S. Marines advancing along the eastern side of the peninsula near the Chosin Reservoir and sent them reeling back to the port of Hungnam. Admiral Doyle brought up his squadron – seven carriers, the battleship *Missouri*, two heavy cruisers, eight destroyers, and three rocket ships. The rescue force laid down a ring of fire that kept the Chinese at bay long enough for the Navy to sea-lift 105,000 American and Korean troops, 91,000 Korean civilians, and 350,000 tons of supplies and equipment to Pusan.

MacArthur Replaced

The setback drove United Nations forces fifty miles south of the 38th Parallel, enabling Chinese forces to recapture Seoul. MacArthur made the mistake of blaming the reversals on presidential constraints. Annoyed by MacArthur's cavalier insinuations, Truman recalled him and on April 11, 1951, replaced him with Lieutenant General Matthew B. Ridgeway. By then, more naval power had reached the Far East, enabling Ridgeway to mount a counter-offensive and form a new battle line just north of the 38th Parallel. Truce talks began in July, 1951, but fighting continued for two more years. For the individuals in the armed forces – mostly reservists or draftees – there was no limit on the strain, hazard, or boredom of the conflict. Although mitigated by a program of rapid rotation, the situation, acceptable in nineteenth century wars fought by regulars, damaged morale in 1951. Absence from home created tensions, as did the piecemeal contributions of men and resources from United Nations forces. The fighting men were not happy with the political leadership that drew them into a limited war, and they never stopped grumbling until July 27, 1953, when the conflict came to an end.

For those who in 1950 contended that navies were obsolete, the war in Korea proved otherwise. Unlike predictions made by warring factions in the armed services, it had not been a nuclear war, but a war fought much like the Italian campaigns in 1943-44 with amphibious landings, carrier strikes, shore bombardment, logistical and convoy support, conventional weapons, and, unlike Italy, forced evacuations. But it had also been a political war fought to a greater degree against Red China, and one which irritated United Nations pilots by forbidding them to bomb targets in Manchuria. After three

Navy pilots called themselves "heckler pilots" because all they did day and night was to bust up railroads, bridges, and roadways to gain an advantage for American negotiators at the peace table. One night heckler pilot who remained behind for peacekeeping in Korea expressed his disdain in a poem:

It weren't no fun in 51
Tried and True in 52
Still out to sea in 53
Don't want no more in 54
Still alive in 55
Amidst the blitz in 56
Almost in heaven in 57
No homecoming date in 58
Remain on the line in 59
Pack up your ditty in 1960
To hell with this poem
We want to come home.

FROM *The Sea War in Korea*, COMMANDER MALCOLM W. CAGLE.

years of fighting, the cease-fire agreement accomplished nothing more than to revert to the original 38th Parallel, leaving Korea divided as before.

The Navy won its share of laurels during the Korean War and proved its indispensability. Truman sacked Secretary of Defense Johnson, work resumed on the supercarrier *United States*, and six even larger carriers of the new 78,000-ton Forrestal class were laid down. Armed with planes capable of delivering nuclear bombs, these carriers broke the monopoly the Air Force had on strategic bombing.

Below: *The USS* Triton *(SSN 586), a nuclear-powered submarine and part of the Navy's modernization program, became the first vessel to circumnavigate the earth submerged. Her voyage lasted 84 days and covered 41,519 miles, closely following the route covered by Magellan 350 years before.*

HYMAN RICKOVER AND THE USS *NAUTILUS*

On September 30, 1954, the USS *Nautilus*, America's first atomic-powered submarine, went into commission at Groton, Connecticut. *Nautilus* evolved from the tenacity and creative energies of one man, Admiral Hyman G. Rickover, who began badgering the Atomic Energy Commission to develop a nuclear reaction plant when he was still a captain. He soon developed the reputation as "the cleverest, the most cunning, and the rudest man in the whole United States Navy," but the distinction did not deter him in the least. The brilliance of the man overshadowed his irascibility to such an extent that even those he antagonized, among them senior naval officers, seemed not to mind.

Rickover had one goal that passionately absorbed him for the rest of his life – to transform the steam-powered Navy into a nuclear-powered fleet. To accomplish this end he walked over anyone or anything in his way. Historian Stephen Howarth wrote of him: "He was abusive, manipulative, impatient, ill-tempered, stubborn, arrogant, and capable of enraging more people in a shorter time than anyone who never met him would believe possible. As his enemies in the Navy and Congress acknowledged, he was close to being a genius. They all acknowledged him as the 'father' of America's nuclear Navy."

At 11:00 a.m. on January 17, 1955, the blunt-nosed, black-hulled 3,530-ton *Nautilus*, identified only by numbers 571, moved silently down the Thames River and past Groton. She carried no guns on her deck. A streamlined sail housed her periscopes and radio antennae, replacing the conning towers of the old diesel submarines. On her bridge stood Admiral Rickover, by now the Navy's leading expert on nuclear propulsion. Despite his less than affable personality, the Navy had given him dual responsibility, making him chief of both the Nuclear Propulsion Division of the Bureau of Ships and the Naval Reactors Branch of the Atomic Energy Commission. As *Nautilus* moved into Long Island Sound, Commander Eugene Wilkinson sent the first ever signal of its kind: "UNDER WAY ON NUCLEAR POWER."

For *Nautilus* and Rickover, it was only the beginning. On August 3, 1958, after an eleven-day voyage from Honolulu, *Nautilus* went under the Arctic ice cap, and in a pioneering voyage crossed the North Pole and resurfaced in the Atlantic. Rickover continued his work, and by 1957 had twenty-one nuclear submarines either built or under construction, and three of them armed with the new fleet ballistic missiles.

On November 19, 1973, Rickover received his fourth star. Eight years later he retired from the Navy at the age of eighty-one, remaining active as the presidential adviser on nuclear science.

Above: *The USS Nautilus (SSN 571) became the world's first nuclear-powered submarine. On August 3, 1958, Comdr. William R. Anderson took her under the polar ice and reached the North Pole.*

Left: *Following that lead but much later, on May 6, 1986, the USS Ray (SSN 653), Hawkbill (SSN 678), and Archerfish (SSN 678) established another first by rendezvousing at the Pole.*

Left: *A Navy TV-2 jet trainer guides a jet-powered Regulus-1 unmanned drone during 1958 flight exercises over the United States.*

Truman finally faced up to the challenges of communism and asked Congress to fund a five-year preparedness program costing $50 billion. In 1952 he got most of what he wanted for the Navy – 173 new combat ships, modernization of 291 vessels, another supercarrier, and the first atomic-powered submarine.

The first nuclear submarines carried conventional torpedoes, but men like Admiral Arleigh Burke, CNO, wanted the boats designed and fitted with guided missiles. Supersonic ramjet-powered missiles like the Rigel and Regulus I were byproducts of World War II technology. In 1955 Rear Admiral William F. Rathbon, Jr., formed a special projects group to develop a ballistic missile. Five years later the nuclear-powered submarine *George Washington* received the first Polaris missiles – a weapon guided by a very accurate inertial navigating system – and fired the first test shot on July 20, 1960, while submerged off the coast of Florida.

NUCLEAR SURFACE SHIPS

After nuclear power became installed on submarines, the Navy applied the technology to every type of vessel ranging from the new 89,600-ton carrier *Enterprise* to the 7,600-ton guided missile frigate *Bainbridge*. In 1964 both these vessels went to sea accompanied by the latest nuclear-powered 17,000-ton cruiser *Long Beach*, and together they sailed around the world without refueling or re-provisioning. All carried the new Polaris missiles.

Never during peacetime had the Navy made

such giant strides toward building its defense-offense capability. The submarine fleet armed with Polaris-Poseidon weapon systems became one of the three basic components of the nation's deterrent to nuclear war, the other two being the Strategic Air Command and the land-based intercontinental missiles buried in silos in the West.

So that nuclear submarines could spend most of their time on station, they operated with two full crews, one Blue and the other Gold. When Crew Blue returned from a two-month patrol, Gold would take the boat out for the next tour of duty. Rotation of crews boosted morale and guaranteed a corps of trained personnel for the silent

Below: *On July 31, 1964, during Operation Sea Orbit, the guided-missile frigate USS* Bainbridge *(CGN 25) carries out maneuvers with the cruiser* Long Beach *and the carrier* Enterprise, *three nuclear-powered warships on a non-stop, non-refueled round-the-world trip.*

▶ **OCTOBER 6:** *Bainbridge*, the first nuclear-powered, guided-missile frigate, is commissioned.

OCTOBER 14: The Cuban Missile Crisis begins.

OCTOBER 24: The U.S. Navy "quarantines" Cuba.

OCTOBER 28: The Cuban Missile Crisis is resolved.

1963

APRIL 10: The nuclear submarine *Thresher* is lost with all hands.

1964

MAY 13: The Sixth Fleet forms the first nuclear-powered task group.

AUGUST 2: The Tonkin Gulf incident escalates the Vietnam War.

AUGUST 5: First naval strike is made on North Vietnam.

Right: *The Navy commissioned the first nuclear-powered carrier* Enterprise *(CVAN 65) on November 25, 1961. Called at the time "the largest moving structure ever built by man," she was 1,123 feet long, displaced 85,830 tons, cruised at more than 30 knots, and carried a crew of 4,600. Her flight deck covered four and one-half acres and handled up to a hundred aircraft.*

and stressful stalking operations performed deep below the northern seas. With improving listening and tracking devices, technology changed rapidly and frequently on nuclear submarines, as did the missiles themselves. Trident missiles with a range of 6,000 miles replaced the Poseidon systems. Before the advent of satellites, the Navy's nuclear submarine fleet became the underwater arm of national defense, always ready to retaliate to a nuclear attack.

NUCLEAR ARMS RACE

As the nation became embroiled in a race with the Soviet Union for nuclear supremacy, none of America's deterrents came too soon. Communist expansion threatened everywhere, from Europe to the Middle East, Africa, and Asia. But for a decade following the Korean War, the Navy kept the peace without firing a shot or launching a missile in an act of war. Without sea power, the United States could not have thwarted the Soviet Union from dominating the Middle East and cutting off oil supplies to the West.

The Middle East crisis began in Iraq when on July 14, 1958, the Iraqi army overthrew the pro-Western government. Lebanon's president, fearing a similar blood bath in his own country, asked President Eisenhower for military assistance. Having promised any legitimate Mid-Eastern gov-

ernment support should they need it, Eisenhower sent the Sixth Fleet. Within hours the carriers *Saratoga*, *Essex*, and *Wasp*, accompanied by cruisers, destroyers, and amphibious vessels loaded with Marines, appeared off Beirut. On the afternoon of July 15, Marines moved through startled bathers on the beaches and captured Beirut's airport. No insurrection took place, new elections were held, the situation in Lebanon stabilized, and the Americans departed uncertain of whether a crisis ever existed. The rush to rescue Lebanon did not go unnoticed by the Soviet Union or its ally Egypt. To Lebanon's call the Sixth Fleet had responded swiftly and with force, using unrestricted maneuverability that the Soviet Union could not match.

While the Sixth Fleet operated off Lebanon, Red China decided the time had come to test American resolve in the Far East. As a stepping-stone to the recovery of Taiwan, the Chinese military set their sights on recovering two islands occupied by Nationalists – Quemoy and Matsu, four miles off the mainland. The Nationalists tenaciously defended the islands, garrisoning them with 100,000 men. On August 23, 1958, the Red Chinese began bombarding the island of Quemoy and continued to do so day after day. Eisenhower sent the Seventh Fleet, instructing Admiral Burke to aid the Nationalists without engaging the Communists. Burke tested the resolve of the Communists by placing the fleet in range of the enemy's shore batteries without

Left: *On September 10, 1961, the Navy commissioned the first nuclear-powered, guided-missile cruiser, the USS* Long Beach *(CGN 9). She carried two 5-inch guns, one twin Talos launcher, two twin Terrier launchers, and one ASROC launcher.*

firing upon them. The Communists confined their artillery fire to the islands. While using Nationalists on Taiwan to fight their own war, Burke supplied them with landing craft, air cover, and Sidewinder heat-seeking missiles for their aircraft. The Sidewinders enabled the Nationalist air force to drive the MiGs from the skies, and the U.S. Navy's superiority in weapons thwarted Red China's effort to recover the islands.

CUBAN MISSILE CRISIS

Communist expansion in the West reached its high-water mark in 1962 when the Soviet Union made a desperate attempt to place missiles with nuclear warheads in Cuba. Since Fidel Castro's seizure of the island in 1959, Cuba had become a festering hotbed of communist influence. Intelligence operatives on the island confirmed the arrival of Russian engineers, heavy earth-moving equipment, and sophisticated instrumentation. U.S. reconnaissance aircraft spotted unusual construction underway. Refugees from Cuba related mysterious activities deep inland but, since Russia had never deployed missiles beyond its own borders, President John F. Kennedy at first dismissed the threat. The president awakened to the vulnerability of the United States only after U-2 planes soaring high over Cuba snapped dozens of photos showing actual construction of missile sites in western Cuba,

Soviet Ilyushin Il-28 bombers sitting on enlarged Cuban airfields, and missiles with a range of 2,200 miles being unloaded and transported to launching sites.

Kennedy had waited almost too long to come to grips with a problem that for months had begged for decisive action. In one stroke Soviet Premier Nikita S. Khrushchev had threatened to neutralize America's superiority in ballistic missiles by installing deadly nuclear weapons capable of

Below: *Two sailors on board the* James Madison *(SSBN 627) remove the cover of a Poseidon missile launcher to inspect the tube. The Poseidon has a launch weight of 60,000 pounds, is 34 feet in length, and has a range of 2,800 miles.*

Above right: *On October 14, 1962, an American U-2 reconnaissance plane spotted a Russian ship carrying six missile transporters in Cuba's Casilda Port. A later U.S. reconnaissance plane caught its own shadow during a fly-over (lower right).*

incinerating the nation's capital with the push of a button. Kennedy and his advisers considered their options – a naval blockade of Cuba, an invasion of the island, diplomatic negotiations through the United Nations, or an air strike. He settled for a "quarantine," a fancy word for a blockade, which could be applied only during time of war. The Organization of American States agreed to support the quarantine by a vote of 19-0, with Uruguay abstaining. Implementing the task fell to Admiral George W. Anderson, Jr., CNO, who assured the president that "the Navy will not let you down."

MASSIVE NUCLEAR FORCE

On October 21 Kennedy confessed to the public that the Soviet Union had placed ballistic missiles in Cuba and that all vessels carrying additional weapons to the island would be interdicted and turned back. The president ended the speech with an appeal to Khrushchev to remove the weapons, warning him that B-52 bombers armed with nuclear bombs were on standby, Polaris-armed submarines were in position, and 156 ICBMs were ready to be launched against the Soviet Union. Kennedy emphasized that the quarantine was a peaceful act, and any aggressive action would first have to come from the Soviet Union. American forces were fully prepared to invade Cuba and, if necessary, initiate an all-out nuclear attack on Russia. As he spoke 183 U.S.

Navy ships, including eight carriers and an invasion force of 30,000 Marines augmented by dozens of multi-national ships under Admiral Robert L. Dennison began fanning across a 500-mile arc northeast of Cuba. After sending the message to Khrushchev "in the clear" and not in code, everyone in the White House held their breath. The Soviet premier responded in a predictable manner, on the one hand charging Kennedy with lying to the public and on the other hand threatening war if American "pirates" boarded a Russian vessel. Work continued on the missile sites, and the tempest boiled hotter as twenty-five Soviet vessels neared the quarantine zone.

On October 25 word reached the White House that eight freighters chartered or operated by the Soviets had stopped at the quarantine line. Others had turned back. The Navy examined those that stopped, and if not laden with contraband they were passed through to Cuba. It soon became evident that the Russians had lost their nerve. "We're eyeball to eyeball," Secretary of State Dean Rusk jubilantly declared, "and I think the other fellow just blinked."

The crisis wound down on October 28 when Khrushchev admitted defeat and informed Kennedy that "the arms which you describe as offensive" would be dismantled and returned to the Soviet Union. Both men had gambled with nuclear war in the most dangerous, direct Soviet-American confrontation since the beginning of the Cold War. Khrushchev lost because he underestimated American resolve. Because the United

States had backed off during a Soviet-aided spat on behalf of Egypt over the Suez Canal and refused to interfere in the Hungarian rebellion, Khrushchev had believed the United States would not interfere in Cuba. But in the western hemisphere the Soviets suffered an unexpected defeat because of America's dominant sea power. In Moscow, Khrushchev's political support hit the skids. Two years later he toppled from power.

Had President Kennedy not been so emboldened by his success in ending the Cuban missile crisis, the United States may never have taken a major role in the defense of South Vietnam, in a war that had been raging with communist-controlled North Vietnam since World War II. At the time of Kennedy's inauguration in 1961, the American presence in Vietnam numbered about 800 advisers. Prior to his assassination in November, 1963, Kennedy poured into Vietnam 23,000 men, most of whom came from the armed services. After Lyndon B. Johnson assumed the presidency, the commitment to eliminate the North Vietnamese-supported Viet Cong guerrilla campaign resulted in the deployment of ever increasing numbers of American troops.

To bolster his aggressive stance on the Vietnam

Left: During the Cuban missile crisis, the old venerable carrier Essex *(CVS 6) made an appearance to search for Russian submarines while en route to Guantanamo. Updated with the latest SQS-23 Sonar and new electronic counter-measures equipment,* Essex *also carried the latest in antisubmarine aircraft – Grumman S2F Trackers (foreground), Sikorsky HSS-2 Sea King helicopters, and Grumman WF-2 Tracers.*

► **1966**

APRIL 10: PBRs, water-jet-propelled Navy patrol boats, begin operating in Vietnam waters.

MAY 9: Air-cushioned craft (PACVs) begin operating off South Vietnam.

JUNE 12: An F-8 Crusader brings down a MiG-17 with the first Sidewinder missile kill.

1967

FEBRUARY 26: A-6 Intruders from *Enterprise* mine North Vietnam waters.

MARCH 11: Walleye, the first television-guided air-to-surface bomb, is used on Sam Son, North Vietnam.

APRIL 24: Carrier planes launch the first attacks on enemy airfields.

Below: *In April 1965, 3,000 Marines from the 9th Marine Brigade, transported to Vietnam from Okinawa by the 7th Fleet transport USS* Mount McKinley *(LCC 7), land near Da Nang to reinforce 4,000 men from the same brigade who landed a month earlier.*

Left: *Drawn into the Cuban missile crisis, the nuclear-powered carrier* Enterprise *(CVAN 65) punctuated America's readiness for war as she headed for the communist-controlled island with armed AD-6 Skyraiders ready to launch strikes against predetermined targets.*

War, Johnson needed an "incident" to rally the support of all Americans. On August 2, 1964, such an incident occurred in the Tonkin Gulf when the destroyer *Maddox*, while carrying out an electronic-surveillance mission off North Vietnam, was attacked by three motor torpedo boats. Helped by aircraft from the carrier *Ticonderoga*, USS *Maddox* beat off the attack. Two days later the destroyer *Turner Joy* joined *Maddox* on her next patrol. That night technicians on board both vessels picked up radar blips and believed they were about to be attacked by several small vessels. In the aftermath of the firing and the confusion to evade torpedoes that followed, the destroyer crews began to question whether they had been attacked at all. Night-flying planes from *Ticonderoga*, also using radar, confirmed the absence of other surface vessels anywhere in the area.

FIRST BOMBS ON VIETNAM

Johnson, however, had his incident, and on the morning of August 5 he ordered aircraft from *Ticonderoga* and *Constellation* to bomb naval bases and oil-storage installations along 100 miles of the North Vietnamese coast. Sixty-four sorties destroyed twenty-five patrol boats and ninety percent of the petroleum stored in the target areas. Lieutenant (jg) Richard A. Sather, flying an A-1H Skyraider, became the first Navy pilot to lose his life in Vietnam, and Lieutenant (jg) Everett Alvaraz, flying an A-4E Skyhawk, was shot down, pulled from the water by North Vietnamese, and spent the next eight years in a prison camp. President Johnson had his war, and on August 10, 1964, Congress passed a resolution giving him blanket authority to "take all necessary measures to repel any armed attack against

Left: *In January 1969, F-4B Phantoms from VMFA-542, Group 11, 1st Marine Aircraft Wing, speed north on their way in a support mission for Marines assigned to the I Army Corps. Phantoms carried six Sparrow III missiles, or four Sparrows and four Sidewinders.*

the forces of the United States," and to assist any member of the Southeast Asia Treaty Organization. From the comfort of his oval office in the White House, Johnson underestimated the determination of Vietnamese communists and their many neighboring friends.

After assuring the American public that "we seek no wider war," Johnson began sending a half-million men to Vietnam, among them 85,000 Marines and 38,000 sailors. Not many days passed before senior naval officers began to quietly question whether a communist takeover of South Vietnam really imposed any threat to the United States or her interests. If America was to play a role, they believed it should be limited to providing the South Vietnamese with naval and air forces, and perhaps a small number of ground troops to act in a strictly advisory capacity. Among themselves the admirals expressed another concern. Most of their ships dated back to World War II, and funds needed to replace obsolete vessels would be diverted to pay for a needless war.

Much of the fighting centered on the so-called Demilitarized Zone between the two Vietnams, where Marines supported by 26,000 Seabees had been deployed at Da Nang and Hue. The Seventh Fleet, using Task Force 77, ran supporting operations from offshore, sending sorties over North Vietnam's supply lines and Hanoi's industrial centers. Battleships, cruisers, and destroyers patrolled the thousand-mile coastline, coordinating their fire in close support of forces of the Army and the Marine Corps. Task Force 115, formed of cutters, minesweepers, and patrol boats, hunted along shore for junks transporting supplies to the Viet Cong.

RESTRICTIONS ON PILOTS

Task Force 77 had too many restrictions to prosecute a winnable war, and the pilots knew it. In certain sections of North Vietnam they could bomb bridges, barracks, power stations, railroads, and industrial plants. In other areas, such as the important ports of Haiphong, Hon Gai, and Cam Pha, they could bomb nothing for fear of hitting Soviet supply ships, which were numerous and loaded with arms and equipment for the North Vietnamese. Naval personnel called them the president's "self-designated sanctuaries." Johnson annoyed Navy pilots from time to time by calling off the bombing and then authorizing it again. He would not allow the Navy to mine seven of North Vietnam's most important harbors, but later, on May 8, 1972, the new president, Richard M. Nixon, did.

The North Vietnamese had no air force. What MiG fighters they had were shot down early in the war. But what the enemy did have were

▶ **SEPTEMBER 1:** Paul R. Ignatius becomes the 59th Secretary of the Navy.

1968

JANUARY 22: The intelligence-collecting ship *Pueblo* is captured off North Korea.

JANUARY 30: The Tet Offensive begins.

MARCH 31: President Johnson declares he will not run for re-election and calls for peace talks.

SEPTEMBER 29: Vice Admiral Elmo R. Zumwalt, Jr., assumes command of naval operations off Vietnam.

OCTOBER 31: President Johnson orders the stopping of the bombardment of North Vietnam by all services.

1969

JANUARY 25: Truce talks begin in Paris.

JUNE 1: The South Vietnamese Navy assumes full responsibility for patrolling coastal sectors.

JUNE 8: The first troop withdrawals begin.

JULY 20: Apollo 11 capsule lands on the moon.

AUGUST 5: The first POWs are released from North Vietnam.

Right: *The USS Enterprise joined the Vietnam War with her deck loaded with A-4 Skyhawks. Unlike many carrier planes, the A-4's delta wings did not fold. Most A-4 series aircraft carried both air-to-air and air-to-ground missile launcher systems and bombs.*

THE *PUEBLO* AFFAIR

After years of cutbacks, the remaining resources of the Seventh Fleet became so committed to Vietnam that they could not respond to emergencies in other sectors of the Far East. When the intelligence-collection ship USS *Pueblo*, Commander Lloyd M. Bucher, strayed into North Korean waters on January 22, 1968, the United States could not respond militarily short of launching nuclear missiles. In a puzzling affair that took months to unravel, Bucher surrendered without a fight, having let his pair of .50-caliber machine guns freeze fast under their tarpaulins. Having no naval or air forces nearby to come to his rescue, Bucher followed his captors into Wonsan harbor. With one man mortally wounded and three others hit, among them himself, Bucher believed he had no other alternative but to surrender. He failed to destroy the ship's electronic equipment, which undoubtedly ended up in Russian hands.

Secretary of the Navy Paul R. Ignatius ordered an investigation and learned that Bucher had radioed for help when his ship was first threatened. No U.S. ship or aircraft arrived at the scene because none was in range to do so. Ignatius then discovered that the incident occurred because of poor command procedures, resulting in part from too many federal agencies and commands being involved in directing the ship's covert operations. Though Bucher remained accountable for the ship, no controlling authority would assume responsibility for the mission. Eleven months later the United States issued an apology – which it later repudiated – to North Korea for the sole purpose of recovering eighty-two members of the crew. After the men returned home a court of inquiry recommended that Bucher and another officer be tried for failing to fight the ship and allowing sensitive electronic equipment to be captured. The Secretary of the Navy overruled the recommendation, allowing that the men had "suffered enough."

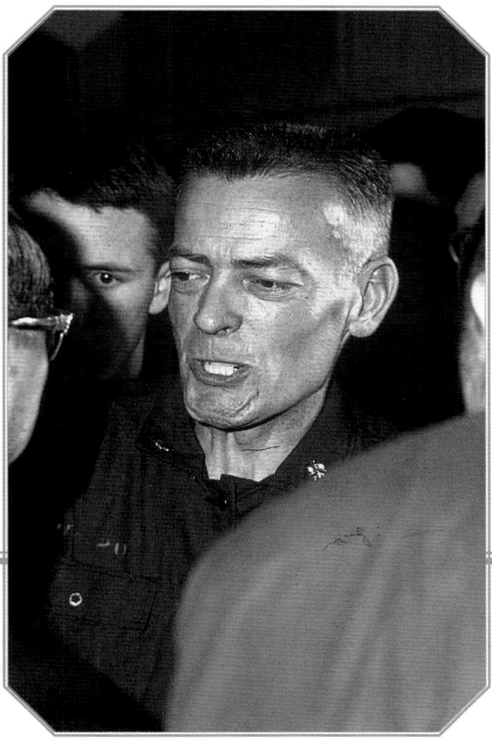

advanced antiaircraft systems in the form of Soviet-made, radar-directed SAMs (surface-to-air missiles). On night bombing runs during August 11-12, 1965, SAMs brought down one of *Midway*'s F-4 Phantom II jets. On the following night one A-1 Skyraider, two A-4 Skyhawks, and two F-8 Crusaders from the carriers *Midway* and *Coral Sea* were shot down while searching for SAM sites – the worst day for the Navy air arm since the fighting began. By March 31, 1968, Task Force 77 had lost 300 planes and 83 pilots and crewmen over North Vietnam. Another 200 fliers had either been captured or reported missing. For the third time since 1965, Johnson called another halt to bombing attacks, this time limiting sorties to the panhandle area south of the 20th Parallel. Had President Johnson permitted the bombing of enemy ports early in the war, fewer SAMs would have made it into North Vietnam. No pilot in the Navy could understand how the president could micro-manage the war in Vietnam from the White House and expressed few kind words for their blundering commander-in-chief.

The North Vietnamese also had no navy, and there were no naval battles. All three U.S. carriers ranged independently, accompanied only by their escorts. In flying weather their attacks on enemy positions were coordinated, constant, and routine. Each carrier launched ships for twelve-hour periods, recovered them, and then took a twelve-hour respite to rest and rearm before flying the next sorties. The carriers never left their stations. The Seventh Fleet's Service Force, based in Subic Bay in the Philippines, made the 700-mile jaunt to replenish the carriers with fuel, ammunition, and supplies.

Above: *On January 22, 1968, the intelligence collection ship* Pueblo *(AGER 2) is surrounded and fired upon by North Korean patrol boats in international waters off the east coast of North Korea.*

Left: *Lt. Comdr. Lloyd M. Bucher is unable to protect* Pueblo *because his pair of .50-caliber machine guns on the ship's bridge had frozen fast under their tarpaulins. Having no U.S. naval or air support within range, Bucher surrenders the ship and takes it under North Korean escort into Wonsan harbor. He is seen here after his release.*

▶ AUGUST 21:
Secretary of Defense
Laird cuts the
defense budget by $3
million.

1970

APRIL 29:
American and South
Vietnamese forces
invade Cambodia.

MAY 6: Navy PBRs
enter Cambodia on
the Kham Span
River.

AUGUST 3: The
submarine James
Madison launches
the first multi-
warhead Poseidon
nuclear missile.

Above right: *A
monitor (MON) from
River Assault Flotilla
I uses an Army M10-
8 flame thrower to
scorch an enemy
ambush position
along the Mekong
Delta.*

Below: *An armored
assault support
patrol boat (ASPB)
from River Assault
Flotilla I, a joint
Navy/Army force,
operates up the
Mekong River and
into the Rung Sat
Special Zone.*

In the 4,000-mile system of canals and estuaries in the sweltering Mekong Delta south of Saigon, Task Force 177 used shallow-draft monitors fitted with one 105mm howitzer or 81mm mortar, two 20mm and three .30-caliber machine guns, and two 40mm high-velocity grenade launchers. In place of a howitzer or mortar, some monitors carried two army M10-8 flamethrowers. On occasion, sailors could be found carrying bows and arrows, handy weapons for hurling a burning wad into a bamboo hut.

Known as the "battleships" of the riverine fleet, monitors transported armored troop carriers (ATCs) to hot spots in the Ninth Army Division sector. ATCs carried their own batteries, usually two 20mm guns, two to six .30- and two .50-caliber machine guns, one 40mm high-velocity grenade launcher, and two 40mm low-velocity grenade launchers. ATCs also carried landing platforms for the UH-1D Huey helicopter, which was used for evacuating the wounded.

OPERATION GAME WARDEN

For riverine vessels, no duty was any more hazardous than Operation Game Warden, where firefights with Viet Cong hidden in the jungle could erupt at any time. The monitors were reminiscent of the Mississippi River ironclads used by Admiral David D. Porter during the Civil War. They were slow — their top speed being about eight knots — and their purpose was to protect transports and to knock-out guerrilla positions concealed in the jungle. Vessels of the task force also worked out of Da Nang, escorting LSTs and smaller amphibious vessels up the Perfume and Cua Viet Rivers, waterways swarming with guerrillas and floating mines. In 1968, members of a single unit earned one Medal of Honor, six Navy Crosses, and 500 Purple Hearts.

Augmenting Task Force 117 were the speedy steel-hulled assault support patrol boats (ASPBs) of Task Force 116. Converted from LCMs (Landing craft, medium), these boats were powered by three gas turbines driving three water jets

Above: *During Operation Game Warden, the shallow-draft PBR river patrol boat became the workhorse of the Navy on inland waters. With four- or five-man crews, the PBRs patrolled the rivers of South Vietnam, carried machine guns and a grenade launcher, and operated with an air support wing of Army helicopters.*

Left: *Navy SEALs (Sea-Air-Land) performed every type of mission imaginable, from commando raids in the jungle to underwater demolition. On January 20, 1967, they used a mechanized landing craft in the Rung Sat Zone to attack an enemy position and set fire to the Viet Cong village in the background.*

Right: *The Navy's
patrol Air Cushion
Vehicle (ACV) came
into use during
Operation Game
Warden and was used
almost exclusively in
the Mekong Delta. It
served a utilitarian
purpose in Vietnam
during shallow water
missions but had little
value in direct combat
with the enemy.*

at speeds up to forty knots. They carried a light-weight 105mm howitzer, and two 20mm cannon mounted in a tank-like turret. A smaller remote-controlled forward mount contained two 20mm cannon and a 40mm grenade launcher. ASPBs were usually commanded by a petty officer with a crew of four or five, some having been cooks and yeomen. Their 12-hour patrols took them up the steamy, winding Mekong Delta where they spent long hours inspecting junks and sampans for contraband. Men suffered from boredom, mosquitoes, fatigue, humidity, torrential downpours, occasional ambushes, booby traps, and carefully camouflaged floating mines.

AMBUSH IN THE DELTA

Men of the river patrol boats (PBRs) never knew what to expect when interdicting junks and sampans. On one occasion in October, 1966, *PBR 105* and *107* were idling off Ngo Hiep Island in the Mekong Delta when they came across a pair of junks and eight sampans huddled together near shore. As Petty Officer James E. Williams's PBR approached, hundreds of Viet Cong hidden behind the bulwarks opened with a heavy fusillade that was augmented by automatic fire from shore. Williams exposed himself to withering fire to get his men to their guns, after which he called for helicopter support. Three hours later night fell and the enemy could no longer be seen. Williams

turned on searchlights, at the same time drawing the fire of the enemy. By dawn the sampans had vanished. Most of the VC's vessels had been sunk and an ammunition junk blown to bits. For extraordinary heroism, Williams received the Medal of Honor. Such fights were common. One out of every three riverine sailors was killed or wounded in the skirmishes.

On July 29, 1968, Operation Game Warden expanded up to the Cambodian border, taking Navy SEALs (Sea Air Land) on special missions deep into the country itself. SEALs often used a volunteer from the South Vietnamese Special Forces dressed as a Viet Cong to question the locals concerning the whereabouts of the enemy. These insertions were usually intelligence-gathering missions, but they often resulted in sudden firefights that required helicopter support. One SEAL mission collided with a heavy force of Viet Cong and had to call in monitor support to extricate themselves after withdrawing to the water. Each man took a wounded buddy wrapped in a life jacket and towed him to safety. In one such act of heroism, Engineman Second Class Michael E. Thornton saved the life of his superior officer and received the Medal of Honor.

Four-man strike assault boats (STABs) operated far up the Mekong Delta and into Cambodia. STAB patrols moved at high speed along the riverbank, a man at each gun mount, but not always fast enough to evade fire from guerrilla AK-47s or the occasional grenade. Just before the United States pulled out of the war, the Navy

Left: *SEALs use a strike assault boat (STAB) to make a high-speed river patrol close to the Cambodian border on June 20, 1967.*

turned all the PBR boats over to the South Vietnamese.

On January 25, 1969, truce talks between the United States and North Vietnam began in Paris. Before the close of the year, the South Vietnamese Navy assumed responsibility for patrolling a large section of the coast and waterways. President Richard M. Nixon began removing troops, and Secretary of Defense Melvin R. Laird sliced $3 billion from the defense budget.

WITHDRAWL FROM 'NAM

For Americans the withdrawal process remained agonizingly slow. On June 26, 1971, the 3rd Marine Amphibious Brigade, the last Marine combat unit in South Vietnam, departed from Da Nang. Not until April 1, 1972, were all U.S. Navy personnel removed from South Vietnam, but for many months to come the Seventh Fleet remained offshore, shelling harbors and flying air missions over North Vietnam. After both parties signed a peace accord on January 27, 1973, the Navy remained behind to sweep mines from coastal North Vietnam.

The Vietnam War left a bad impression on many Americans, including those who fought it and those who remained behind after it ended. On April 12, 1975, Marine Corps helicopters had to remove embassy personnel from Cambodia's

besieged capital. Seventeen days later Navy and Marine helicopters from Seventh Fleet carriers evacuated 9,000 civilian and military personnel from Saigon, among them 989 Marines who had been inserted to cover the operation. The final flight came from the rooftop of the American embassy on April 30 as North Vietnamese tanks rolled into the city. The United States got her men back but left Southeast Asia in the hands of the communists. The Navy performed its role and met every expectation of the government, but nobody came home happy about the outcome.

Above: *On April 29, 1975, Navy crewmen on the USS* Blue Ridge *carry Vietnamese children who have been flown to the ship by South Vietnam helicopters. After landing the children, all the helicopters were pushed over the side or ditched by their pilots.*

TERRORISM & THE GULF WAR

In 1959 the Navy reorganized and established four new bureaus – Naval Weapons, Ships, Yards and Docks, and Supplies and Accounts. The new departments lasted seven years. With rapid advancements in technology, especially in submarine, missile, and nuclear warfare. On May 1, 1966, the Navy replaced the four bureaus with six commands reporting to the Office of Naval Material: Ordnance Systems, Air Systems, Ship Systems, Electronic Systems, Supply Systems, and Facilities Engineering. The Navy then coupled the Office of Naval Material with the Bureau of Naval Personnel and the Bureau of Medicine and Surgery and placed them directly under the Chief of Naval Operations (CNO).

On July 1, 1970, forty-nine-year-old Admiral Elmo R. Zumwalt, Jr., became the youngest four-star admiral and the youngest CNO in the history of the Navy. Zumwalt's star began to rise in 1968 when he became Commander, U.S. Naval Forces, Vietnam. The Navy recognized his abilities and elevated him to rear admiral two years before he was technically old enough to be one, and the rapidity with which he "Vietnamized" naval operations in Southeast Asia so impressed Congress that they approved his controversial appointment to CNO.

The depressing combination of deteriorating combat ships combined with an unpopular war had worn down almost everyone but Zumwalt. He launched a two-pronged campaign to modernize the fleet and abolish the Navy's antiquated

> '*When I joined the Navy, all the enlisted men lived on board; the ship was home. This was a very severe cultural change – when the ship was no longer a home, but a place to go and work. This caused great stresses that didn't exist before.*'
>
> CAPTAIN ROGER BARNETT TO STEPHEN HOWARD, IN *TO SHINING SEA*.

personnel policies. A flurry of directives emanating from his office in the Pentagon, known as "Z-grams," delighted younger officers and enlisted personnel but troubled career professionals. They feared that the changes, abetted by the social revolution sweeping the nation, would erode long-standing traditions and relax discipline. Zumwalt understood the impact of the social changes that came with the Vietnam War and the Johnson administration. He let his bushy eyebrows grow untrimmed and sported long sideburns. He permitted sailors to grow beards, choose their own hairstyles, wear civilian clothes on liberty, and keep vehicles on naval bases. He also made the predominantly white male Navy more accessible to women, blacks, and other minorities, and he made the service more attractive by giving officers and enlisted men longer tours of duty ashore to be with their families. Not all sailors agreed with the new "homeporting" regulations, since they preferred the traditional economy of being able to live on their ship.

Liberalizing the standards of the Navy also had a downside. Racial violence erupted on four ships where small groups of young blacks attacked whites. Zumwalt ordered an investigation and discovered that the disorderly blacks had been enlisted in specialized job classifications for which they had no skills and could not qualify for advancement in a navy growing by leaps and bounds technologically. Critics of the

Right: *When it came to quarters on the submarine USS* La Jolla *(SSN 701), commissioned on October 24, 1981, some of the crew bunked on racks beside the ship's Mk 48 torpedoes.*

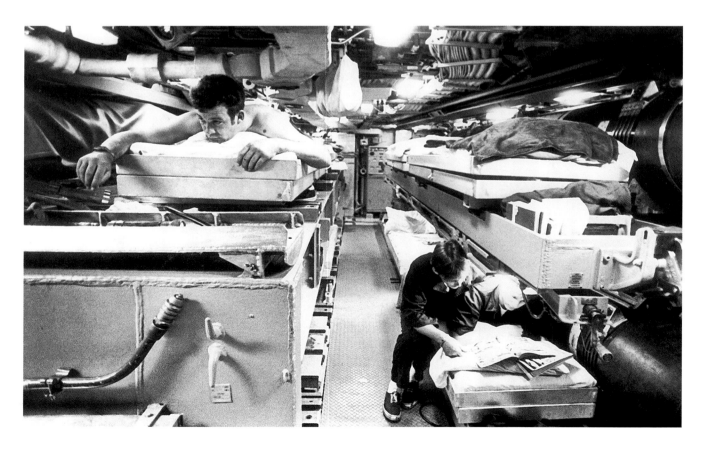

fast-paced reforms blamed Zumwalt, but the admiral attributed the problems to the social turmoil spreading across the nation. He did not like the raised clenched-fist salutes of black protesters, but when President Nixon demanded that the men be dishonorably discharged, Zumwalt ignored the order. He re-emphasized the importance of promoting equality within the service, writing, "I considered the tumult not as a warning to take a defensive posture, but as an opportunity to nail equal treatment for minorities and women so firmly in the Navy that anyone would have trouble removing it."

SOVIETS OUTMATCH NAVY

When on July 1, 1974, Zumwalt turned the office of CNO over to Admiral James L. Holloway III, he also turned over enormous problems – the Soviet Union had entered the race for mastery of the seas. The presence of Soviet warships in the Mediterranean had prevented the Sixth Fleet from mixing into the Arab-Israeli War of 1967, the Jordanian crisis of 1970, and the Yom Kippur War

Left: *The USS* Georgia *(SSBN 729) was one of ten nuclear-propelled Ohio-class submarines to go into commission during the 1980s. Fully integrated crews – blacks, whites, and latinos – learned to work in harmony as they handled the controls at their dive stations.*

Left: *Three of the Navy's new carriers were the giant 1,090-foot* Nimitz *(1975),* Dwight D. Eisenhower *(1977), and* Carl Vinson *(1982), with displacements of 91,400 tons. Powered by two A4W nuclear reactors, the carriers could steam at 33 knots and carry ninety fixed-wing aircraft and helicopters. The completion of the carriers was delayed by the Vietnam conflict. When finally commissioned they could do most anything from controlling the sea to hunting submarines or launching air attacks deep into enemy territory.*

▶ 1976

MARCH 28: An A-6 Intruder makes the first successful launching of a Tomahawk cruise missile.

JULY 6: The first women are sworn in at the Naval Academy.

NOVEMBER 13: The USS *Los Angeles*, the newest class of nuclear submarines, is launched.

1977

JANUARY 18: The first new, long-range Trident missile is launched at Cape Canaveral.

1978

FEBRUARY 1: The USS *Barb* makes the first successful launch of a Trident missile from a submarine.

FEBRUARY 9: The first Navy Fleet Satellite Communications System is placed in space.

Right: The earlier Ohio-class strategic missile submarines such as the USS Lafayette *(SSBN 616) carried 16 Trident C-4 missiles in their tubes. After 1981, all Ohio-class submarines were fitted with 24 tubes for either Trident C-4 or D-5 SLBMs.*

of October, 1973. During the latter conflict, Zumwalt strengthened the Sixth Fleet to sixty-five vessels, only to find his force outmatched by ninety-eight Soviet ships. The affair triggered a worldwide alert, the first since the assassination of President Kennedy, and it occurred during President Nixon's troubling Watergate scandal. Zumwalt later dolefully admitted that "we lacked either the military strength or the stable domestic leadership – one or the other might have been enough – to have supported the Israelis."

CALL FOR LARGER SHIPS

To address needed material changes in the Navy, carrier admirals sought larger ships, such as the 91,400-ton *Nimitz*. But with the development of cruise missiles, nuclear-tipped weapons, and highly sophisticated torpedoes, other officers pointed to the vulnerability of large surface vessels, preferring instead that funds be spent on building more submarines and antisubmarine vessels. Hardly behind the scenes, seventy-six-year-old Admiral Rickover demanded that all future warships be nuclear-powered, despite the higher cost and the consequence of being compelled to build fewer ships. While Holloway debated the needs of the Navy, Admiral Rickover, in his characteristic manner, informed Congress that he would rather command the Soviet submarine fleet because if it came to war, he would have a better chance of winning it.

Zumwalt also left a few pieces from the 1972 Mid-East War unfinished, the clearing of the Suez Canal of mines and sunken vessels deposited there by Egypt. On June 5, 1975, the guided-missile cruiser *Little Rock*, flagship of the Sixth Fleet, made the first transit through the canal, but minesweeping operations continued for another six weeks.

Following President Nixon's resignation, neither Gerald Ford, who succeeded him, nor Georgia Democrat Jimmy Carter, who won the presidential election in 1976, did anything to bolster the needs of the Navy. Carter had been a naval officer during World War II but he seemed oblivious to the growing gap in power between a Soviet Navy with 446 combat vessels and a rapidly declining U.S. Navy with 217.

Having entered another era of progressive depletion, this time under the Carter administration, senior naval officers became utterly perplexed. Harold Brown, Carter's shortsighted Secretary of Defense, seemed oblivious to the festering problems in the Mid-East when he tried to redefine the Navy's role as mainly "to protect the sea lanes of communication between the United States and Europe." Admiral Holloway predicted that if Brown's limited view of the world prevailed, the United States would by the turn of the century be unable to protect its sea-lanes, much less fulfill its peacetime or wartime tasks. Nor had the Carter administration taken notice of the turmoil in the Mid-East when making decisions affecting the Navy's future. Iran revolted against the shah, and the Soviet Union threatened to invade Afghanistan. Preoccupied by problems with Iran, three months passed before Carter took interest in Afghanistan. The Kremlin ignored Carter's eleventh hour warnings and on December 27 sent troops into Afghanistan.

On November 4, 1979, after many months of harassing Americans in Iran, Muslims stormed the U.S. embassy in Tehran and took hostages, by any other definition an act of war. A month later another mob raided the U.S. embassy in Tripoli, but diplomatic personnel escaped unharmed. Carter dispatched a carrier group to the Arabian Sea without clearly explaining the task group's mission. The Iranians, perhaps understanding

Comparison of naval strength – 1978		
	United States	Soviet Union
Carriers	21	3
Nuclear submarines	68	84
Other submarines	51	210
Ballistic nuclear ships	41	58
Other combat vessels	36	91
Totals	**217**	**446**

OPERATION BLUE LIGHT

On April 24, 1980, the U.S. Navy and Air Force combined in a daring attempt to rescue American hostages held in Tehran. At the time, the Navy had twenty-seven ships positioned in the Arabian Sea. The operation called for six Air Force C-130 transports to fly from Egypt and rendezvous with eight RH-53D helicopters launched from the USS *Nimitz.* Each air group would carry special forces commandos and meet at Desert One, a staging point two hundred miles from Tehran.

On the way to Desert One, two of the helicopters experienced mechanical trouble and turned back. A third helicopter conked out while landing in a whirl of flying sand. Because a minimum of six helicopters was needed for the rescue, Colonel Charles Beckwith aborted the mission. On departure a fourth helicopter, its rotating system becoming clogged with sand, collided with one of the transports, killing five airmen and three Marines.

The embarrassing attempt diminished the fragile esteem of the armed forces of the United States at home and abroad and gave encouragement to the Soviet Union and their friends in the Mid-East to take reckless chances. The botched mission also contributed to President Carter's inability to win a second term. The bad experience, however, provided a valuable observation. Helicopters could not operate in desert conditions without major design changes, and ten years later the United States would need aircraft and vehicles that could.

Above: On April 24, 1980, sand-colored RH-53D helicopters wait on the deck of the USS Nimitz *for take-off on an ill-conceived mission to Desert One.*

Left: The map of the Desert One mission illustrates the long, circuitous route taken by the Air Force C-130 transports to rendezvous with helicopters launched from the Arabian Sea.

Carter better than he understood himself, ignored the show of force and held the hostages until Ronald Reagan took office.

After fifteen years of abject melancholy, the Navy received a new stimulus when Ronald Reagan attained the presidency. Anyone who questioned what an aging, ex-movie star might know about naval affairs got their answer when Reagan appointed Casper M. Weinberger Secretary of Defense, and thirty-eight-year-old John F. Lehman, Jr., Secretary of the Navy. Weinberger immediately increased defense expenditures over Carter's budget by 11 percent for fiscal year 1981 and by 15 percent for 1982, adding $9.5 billion to the naval program. Lehman articulated his perception of the new Navy, promising that by 1990 the service would hold "outright maritime superiority over any power...which might attempt to prevent our free use of the seas and the maintenance of our vital interests worldwide." He envisioned fifteen carrier battle groups, 100 nuclear attack submarines, and four surface battle groups, which meant renovating World War II battleships. Few believed him, but on February 4, 1981, defense spending included the reactivation of the battleships *New Jersey, Iowa,* and *Oriskany.* Recommissioning old-line battleships became a contentious issue among some admirals, but Lehman demanded them, arguing that they were the heaviest armored vessels afloat, and if battleships should be suddenly needed the

▶ **APRIL 6:** Colonel Margaret A. Brewer is nominated to become the first woman brigadier general in the Marine Corps.

NOVEMBER 1: For the first time, nine women ensigns are assigned to five non-combatant vessels of the Atlantic Fleet.

1979

APRIL 1: Twenty-six-year-old Lieutenant (jg) Beverly Kelly becomes the first woman to captain a U.S. warship.

NOVEMBER 4: The Iranian hostage crisis begins.

Right: *The USS* Iowa *(BB 61), commissioned in 1943, continued to receive the latest upgrades in technology. Recommissioned in 1984 with Harpoon and Tomahawk missiles, she test fires one of the latter during exercises.*

enemy would not give the country time to build them.

On December 28, 1982, the battleship *New Jersey* – a veteran of World War II, Korea, and Vietnam – became the first of the giant vessels to go back into commission. Updated with the latest weapons, she carried sixteen Harpoon missiles with ranges of 50-60 miles and thirty-two Tomahawk cruise missiles with ranges up to 500 miles. As the range of upgraded Tomahawks, tipped with nuclear warheads, increased to 1,500 nautical miles, the Navy refitted the old battleships with launchers to carry the new weapons.

MID-EAST TERRORISM

Reagan also demonstrated that the United States was not to be pushed around by the Soviet Union or anybody else. During the Syria-Israeli war in 1981, the Sixth Fleet maintained a strong presence in the Mediterranean. When Colonel Muammar Qadaffi declared the entire Gulf of Sidra as Libyan territorial waters, the United States rejected the claim. On August 18 Qadaffi sent Libyan Su-22 Fitter fighters to assert his demands, and two F-14 Tomcats from the carrier *Nimitz* shot them down.

A year later war erupted between the Palestine Liberation Organization (PLO) in Lebanon and invading Israeli forces. Though mindful of how close America had come to war with Soviet naval forces during the Yom Kippur War of 1973, Lehman, on August 18, 1982, nonetheless dispatched 800 Marines from the 32nd Marine Amphibious Unit to cooperate with French and Italian detachments in the removal of 12,000 Palestinians from Beirut. By September 10, the entire community had been transferred to merchant vessels protected by the Sixth Fleet.

On September 29, 1,200 Marines under Colonel James M. Mead returned to Lebanon and joined French and Italian forces in a Multinational Peacekeeping Force. Seven months later, April 18, 1983, terrorists exploded a truck bomb outside the U.S. Embassy in Beirut, killing 61 persons, among them one Marine and 17 American civilians. The bombing signaled the beginning of more terrorist actions. At 6:25 a.m. on October 23, a Mercedes truck loaded with 2,000 pounds of high explosives crashed through barricades outside the headquarters building of the 24th Marine Amphibious Unit. The explosion killed 241 Marines and wounded 70. Minutes later, a second truck struck the French compound, killing 58 more peacekeepers.

The situation in Lebanon continued to worsen. Lehman pulled the battleship *New Jersey* off the east coast of Central America and ordered her to Lebanon. On December 4, Syrian antiaircraft and Russian-built surface-to-air batteries shot down

Left: *Commissioned on September 9, 1989, the nuclear-propelled USS Pennsylvania (SSBN 735) was the tenth Ohio-class submarine put to sea. At 560 feet overall, she displaced 18,750 tons submerged and could make 30 knots below the surface. She carried 24 tubes for Trident missiles and four 21-inch tubes amidships for Mk68 torpedoes.*

'We cannot and will not abstain from forcible action to prevent, preempt, and respond to terrorist acts when conditions merit the use of force.'

ROBERT C. McFARLANE,
MARCH, 1985.

Left: *U.S. Marines landed in Lebanon on a peacekeeping mission on August 25, 1982. A year later a terrorist suicide-driver bombed the headquarters building of the 24th Marine Amphibious Unit, compelling Marines to take to the street to hunt for suspects and to protect American interests.*

two Navy reconnaissance planes twenty miles east of Beirut. At the cost of two more aircraft, A-6 Intruders and A-7 Corsairs from the carriers *Independence* and *John F. Kennedy* retaliated and bombed six Syrian positions in the mountains. On December 14, *New Jersey* opened on enemy positions with 16-inch shells, the first fired anywhere in the world since 1969.

While the Sixth Fleet tried to keep the peace in the Mid-East, Cuban and Nicaraguan communists, supplied with arms from Russia, attempted to incite a Marxist revolution in the small Central American country of El Salvador. Navy SEALs went ashore during 1983 on covert missions and remained there for more than a year while carrier groups, exercising offshore, turned around Soviet arms-supply vessels heading into Nicaragua.

Reagan believed that the best way to prevent wars was to impede them before they escalated, but by 1985 fighting had taken a back seat to more

▶ **1980**

APRIL 24: The Iranian rescue mission ends in failure.

MAY 28: The first fifty-five women cadets graduate from the Naval Academy.

1981

FEBRUARY 5: John F. Lehman, Jr., becomes the sixty-fifth Secretary of the Navy.

AUGUST 19: Navy Tomcats shoot down two Libyan planes over the Gulf of Sidra.

NOVEMBER 11: The USS *Ohio*, the first of the Navy's new nuclear-powered, ballistic missile submarines, is commissioned.

Above right: *On October 25, 1983, a joint force of U.S. Navy SEALs and Marines land on six Grenada beaches (see arrows) during Operation Urgent Fury, and Army Ranger parachutists land on an unfinished 9,000-foot airstrip built by Cuban forces at Point Salinas.*

OPERATION URGENT FURY — GRENADA

On October 19, 1983, four days before the Beirut bombing of Marine headquarters, a Marxist coup overthrew Grenada's government after a communist general murdered the commonwealth's president. The former British colony of Grenada, a 133-square-mile island in the eastern Caribbean, lay 1,600 miles from Florida. If given the time to fortify, the island would have provided communists with the same military advantages as had Cuba. Soviet aid had already supplied a naval base, military installations, and storage facilities for an arms buildup. One thousand Americans lived on the island, most of them students attending St. George's University Medical School.

President Reagan had no intention of allowing the USSR to build a base in the Caribbean. He diverted to Grenada a task force of twelve ships and 1,900 Marines en route to Lebanon. On October 25, at the invitation of the Organization of Eastern Caribbean States, Reagan issued orders to Vice Admiral Joseph Metcalf, Jr., to occupy the island.

Early on the 25th Metcalf put SEALs ashore to infiltrate the capital of St. George's and secure Government House, where insurgents had held Governor General Sir Paul Scoon captive since the coup. At 5:36 a.m. helicopters from USS *Guam* landed 400 men from the 22nd Marine Amphibious Unit on Pearls Airport, Grenada's only operational airfield. Thirty minutes later C-5A and C-130 transport aircraft from Barbados dropped parachutists on a new unfinished 9,000-foot airstrip being built by Cubans on Point Salinas. By 8:50 a.m. American forces secured every target area except for Government House at St. George's, where SEALs had been surrounded and besieged mainly by Cubans. On the morning of October 26, Marines secured Government House and, on the following day, the entire island. American casualties were light — 18 killed and 116 wounded. During the mopping-up campaign combined American forces discovered unmistakable signs of a major communist military buildup augmented by the presence of 49 Russian, 24 North Korean, and 13 Eastern European diplomats and advisers. The American invasion force collected 638 Cuban prisoners, found warehouses crammed with Soviet arms, and located documents revealing plans for establishing a garrison for 6,800 Cuban troops.

Before the invasion the U.S. State Department failed to remind Reagan that Grenada, though no longer a British colony, was still a commonwealth with Queen Elizabeth as head of state. Britain expressed considerable displeasure when the United States muscled into her domain. Two years later, when the Queen visited the island, a correspondent from the London *Times* observed that, "Ronald Reagan would have drawn bigger crowds. He is so revered [here]....Loyalties are now to Washington, not London."

Left: *During the mopping up process, a Marine from the 22nd Amphibious Unit steers a Cuban "soldier" into a hurriedly constructed stockade.*

Left: *The guided-missile cruiser USS* Ticonderoga *(CG 47) became the first of her class. By 1994, the Navy had commissioned 24 such ships with Aegis weapon systems. In the stern* Ticonderoga *carried Harpoon canisters and a Mk26 missile launcher, shown being fired.*

insidious forms of warfare. In that year alone, the State Department reported nearly 700 international terrorist incidents mainly emanating out of the Mid-East. American citizens and servicemen were getting killed everywhere they went.

ACHILLE LAURO INCIDENT

On October 7, 1985, four Palestinian passengers hijacked the cruise liner *Achille Lauro* at gunpoint and demanded the release of fifty Palestinians jailed in Israel. The guided-missile destroyer USS *Scott* shadowed the captured vessel, and the carrier USS *Saratoga* went on alert. After murdering one crippled passenger, the terrorists accepted a deal brokered by Egypt, and on October 9 they disembarked unmolested at Port Said. American intelligence learned that the terrorists intended to fly to Tunis on an Egyptian airliner. Reagan authorized that the plane be intercepted so long as no harm came to other passengers.

On the evening of October 10, the carrier *Saratoga* launched two E-2C Hawkeye aircraft to watch for the Egyptian flight carrying the terrorists. *Yorktown*, steaming in company with *Saratoga*, carried a sophisticated radar system capable of monitoring anything in the air in the eastern half of the Mediterranean and hundreds of miles inland. After *Yorktown*'s radar spotted the Egyptian airliner, four F-14 Tomcat fighters from *Saratoga* closed on the aircraft, surrounded it, and forced it to land at Rome. Both acts, the first bred by terrorists who captured *Achille*

Lauro, and the second propagated by American fighter aircraft forcing a plane of a sovereign nation to land at an airport against the pilot's wishes, caused quite a commotion internationally and especially in Italy and Egypt. Most people in the western world condoned the act as a necessary strike against terrorism. Libyan leader Qadaffi felt differently and sent terrorists to set off explosives at Rome and Vienna's airports.

By January, 1986, the center of gravity for terrorism had shifted to Qadaffi. On the 26th Vice Admiral Frank B. Kelso, commanding two battle groups, moved the carriers *Saratoga* and *Coral Sea* into position off the Gulf of Sidra and maneuvered off Libya. Qadaffi had announced that any American ship or airplane penetrating the Gulf

Below: *A Grumman swing-wing F-14A Tomcat, armed with six Phoenix missiles, prepares to launch from the deck of the USS* Saratoga. *Mounted under the Tomcat's nose is a TV optical system and deceptive jamming system. Four F-14s forced down an Egyptian airliner which was under the control of terrorists.*

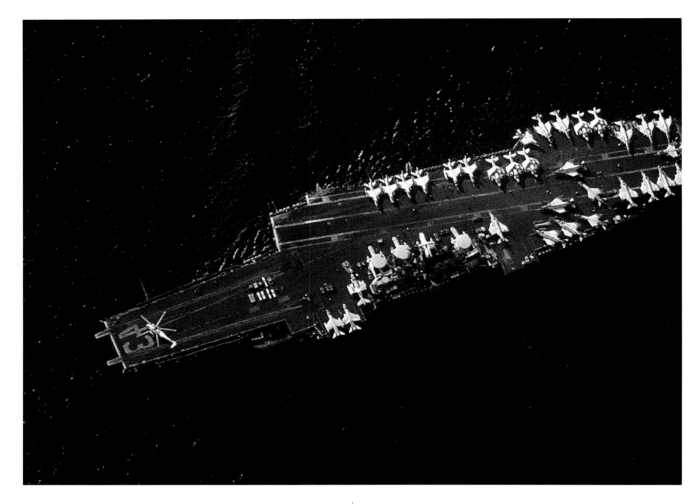

Above right: *An overhead shot of the USS* Coral Sea *(CV 43) shows a deck jammed with a variety of aircraft.* Coral Sea *launched strikes against Libyan military targets in 1986.*

Below: *Images from Pave Tack laser-guided delivery system show Soviet-made Libyan Il-76 military transports just prior to the strike.*

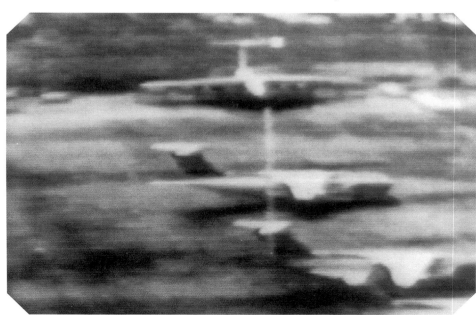

and entering his so-called "Line of Death" would be attacked and destroyed. On the first day of operations, Libyan MiG-25 Foxboats approached one of the American Combat Air Patrols but were intercepted and chased away without a shot being fired. The third carrier group led by the USS *America* joined Kelso's Sixth Fleet, making it stronger than it had been for years. For eight weeks the minuet with Libyan aircraft continued until March 24 when the guided-missile cruiser USS *Ticonderoga* crossed the "Line of Death" into waters recognized by everyone but Qadaffi as international. That afternoon carrier aircraft also penetrated the "Line" and evaded two surface-to-air missiles fired from Libyan shore batteries.

Kelso now found reason to retaliate. That night an A-6 from USS *America* sank a Libyan missile patrol boat, and A-7s and A-6s from *Saratoga* and *Coral Sea* struck land-based SAM sites, sank a missile corvette, and damaged another. Qadaffi responded by launching more terrorist attacks, blowing up a TWA (Flight 847) airliner and bombing a German discotheque jammed with U.S. servicemen.

AIR STRIKE ON LIBYA

President Reagan had seen enough of Qadaffi's methods and ordered an air strike. On April 10, 1986, dozens of carrier aircraft struck Benghazi's Benina airfield and military barracks, terrorist training bases at Sidi Bilal, and Tripoli's military airport and barracks. The night attack came as a complete surprise to Qadaffi and the rest of the world. All the target areas were hit. The U.S. Navy lost only one plane, possibly from mechanical failure. Reagan had hoped to dispose of Qadaffi. Instead, at least a hundred Libyan and foreign nationals died, including one of the colonel's adopted children. The propaganda emanating from the child's unfortunate death made it difficult for other nations to accept bombing runs as a means of curbing terrorism. Reagan could find few other ways to discourage terrorism aside from attacking its center of gravity, though he cautioned, "We must be careful that we do not appear as terrorists ourselves."

BENINA AIRFIELD
15 APR 86

DESTROYED F-27

DAMAGED MI-8/HIP

DESTROYED MI-8/HIP

Left: *Aerial photos taken after the April 14, 1986, surprise air attack on Benina Airfield, Libya, show the military assets destroyed during the missio*

With Reagan in office, the Navy grew in leaps and bounds. On October 25, 1986, the nuclear carrier *Theodore Roosevelt* was commissioned, bringing the nation's carrier strength to fifteen. By the end of 1987, the Navy had grown to 509 ships with still more on the way. By adding eighty more in 1988, the 600-ship Navy envisioned by Reagan and Lehman was well in sight. Defense expenditures, especially for the Navy, were enormous, incomprehensible, and unacceptable to members of a Democrat-controlled Congress. They shook their heads at the huge growth in the nation's debt and its effect upon the domestic economy, interest rates, and the shrinking value of the American dollar. Reagan had an objective less visionary opponents failed to comprehend – to bankrupt communism by forcing the Soviet Union into an arms race they could not financially sustain.

GRAMM-RUDMAN BILL

When congressional budget cutters went to work during Reagan's second term, naval expenditures became the primary target, mainly because big-ticket items like nuclear-powered carriers and Ohio-class submarines cost billions. In 1985 Congress passed the Gramm-Rudman Bill, legislation designed to control the growing national debt by balancing the budget for the next five years. Naval advocates derided the bill, one expert lamenting, "If Gramm-Rudman stays in force for the full five years, the U.S. Navy will suffer its greatest defeat since Pearl Harbor." Another policy analyst declared, "Gramm-Rudman! The very words conjure up images of faceless bureaucrats wielding meat cleavers with no regard for priorities…." The legislation so annoyed Secretary of the Navy Lehman that on April 11, 1987, he resigned. Ex-Marine James H. Webb filled the post for less than a year. Having watched the budget-cutters snip away at Navy expenditures and having no power to stop them, Webb also resigned.

In 1987 the U.S. Navy had more to worry about

Below: *On April 18, 1987, an Iranian oil platform goes up in smoke after being struck in a reprisal attack by Navy aircraft from the carrier* Enterprise *during the Iran-Iraq War.*

► 1984

FEBRUARY 7:
President Reagan
withdraws Marines
from Lebanon.

1985

OCTOBER 7: Four
Palestinians hijack the
cruise liner *Achille
Lauro.*

OCTOBER 10:
Aircraft intercept an
Egyptian plane
carrying Palestinian
hijackers, forcing it to
land at Rome.

1986

JANUARY 26: Navy
surveillance of Libya
begins.

MARCH 24: Libyan
shore batteries fire on
American aircraft.

APRIL 10: Carrier
aircraft bomb Tripoli
and Benghazi.
1987

Above right: *Aircraft
on carriers do not get
very far on their own.
Mobile transports
shuttle F-14A Tomcats
about the deck of the
USS* Dwight D.
Eisenhower.

than budget cutting. The long, bloody war between Iraq and Iran threatened to disrupt the transportation of oil from the Persian Gulf. Both combatants showed no compunction about capturing or firing upon unguarded vessels under neutral flags. To ensure supplies of oil, the United States joined the navies of Western Europe escorting tankers and merchant ships through the war zone. Reagan permitted Kuwaiti tankers to fly the American flag, and because Kuwait was supporting Iraq, the president involved the U.S. Navy in Iraq's war with Iran. This relationship seemed to make little difference to Iraqi pilots. Off Bahrain on May 17, an Iraqi F-1 Mirage jet fired two Exocet missiles at the frigate USS *Stark*, killing thirty-seven Americans. Two months later a floating mine, ostensibly the work of Iranians, blew a huge hole in the supertanker *Bridgeton*, a Kuwaiti vessel flying the Stars and Stripes. Being a double-hulled, steel-plated vessel, *Bridgeton* completed her voyage. On September 21, a helicopter from the frigate USS *Jarrett* spied an Iranian boat in the act of laying more mines and blew it up.

Iranian mines fished from the Persian Gulf were old-fashioned Russian devices that exploded upon contact – exactly the kind used to damage *Bridgeton*. They infested the Gulf, and because that particular design could last for decades, they represented a permanent danger to shipping. If the mines broke free and floated away, they became indiscriminating. Navy minesweepers worked constantly to remove them from harbors and along heavily traveled routes, but on April 14, 1988, a drifting mine struck the

frigate USS *Samuel B. Roberts*. It opened a huge hole and lifted the vessel's stern 10-12 feet out of the water. The ship survived the blast and no one was killed, but several men were severely injured.

On April 18 the U.S. Navy took revenge on Iranian outposts, which happened to be a number of old oil platforms used by Iranians for launching operations against neutral merchantmen. In the largest naval battle conducted by American warships since 1945, aircraft from the carrier *Enterprise*, using advanced guidance systems on bombs and missiles, led the attack against Iranian forces clustered around the oil platforms, sinking one cruiser and several gunboats. Destroyers using armor-piercing shells containing high explosives shattered the platforms, set them afire, and rendered them useless.

PASSENGER PLANE DOWNED

The guided-missile frigate *Vincennes* arrived in the Persian Gulf where terrorism and undeclared warfare preoccupied the attention of most servicemen. She carried the latest high-tech instrumentation, an Aegis weapon system, four-screen SPY-1A radar, and a superbly trained crew – everything neatly integrated to accurately differentiate between friendly and hostile aircraft. The vessel carried only two guns capable of engaging surface craft. On July 3, 1988, when several speedy Iranian gunboats opened on her, *Vincennes* returned the fire. After one of her guns jammed, she was forced to make erratic course changes to keep the other gun bearing on the enemy. The crew had already reached a state of uneasiness when communications reported an aircraft descending directly towards them. Having been briefed on terrorist actions, the men studied the plane and concluded that it intended to take aggressive action, so they shot it down. The moment of exhilaration soon passed when the captain learned that his men had destroyed Iran Air Flight 655 and killed all 290 persons aboard.

The investigation of the Iran Air tragedy drew one important conclusion from the accident. Weapon technology and guidance systems which enabled a warship to fight across far greater distances still left decisions in the hands of personnel who, often under stress, had to analyze and interpret incoming information and decide how to respond to it. Machines could not do all the thinking. To a certain degree people remained imperfect, regardless of the sophisticated tools used to determine their actions.

COLD WAR ENDS

Though warring factions in the Mid-East continued to dominate the attention of the Navy, Ronald Reagan won his war with the Soviet Union. In 1987 General Secretary Mikhail Gorbachev admitted being driven into national bankruptcy caused by military competition with the United States. Reagan's bloodless war with the USSR cost a tremendous amount of money, but a hot war would have cost immeasurably more. At the end of the year he signed a treaty with Gorbachev as the first step in reducing the stockpile of nuclear weapons, and the forty-year Cold War between East and West ended with the dissolution of the Soviet Union. When Reagan left office in 1989, he turned a different world over to his predecessor, George Bush.

The eight-year war between Iraq and Iran had also ended, but a new problem began to simmer in the boiling cauldron of the Mid-East. The situation at first remained obscure, however. Under the Bush administration, Congress envisioned less need for costly armed forces and began to contemplate ways to spend the money saved. The question of what to cut first centered on the armed services. Congress predicted that future wars would not likely require ground troops, the same erroneous approach to national defense articulated after World War II and after every war since. They even debated which to dissolve; the Army or the Marine Corps, based on the theory

Left: *During the Iran-Iraqi War, Iranian vessels planted mines off many of the ports in the Persian Gulf. Fishing them out became the work of the Navy and the U.S. Special Operations Command SEALs, who defused the detonators and hauled the mines on board a minesweeper.*

that one ground force would be enough.

CNO Admiral Trost took the initiative and redefined the post-Cold War Navy's future role by specifying its three governing principles as: a deterrent force strong enough to discourage any enemy from considering an attack on the United States; an attack force capable of deploying rapidly in a crisis; and a Navy of alliances with nations of the world who shared a common interest in mutual protection. Trost's lucid perception on the U.S. Navy in the 21st century compares in stature with Alfred Thayer Mahan's perception of the Navy for the twentieth century. Much had changed during the hundred years that separated the two men, but each succinctly articulated the role of the Navy at a time when it needed to be redefined. In Trost's view of the world, federations of mutual assistance had grown in importance, and he probably saved the Navy from deep cuts by his stated conviction that, "By defending our allies we defend ourselves." General Colin Powell, at the time Chairman of the Joint Chiefs of Staff, though not a Navy man, sharply sensed the validity of Trost's philosophy and demonstrated no interest in gutting the Navy to preserve the other forces. For fiscal 1991, Secretary of Defense Richard Cheney kept the cuts to the minimum, retaining for the Navy 546 combat ships. Trost,

'When a crisis confronts the nation, the first question often asked by policymakers is: 'What naval forces are available and how fast can they be on station?' '

ADMIRAL CARISLE A. H. TROST, CNO, MAY, 1990.

▶ **APRIL 11:** Secretary of the Navy Lehman resigns in frustration over cuts in naval expenditures and is replaced by James H. Webb.

MARCH 7: The United States agrees to protect Kuwaiti commerce.

MAY 17: An Iraqi jet damages the USS *Stark*.

OCTOBER 19: U.S. Navy launches its first attack against Iranian oil platforms.

DECEMBER: The Navy attains peak strength of 588 ships.

Right: *Transporting supplies to the Persian Gulf for Desert Shield required the urgent mobilization of freighters. The old but still available* Cleveland (LPD 7) *is rushed into service and loaded with military equipment and supplies for the Gulf.*

DESERT SHIELD

Within a week after Iraq invaded Kuwait, President George Bush put emissaries to work around the world and with friendly nations in the Middle East to build a coalition. He also authorized Desert Shield, the buildup of forces in Saudi Arabia to oust the Iraqi Army from Kuwait if Saddam Hussein refused to withdraw peacefully. As the Navy geared-up for the task ahead, Secretary of State James Baker opened discussions with Iraqi minister Tarig Aziz, warning what would happen if Iraqi troops did not withdraw. While Bush took action, majority party Democrats in Congress blustered and debated over the issue of war.

The demands of Desert Shield descended upon the Navy in the form of less glamorous jobs – providing sealift vessels for transferring to Saudi Arabia 45,000 Marines with tanks, ammunition, heavy equipment, and supplies. In the incredibly short time of thirteen days, the first ships from Diego Garcia in the Indian Ocean began unloading troops on Saudi Arabia. Because of a shortage in transports, two brigades had to be airlifted with all their equipment, one from California and the other from Hawaii. At Camp Lejune, North Carolina, the 4th Marine Expeditionary Brigade embarked on thirteen amphibious vessels. From different points around the globe, giant C-5 and C-141 cargo planes began transporting ninety-five percent of the armor, heavy equipment, fuel, ammunition, and supplies needed to sustain operations on the ground.

The Military Sealift Command activated eight fast cargo ships, and dispatched nineteen prepositioning ships to carry munitions and supplies for the joint services and a Navy field hospital. The eight cargo ships picked up the 24th Army Infantry Division (Mechanized) from Savannah, along with many of the M1 Abrams battle tanks that would distinguish themselves in Desert Storm. By August 7 other battle carrier groups with cruisers and destroyers departed from their stations and headed for the Gulf, among them *Saratoga* and *John F. Kennedy*, both from the East Coast and packed with aircraft. In December two more carriers, *Theodore Roosevelt* and *America*, got underway from Norfolk, just in time for Desert Storm.

On August 22, the Navy called up its "selected reserves," and thousands of men and women, many in specialist capacities, packed suitcases, and began trundling off to assignments in the Gulf. Nor did the Navy forget the Coast Guard, calling it into active service for the first time since World War II. By October, as land forces neared their peak, more than 100,000 sailors, Coast Guard personnel, and Marines were at sea against Iraq.

On January 15, 1991, United Nations forces were all in place for Desert Storm, waiting to see whether Saddam Hussein would remove his troops from Kuwait. The world also waited for the U.S. Congress, which continued to debate American involvement. Finally, on January 12 the House voted 250-183, the quarreling Senate 52-47, and Desert Storm was approved.

Now began the effort to put the resources into play for halting the advance of the Republican Guard and hurling the Iraqis out of Kuwait. For every mission the ships, aircraft, and men of the Navy were ready.

Left: *A Tomahawk missile, fired from the USS* Wisconsin *(BB 64) during Desert Storm, heads for a target in Iraq. As the 18-foot 2-inch missile with the thousand-pound warhead gains altitude, stub wings and tail fins open as it is guided toward the target.*

Powell, and Cheney did not anticipate a war with Iraq in 1990.

As Admiral Trost emphasized, alliances were important, especially with countries crucial to the interests of the United States. Since 1949 Persian Gulf countries like Saudi Arabia and Kuwait had depended upon America to maintain a presence off their shores. On August 2, 1990, when Saddam Hussein sent the fourth largest army in the world into Kuwait, the U.S. Navy was already in the Persian Gulf providing maritime superiority and the foundation for a powerful thirty-three-nation military coalition. A battle group formed around the carrier *Independence* moved quickly into the Gulf of Oman. A second battle group formed around the carrier *Dwight D. Eisenhower* moved from the eastern Mediterranean into the Red Sea. On arrival, both battle groups were ready for immediate and sustained operations.

When President Bush ordered Desert Shield – the deployment of troops to defend Saudi Arabia – more than 240 ships responded to the call, the largest number of U.S. warships assembled in a single theater since World War II. In the fastest strategic sealift in history, the Navy transported 18.3 billion

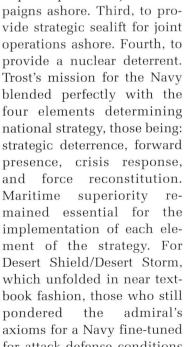

pounds of equipment and supplies to sustain the forces on the ground. Urged by the United States, the United Nations implemented trade sanctions against Iraq, severing Saddam Hussein from his economic lifeline.

By 1990, Admiral Trost had restructured the U.S. Navy to provide four essential military capabilities. First, to control the sea, thereby ensuring use of the oceans for economic and military purposes while denying the same privilege to opponents in time of war. Second, to project power ashore using aircraft, naval gunfire, cruise missiles, and Marine forces, the latter either in support of sea-control or participation in joint campaigns ashore. Third, to provide strategic sealift for joint operations ashore. Fourth, to provide a nuclear deterrent. Trost's mission for the Navy blended perfectly with the four elements determining national strategy, those being: strategic deterrence, forward presence, crisis response, and force reconstitution. Maritime superiority remained essential for the implementation of each element of the strategy. For Desert Shield/Desert Storm, which unfolded in near textbook fashion, those who still pondered the admiral's axioms for a Navy fine-tuned for attack-defense conditions

Left: *The USS Louisville (SSN 724), while submerged in the Red Sea, also launched long-range Tomahawk land attack cruise missiles on the opening day of Desert Storm. Of 288 Tomahawks fired at Iraqi targets, twelve were fired from submarines.*

▶ **1988**

FEBRUARY 22:
Secretary of the Navy
James H. Webb resigns.

APRIL 18: U.S. Navy
strikes Iranian Navy
vessels and oil
platforms.

JULY 3: *Vincennes*
shoots down Iran Air
Flight 655, mistaking
it for an Iranian F-14.

Below: *An F/A-18
Hornet (left) waits on
the deck of a carrier
for assignment. Navy
and Marine Corps
pilots flew more
F/A–18s during Desert
Storm than any other
aircraft. Docked at
right is an E-2C
Hawkeye, the highly
sophisticated
AEW/AWACS aircraft
used on the USS
Saratoga during
combat and
reconnaissance
operations over Iraq.*

> '*Soldiers, sailors, airmen and marines of the
> United States Central command, this morning at
> 0300, we launched Operation DESERT STORM, an
> offensive campaign that will enforce the United
> Nations' resolutions that Iraq must cease its rape
> and pillage of its weaker neighbor and withdraw its
> forces from Kuwait. My confidence in you is total.
> Our cause is just! Now you must be the thunder
> and lightning of Desert Storm. May God be with
> you, your loved ones at home, and our Country.* '
>
> GENERAL H. NORMAN SCHWARZKOPF,
> JANUARY 16, 1991,
> IN A MESSAGE TO HIS COMMAND.

were about to witness it in live action.

At "H-hour" January 17, 1991, Desert Storm
began with a shattering attack on Iraq's air
defenses and command and control posts. Two
U.S. battleships, nine cruisers, five destroyers,
and two nuclear powered submarines in the
Persian Gulf and Red Sea launched the first 100
Tomahawk land attack missiles (TLAMs). It must
have come as quite a shock to fishermen when a
fiery Tomahawk, launched by the submerged USS
Louisville, spurted from the depths of the Red
Sea.

A carefully crafted joint strategic air campaign
struck heavily defended targets in the vicinity of
Baghdad. Tomahawks and other precision-guided
projectiles used by the joint forces demonstrated
a revolution in the art of warfare for which the

Iraqis were totally unprepared.

From the day hostilities began until the cease-
fire, Navy and Marine Corps pilots, using both
fixed and rotary wing aircraft, flew sorties off six
carriers and several amphibious ships posted in
the Red Sea and the Persian Gulf. Some units
operated from ground and makeshift airstrips
ashore. Their mission consisted of four phases.
First: to gain air superiority by destroying Iraq's
strategic capabilities, which was accomplished in
seven days. Second: to knock out the enemy's air
defenses in the Kuwaiti area. Third: to attack the
Iraqi Army in Kuwait while maintaining the first
two phases. Fourth: to give air support to ground
operations.

Flights from the Red Sea averaged 3.7 hours
and required airborne refueling from KC-10 or
KC-131 Air Force tankers at both ends. Navy EA-
6B Prowlers (defense suppression aircraft) aided
air attacks, using electronic countermeasures to
jam and then direct the destruction of enemy
radar. If the Navy's defense suppression was not
available, the sorties did not fly. Augmented by
U.S. Air Force units flying out of eastern Turkey
and Saudi Arabia, the combined air strike forces
surrounded Iraq with a virtually impenetrable air-
cap. Naval tactical aircraft used high-speed anti-
radiation missiles (HARM) to destroy radar sites,
command centers, Scud missile launchers, elec-
trical power plants, and the enemy's nuclear, biological, and chemical weapons facilities. During
forty-three days of offensive combat operations,
more than 1,000 Navy and Marine Corps aircraft

Left: *The Ticonderoga-class guided-missile cruiser* San Jacinto *(CG 56) carries six highly specialized radar systems, four sonars, and five fire control systems as part of her Aegis instrumentation.*

flew close to 30,000 sorties. The presence of U.S. naval forces on both flanks of the Arab coalition ensured the continued flow of logistics throughout the war and enabled the Gulf States to participate throughout the conflict without fear of Iraqi retaliation.

During the first day's action, four Navy Hornets on a bombing mission intercepted two Iraqi MiG-21s at seven miles. Switching their F/A-18 strikefighters from bombing profile to air-to-air, the pilots downed both aircraft using Sidewinder missiles, producing the Navy's only air-to-air kills of the conflict. After losing ninety aircraft in combat operations, Iraqi pilots realized they could not compete with America's targeting technology and flew 122 MiGs to safety in Iran. Iraqi aircraft had used air-launched Exocet missiles during the eight-year war with Iran, and their retreat from the skies came as some relief to coalition ships in the Gulf.

DAY AND NIGHT BARRAGE

For Saddam Hussein's forces, fighting against advanced technology must have been a dizzying experience. Three weeks into the campaign, Intruders and Hornets using Harpoon missiles, and Skipper and Rockeye bombs, sank or disabled most of Iraq's missile gunboats, minesweepers, patrol boats, and Silkworm anti-ship missile sites. Though Iraq's Navy might be described as a joke, it had enough missile-armed fast attack boats to cause trouble if not eliminated early in the action.

On January 29, and after the start of the ground campaign on February 24, Navy and Marine Corps Harriers and Intruders shifted from hitting

stationary targets to strikes against roving quarry such as tanks and truck convoys. The Navy's newest aircraft, such as the F/A-18D night attack Hornets, prevented the enemy from moving masses of men and materiel at night.

Keeping carrier-based planes in the air was no small task for the Navy. Launching up to 140 sorties a day from a single flight deck kept 30,000 men busy around the clock, refueling, repairing, refitting, and rearming 500 aircraft every day, seven days a week. Without doubt, their performance and mission statistics were unparalleled in modern warfare.

The war at sea involved a multinational force of 115 U.S. and 50 allied warships. They had already severed Iraq's economic lifeline when the first cruise missile fired by the Aegis cruiser USS *San Jacinto*, stationed in the Red Sea, arced into Baghdad. The USS *Wisconsin*, the Tomahawk strike commander in the Persian Gulf, fired twenty-four missiles during the first two days of

Above: *An F/A-18D Hornet wings toward Iraq with Sidewinder AAMs on the wingtips, a pair of Sparrows, at least one Harpoon anti-ship missile, and two 330-gallon fuel tanks connected to her wings.*

► 1990

AUGUST 2: The Iraqi Army invades Kuwait.

AUGUST 5: Evacuations begin at Monrovia, Liberia.

AUGUST 7: President Bush initiates Desert Shield.

AUGUST 17: The Navy activates the Ready Reserve.

AUGUST 19: Vice Admiral Henry H. Mauz, Jr., is named Commander, U.S. Naval Forces, Persian Gulf.

Right: *The USS Wisconsin (BB 64), another of the upgraded battleships from World War II, opens on Iraqi targets with her 16-inch guns.*

Below: *Carriers kept a number of MH-53E Sikorsky Sea Dragons available for a variety of missions in the Persian Gulf. It was the heaviest lift helicopter outside of the former Soviet Union and was used extensively for hunting mines.*

the campaign. Before the Gulf War ended, 288 Tomahawks would be fired at strategic targets. Senator Sam Nunn, chairman of the Senate Armed Service Committee, observed that cruise missiles "[cost] a lot of money, but when you look at the precious savings in lives, I think the dollars are well invested." The Navy also used the first stand-off land-attack missile (SLAM), a variant of the Harpoon which allowed carrier pilots to attack high-value targets from more than fifty miles away.

Forty miles off the coast of Kuwait, Iraqi troops had established observation posts on nine of the Dorrah oilfield platforms. Early in Desert Storm the guided-missile frigate USS *Nicholas* and the Kuwaiti fast attack craft *Istqlal* launched a dangerous nighttime attack on the southernmost platforms. SH-60 Seahawk helicopters from *Nicholas*, joined by embarked Army AHIP helicopters, attacked two of the northernmost platforms from the rear. The choppers launched a volley of precision-guided missiles that struck both targets and touched off a store of ammunition that blew both platforms apart. While Iraqis stared at the enormous conflagration illuminating the sky, *Nicholas* and her consort moved on the remaining platforms, capturing them all and taking twenty-three prisoners, the first of the war.

SHORE BOMBARDMENT

In final preparation for the ground war, the guided-missile frigates *Curts* and *Nicholas*, using advanced mine-avoidance high-resolution sonar, led the battleship *Missouri* within range of an enemy command post near the Saudi border. On February 3, for the first time since Korea, *Missouri* fired her 16-inch guns in combat, sending 2,700-pound shells into prefabricated concrete structures along the Kuwaiti coast. During a three-day period *Missouri* fired 112 16-inch shells at enemy positions. On February 6, the recommissioned battleship *Wisconsin* relieved *Missouri* and fired eleven shells across nineteen miles to destroy an Iraqi battery in southern Kuwait. The two battleships alternated their positions on the gun line, blasting bunkers and artillery sites near Khafji while Marine detachments ran night reconnaissance missions into southern Kuwait.

Several minesweepers, joined by MH-53E Super Stallions of the Mine Countermeasures Helicopter Squadron and British Sea King helicopters, discovered Iraqi mines in waters well beyond the 12-mile international line. The amphibious assault flagship USS *Tripoli* embarked the choppers and began sweeping sixty miles east of the Kuwaiti coast, initially clearing a 1,000-yard path fifteen miles long and broadening it as the sweep approached Faylaka Island off Kuwait. On February 18 the Aegis missile cruiser *Princeton* reported Iraqi fire control radars and Silkworm missile sites ahead, causing the sweeping operation to move out of range. As the ships withdrew, *Tripoli* and *Princeton* struck mines. Though both vessels sustained damage, they remained on duty until relieved. A later investigation of the minefield revealed 1,000 mines anchored in an arc from the Saudi-Kuwaiti border to Faylaka.

As "G-Day" approached, unmanned air vehicles (UAVs) and F-14 Tomcats, equipped with Phoenix missiles and tactical air reconnaissance pod systems (TARPS), flew real time and near-real-time tactical missions over areas prepared to support the ground offensive. Iraq had no eyes over the battlefield, and General Schwarzkopf's deceiving tactics compelled the enemy to concentrate its forces along its defensive center on the eastern Saudi-Kuwaiti border and on the beaches. Under a screen of aircraft and artillery, Schwarzkopf moved 250,000 troops far to the west for an "end run" that would cut off the Iraqi Army's roads of escape north and west of Kuwait.

On February 21 a massive 31-ship amphibious task force with 17,000 Marines on board moved into the mine-swept corridor in preparation for the launch of Desert Storm. Their war-fighting skills would never be needed, but their preparation would not be in vain. They were at the core of a deception that would play a key role in the swift coalition victory.

FEINT MANEUVER

On the 23rd, the night before the ground offensive began, the amphibious task force battleships *Wisconsin* and *Missouri* opened on Faylaka Island in a massive pyrotechnic display, mainly to delude the enemy into believing that the main attack would come from the Gulf. Iraqis manning a Kuwaiti Silkworm site fired two missiles at *Wisconsin*. The first dropped harmlessly into the sea, and the British destroyer HMS *Gloucester* intercepted and destroyed the other with two Sea Dart missiles.

While maneuvers off Faylaka Island held the attention of 80,000 Iraqis, the coalition's end run began. On February 24, 36,000 men of the 1st and 2nd Marine Divisions, supported by the 3rd

Below: A UH-46D Sea Knight helicopter shuttles between her mother craft, the USNS replenishment ship Spica *(T-AFS-9), and the battleship USS* Wisconsin *(BB 64) during operations in the Persian Gulf.*

▶ 1991

JANUARY 3: The Navy and Marine Corps evacuate citizens from warring Somalia.

JANUARY 17: The Desert Storm air attack begins.

FEBRUARY 2: The Iraqi Navy is rendered combat-ineffective.

FEBRUARY 14: The Desert Storm land attack begins.

FEBRUARY 28: The Persian Gulf cease-fire begins.

Right: *During Desert Shield/Desert Storm, women performed multiple roles, including the maintenance and repair of aircraft operating from the decks of carriers.*

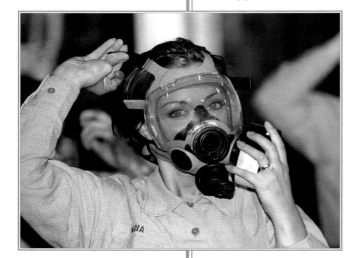

Above: *Women in the Persian Gulf went through much the same training as men, right down to adjusting the chemical warfare masks to ensure the proper fit.*

WOMEN SERVING IN THE PERSIAN GULF

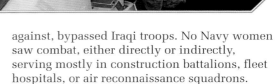

At the outbreak of Desert Storm, there were 37,000 military women in the Persian Gulf – 3,700 in the Navy and 2,200 in the Marine Corps. They served in all of the hundreds of occupations open to them, excluding certain specified combat roles. They were administrators, air traffic controllers, logisticians, mechanics, ammunition technicians, ordnance specialists, and, among other occupations, helicopter and reconnaissance aircraft pilots. Some served on hospital, supply, ammunition, and oiler vessels, others as public affairs officers and chaplains. They endured the same hardships as their male counterparts, commanding brigade, battalion, company, and platoon-sized units in combat service support areas.

Though women did not serve in U.S. units whose missions entailed direct contact with the enemy, five were killed and twenty-one were wounded in action. Two women became prisoners of war, and one struck a mine while driving a truck, but escaped without injury. Four Marine women received the Combat Action Ribbon, having been engaged by, and returned fire against, bypassed Iraqi troops. No Navy women saw combat, either directly or indirectly, serving mostly in construction battalions, fleet hospitals, or air reconnaissance squadrons.

Substantial social and cultural differences existed in Saudi Arabia with respect to women, but they did not change the American military's role in Desert Shield or Desert Storm. The Saudi government accepted females performing military responsibilities, but outside of those duties women had to respect the host country's cultural distinctions. As one Marine officer observed, "[Women] endured the same living conditions, duties, and responsibilities....They performed professionally and without friction of special consideration." The Gulf War redefined the role of women in the services. The Department of Defense policies are now "not designed to shield women from all hostilities, but are designed to limit their exposure to a level which is less than that in direct combat," which means "closing with the enemy by fire, close combat or counterattack."

Marine Aircraft Wing and Navy air power, swept around the enemy flank. The Marines, joined by the U.S. Army 1st Brigade and the 2nd Armored Division, had to cross two belts of minefields, climb 12-foot high sand berms, and deal with barbed-wire defenses, booby traps, and fire trenches, all the while under attack from Iraqi artillery. Marine aircraft attacked in waves as engineers shot line charges and formed makeshift bridges over trenches.

The sheer speed of the offensive shocked the enemy. The Marines used only a small percentage of their ammunition. Iraqis fought briefly, surrendering so rapidly that they often impeded progress. General Schwarzkopf was elated with the outcome, declaring: "It was a classic, absolutely classic military breaching of a very, very tough minefield....They went through the first barrier like it was water. Then they brought both divisions steaming through that breach. Absolutely superb operation – a textbook, and I think it will be studied for many, many years to come as the way to do it." The general had reason to be proud. Only eighty-eight Americans were killed, twenty-eight of whom died when a Scud penetrated the defensive screen and fell upon a compound in Dhahran, Saudi Arabia.

To hold the Iraqi Army in position near the coast, Marine helicopters from the amphibious task force conducted strikes against Faylaka, Bubiyan, and Kuwaiti beaches. By the time the enemy realized that the main attack was not headed their way, coalition victory was less than twenty-four hours away. By then, the 16-inch guns of *Missouri* and *Wisconsin* had poured more than a million pounds of ordnance at Iraqi targets.

After the cease-fire ended ground hostilities, U.S. and British ships continued to work offshore, clearing mines and enforcing U.N. sanctions. Unmanned aircraft (UAVs) from battleships performed reconnaissance missions along the coastline. Over Faylaka Island, one of *Missouri*'s UAVs observed hundreds of Iraqis waving white flags, marking for the first time an enemy unit surrendering to an unmanned aircraft.

The Kuwaiti cleanup took much longer than the war. "The Iraqis might have agreed to a cease-fire," said Rear Admiral Raynor A. K. Taylor from the USS *La Salle*, "but their mines have not yet surrendered. There are lots of them out there." The 21-vessel minesweeping operation proved especially difficult because of the enormous amount of oil spilled by Iraqis into the Gulf, hampering mine-sighting efforts and the work of divers. Only half of the Iraqi mines were found.

SMART WEAPONS TESTED

The war with Iraq gave the United States a marvelous opportunity to test under live conditions their "smart" weapon technology. It worked magnificently, totally defeating the effectiveness of the Iraqi Army and its highly vaunted Republican Guard. Defense Secretary Cheney summarized the outcome with an astute observation, when he said, "Everybody talks about the wonder weapons, but the most impressive capability we have is our people."

In the midst of Desert Shield/Desert Storm, two other hotspots on opposite sides of Africa embroiled the Navy and the Marine Corps in another crisis. On August 5, 1990, a task force of Marines rushed into Liberia and began to evacuate 330 U.S. citizens and 2,690 Liberian, Italian, Canadian, and French nationals by helicopter from war-torn Monrovia. Because the evacuations were painstakingly made from embassies, they

did not end until January 9, 1991, and became the longest-running non-combatant evacuation in recent naval history.

In early January, 1991, another crisis caused the amphibious assault ship *Guam* and the amphibious transport *Trenton* to rush the 4th Marine Expeditionary Brigade to the coast of Somalia. Marines went ashore at Mogadishu and set up defensive positions around the U.S. embassy. Helicopters landed and began evacuating 260 citizens from thirty nations, including fifty-one Americans. With all the evacuees safely on board, the ships steamed back to the North Arabian Sea and rejoined Desert Shield. The incident in Somalia would lead to new problems for the next president, a chief executive who would initiate the questionable practice of using military assets for nation building.

The effectiveness and the combat-readiness of the U.S. Navy during the Persian Gulf War can be attributed to the willful efforts of presidents Reagan and Bush to keep the nation strong and make the necessary investments in manpower, technology, and the capital assets of modern warfare. The unanswered question in 1992 was whether future administrations and the Congress would continue to fund military preparedness and use those resources as they were intended — to protect the interests of the United States.

Above: The Navy used the Sikorsky HH-60H Seahawk as a replacement for the Army's HH-1K Huey. The helicopter served well in Desert Storm, carrying eight SEALs in support of special operations.

Left: Battleships and carriers used unmanned aircraft (UAVs) for short-range reconnaissance missions over enemy-held territory. Iraqi soldiers had never seen such a craft, and several of the enemy attempted to surrender to one!

CHAPTER TEN

THE NEW TECHNOLOGY

The accelerating pace of technological change has transformed the way we think about national security. No longer is there a Nazi Germany, an imperial Japan, or a Soviet Union, but there is a constant clash of religious and ethnic rivalries emanating out of the Middle East, North Africa, and the Balkans. There is also an awakening of a potent military power in China and many troublesome aspects of a nuclear India. On the surface, there is no single clear and present danger to the security of the United States, but the potential for conflict is growing as rogue nations acquire devastating weapons. There must be a clear strategy beyond President William Jefferson Clinton's attempts at nation building and peacekeeping in areas of the world posing no threat to the interests or the alliances of the United States.

The swift and devastating victory over Iraq created the impression that the nature of warfare had changed. The Navy played an immensely important role in destroying the morale of the Iraqi military with a lethal barrage of airpower, stealth, anti-radio-frequency technology, and cruise missiles. Precision firepower and surgical strikes shifted the battlefield advantage away from the tactical defensive promoted by Russia to a tactical attack force that could not be detected before it struck. The Iraqis lacked the cunning of the North Vietnamese and made absurd tactical judgments in fighting a war that they lost too easily.

Having defeated George H. W. Bush in the 1992 elections, Clinton became the new president and commander in chief. Like many of his peacetime predecessors, he promised to cut the cost of government and did so by reducing expenditures for the armed forces. The president was not a military man, having avoided service during the Vietnam War, and he probably watched the progress of the Gulf War, as did most Americans, with eyes fixed firmly to a television as the news media portrayed the conflict as a video game.

After cutting defense expenditures, too much of the remaining money went to funding bad decisions, such as nation building in places like Somalia and an all too anxious rush into the Balkans on peacekeeping missions having no exit strategy. Politicians robbed billions from defense funds for pork-barrel projects. Congress and the president blocked innovations needed to improve the country's defenses against nuclear attack. Sending expensive cruise missiles and strategic bombers into places like Sudan, Afghanistan, Kosovo, and Serbia have deprived the defense establishment of training and resources needed to advance the evolution of new technology and the tactics to support it. It has been difficult for many in government not to think of the military as an elaborate extension of the Peace Corps.

Strategic Defense

After World War II the U.S. Navy became the most technically complex of all the armed services. It is the only service capable of waging war at sea, in the air, on the ground, and in space. During the many technological transformations of the twentieth century, the Navy participated in all of them, constantly reconfiguring itself. Its weapons of choice have moved from dreadnoughts to Trident missiles. It has constantly tried to maintain a balanced fleet, one that could

Right: *When the call went out for Desert Shield, the Navy stepped up to the task and sent their best technology in the way of carriers and Aegis guided-missile cruisers (center) and destroyers into a live proving ground for the new weaponry.*

reach into the Soviet Union while at the same time project American power into places like Vietnam, Iraq, and Yugoslavia. The security of the nation during the next century must be the cornerstone of strategic defense because the world, with the proliferation of nuclear weapons in the hands of renegade countries, has become more dangerous and far less predictable.

The Persian Gulf War left unresolved a number of important issues, the most onerous being Saddam Hussein. He remained in power to nurse a deep hatred toward the country that led the coalition, defeated him in battle, established a no-fly zone, and inserted into his country a rigorous weapons inspection regime. Months after Clinton assumed office, intelligence sources reported that Iraqi terrorists planned to assassinate George Bush during his April 14, 1993, visit to Kuwait. After Kuwaitis seized two cars containing remote-control devices and several hundred pounds of explosives, and interrogated the suspects, the plot was confirmed. In June, 1993, Clinton approved a retaliatory cruise missile

Left: *In a fiery eruption, a Tomahawk cruise missile is fired from a vertical launch port.*

SOMALIA

On August 18, 1992, the venture into Somalia started as a relief mission to prevent millions from starving. Marine Brigadier General Frank Libutti ran the operation with 570 personnel and predicted that Operation Provide Relief would be wrapped-up by January 20, 1993. A short time later the United Nations sent 500 Pakistanis to Mogadishu to protect the supply convoys from being hijacked or prevent "taxes" from being extorted by armed militia groups. Frustrated by interference from warlords, President Bush initiated Operation Restore Hope and sent Lieutenant General Robert B. Johnson and the 1st Marine Expeditionary Force to Somalia to ensure the success of the humanitarian effort.

General Johnson planned on getting his forces into Somalia quickly and quietly. Early on December 9, SEALs swam ashore at Mogadishu, followed closely by reconnaissance Marines in rubber boats. Their arrival on the beach was met by the glare of video lights and photoflashes. Someone in the United Nations had let the so-called cat out of the bag. Mobs of reporters lined the beach and demanded interviews while Americans, halfway around the world, watched the broadcast of a live landing that met no resistance. Bemused Marines, supported by helicopters and assault amphibious vehicles, established checkpoints, occupied the vacated U.S. Embassy compound, secured the port and airfield, and began manning roadblocks and confiscating weapons. The so-called Somali militia carried old-fashioned small arms, the largest of which could be mounted on the back of a pickup truck, but on the day the Marines landed most of the armed thugs had already retreated

underground with their weapons.

What began as a humanitarian mission under President Bush quickly deteriorated in May 1993 into a peacekeeping and nation building mission under President Clinton. Bush's exit strategy depended upon a truce between the two warlords occupying Mogadishu, and on December 28, 1992, the two head clansmen met in the most strife-torn section of the city and reached a temporary agreement. Four months later General Johnston's joint task force closed down the famine-relief operation, turned it over to a U.N. force under a Turkish general, and commenced the nation building phase. The operation quickly ran into trouble, and American Marines began taking casualties. President Clinton had acceded too much authority to the United Nations, resulting in a faulty lack of direction, a lack of political and military insight, and no wise and firm guidance. Clan activity intensified, and the muddling U.N. effort all but collapsed. In October, 1993, the U.S. Navy began evacuating its force after the deaths of eighteen Americans. Multinational troops attempted to continue the work of nation building, but in March, 1995, the U.N. aborted the mission and called upon the U.S. Navy to withdraw its forces.

Above: *When the Navy SEALs hit the beach at Somalia, they came prepared for a firefight. Somewhat to their astonishment, they found only newsmen and lights for TV cameramen.*

▶ **1993**

JANUARY: President Clinton authorizes strikes against Iraq.

MAY: The Somalia peacekeeping/nation building phase is initiated.

JUNE 27: Tomahawk missiles are fired into Baghdad in reprisal for assassination attempt on President Bush.

JULY 1: Relief flights authorized for Bosnia.

OCTOBER: The U.S. Navy begins the withdrawal of American troops from Somalia.

attack, and on the 27th the destroyer USS *Peterson* and the cruiser *Chancellorsville* fired twenty-three Tomahawk missiles at the Iraqi headquarters in downtown Baghdad. Three missed the target, fell upon nearby neighborhoods, and killed eight civilians. The strike generated a little sympathy for Saddam Hussein.

One of the lessons learned in Somalia was that impressive technology does not always work in places having no center of gravity. Eliminate a warlord and another fills his shoes. Nations cannot be built around thugs. The same can be said of Bosnia, ruled until 2000 by Serb potentates.

During the years following the death of Yugoslav leader Josip Tito, relations with Western nations continued to improve until 1991 when Croatia and Slovenia defected and became sovereign nations. A year later the first clashes began in Bosnia between Serbs, Muslims, and Croats. Serbs made up thirty-one percent of Bosnia but in 1992 seized seventy percent of the country before Bosnia declared its independence. Once again President Clinton stepped into a factional clash without a clear exit strategy and committed the Navy, Marine Corps, and other services to a limited peacekeeping role which nine years later still continued. In this instance the center of gravity was Serbian President Slobodan Milosevic in Belgrade, a friend of the former Soviets, and his 100,000 troops of the Ministry of Interior, not the Yugoslav Army.

Secretary of Defense William Perry stationed

> *'Our retreat from Somalia was not due to the public's revulsion of seeing casualties on television but to their sense that the political leadership had no clear policy in Africa and that lives were being wasted.'*
>
> ANDREW P. ERDMANN.

one battle carrier group in the Adriatic. The ships played a key role in enforcing the maritime embargo and provided a mobile base for Navy and Marine aircraft. Navy and Marine Corps pilots flew missions over Bosnia from several airfields in Italy, among them Aviano. Navy P-3s flying out of Sigonella provided most of the maritime sorties flown; carrier- and land-based F-14 and F/A-18 fighter aircraft and E-2C Hawkeye and EA-6B Prowler reconnaissance aircraft flew another 8,000 sorties. The Navy fired thirteen Tomahawk cruise missiles at several well-defended Serb targets near Bihac, all to little avail. The munitions delivered by Navy and Marine Corps aircraft were mostly precision-guided, but adverse weather and heavy foliage reduced the weapons' effectiveness. Because the shadowing effects of Bosnia's mountainous terrain limited the effectiveness of satellite reconnaissance, the Navy relied heavily on aircraft systems such as those on the E-2C Hawkeyes to accomplish recce missions.

"MISSION IMPOSSIBLE"

In 1995, U.N. Secretary General Boutrous Boutros-Ghali finally admitted that keeping the peace in a nation where there was no peace to keep had become "mission impossible." The average American believed that the United States'

Right: *An incoming Lockheed P-3 Orion taxis to a stop at NAS Whidbey Island. Though intended primarily as a long-range maritime reconnaissance aircraft, it can be equipped with a variety of torpedoes, mines, and depth bombs in the weapons bay and Harpoons on the wings.*

Left: *A Navy controller on the deck of the USS Saratoga communicates with the pilot of an E-2C Hawkeye as the aircraft takes to the air on a reconnaissance mission. The E-2C became indispensable in air combat activities and the drug war.*

role in Bosnia should have been limited to arming the Bosnian Muslims. President Clinton believed in peacekeeping and nation building. By then, the United States and its allies had flown more than 109,000 sorties, just slightly fewer than those flown during the Gulf War. In 2001, Bosnia and its neighboring countries remained a volatile region still rife with ethnic hatreds.

FUNDED TERRORISM

During the Bosnian affair, another terrorist regime took American lives. In the 1990s Islamic leader Osama bin Laden began to emerge as a terrorist without a country. Son of a Saudi billionaire, bin Laden had gone to Afghanistan in the 1980s to fight the Soviets. He built his own quasi-military organization, and after the Soviets pulled out of Afghanistan, he became dedicated to driving Western influences out of the Arab world. He provided funding for terrorist groups and was suspected of financing the 1993 bombing of New York's World Trade Center, and subsidizing the warlords of Somalia. In 1995 he supported the bombing of a building in Riyadh used by the American military and the 1996 Khobar Tower bombing in Dhahran, killing nineteen American airmen. In 1996 he called for a holy war against the United States, and in 1998 told ABC News, "We do not differentiate between those dressed in military uniforms and civilians: they are all targets." Though warned, Americans were not prepared when on August 7, 1998, bin Laden's emissaries bombed the U.S. embassies in Nairobi, Kenya, and Dar es Salaam, Tanzania, killing in all 224 people, including twelve Americans, and injuring more than 4,800 people. More recently, bin Laden's name was also connected with an attempt to sink the USS *Cole* which was refueling in a Yemeni harbor, as well as the hijacking of

airliners used in the devastating suicide attacks that destroyed the twin towers of the World Trade Center in New York, damage to the Pentagon in Washington, D.C., and what was believed to be an attempt to attack Camp David in Maryland - all in the space of a few minutes on September 11, 2001.

On August 20, 1998, Clinton authorized a strike against bin Laden's bases. U.S. Navy surface ships and submarines in the Red Sea and Persian Gulf fired approximately seventy Tomahawk cruise missiles against terrorist targets in Khartoum (Sudan), and Khost (Afghanistan). The Tomahawks struck four different terrorist training camps in Afghanistan, killed 21 people and injured 30, but missed bin Laden. In Sudan, missiles struck a candy factory and a pharmaceutical plant in downtown Khartoum, the latter being suspected of producing an agent used in manufacturing nerve gas. There being no evidence to support White House allegations that Sudan's pharmaceutical plant produced toxic substances or that bin Laden was in any way connected with the facility, the incident raised questions about

Above: *The destroyer USS* Cole *(DDG 67) became the unsuspecting victim of Middle East terrorists when she pulled into a port of Yemen. The explosion opened a hole on her beam through which a truck could drive.*

▶ **1994**

Combat operations begin in Bosnia.

1995

March 1995: The U.S. Navy begins the withdrawal of U.N. troops from Somalia.

July 6: The Navy releases plans for its "Navy Theater Ballistic Missile Defense" system for 2005.

1998

August 20: President Clinton authorizes Tomahawk attacks on Sudan and Afghanistan.

Above right: *A U.S. Special Operations Command "Civil Affairs" poster of Slobodan Milosevic punctuates the troubled times in the former Yugoslavia. It took more than a month of bombing by Air Force and Navy aircraft to suppress the pugnacious Serbian president.*

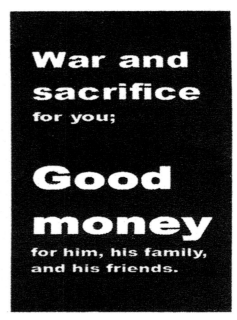

> 'We launched on time, significantly ahead of the strike force. Our check-in, progress to station, systems, and theater communications were exactly as planned. The main force was on its way, as scheduled....I remember wondering whether it was really going to be this simple. How could it be this smooth? The EA-6B Prowlers set up their suppression orbits, and the strike fighters continued on to their targets. They were in and everything was still working....The strike fighters delivered their weapons on target, on time. The U.S. Navy had arrived. We presented a new, unpredictable force to the enemy. We added a new threat axis to the picture. We provided lethal and precision accuracy and control of the nighttime skies. We had made an impact, exactly as planned. '
>
> Commander Wayne D. Sharer, leading a squadron of Hawkeyes, recalling the first strike over Kosovo.

President Clinton's rush to use Tomahawk missiles when all the facts were not known. As President Reagan once warned, "We must be careful that we do not appear as terrorists ourselves."

Whether the involvement of the United States military in Kosovo during 1999 resulted from terrorist acts of ethnic cleansing by Milosevic's Serbian army or as a deflection from President Clinton's impeachment is still arguable. Unlike Bosnia, the bombing of Kosovo and Serbia was done under the auspices of the North Atlantic Treaty Organization (NATO) and was judged by the participants as a success. Soldiers, sailors, and airmen performed remarkably well at the tactical level. Too many mistakes were made at the strategic and operational levels, mainly because political restrictions and interference hampered the ability of NATO's planners to articulate strategic guidance to theater commanders. Strategic objectives were ambiguous when the air cam-

paign began on March 24, 1999, and remained unclear until the last bomb fell on June 10. The center of gravity was still the forces of the Ministry of Interior and Slobodan Milosevic, who was weakened by the bombing but remained in power until the 2000 election. For the United States military the one-sided fray served as another demonstration of American weapon technology and another indeterminate and expanded role as peacekeepers.

Objectives not Specific

When the NATO bombing campaign began over Kosovo and Serbia, Secretary of Defense William Cohen stated that the strategic objective was to degrade and damage the military and security structure that President Milosevic was using to depopulate and destroy the Albanian majority in Kosovo. NATO's objectives were less than specific, and the U.S. Navy did not have time to ask many questions. Using operations against Bosnia as a pattern, Cohen sent a carrier force to the Adriatic, and Navy and Marine Corps pilots began flying sorties off the carriers and out of Italy.

Two systems guided the air attacks. Special Operations teams landed in Kosovo to locate and mark lucrative ground targets for the Army Tactical Missile System (ATACMS). The system used enhanced global positioning and could deliver a variety of missiles at targets anywhere in Kosovo and well into Serbia. ATACMS worked day or night and could direct laser-guided bombs dropped by aircraft at high altitudes or Hellfire missiles fired by helicopters skimming the hillsides. The Navy used twin-engined E-2C Hawkeyes launched from carriers, which when airborne became the pinnacle command, control, and combat direction and detection platform for the self-contained naval strike forces. They brought to strike planning teams the data for organizing sorties, but they were also vulnerable to surface-to-air missiles.

The problem with the Kosovo operation was that it focused almost entirely on weapons technology and not enough on the relationship between policy and strategy, strategy formulation, operational planning, and operational thinking. Smart weapons, computer systems, and information warfare may not be enough to win the next battle. The mistakes in Kosovo, which go beyond the accidental bombing of the Chinese Embassy in Belgrade, should serve as a wake-up call rather than a cause for self-congratulation. NATO's meddling and reversal of the decisions made by General Wesley Clark, the Supreme Allied Commander, Europe, raises questions as to whether NATO is any longer a cohesive organization capable of waging war against anything other than a pathetically weak nation. If General of the Army Dwight D. Eisenhower had to contend with NATO bureaucrats during World War II, the world might still be waiting for the opening of a second front.

DECISIVE RESCUE

When Air Force Captain Scott O'Grady got shot down over Bosnia, Admiral Leighton Smith, commander of NATO forces Southern Europe, did not wait for permission from a bureaucrat to rescue the pilot. He sent Marine Colonel Martin Berndt and a helicopter team into the Bosnia hills to pull O'Grady out. "I had sent a message to the Bosnia commanders," Smith later told reporters, "saying, 'I'm coming in to get him out. Stay out of my way.'" Six days later Colonel Berndt, a strapping Marine, picked up O'Grady's signal, and "reached out and hauled him into the cockpit." When the helicopter deposited O'Grady on the USS *Kearsarge*, Smith met him on the flight deck and said, "I haven't the foggiest idea what it is to be a hero, but I can tell you to get ready. The next six days may be just as hard as the last six." Smith acted in the tradition of the Navy – quickly and decisively.

The war in Vietnam taught us that emphasis on tactics and technology does not always ensure complete victory. Iraq is still a menace to the world because Saddam Hussein is still in power. Peacekeepers are still putting their lives at risk around the world, and terrorism is as rampant as ever. No incident occurs anywhere in the world that does not require the services of a combat-ready Navy.

A larger question becomes: what if terrorist attacks become nuclear? Each year that passes, renegade countries expand their technological capabilities through nations such as China,

Above: *The Sikorsky CH-53E/MH-53E Sea Stallion/Sea Dragon was developed specifically for the Navy and the Marine Corps and is used for a multiplicity of missions, including night operations, combat search and rescue, and mine detection.*

Left: *The rescue by the Navy of downed Air Force Captain Scott O'Grady in Bosnia made headline news. O'Grady, usually a smooth-shaven officer, looks like he had been through the wringer when the Navy brought him safely aboard the USS Kearsarge.*

> '*In the Kosovo crisis of 1999, the lessons of operational war fighting learned during the Gulf War were forgotten. The lack of focus on the proper centers of gravity allowed Serb forces...to operate in Kosovo unharmed. If the current obsession with technology and targeteering is not reversed, our ability to use military force decisively against a strong opponent could be crippled severely* '
>
> DR. MILAN VEGO,
> NAVAL WAR COLLEGE.

Russia, and North Korea, while those countries, within their own boundaries, work assiduously at perfecting greater weapons of war. While the U.S. Navy can do little to prevent a terrorist from driving a nuclear device into New York and incinerating the city, it can, with sufficient funding, fulfill its obligation for national defense by intercepting weapons of mass destruction directed at the United States from offshore.

The assets of the U.S. Navy continue to dwindle, despite the many deployments and the number of concurrently running tasks that existed during the 1990s.

▶ 1999

MARCH 24: The bombing of Serbia begins.

JUNE 10: The bombing of Serbia ends.

2000

NOVEMBER 13: Over the past nine years, the U.S. Navy is reduced to sixty percent of its Gulf War readiness.

Today the Navy operates only three fleets, the 5th, 6th, and 7th, and five carrier groups, centered around the carriers *Abraham Lincoln* (Arabian Gulf), *Carl Vinson* (Pacific Ocean), *Enterprise* (Atlantic Ocean), *George Washington* (Mediterranean), and *Kitty Hawk* (Sea of Japan). Two-thirds of the fleet is not deployed. This raises questions of readiness.

Since the mid-1990s, the Navy has been building a two-tiered structure around the Theater Ballistic Missile Defense (TBMD) system – a "lower tier" for limited area defense, and an "upper tier" for theater-wide defense capable of engaging supersonic long-range missile attacks. Because of political debate over "SDI," the Strategic Defense Initiative, or what the Reagan administration called "Star Wars," the Clinton administration and Congress allowed the program to languish at the expense of national defense. The Navy has now moved the date of implementation out to the year 2005, but much of the work has been planned and partially implemented.

The Navy Area (lower tier) Defense (NAD) system was designed to perform the function of "goalkeeping" and is centered around the SM2 Block IVA area defense interceptor missile, which is due to become operational in 2003. The Block IVA missile has a boosted, high-mach, long-range, solid-fuel, "dual mode" (infrared and semiactive radio frequency) homing and a blast-fragmentation warhead specifically enhanced for the role of destroying incoming enemy missiles, such as

Scuds. Being proximity-fused, it does not suffer the drawback of kinetic-energy hit-to-kill systems. Like the proposed next-generation Patriot PAC-3 missile, the SM2 Block IVA will be multi-mission-capable and lethal against cruise missiles or manned aircraft. NAD will be the sole naval active defense system capable of engaging low-apogee, short-range missiles because the "upper tier" interceptor functions only outside the atmosphere, above forty-four miles.

ANTI-BALLISTIC MISSILES

The Navy Theater-Wide (NTW) (upper tier) system defends against ballistic missiles outside the atmosphere, and instead of "goalkeeping" performs the role of "gatekeeping." The only weapon available for performing this function is the SM3/LEAP KKV (Kinetic Kill Vehicle) interceptor measuring 21.5 feet in length. It has a four-stage system with a Mark 72 booster and a Mark 104 solid rocket motor that it shares with the interceptor. It is scheduled for deployment in 2005-2007, depending upon funding.

An Aegis ship carrying LEAP missiles depends more upon being in the defended area than being near the defended target, the "area of negation" being the range of water over which Aegis ships can intercept missiles en route from a hostile launch area to an assortment of targets. A single Aegis cruiser off South Korea could protect most

---

THE US NAVY – 2000

Navy strength: 2000

Total ships:	318
Ships on deployment:	100 (31 percent of total)
Submarines on deployment:	11 (20 percent of force)
Personnel on deployment:	46,249
Total operational aircraft:	4,108
Total Navy personnel:	
Active duty:	373,193
Officers:	53,550
Enlisted:	315,471
Midshipmen:	4,172
Ready Reserve:	183,942
Civilians:	184,044

In 1988, the U.S. Navy operated a fleet of 589 vessels. In 1991, after the Persian Gulf War, Congress trimmed the number to 546. Each cut also reduced the number of personnel in the service. Following the Gulf War, Congress and the Clinton administration continued to cut the armed services and the budget needed to fund the Navy of 2005. By the end of the year 2000, the Navy had been reduced by forty percent, and the majority of the ships will not be placed on deployment for lack of funding. As one observer noted, "One of the more infamous and disquieting statements made by a public official in recent years about the role of the military is attributed to Madeline Albright [Secretary of State under the later Clinton administration]. While serving as ambassador to the United Nations she reportedly told then-Chairman of the Joint Chiefs of Staff, Colin Powell, 'What's the point of having this superb military you are always talking about, if we can't use it?'" Ms. Albright preferred to use the money for nation building and endorsed the cuts.

THE MODERN AMERICAN AIRCRAFT CARRIER

Left: *Commissioned in 1965, the multi-purpose carrier USS America (CV 66) has undergone continuous changes to keep it technologically current. Fully loaded, she displaces 85,490 tons and carries a complement of 141 officers and 2,705 enlisted men. Though smaller than the nuclear-powered Nimitz-class carriers, she nonetheless carries eighty aircraft and two 8-tube Sea Sparrow launchers.*

By the 1990s, no ship in the Navy cost more to build and operate than a nuclear-powered, two-reactor aircraft carrier that displaced 95,000 tons. The ship carried about a hundred planes: F-14A Tomcats and F/A-18 Hornets; reconnaissance and guidance E-2C Hawkeyes, EA-6B Prowlers, S-3A Vikings; and SH-3H Sea Kings and H-46 Sea Knight helicopters. Tomcats attained speeds of Mach 2.4 at 50,000 feet and carried a variety of Phoenix, Sparrow, and Sidewinder missiles and a 20mm Vulcan cannon. Hornets achieved a maximum speed of 1,185mph and carried a mixture of Sidewinders, Sparrows, and 17,000 pounds of bombs, missiles, and rockets, including HARM, SLAM, and Harpoon.

The typical nuclear-powered supercarrier, such as the USS *United States* (CNV-75), cost $6.5 billion and could steam at 30 knots for fifteen years without refueling. The flight deck occupied 4.5 acres, being 1,092 feet long and 251 feet wide. From keel to mast (244 feet) she contained 3,360 compartments and spaces and attained the size of a 24-story building. She carried four aircraft elevators, four aircraft catapults, and 6,200 men and women. Each of her four propellers weighed 66,200 pounds and were 21 feet in diameter. Her rudders weighed 65.5 tons each, more than most of the vessels that fought for the Continental Navy.

For weapons she carried three eight-tube Sea Sparrow launchers and four multi-barreled 20mm Phalanx guns.

For the comfort of the officers and crew, the carrier provided enough air conditioning to cool 800 homes and distilled enough salt water to provide the daily freshwater needs of 2,000 families. The ship generated enough electricity to power fifty broadcasting stations operating concurrently and provided light for 29,000 fixtures. More than 18,000 meals were served each day, the average breakfast run consisting of 10,000 eggs, 10,000 pancakes, 2,700 pounds of meat, and unlimited coffee. The average crew earned a total of $900,000 a month, and as a group were the most technically trained and versatile branch of the armed services. If the men and women who served on aircraft carriers needed further instruction, the ship carried enough technical manuals to reach from the ground to the tip of the Washington Monument (555 feet).

On board, the carrier provided recreational facilities and social amenities. One of the favorite off-duty pastimes was boxing, a popular sport during holidays at sea.

Below: *In a compartment several yards below a carrier's waterline, enlisted men manhandle a rack of aircraft bombs a few paces away from the ship's bomb elevator.*

Right: *Arleigh Burke-class Aegis destroyers (foreground) began coming off the production line in 1991 and are still coming. They are light, swift, and loaded with instrumentation. They carry 29 cells forward and 61 cells aft for Tomahawks, two quad canisters for eight Harpoons, and six 12.75-inch torpedo tubes.*

of that country and Japan. By being forward-deployed, near a launch site that can fire ballistic missiles at many targets in a great arc, the NTW has the capability of defending an area covering tens of thousands of square miles. Different versions of SM3/LEAP missiles are currently going through tests.

OUT OF ATMOSPHERE DISPERSION

Guidance technologies used in such an extremely long-range system include missile command uplink and inertial Global Positioning System, and imaging infrared terminal homing. The interceptor warhead is the LEAP itself, a small, forty-pound projectile containing no explosive charge. Maneuvering autonomously with thrusters, it homes on the infrared signature of the hot ballistic missile, closing for the kill at 2.8 miles per second, more than three times the velocity of the fastest rifle bullet. If the hostile missile is carrying a chemical, biological, or nuclear payload, the components will be shattered and dispersed outside the atmosphere. While the SM2/LEAP should be extremely effective against medium-range ballistic missiles, it does not have the speed to overtake intercontinental ballistic missiles (ICBMs), which run at 3.75-4.38 miles a second.

The Aegis SPY-1 radar acts as primary sensor for the Navy's missile defense system and is capable of tracking hostile missiles at ranges over 310 miles. SPY must first search for and locate a hostile missile before the Aegis system can compute

'The primary purpose of forward-deployed naval forces is to project American power from the sea to influence events ashore in the littoral regions of the world across the operational spectrum of peace, crisis, and war. This is what we do.'

ADMIRAL JAY L. JOHNSON

the track. Radar range-tracking is highly dependent on cross-sectioning the target through the battlespace by cooperative tracking between two Aegis ships. The forward ship transmits track data to a consort downrange until the second ship can acquire the target. The system works best when the tracking vessels are not underneath the target but well off to the side. By 2005, cueing to Aegis will be primarily a function of the U.S. Space Command. Until then, the Navy will depend upon its SPY radar and sensor help from the Air Force AWACS Eagle, which has a system with sufficient accuracy to pass a single-beam cue to SPY.

Challenges to the capabilities of the two SM2 systems have been both technical and political. Russia has fought the development of the system on the basis of the 1972 Anti-Ballistic Missile Treaty, but both the Department of Defense and Congress have agreed that the Navy's SM2 systems comply with the terms of the treaty (which in 2001 President George W. Bush described as

Left: *Before being damaged by a terrorist bomb in the harbor of Yemen, the destroyer USS* Cole *(DDG 67) demonstrates the launching of a Tomahawk cruise missile from one of her forward cells.*

belonging to a past era).

The Navy must have enough Aegis cruisers and destroyers capable of performing antimissile deterrent patrols in distant and isolated areas. Cruisers can remain on station longer than destroyers because they carry more fuel. A cruiser also carries a third more vertical-launch missiles than a destroyer. Because weapon systems have become so complex, an Aegis ship must carry Tomahawks, SM2 Block IVA, and the SM2/LEAP missiles, all of which are too heavy to be transferred at sea and offloaded into the vessel's vertical launching stations. The Aegis ship will also carry four-missile packs of the "Evolved Sea Sparrow," vertical-launch antisubmarine rockets, several different varieties of Tomahawk land attack missiles, perhaps anti-armor Tomahawk (TSTARS), and a navalized version of the Army Tactical Missile System. Only one of these missiles, the SM2 Block IVA, is a true multi-mission weapon with capability against aircraft, cruise missiles, and theater ballistic missiles. By 2005, there will be more than 5,500 vertical launching stations to fill with attack-defense missiles, and there will be a need for more Navy bases to keep Aegis ships armed and fueled.

The future carrier battlegroup planned for 2005 is likely to include four Aegis destroyers and two Aegis cruisers. Each destroyer will carry ninety vertical missile launch cells, and each cruiser 122. Each vessel will carry four antisubmarine rockets, the balance of the space being occupied by SM2s (seventy percent) and Tomahawk land attack missiles (thirty percent), giving each destroyer a total of sixty defense interceptor missiles and each cruiser a total of eighty-two.

The profile of the 2005 Navy has been planned with emphasis on national defense and the obliteration of mid-range missiles fired upon the United States and its allies by hostile or rogue nations. Sophisticated systems do not always work as well as their creators and tacticians envision. During attacks on Iraq, cruise missiles went astray and landed in neighborhoods. Because of inaccurate intelligence, a candy factory and a pharmaceutical plant in Khartoum and the Chinese embassy in Belgrade were blown to pieces with much loss of life. After extraordinar-

Below: *New vessel concepts are continuously coming off computerized drawing boards. Whether the carrier of the future will have the bridge and control tower amidships remains to be seen, but the concept gives the ship a more natural balance.*

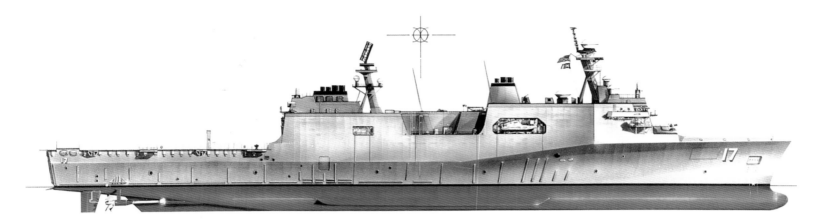

Above and right: *The assault ship of the future will contain an Aegis system for detecting and positioning enemy missiles fired from greater distances and coordinating their destruction with comparable systems on the land, on the sea, and in the air. Such craft will be armed with missile attack/defense systems, augmented by their own squadron of specially designed aircraft, such as tilt-rotor Ospreys and Harrier jets (or Joint Strike Fighters).*

'*There is a revolution at sea. The Navy is in the midst of a fundamental change in the way it designs, builds, and fights ships. The surface Navy is the vanguard, but the changes are so fundamental that eventually the warfighting structure of the entire Navy will change.*'

VICE ADMIRAL JOSEPH METCALF III.

ily accurate weapons such as GPS-guided bombs hit the embassy in Belgrade, it is easy to understand why the Chinese did not believe that the targeters had simply erred. Clausewitz's theory of "friction" emphasizes that even the most reliable technological systems perform less than perfectly under the tremendous pressure of war. The theory stresses the importance of centralized planning but decentralized execution, at which the Navy excels.

GPS-guided bombs that struck the Chinese embassy, known as JDAMS or Joint Direct Attack Munition System bombs, do not require a pilot to see the target. For JDAMS, and most strategic weapons, accuracy depends mainly on the coordinates fed into the weapon system. The targeter is seldom in the war zone. He looks at photographs and tries to register them against GPS coordinates, a process called mensuration. Without a person at the target holding a GPS receiver, the targeter can never be absolutely certain that his coordinates are correct or that the target has not been moved. The process is complicated by not always having an absolutely precise read on the orbit of the satellite that took the pictures, if that is where they came from. Another complication is the age of the satellite sensor systems; many of the satellites were put into orbit during the Reagan administration. A very small error in collected data can create a rather large error in mensuration, causing bombs to strike something other than the intended target. Mistakes like the Chinese embassy bombing work against defense efforts. Politicians take little interest in understanding weapons systems, but they hold the purse strings. Accidents tend to make them less generous.

Recently, the Joint Chiefs of Staff fashioned a

new military doctrine – Joint Vision 2010. It emphasized attacking with long-range weapons an enemy's center of gravity with such destruction as to cause the enemy to collapse without his forces having ever entered combat. Satellites would dominate such a war, collecting data about the enemy and transmitting the vital navigational information to ships carrying precision weapons. Space systems have already given missile-armed non-carrier surface ships the reach, though not the weight of fire, of aircraft carriers. Whether the new kind of warfare gets off the ground by the year 2010 will depend to some degree upon whether the Navy is able to meet its targets for the year 2005.

An enemy's center of gravity is not always easy to hit. Cruise missiles fired into Osama bin Laden's terrorist camp in Afghanistan destroyed the camp but not the center of gravity. Bin Laden is the terrorist group's center of gravity, but he moves about. Fixed targets are easier to hit.

The problem with Joint Vision 2010 could be its dependence upon surface vessels. The proliferation of commercial space systems has made global surveillance nearly continuous, making it easier for other nations to gain the same capabilities as the U.S. Navy by tapping into non-military satellites. Within the next decades, the only viable fleet may be one under water.

FUTURE WARS

The twentieth century survived without a war of ballistic missiles capped with biological, chemical, or nuclear warheads. The twenty-first century may not be so fortunate. In the new millennium the officers and men who go to sea in the U.S. Navy carry an enormous burden. They must personally contribute to the defeat of any enemy – terrorist or nation – who would use such weapons. There will be other wars, and the Navy must be given what it needs to fight them.

The seas are no longer lonely, nor are the skies. The tall ships of sail are gone forever. In their place are submarines, carriers, battleships, cruisers, and the serious business of protecting the world from those who seek to destroy it. It is on the sailors of the new technology who "go down to the seas again" that we depend for survival. Planet Earth is no longer a simple place on which to live.

But the simple sailor is still among us, and to him we owe our past and future. At the dedication of the Lone Sailor Memorial on June 23, 1987, Herman Wouk, the first recipient of the "Lone Sailor Award," paid this tribute at the unveiling of the statue:

"The Lone Sailor is one of those self-sacrificing brave spirits. I know him well.

"I saw him on the forecastle as we approached

an invasion beach in the dawn, in his kapok jacket and his steel helmet, at his battle station by the number one gun, ready for anything that would come. I saw him in the wheelhouse and in the radar shack during a typhoon, when our old minesweeper was rolling at 40 or 45 degrees, standing by his station and doing his job.

"I saw the Lone Sailor…on the forecastle as we steamed homeward for a Navy yard overhaul, passing from the warm Pacific to the cold December waters of Northern California; his hands jammed in his peajacket pockets, his eyes gazing toward the Golden Gate and toward home.

"But if I know him, and I think I do, the Lone Sailor looks beyond the shores of battle and the shores of home to a distant shore, and to the quintessence of the American dream. He looks to the day when the nation will not lift up sword against nation, neither will they learn war anymore.

"Until that day comes, he stands at his station, ready to do his job. And, I think it is because I have spoken up for him that you give me this most moving honor; because in truth you are honoring him, the Lone Sailor."

Above: *A Navy honor guard stands at attention during the ceremonial dedication of the Lone Sailor Memorial in Washington, D.C., on June 23, 1987.*

BIBLIOGRAPHY

Abbazia, Patrick. *Mr. Roosevelt's Navy.* Annapolis: U.S. Naval Institute, 1975.

Abel, Elie. *The Missile Crisis.* Philadelphia: J. B. Lippincott Company, 1966.

Alden, John D. *The American Steel Navy.* Annapolis: Naval Institute Press, 1972.

Alexander, John W. *United States Navy Memorial: A Living Tradition.* Washington:United States Navy Memorial Foundation, 1987.

Allen, Gardner W. *Our Navy and the Barbary Corsairs.* Boston: Houghton, Mifflin Company, 1905.

_____. *Our Naval War With France.* Boston: Houghton Mifflin Company, 1909.

Allen, Thomas B., and Polmar, Norman, et al. *War in the Gulf.* Atlanta: Turner Publishing, Inc. 1991.

Bacevich, A. J. "After Kosovo: SACEUR No Longer," U. S. Naval Institute Proceedings, 126 (July, 2000), No. 7, 2.

Barlow, Jeffrey G. *Revolt of the Admirals.* Washington: Brassey's, 1998.

Barney, Mary. *A Biographical Memoir of the Late Commodore Joshua Barney.* Boston: Gray and Bowen, 1836.

Bauer, K. Jack. *The Mexican War, 1846-1848.* New York: Macmillan Publishing, 1974.

Baxter, James P. *The Introduction of the Ironclad Warship.* Cambridge, Mass.: Harvard University Press, 1933.

Beach, Edward L. *The United States Navy: 200 Years.* New York: Henry Holt and Company, 1986.

Bennett, Frank M. *The Steam Navy of the United States.* Pittsburgh: Warren Publishing, 1896.

Bonds, Ray, ed. *The Vietnam War: The illustrated history of the conflict in Southeast Asia.* London: Salamander Books, 1983.

Buell, T. B. *Master of Sea Power: A Biography of Fleet Admiral E. J. King.* Boston: Little, Brown and Company, 1980.

Burton, David H. *Theodore Roosevelt: Confident Imperialist.* Philadelphia: University of Pennsylvania Press, 1968.

Cagle, Malcolm W. and Manson, Frank A. *The Sea War in Korea.* Annapolis: U. S. Naval Institute, 1957.

Chappelle, Howard I. *The History of the American Sailing Navy.* New York: W. W. Norton and Co., 1949.

Clark, William Bell, and Morgan, William James, et al. Naval Documents of the American Revolution. 9 vols. Washington, D.C.: Government Printing Office, 1964-.

Clark, William Bell. *Lambert Wilkes: Sea Raider and Diplomat.* New Haven: Yale University Press, 1932.

_____. *Ben Franklin's Privateers: A Naval Epic of the American Revolution.* Baton Rouge: Louisiana State University Press, 1956.

_____. *Captain Dauntless: The Story of Nicholas Biddle of the Continental Navy.* Baton Rouge: Louisiana State University Press, 1949.

Coletta, Paolo. *American Secretaries of the Navy.* 2 vols. Annapolis: Naval Institute Press, 1980.

Cushman, John H. "Somalia, Phase II...Phase III?" U. S. Naval Institute Proceedings, 119 (November, 1993), No. 11, 13.

_____. "To Win on the Ground in Kosovo," U. S. Naval Institute Proceedings, 125 (June, 1999), No. 6, 2.

Daniels, Josephus. *Our Navy at War.* Washington, D.C.: Pictorial Bureau, 1922.

Davis, Burke. *The Billy Mitchell Affair.* New York: Random House, 1967.

Davis, George T. *A Navy Second to None.* Westport, Conn.: Greenwood Publishers, 1971.

Davis, William C. *Duel Between the First Ironclads.* New York: Doubleday & Company, 1975.

Dolan, Edward F. *America in the Korean War.* Brookfield, Conn.: The Millbrook Press, 1998.

Dorr, Robert F. *Desert Shield; The Build-Up: The Complete Story.* Motorbooks International, 1991.

Dutton, Charles J. *Oliver Hazard Perry.* New York: Longmans, Green and Co., 1935.

Eichelberger, K. L., "Making the Navy's Case in Somalia," U.S. Naval Institute Proceedings, 121 (May, 1995), No. 5, 126-28.

Field, James A. *History of United States Naval Operations Korea.* Washington: Government Printing Office, 1962.

Fiske, Bradley A. *From Midshipman to Rear Admiral.* New York: The Century Co., 1919.

Fitzpatrick, John C., ed. *The Writings of George Washington.* Vol. 23. Washington D.C., Government Printing Office, 1937.

Fowler, William M., Jr. *Rebels Under Sail: The American Navy During the Revolution.* New York: Charles Scribner's Sons, 1976.

Friedman, Norman. *Seapower and Space: From the Dawn of the Missile Age to Net-Centric Warfare.* Annapolis: Naval Institute Press, 2000.

_____. *The Naval Institute Guide to World Naval Weapons Systems, 1991-1992.* Annapolis: Naval Institute Press, 1991.

_____. "Bosnian Crisis Defines New Limits on U.S. Power," U.S. Naval Institute Proceedings, 121 (February, 1995), 91-92.

_____. *Desert Victory: The War for Kuwait.* Annapolis: Naval Institute Press, 1991.

Gimpel, Herbert J. *The United States Nuclear Navy.* New York: Frederick Watts, Inc., 1965.

Goldsborough, Charles W. *United States Naval Chronicle.* Washington: J. Wilson, 1824.

Gregory, Barry. *The Vietnam War.* Vols. 5, 6, 9. Freeport, N.Y.: Marshall Cavendish Ltd., 1988.

Grider, John M. *War Birds.* E. W. Springs, ed. Fort Mill, S.C.: privately printed, 1951.

Guttridge, Leonard F. and Smith, Jay D. *The Commodores.* New York: Harper & Row, Publishers, 1969.

Halsey, William F. and Joseph Bryan III. *Admiral Halsey's Story.* New York: Whittlesey House, 1947.

Hart, Robert A. *The Great White Fleet.* Boston: Little, Brown & Company, 1965.

Hearn, Chester G. *George Washington's Schooners: The First American Navy.* Annapolis: Naval Institute Press, 1995

_____. *Gray Raiders of the Sea.* Camden, Maine: International Marine, 1992.

_____. *The Capture of New Orleans, 1862.* Baton Rouge: Louisiana State University Press, 1995.

_____. *Admiral David Glasgow Farragut: The Civil War Years.* Annapolis: Naval Institute Press, 1997.

_____. *Admiral David Dixon Porter: The Civil War Years.* Annapolis: Naval Institute Press, 1996.

Heinl, Robert D., Jr. *Soldiers of the Sea.* Annapolis: U. S. Naval Institute, 1962.

Herrick, Walter R., Jr. *The American Naval Revolution.* Baton Rouge, La.: Louisiana State University Press, 1966.

Hooper, Edward Bickford, and Oscar P. Fitzgerald, et al. *The United States Navy and the Viet Nam Conflict.* 2 vols. Washington: Naval Historical Center, 1976, 1986.

Hough, Richard. *Dreadnought: A History of the Modern Battleship.* London: Michael Joseph, 1965.

Howarth, Stephen. *To Shining Sea: A History of the United States Navy, 1775-1991.* New York: Random House, 1991.

Huchthausen, Peter A. "Back to the Balkans," U. S. Naval Institute Proceedings, 119 (June, 1993), No. 6, 43-49.

Humble, Richard. *U. S. Navy.* New York: Arco Publishing, Inc. 1975.

Isaacs, Jeremy, Downing, Taylor. *Cold War, 1945-1991.* Boston: Little, Brown and Company, 1998.

Jackson, John W. *The Pennsylvania Navy, 1775-1781: The Defense of the Delaware.* New Brunswick, N.J.: Rutgers University Press, 1974.

Joss, John. *Strike.* Novato, Cal.: Presidio Press, 1989.

Kelly, Mary Pat. "Rescue: Out of Bosnia," U.S. Naval Institute Proceedings, 121 (July, 1995), 52.

Knox, Dudley W. *A History of the United States Navy.* New York: G. P. Putnam's Sons, 1948.

Kosnick, Mark E. "The Military Response to Terrorism," Naval War College Press Review (Spring, 2000), 1-30.

Langston, Bud, and Bringle, Don. "Operation Praying Mantis," U. S. Naval Institute Proceedings, 115 (May, 1989), No. 5, 54-70.

Lippard, Karl C. *The Warriors: United States Marines.* Lancaster, Tex.: Vietnam Marine Publications, 1983.

Lloyd, Christopher. *The Navy and the Slave Trade.* London: Frank Cass & Co., 1968.

Long, David F. *Nothing Too Daring: A Biography of Commodore David Porter, 1780-1843.* Annapolis: Naval Institute

Press, 1970.

Lord, Clifford L. *History of United States Naval Aviation*. New York: Arno Press, 1972.

Lundstrom, John B. *The First South Pacific Campaign*. Annapolis: U. S. Naval Institute, 1976.

Mahan, Alfred Thayer. *Sea Power in its Relations to the War of 1812*. 2 vols. New York: Haskell House Publishers Ltd., 1969.

_____. *The Influence of Sea Power Upon History, 1660-1783*. Boston: Little, Brown and Company, 1918.

_____. *The Influence of Sea Power in its Relation to the War of 1812*. Boston: Little, Brown & Company, 2 vols., 1905.

_____. *From Sail to Steam*. New York: Harper Brothers, 1907.

_____. *The Gulf and Inland Waters*. New York: Charles Scribner's Sons, 1883.

Metcalf, Joseph III, "Revolution at Sea," U.S. Naval Institute Proceedings, 114 (January, 1988), No. 1, 34-39.

Milholland, Ray. *The Splinter Fleet*. Indianapolis: Bobbs-Merrill Co., 1936.

Miller, Francis Trevelyan. *The Complete History of World War II*. Chicago: Progress Research Corporation, 1948.

Miller, Nathan. *Sea of Glory: The Continental Navy Fights for Independence, 1775-1783*.New York: David McKay Company, Inc., 1974.

_____. *The U. S. Navy, An Illustrated History*. New York: American Heritage Publishing Company, 1977.

Milligan, John D. *Gunboats Down the Mississippi*. Annapolis: Naval Institute Press, 1965.

Millis, Walter. *Road to War*. Boston: Houghton Mifflin Co., 1935.

Mitchell, Donald W. *History of the Modern American Navy*. New York: Alfred A. Knopf, 1946.

Morison, Elting E. *Admiral Sims and the Modern American Navy*. New York: Russell and Russell, 1968.

Morison, Samuel Eliot. *John Paul Jones: A Sailor's Biography*. Boston: Little, Brown & Company, 1959.

_____. *The Battle of the Atlantic*. Boston: Little, Brown and Company, 1947.

_____. *"Old Bruin": Matthew Calbraith Perry*. Boston: Little, Brown & Co., 1967.

_____. *The Rising Sun in the Pacific*. Boston: Little, Brown and Company, 1948.

_____. *The Two-Ocean War*. Boston: Little, Brown and Company, 1963.

Morris, Richard K. *John P. Holland*. Annapolis: U. S. Naval Institute, 1966.

Naval Documents Related to the United States Wars with the Barbary Powers. Dudley Knox, W. ed. 4 vols. Washington: Government Printing Office, 1939.

Naval Documents Related to the Quasi-War Between the United States and France. 7 vols. Washington: Government Printing Office, 1935.

Naval History Division. Civil War Naval Chronology, 1861-1865. Washington, D.C.: Government Printing Office, 1971.

Naval Theater Ballistic Defense (TBMD) Operational Requirements Document. Washington, D.C.: U.S. Navy, 1995.

Neeser, Robert W., ed. *Letters and Papers Relating to the Cruises of Gustavus Conyngham*. New York: Naval History Society, 1915.

Niven, John. *Gideon Welles, Lincoln's Secretary of the Navy*. New York: Oxford University Press, 1976.

O'Gara, Gordon C. *Theodore Roosevelt and the Rise of the Modern Navy*. Princeton: Princeton University Press, 1943.

Paine, Ralph D. *The Ships and Sailors of Old Salem*. Chicago: A. C. McClurg & Co., 1912.

Paullin, Charles Oscar. *Diplomatic Negotiations of American Naval Officers, 1778-1883*. Baltimore: The Johns Hopkins Press, 1912.

_____. *Paullin's History of Naval Administration, 1776-1911*. Princeton: Princeton University Press, 1966.

Polmar, Norman. *The Naval Institute Guide to the Ships and Aircraft of the U.S. Fleet*. Annapolis: Naval Institute Press, 2000.

Potter, E. B. *Nimitz*. Annapolis: U.S. Naval Institute, 1976.

Richards, T. A., "Marines in Somalia: 1992," U.S. Naval Institute Proceedings, 119 (May, 1993), No. 5, 133-36.

Roosevelt, Theodore. *The Naval Operations of the War Between Great Britain and the United States, 1812-1815*. Boston: Little, Brown and Company, 1901.

Rees, David, ed. *The Korean War: History and Tactics*. New York: Crescent Books, 1984.

Sandler, Stanley, ed. *The Korean War: An Encyclopedia*. New York: Garland Publishing, 1995.

Scharf, J. Thomas. *History of the Confederate States Navy*. New York: Rogers and Sherwood, 1887.

Sharer, Wayne D. "The Navy Way Over Kosovo," U.S. Naval Institute Proceedings, 125 (October, 1999), No. 10, 26-29.

Simmons, Dean, and Gould, Phillip, et al, "Air Operations over Bosnia," U.S. Naval Institute Proceedings, 123 (May, 1997) No. 5, 58-63.

Sims, William S. *The Victory at Sea*. Garden City, NY: Doubleday, Page & Co., 1920.

Smelser, Marshall. *The Congress Founds the Navy*. South Bend, Ind.: University of Notre Dame Press, 1959.

Smith, S. E. *The United States Navy in World War II*. New York: William Morrow and Company, 1966.

Soley, James Russell. *Historical Sketch of the United States Naval Academy*. Washington: Government Printing Office, 1876.

Sprout, Harold and Margaret. *The Rise of American Naval Power, 1776-1918*. Princeton: Princeton University Press, 1966.

Stout, Jay. *Hornets Over Kuwait*. Annapolis: Naval Institute Press, 1997.

Sweetman, Jack. *American Naval History: An Illustrated Chronology*. Annapolis: Naval Institute Press, 1984.

Swicker, Charles C., "Ballistic Missile Defense from the Sea: The Commander's Perspective," Naval War College Press Review, 199 (Spring, 1997) 1-27.

Tilley, John A. *The British Navy and the American Revolution*. Columbia, S. C.: University of South Carolina Press, 1987.

Truver, Scott C. "Gramm-Rudman and the Future of the 600-Ship Fleet," U.S. Naval Institute Proceedings, 113 (May, 1987) No. 5, 111-123.

Vego, Milan. "Wake-Up Call in Kosovo," U.S. Naval Institute Proceedings, 126 (October, 2000), No. 10, 66-70.

Wallace, Willard M. *Traitorous Hero: The Life and Fortunes of Benedict Arnold*. New York: Harper and Brothers, 1954.

Warner, Oliver, et al. *The Encyclopedia of Sea Warfare from the First Ironclads to the Present Day*. New York: Thomas Y. Crowell Company, 1975.

Watson, H. W. *Battleships in Action*. Boston: Little, Brown & Company, 1926.

Wescott, Allan, ed. *American Sea Power Since 1775*. Philadelphia: J. B. Lippincott Company, 1947.

West, Richard S., Jr. *Mr. Lincoln's Navy*. New York: Longmans, Green and Company, 1957.

Wheeler, Richard. *In Pirate Waters*. New York: Thomas Y. Crowell Company, 1969.

White, J. A. *The Diplomacy of the Russo-Japanese War*. Princeton: Princeton University Press, 1964.

Wilkie, Robert. "Set and Drift, Navy 2001: Back to the Future," Naval War College Press Review (Spring, 2000), 1-12.

Wimmel, Kenneth. *Theodore Roosevelt and the Great White Fleet*. Washington: Brassey's Inc., 1998.

Wohlstetter, Roberta. *Pearl Harbor: Warning and Decision*. Stanford, Cal.: Stanford University Press, 1962.

Zumwalt, Elmo R.,Jr. *On Watch*. New York: Triangle Books, 1976.

INDEX

Ship names are in *italics*. Page numbers in *italic* type indicate reference in a caption to an illustration.